Grow Your Business with AI

A First Principles Approach for Scaling Artificial Intelligence in the Enterprise

Francisco Javier Campos Zabala

Apress®

Grow Your Business with AI: A First Principles Approach for Scaling Artificial Intelligence in the Enterprise

Francisco Javier Campos Zabala
Cambridge, Cambridgeshire, UK

ISBN-13 (pbk): 978-1-4842-9668-4   ISBN-13 (electronic): 978-1-4842-9669-1
https://doi.org/10.1007/978-1-4842-9669-1

Managing Director, Apress Media LLC: Welmoed Spahr
Acquisitions Editor: Shiva Ramachandran
Development Editor: James Markham
Editorial Project Manager: Shaul Elson

Cover designed by eStudioCalamar

Distributed to the book trade worldwide by Apress Media, LLC, 1 New York Plaza, New York, NY 10004, U.S.A. Phone 1-800-SPRINGER, fax (201) 348-4505, e-mail orders-ny@springer-sbm.com, or visit www.springeronline.com. Apress Media, LLC is a California LLC and the sole member (owner) is Springer Science + Business Media Finance Inc (SSBM Finance Inc). SSBM Finance Inc is a **Delaware** corporation.

For information on translations, please e-mail booktranslations@springernature.com; for reprint, paperback, or audio rights, please e-mail bookpermissions@springernature.com.

Apress titles may be purchased in bulk for academic, corporate, or promotional use. eBook versions and licenses are also available for most titles. For more information, reference our Print and eBook Bulk Sales web page at http://www.apress.com/bulk-sales.

Any source code or other supplementary material referenced by the author in this book is available to readers on GitHub (https://github.com/Apress). For more detailed information, please visit https://www.apress.com/gp/services/source-code.

Paper in this product is recyclable

For Sarah.

You have been my rock through thick and thin. You have supported me through the long hours of writing, and you have always been there. I am so grateful for your love and support.

To our four remarkable children, James, Sofia, Harry, and Lily.

You not only brought your keen insights to this book by co-authoring a chapter, but also bring joy, inspiration, and purpose to my every day. This book is proof that we can achieve great things together.

And in memory of my parents, Maria and Diego.

Your sacrifices laid the path for my journey. They gifted me an education that was more than knowledge - it was the ability to dream, to strive, and to create. Even in your absence, you continue to shape who I am.

This book is dedicated to you all, my family, who have been my greatest teachers. In each page, in every line, your influence is there. Thank you.

I hope this book will help others achieve their dreams, just as you helped me achieve mine.

Table of Contents

About the Author

Francisco Javier Campos Zabala is a passionate technology leader with a background in delivering innovative tech transformations within the marketing adtech, telco, financial services, and healthcare sectors. Previously, he spent a decade as a management consultant at Accenture, working on strategy, product, analytics, and technology. He has led several digital/business transformations, scaling high-performing teams in technology and data science with a product-centered mindset and agile best practices. He has shaped governance models to create and scale breakthrough innovation and is a regular public speaker on innovation and AI at large tech events such as LondonTech week, BBC, NASA, IDC, and the Gartner IT Symposium. From 2020 to 2022, Javier served on an exclusive 21-member panel of industry experts to craft the Bank of England's guide on accelerating use of AI within the financial services industry.

Acknowledgments

As Sir Isaac Newton famously stated, "If I have seen further it is by standing on the shoulders of giants." The completion of this book stands as a testament to this timeless insight. The invaluable wisdom, guidance, and support of those around me have greatly influenced this work. I have been extraordinarily fortunate to have been enveloped by such an amazing community throughout my professional journey.

I am deeply grateful to have been part of remarkable organizations like Accenture and WPP. These companies not only provided a robust foundation for learning and exploration but also fostered a nurturing environment that brought together some of the most gifted and inspiring individuals I've had the pleasure to work alongside. The wisdom I've gathered from these experiences has directly shaped the insights presented in this book.

Moreover, my deepest thanks go to those who have endorsed this book, whose faith in this project and thoughtful words have added depth and validation. In no particular order, I am humbled from the support of Zahra Bahrololoumi, Dimitris Bountolos, Laia Collazos, Ashley MacKenzie, Greg Douglass, José María De Santiago, Jakob Nielsen, Chris Cowan, Alvaro de Nicolas, John McHarry, John Donnarumma, Charles Butterworth, Carlos Catalan, and Matthew Cross. Your contributions have been invaluable.

Indeed, this book has been built on the collective wisdom, experience, and talents of a diverse and vibrant professional community. To all my colleagues, mentors, and collaborators at Accenture, WPP, and beyond and to those who gave their support and endorsement, please accept my heartfelt gratitude.

Introduction

You are picking up this book at one of the most exciting times in human history. We are approaching a point in history like no other, the birth of Artificial General Intelligence (AGI), a new technology that will outsmart us in all aspects, opening a series of possibilities for humanity that were inconceivable until now.

We will explore detailed definitions of all types of AI, but it is useful to introduce some terminology now. This book primarily uses "AI" to refer to the current form of artificial intelligence, also known as "narrow AI." These systems excel in specific tasks but lack the flexibility and adaptability of human intelligence. For instance, an AI may play chess at an expert level but lacks the capacity to learn other games.

Next, we encounter "Artificial General Intelligence" (AGI), a level of AI that surpasses task-specific constraints. AGI systems possess the ability to understand, learn, and apply knowledge across diverse tasks, much like humans.

Lastly, "Superintelligence" denotes AI that's advanced beyond AGI to a stage where its intellectual capacities far exceed those of humans, heralding an era of unparalleled technological advancement.

It's important to note, though, that AGI and Superintelligence are largely theoretical at this stage. While we've made remarkable progress with narrow AI, the journey toward AGI and Superintelligence is replete with uncertainties. We may be nearing AGI, but the timeline and method of its realization are unknown. Superintelligence, while intriguing, may forever remain a theory. Thus, our quest toward advanced AI forms is an exciting yet uncertain exploration of technological potential.

The history of economic development is a history of technological innovation. The Industrial Revolution, which occurred in the late 18th and early 19th centuries, radically altered the way goods were produced and distributed. It introduced the advent of mechanized production, steam power, and improved transportation methods, setting the stage for subsequent technological leaps such as the introduction of electricity and the development of digital technology. The Information Revolution, which is still ongoing, is being driven by the development of new computing technologies, such as the transistor and the microprocessor.

AI is the next major technological revolution. It has the potential to automate many tasks that are currently performed by humans, and to create new products and services that we can't even imagine today. By combining advanced algorithms with powerful computational resources, AI systems can process and analyze vast amounts of data, make predictions, and solve complex problems far more efficiently than human beings. As a result, AI has the potential to transform countless industries, create new economic opportunities, and greatly improve the quality of life for people around the world.

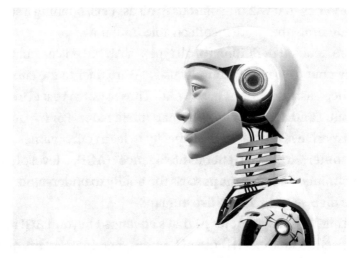

Is super-AI the next stage in human evolution?

Here are some specific areas where AI is already starting to have a major impact:

- **Autonomous vehicles**: AI-powered self-driving cars have the potential to revolutionize transportation. They could make our roads safer, reduce traffic congestion, and make it easier for people to get around.

- **Healthcare**: AI could be used to diagnose diseases, develop new treatments, and provide personalized care to patients.

- **Education**: AI could be used to create personalized learning experiences for students and to provide real-time feedback and support.

- **Customer service**: AI could be used to provide 24/7 customer service and to resolve customer issues more quickly and efficiently.

- **Manufacturing**: AI could be used to automate many manufacturing tasks and to improve the quality and efficiency of production.

- **Agriculture**: AI could be used to improve crop yields, reduce water usage, and protect crops from pests and diseases.

These are just a few examples of the many ways that AI could impact our lives. As AI continues to develop, it is likely to have an even greater impact on society and the job market. It is important to start thinking about how we can prepare for this future, and how we can ensure that AI is used for good.

AI's Full Potential

There are many reports published by the top research and consulting institutions on the AI's potential to the global economy. These studies have been created before the latest release of Generative AI, which means they could have underestimated the full potential value.

According to a report by McKinsey Global Institute[1] on the impact of AI on the world economy, artificial intelligence has the potential to incrementally add 16% or *around $13 trillion by 2030* to current global economic output – an annual average contribution to productivity growth of about 1.2 percent between now and 2030. Another of the top management consultancies, PWC[2] shows a $15.7 trillion potential contribution to the global economy by 2030 from AI.

Finally, one of the greatest AI pioneers, Stuart Russell, has estimated that AI could raise living standards for *everyone* on the planet,[3] adding 10x in the global GDP or $13.5 quadrillions net present value.

There is already evidence and many reports pointing to substantial large economic benefits that AI will bring to humanity. It is also worth noticing, it is possible these reports are undervalued, as we cannot fully see all the possibilities that will open as AI advances to more and more fields and connects more and more data.

---

[1] www.mckinsey.com/featured-insights/artificial-intelligence/
notes-from-the-ai-frontier-modeling-the-impact-of-ai-on-the-world-economy

[2] www.pwc.com/gx/en/issues/data-and-analytics/publications/
artificial-intelligence-study.html

[3] www.youtube.com/watch?v=ISkAkiAkK7A

Enter the Moloch…

Despite AI's undoubtedly potential benefits to humanity, like all technologies, there are also some risks that are worth highlighting.

Most of Hollywood's movies[4] since the 1960s that have featured AI displayed scenarios where some of the risks turn into reality. In most plots where AI goes wrong, the screenwriter/director anthropomorphizes the AI, and the machines would behave as a "bad" human would do with superpowers. Nevertheless, there is an unspoken assumption which is likely to be incorrect; an intelligent machine will not require all the rest of human traits such as feelings and physical and biological goals – such as survival, reproduction, etc. Like airplanes fly in a very different way than birds, AI machines will think very differently and not need to have exactly all human traits. And there is already evidence that early advanced AI systems such as AlphaGo[5] – which defeated Lee Sedol, the human champion at Go – think very differently to us.

One of the most interesting facts about AI is the concept of "the Singularity," which refers to a hypothetical point in the future when artificial intelligence becomes capable of improving itself at an accelerating rate, leading to rapid advancements in technology that are beyond human comprehension or control.

The idea was popularized by mathematician and computer scientist Vernor Vinge in his 1993 essay "The Coming Technological Singularity,"[6] and it has since been discussed and debated by AI researchers, futurists, and ethicists. Some experts predict that the Singularity could occur within the 21st century, while others argue that it may be much farther away or might not happen at all. Ray Kurzweil's[7] book, *The Singularity is Near*, even predicts that this will happen around 2045.

The Singularity raises important questions about the potential implications of AI for society, ethics, and the future of humanity. In the event of a singularity, there are some important risks that must be discussed and addressed before it is too late.

Indeed, some of the potential risks of a "super-AI" are very dangerous, including an Extinction Level Event, or ELE. The real concern, which has motivated many leading AI scientists and AI industry leaders to write a letter asking for a pause of any more

---

[4] www.imdb.com/title/tt0088247/?ref_=ext_shr_lnk
[5] www.ft.com/content/8474df6a-ed0b-11e5-bb79-2303682345c8
[6] https://edoras.sdsu.edu/~vinge/misc/singularity.html
[7] www.amazon.co.uk/Singularity-Near-Humans-Transcend-Biology-ebook/dp/B000QCSA7C

advanced AI at the time of this book writing,[8] *is goal misalignment between humanity and the machines.* And the danger is that the misalignment could happen naturally without any human giving the machines bad goals. This is better explained with the concept of a "Moloch."

Scott Alexander wrote an influential essay "Meditations on Moloch."[9] Moloch is a Canaanite deity associated in biblical sources with the practice of child sacrifice.[10] In the modern context of game theory, Moloch is unintended self-destructive competition. In other words, it is a force of game theoretical incentives that lead agents within a competitive system to sacrifice everything in order to win individually, but in doing so they destroy the overall ecosystem. It is the God of unhealthy competition. Moreover, no individual agent can unilaterally break out of the dynamic. The situation is a bad Nash equilibrium. A good way to summarize it is as an "unstoppable race to the bottom where everybody is worse off."

Moloch, an ancient deity seen by AI[11]

---

[8] https://futureoflife.org/open-letter/pause-giant-ai-experiments/
[9] https://slatestarcodex.com/2014/07/30/meditations-on-moloch/
[10] www.britannica.com/topic/Moloch-ancient-god
[11] Picture created with Generative AI (OpenAI's DALL-E)

When this is applied to a potential super-AI, it reveals several potential coordination failures that may occur when stakeholders act in their own self-interest, leading to collectively negative outcomes, such as AI Arms Race, Extreme Privacy and Surveillance, Bias and Inequality, and many others.

While nearly everyone in the AI community would agree that these risks exist, they all have a different view as to (1) when the risk could materialize and (2) what to do about it. We will explore both points in different chapters of the book.

This Book at a Glance

The motivation to write this book stems from the fact that while AI has tremendous potential, probably the most powerful technology developed by humanity so far, many businesses are still struggling to implement even basic AI solutions effectively. AI is also evolving at an unprecedented pace, and by the time this book is published, there will have been more incredible advancements. This is the main reason why I decided to explain AI from a First Principles point of view, so the fundamentals will stay even if the algorithms and commercial offerings change quickly. Therefore, I believe that the First Principles approach can help companies navigate the fast-changing AI landscape and derive practical solutions to their business problems.

It's geared toward companies looking to grow their business with AI. Enterprises of all sizes will be able to effectively navigate the fast-changing AI landscape and derive innovative solutions that will drive growth and success, using the First Principles methodology in all the areas discussed in this book, along with the WHY, WHAT, and HOW of AI. Whether you are a business leader, data scientist, or software engineer, this book will provide valuable insights and practical advice on how to harness the power of AI and grow your company.

Indeed, artificial intelligence (AI) is growing at an unprecedented rate and has become a game-changer in the business world. AI has the potential to fundamentally transform how businesses operate and serve customers, in a way not seen before by any technology transformation, making it a critical factor in the success of companies. However, implementing AI at scale can be challenging, and many companies struggle with how to leverage even basic AI to achieve business objectives.

The book is structured into five parts, to provide a comprehensive background on AI so the reader can apply those principles to improve their businesses:

- **Part I, "Introduction and First Principles"**: Here, we will introduce the First Principles methodology, which is based on breaking down complex problems into fundamental principles to derive innovative solutions. This approach will help companies navigate the fast-changing AI landscape and stay ahead of the curve. We will also spend a lot of time understanding why most companies struggle to take full advantage of AI capabilities.

- **Part II, "The WHY of AI"**: We will explore the reasons why companies should invest in AI, including its potential to improve customer satisfaction, increase efficiency, and reduce costs.

- **Part III, "The WHAT of AI"**: We will provide an overview of the various AI technologies available, including machine learning, natural language processing, computer vision, and foundational models, such as large language models. We will also discuss how these technologies can be used to solve business problems and provide value to companies.

- **Part IV, "The HOW of AI"**: We will discuss the practical aspects of implementing AI solutions, including data preparation, model development, and deployment. We will also explore the best practices for effectively managing AI projects.

- **Part V, "The Future of AI"**: How AI could evolve. While it is not possible to predict the future, it is possible to look at key trends to see a few plausible scenarios and plan accordingly.

There is also an appendix of resources for further study and a glossary of common terms related to AI at the end of the book. Any updates can be found at `https://github.com/Apress` and `https://github.com/javcamposz/`.

Reviews from Industry Leaders

This book offers a holistic view of AI, covering everything from the basics of machine learning to the strategic implications of AI for businesses.

—Dimitris Bountolos, Chief Information and Innovation Officer, Ferrovial

Campos expertly navigates the technical complexities of AI and presents real-world case studies that demonstrate its successful implementation in various industries, including financial services, travel and hospitality, and marketing.

—Zahra Bahrololoumi, CBE, CEO UK/I Salesforce

AI is here to stay and is permeating all aspects of a business because of its value. Similar to the rise of digital technologies, this conversation cannot be confined to a select few experts. Javier Campos helps bridge the gap, enabling a more meaningful dialogue in both the workplace and the boardroom.

—Laia Collazos, Chief Data and Analytics Officer at Coca-Cola Europacific Partners

This book doesn't just explain the what and the how of AI; it articulates the why, demonstrating its growing importance in our lives and businesses.

—Ashley MacKenzie, Founder and CEO, Fenestra

The book is an enlightened journey from the technical fundamentals of AI to the clear articulation of the role AI plays in all aspects of business strategy and operations.

—Greg Douglass, Senior Technology Advisor, ex-Accenture

Very well documented, the book includes real examples on successful AI implementations, and also describes the main barriers organizations face when dealing with this fascinating discipline. A well-rounded guide to help put AI at the core of any business strategy.

—José María De Santiago, Partner, Technology Strategy and Transformation, Deloitte

Perhaps the most compelling part of this book is Campos' "First Principles approach." This methodology encourages readers not just to understand AI but to deeply contemplate its fundamental principles and creatively apply them to their unique business challenges.... For those looking to get an edge in the new age of data-driven digital business, this is not just a book – it's an investment in your company's future.

—Jakob Nielsen, Senior Executive, Global CEO Broadlab,
ex-Microsoft, ex-WPP

In an era where technology is becoming the backbone of every successful business, this book serves as a roadmap for entrepreneurs, executives, and decision-makers keen on navigating the AI landscape effectively. I whole-heartedly recommend Grow Your Business with AI *to anyone aiming to understand, embrace, and exploit AI's massive potential.*

—Chris Cowan, Board Advisor and Founder, Costello Ventures

In his essay "Only the paranoid survive," former Intel CEO Andy Grove delineates three indicators of an impending shift: your prime competitor changes, the "mental gun" holding the bullet to shoot your main problem changes direction, and trusted colleagues discuss themes that you don't understand. All of these elements have appeared with AI. Javier Campos' work is a must-read to understand this shift and prepare yourself, your company, and your children for a future that is upon us.

—Alvaro de Nicolas, CEO, DNA Ventures

Javier Campos' book provides a helpful roadmap to allowing you to lever-age AI in business through a pragmatic First Principles approach. With AI at the forefront of all tech, Campos offers vital insights and knowledge, guiding readers easily through AI's diverse applications. An essential read for every business owner.

— John Donnarumma, CIO/CTO in the advertising industry

Understanding the potential for AI and its transformative power for business is a real challenge. Javier Campos guides you expertly through the challenge with this comprehensive and impactful book.

—Charles Butterworth, Managing Director, The Access Group

There should be no debate that AI will both provide great benefit and great harm to both society and businesses. For businesses the unmanaged impact could be profound, from AI-generated cyberattacks to falling on the wrong side of both current and evolving data laws, to releasing products that have flaws. The positive impact potential is equally significant. Where the balance lies between the two will depend on the degree to which leaders across society and business engage proactively in the topic. Businesses must enable their people to learn and experiment while ensuring leaders across all functions have frameworks to enhance the upsides and minimize the risks.

—John McHarry, Former CIO at Global Insights Organization

We are now way past thinking if AI will change our lives; the questions have moved on to when and by how much. The possibilities are both exciting and concerning. This is transformational change. It is difficult to find a contrary view, yet so few companies have the recipe for this change. This is an existential risk to all businesses. This is a must-read book for any business leader.

—Matt Cross, Chief Information Officer, Places for People

As CFO of GroupM Investment, I am always looking for ways to improve our business and drive growth. It is clear that AI will open up countless new opportunities for increased precision and efficiency and make possible to deploy highly personalized campaigns at scale. In this book, Campos provides a clear and concise overview of the potential of AI to help businesses grow.

I found Campos' book to be very informative and helpful. I particularly appreciated his insights into the challenges of implementing AI and the importance of having a clear strategy in place.

—Carlos Catalan, Global CFO, WPP's GroupM Investment

PART I

Introduction and First Principles

CHAPTER 1

Setting the Stage: AI Potential and Challenges

Human history has been closely intertwined with technology, which has been at the heart of a few epochal moments that have transformed the course of civilization. The discovery of fire, the invention of the wheel, the birth of agriculture, the industrial revolution – each of these milestones marked a fundamental shift in the way humans interacted with the world around them. Today, we live through another such revolution – a moment that promises to reshape our lives and redefine our future: the advent of artificial intelligence (AI). This section will provide an overview of AI's transformative power, its growing importance in the modern world, and the key challenges faced by organizations when implementing AI solutions. I will also introduce the "First Principles" methodology, to successfully implement AI.

AI is already transforming industries across the board, from healthcare and finance to manufacturing and logistics. In healthcare, AI is being used to develop personalized treatment plans, improve diagnostics, and optimize patient care.[1] In finance, AI algorithms are helping banks detect fraudulent transactions, automate customer service, and make smarter investment decisions.[2] Also in financial services, AI is also creating new business value from data, such as using transactional data for new use cases.[3] Manufacturing companies are leveraging AI to optimize their production processes, reduce waste, and improve supply chain efficiency.[4] AI's versatility and ability to process vast amounts of data make it a powerful tool for unlocking new opportunities and

---

[1] www.forbes.com/sites/bernardmarr/2018/07/27/how-is-ai-used-in-healthcare-5-powerful-real-world-examples-that-show-the-latest-advances/?sh=6a7292505dfb

[2] www.turing.ac.uk/news/publications/ai-financial-services

[3] www.experian.co.uk/assets/trusso-data-labs-case-study.pdf

[4] www.nist.gov/blogs/manufacturing-innovation-blog/artificial-intelligence-manufacturing-real-world-success-stories

driving innovation in these and many other industries. And as we further develop AI, it has the potential to touch every aspect of our lives, unlocking possibilities we could scarcely have imagined even a few decades ago. From curing diseases that have plagued humanity for centuries to combating climate change, from revolutionizing education to reshaping the global economy – AI holds the key to solving some of the most pressing challenges of our time. As we move forward into this new era, we must embrace the opportunity to harness AI's power for the greater good, using it to build a more equitable, sustainable, and prosperous world for all.

But this monumental shift is not without its challenges. On one hand, from a macro-society point of view, and same as with any powerful tool, AI's potential for positive change is accompanied by a range of risks and ethical concerns. The rapid advancement of AI technologies raises questions about privacy, job displacement, and the concentration of power in the hands of a few. Furthermore, the potential for AI to perpetuate existing inequalities or even create new ones cannot be ignored. There are also risks associated with AI safety – how do we ensure the goals of humans and machines are aligned in the right way? On the other hand, from a micro-enterprise point of view, AI is a foundational technology very different to others; therefore, many enterprises struggle to successfully implement the technology at the pace it is developed.

This first chapter aims to set the stage for our exploration of the opportunities and challenges presented by AI. We will explore the full potential of AI to transform society and enterprises. However, AI implementation is not always straightforward, and businesses can encounter significant challenges. This chapter will introduce the concept of First Principles to establish a solid foundation for AI implementation and decision-making in a fast-paced and rapidly changing environment.

One of the main reasons why it is difficult to implement AI is that technical people and businesspeople speak different languages. Technical experts have in-depth knowledge of AI and its capabilities, but they often lack the business acumen to translate the benefits of AI into financial outcomes for the company. On the other hand, business executives may not understand the technical aspects of AI, making it challenging to make informed decisions about its implementation. Another critical point is the outdated management practices. Peter Drucker, considered by many the founder of modern management[5], set the following as a key principle of enterprise management:

---

[5]www.forbes.com/sites/stevedenning/2014/07/29/the-best-of-peter-drucker/?sh=27228a1c5a96

Marketing and innovation produce results; all the rest are costs.

—Peter Drucker

As you will see in later chapters in this book, in the era of data and AI, you can also generate an enormous amount of value by leveraging data with AI, both the datasets you already have but more importantly the new ones you could generate from your existing operation to fully take advantage of AI. Not all innovation is AI and vice versa, so unless senior management has a deep understanding of data and AI, value will be left unrealized. This is what happens currently in most enterprises.

We also address the challenges in the interaction between humans and technology. Conway's Law, the Innovator's Dilemma, and human biases can all impact the decision-making process and limit the potential benefits of AI. We explore strategies from both technical and businesspeople to communicate more effectively with each other, thus breaking down the barriers that often hinder successful AI implementation.

In the following sections, we delve deeper into the opportunities presented by AI, the challenges in its implementation, and the strategies for successful adoption. By the end of this chapter, you will have a comprehensive understanding of the potential of AI, the difficulties in implementing it, and how to overcome these challenges to grow your company with AI.

AI Potential Benefits: The Size of the Prize

As the world becomes increasingly digitized and data-driven, the importance of AI continues to grow. The top management consulting firms and analyst have produced plenty of reports into the potential value that AI could add to the global economy. For instance, according to a study by McKinsey, AI has the potential to create an additional $13 trillion of global economic activity by 2030.[6] This highlights the immense value that AI can bring to businesses and society. Companies that successfully adopt AI can improve their products and services, enhance customer experiences, and outpace their competitors. Those that fail to adapt risk being left behind in the rapidly evolving technological landscape.

---

[6] www.mckinsey.com/featured-insights/artificial-intelligence/notes-from-the-ai-frontier-modeling-the-impact-of-ai-on-the-world-economy

It is worth spending some time understanding why AI is so important and different from other technologies.

AI: Why It Is Important

AI's ongoing development is reaching a critical juncture, akin to the profound influence of electricity in the 1800s (Figure 1-1). Prior to electricity, factories reliant on steam power were constrained to locations near coal mines. The advent of electricity, however, facilitated the decentralization of power, allowing it to be transmitted remotely and significantly altering industrial and societal organization. A similar paradigm shift is unfolding with AI's transformative potential. It will empower **decentralized decision-making** across organizations as AI-driven insights are disseminated to the frontlines. This is very profound; if you think of your current business processes, every point where a human is currently involved could be potentially automated by AI.

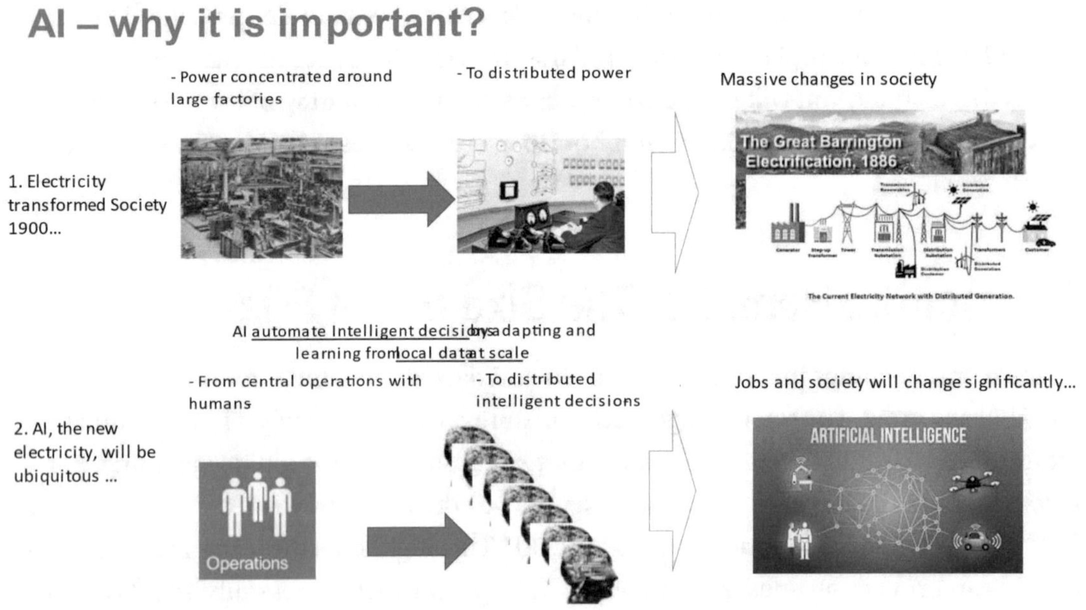

Figure 1-1. *AI is like electricity*

Opportunities in the Enterprise for AI

In this section, we will delve deeper into the opportunities that AI offers for businesses across various industries. We will discuss the potential of AI in decision-making and process optimization, enhancing customer experiences and personalization, unlocking new revenue streams and business models, and reducing costs and driving efficiency.

Chapter 7 and Chapter 11 will go into the details as to how to unlock the potential value that AI can bring to your enterprise; this section will provide an overview.

The full potential of AI for companies is vast and can be challenging to estimate, which is one of the challenges. However, the First Principles approach can help companies to define the problem and opportunity with AI and develop a solid foundation for implementation. The First Principles approach involves breaking down complex problems into fundamental components and building solutions from the ground up. This approach can help companies to identify the key metrics to measure the value of AI and determine the best projects to implement – Chapter 11 and Chapter 7 will provide frameworks to help you uncover the hidden value in your enterprise.

AI's Potential in Decision-Making and Process Optimization

AI has the power to improve decision-making processes by analyzing large volumes of data to identify patterns, trends, and relationships that humans may overlook. This enables organizations to make more informed, data-driven decisions, ultimately increasing efficiency and productivity. For example, AI-driven predictive analytics can help businesses anticipate customer needs and make better inventory management decisions, reducing waste and costs associated with overstocking. This can help companies to make better decisions by providing insights that are not visible through traditional data analysis.

AI can also streamline and optimize business processes through automation and intelligent algorithms. Machine learning algorithms can be used to automate repetitive tasks, freeing up employees to focus on more complex, value-added work. Additionally, AI-powered optimization tools can identify inefficiencies in workflows and recommend improvements, driving continuous improvement.

Enhancing Customer Experiences and Personalization

AI can significantly improve customer experiences by personalizing interactions and providing relevant, timely information. AI-powered chatbots, for instance, can handle routine customer inquiries, providing quick and accurate responses, while freeing up human agents to handle more complex issues. Machine learning algorithms can also analyze customer data to provide personalized recommendations and offers, resulting in increased customer satisfaction and loyalty.

Furthermore, AI can be utilized to analyze customer feedback and sentiment, enabling businesses to better understand their customers' needs, preferences, and pain points. This information can then be used to make targeted improvements to products and services.

Unlocking New Revenue Streams and Business Models

AI has the potential to open new revenue streams and business models by identifying untapped opportunities and enabling businesses to innovate more effectively. For example, AI can be used to analyze market trends and customer preferences to identify new product or service opportunities. Additionally, AI-powered tools can help businesses explore and evaluate new business models, such as subscription-based services or data-driven offerings, ultimately driving growth and diversification.

There are several areas where AI can help increasing revenues for companies:

- **Personalization**: AI can analyze vast amounts of data and provide insights into customer behavior and preferences, which can help businesses offer personalized products and services. For example, Netflix[7] uses AI algorithms to recommend movies and TV shows based on users' viewing history.

- **Sales optimization**: AI can help sales teams optimize their strategies by analyzing data on customer interactions and preferences. Salesforce's Einstein[8] platform provides predictive insights to sales teams to help them target the right customers at the right time.

---

[7] https://research.netflix.com/research-area/machine-learning
[8] www.salesforce.com/uk/products/einstein/overview/

- **Marketing automation**: AI can help automate and streamline marketing activities, such as email campaigns, social media advertising, and content creation. HubSpot's Marketing Hub uses AI[9] to help marketers identify the best times to send emails and which content to promote.

- **Fraud detection**: AI can analyze vast amounts of data and identify patterns that may indicate fraudulent behavior. By doing so, companies can detect and prevent fraud before it occurs.

Reducing Costs and Driving Efficiency

AI can help organizations reduce costs and improve efficiency in various ways. By automating repetitive tasks and streamlining processes, AI can significantly reduce the time and resources required to complete these tasks, resulting in cost savings. Furthermore, AI-powered predictive maintenance tools can help businesses identify equipment that is likely to fail, enabling them to address issues before they become more costly problems.

- **Process automation**: AI can automate repetitive and time-consuming tasks, such as data entry and report generation. For example, UiPath's platform uses AI-powered[10] robots to automate back-office processes.

- **Predictive maintenance**: AI can help reduce maintenance costs by predicting when equipment is likely to fail and scheduling maintenance proactively. Rolls-Royce uses AI to predict when aircraft engines need maintenance,[11] which has resulted in significant cost savings for airlines.

---

[9] www.hubspot.com/artificial-intelligence
[10] www.uipath.com/automation/ai-and-rpa
[11] www.rolls-royce.com/media/our-stories/discover/2021/intelligentengine-harnessing-the-power-of-ai-to-deliver-more-intelligent-engine-inspections.aspx

- **Supply chain optimization**: AI can help optimize supply chain operations by analyzing data on inventory levels, delivery times, and demand forecasts. Walmart uses AI to optimize its supply chain by predicting demand and optimizing its inventory management, including how to make smarter substitutions in online orders.[12]

As you have seen in the numerous examples, AI offers numerous opportunities for businesses to improve decision-making, enhance customer experiences, unlock new revenue streams, and drive efficiency. By embracing these opportunities and adopting a First Principles approach, organizations can successfully harness the potential of AI to transform their businesses and remain competitive in an ever-evolving technological landscape.

Deep Understanding of the Problem

Einstein's quote, "If I were given one hour to save the planet, I would spend 59 minutes defining the problem and one minute resolving it," emphasizes the importance of understanding the problem before implementing any solution. One common mistake that businesses make is jumping straight into implementing AI without neither fully understanding the problem they are trying to solve nor the full capabilities of AI. Without a deep understanding of the problem, businesses risk wasting resources on solutions that do not address the root cause. When it comes to implementing AI, this becomes even more crucial as AI systems are complex and require a clear understanding of the problem to be solved.

To avoid this, businesses should take the time to identify the problem they are trying to solve, understand the underlying causes, and define success metrics. This process requires collaboration between business and technical teams, as well as subject matter experts who can provide valuable insights into the problem.

I have seen many examples during my career as a management consultant and CTO/CIO of projects that, due to many reasons, did not define the problem well. A typical symptom of a project without a solid business requirements base is to have multiple

---

[12] https://corporate.walmart.com/newsroom/2021/06/24/headline-how-walmart-is-using-a-i-to-make-smarter-substitutions-in-online-grocery-orders

"change requests," some with important changes versus the original plan. Finally, it is worth noticing that using agile technologies, while they help reduce wasted effort, cannot fully compensate for a weakly defined project.

Defining the problem requires more than just identifying the pain points. It requires a deep understanding of the underlying issues and the root cause of the problem. Companies should employ techniques that help them identify and define the problem in detail, including its scope and the impact it has on the business. Some of the techniques that can help include:

1. **Baseline**: What exactly is the status of the situation and what needs to be improved. For AI, sometimes people would generate very high expectations, hoping AI would be perfect. However, to generate business value, AI must be better than the current process, not necessarily perfect.

2. **Customer feedback**: Understanding customer needs and pain points is critical in defining the problem that needs to be addressed. Companies can collect feedback through surveys, interviews, or social media listening tools to get a better understanding of their customers' needs. There are several methodologies to do this systematically; I recommend "jobs-to-be-done,"[13] based on the book from Clayton M. Christensen.

3. **Data analysis**: Data analysis can help identify patterns and trends that may be causing the problem. Companies can use data to gain insights into the issue and to validate assumptions.

4. **Process mapping**: Mapping out the current process can help identify bottlenecks and inefficiencies in the workflow. This can help pinpoint the root cause of the problem and guide the implementation of the AI solution.

5. **Stakeholder interviews**: Talking to stakeholders involved in the process can provide a different perspective on the problem. It can help identify issues that may not be immediately apparent and uncover hidden complexities.

---

[13] https://hbr.org/2016/09/know-your-customers-jobs-to-be-done

Companies can gain a deep understanding of the problem they are trying to solve, employing these techniques. This knowledge is essential when designing an AI solution that addresses the root cause of the problem.

To illustrate this point, consider a manufacturing company that was experiencing a high rate of defective products. The initial assumption was that the machines used in production were faulty. However, after conducting data analysis and process mapping, it was discovered that the root cause was an issue with the training of employees operating the machines. By addressing the root cause, the company was able to reduce the rate of defective products significantly.

A deep understanding of the problem is critical to the success of any AI implementation. Companies should employ techniques to help them define the problem in detail, including customer feedback, data analysis, process mapping, and stakeholder interviews. This understanding will help guide the implementation of an effective AI solution that addresses the root cause of the problem.

Why AI Implementation Is Challenging

In this section, we will discuss the challenges organizations face when implementing AI solutions. While the potential of AI to transform society and enterprises is immense, implementing AI can be challenging. These challenges can be grouped into two types: challenges that are generic to all new technology and challenges specific to AI technology.

We will expand on all these issues in Chapter 4 and how to address them.

Challenges Generic to All New Technology

Implementing new technologies in an organization is quite challenging. The management consultant company, McKinsey, surveys the industry regularly, and it is reported **that up to 70% of transformations will end up failing**.[14] There are a few reasons that explain this high rate of failure:

1. **Resistance to change – overcoming technical and cultural barriers**: Implementing new technology requires change, and change can be difficult. Many employees may resist change and

---

[14]www.mckinsey.com/capabilities/transformation/our-insights/
common-pitfalls-in-transformations-a-conversation-with-jon-garcia

be unwilling to learn new tools or methods. They may also fear that the new technology will make their jobs redundant, leading to job loss. Technical challenges may include integrating AI solutions with existing systems, managing computational resources, establishing a right operational culture (e.g., MLOps, which will be covered in later chapters) and scaling AI applications. Cultural barriers, on the other hand, may involve resistance to change or a lack of understanding of AI's potential benefits. Organizations should promote a culture of continuous learning and foster collaboration between departments to overcome these barriers.

2. **Fear of the unknown – lack of understanding and expertise**: Successfully implementing new technology requires knowledge and expertise. AI is still a relatively new technology, and many people are unfamiliar with how it works. This lack of understanding can lead to fear and distrust of the technology. The capabilities of AI are vastly different from traditional methods. People may be unfamiliar with the potential of AI and how it can be used to solve business problems. This lack of understanding can lead to a reluctance to adopt the technology. Organizations can address this barrier by investing in upskilling their workforce, partnering with external experts, and fostering a culture of continuous learning.

3. **Business and strategy alignment**: Ensuring new technology aligns with an organization's overall goals and strategies is crucial. To achieve alignment, organizations should develop a comprehensive strategy that outlines how AI can support their objectives and facilitate regular communication between business and technical stakeholders.

4. **Change management best practices**: Effective change management is essential for successful technology implementation. Organizations should develop a change management plan that outlines objectives, timelines, and key activities, and ensure stakeholder engagement and cultural

alignment throughout the process. **Balancing innovation with risk management.** AI adoption can bring about significant innovations and competitive advantages, but it also introduces new risks. Businesses must strike a balance between embracing innovation and managing risks associated with AI, such as the potential for biased decision-making, security vulnerabilities, and regulatory compliance challenges. Implementing robust risk management processes and adopting a First Principles approach can help organizations navigate these challenges.

Challenges Specific to AI Technology

As well as the reasons generic to any new technology, AI also creates a few specific challenges that need to be addressed for successful AI implementations:

1. **Outdated management guidelines**: Many management guidelines in use today were established in the 1960s and 1970s, and they do not fully account for the rapid advancements in technology and data processing capabilities. As a result, organizations might struggle to adapt to the changes brought about by AI adoption. Business leaders need to update their management approaches to align with the evolving technological landscape and take advantage of the opportunities AI offers.

2. **Language barrier – two groups of people with different languages and motivations**: AI implementation involves two groups of people with different languages and motivations. The first group is the AI experts, who speak the language of data and algorithms. The second group is the business executives, who speak the language of strategy and goals. These groups have different motivations and may not always understand each other's needs or perspectives. This issue is also often referred as "**The two cultures**"[15] (Figure 1-2), paper written in the 1950s by C. P. Snow where he argues that Western society is divided into two distinct cultures: the sciences and the humanities.

---

[15] https://sciencepolicy.colorado.edu/students/envs_5110/snow_1959.pdf

This division, he contends, has led to a breakdown in communication and understanding between the two groups, stymying progress, and collaboration. Finally, the AI expert community also suffers often "**Curse of Knowledge**," which is the phenomenon where experts have difficulty communicating with people who are less knowledgeable in their field. This can impact communication between AI experts and business executives without a tech background. The AI experts may assume that the executives have a level of understanding that they do not, leading to miscommunication and misunderstanding.

Figure 1-2. *The Two Cultures and the Scientific Revolution*

3. **Data and infrastructure**: AI technologies rely on data quality, storage, and processing power. Organizations may face challenges related to data management and infrastructure. To address these issues, businesses should invest in modernizing their data infrastructure, implementing robust data governance policies, and utilizing cloud-based solutions. This can lead to high **Cost and Complexity**: implementing AI can be costly and complex. Companies may need to invest in new hardware, software, and infrastructure to support AI applications. They may also need to hire new personnel with specialized skills, further adding to the cost.

4. **Governance and regulation**: AI adoption brings legal and regulatory considerations, such as data privacy, security, and compliance. Organizations must ensure they meet these requirements by conducting regular audits, establishing a dedicated AI ethics committee, and staying informed about

the latest regulatory developments. There are many countries around the world who, with the rise of AI, are actively working on regulations to govern how the technology is used. Compliance with these regulations can be complex, adding another layer of difficulty to AI implementation.

5. **Metrics and measurement**: Establishing clear key performance indicators (KPIs) and metrics is vital for measuring the success of AI initiatives. Organizations should develop a set of quantitative and qualitative metrics to track progress and evaluate AI's impact on the business.

To illustrate these challenges, consider a company that wants to implement an AI-based chatbot to handle customer service queries. The implementation of the chatbot requires a significant investment in infrastructure and AI expertise. The company may also face resistance from employees who fear that the chatbot will make their jobs redundant. Additionally, the business executives may struggle to understand the technical aspects of the implementation, leading to miscommunication with the AI experts.

Introduction to First Principles Methodology

The First Principles methodology is a powerful tool for problem-solving and innovation that has been used by some of the most successful companies in the world, including SpaceX and Tesla. This methodology involves **breaking down complex problems into their fundamental components and then using basic principles** to develop innovative solutions. This approach can help businesses avoid biases and assumptions and establish a solid foundation for decision-making. This section will provide an overview, and in Chapter 2 we will dive deep into the methodology.

The First Principles methodology has its roots in philosophy (Aristotle) and science (Einstein), where it is used to develop new theories and discoveries. However, it has also been applied in business and technology, where it can help companies to uncover deep issues that may be holding them back from achieving their goals.

At its core, the First Principles methodology involves three key steps:

1. Breaking down the problem into its **fundamental components**

2. Identifying the **basic principles that govern** those components

3. Using those principles to **develop new, innovative solutions**

Companies can follow this approach and develop solutions that are based on fundamental truths, rather than relying on the way things have been done in the past, assumptions, or intuition. This can lead to breakthrough innovations that have the potential to transform entire industries.

Adopting a First Principles mindset in AI implementation offers several benefits (Figure 1-3):

a. **Enhances adaptability**: This is the key reason for using First Principles in AI. The AI field is moving to an incredible pace which has been accelerating in the last few years; therefore, it is very important to understand the fundamental to ensure your AI solutions are designed with the future in mind. By breaking down complex problems into their core components, organizations can better understand the underlying factors driving the problem and adapt their strategies accordingly.

b. **Encourages innovation**: The First Principles approach fosters innovation and allows for the discovery of new, more effective solutions, as it challenges conventional wisdom and question established assumptions.

c. **Enhance problem-solving**: The First Principles greatly enhance the problem-solving capabilities of the teams using them:

   a. **Facilitates collaboration**: The First Principles approach encourages interdisciplinary collaboration and knowledge sharing by fostering an environment in which ideas and expertise from different fields can be brought together to tackle complex challenges.

   b. **Reduces cognitive biases**: The First Principles approach helps to mitigate the impact of cognitive biases and promotes objective decision-making as it encourage focus on fundamental principles rather than relying on pre-existing mental models.

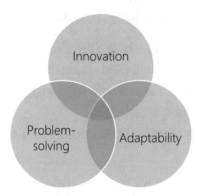

Figure 1-3. *Key benefits of using First Principles methodology*

How the First Principles Approach Can Help Overcome Challenges in AI Adoption

The First Principles approach can help organizations overcome challenges in AI adoption by facilitating the identification of innovative solutions and fostering a culture of continuous learning and adaptability. Some ways in which the First Principles approach can help overcome AI adoption challenges include:

a. **Overcoming outdated management guidelines**: By questioning existing management practices and breaking down organizational silos, the First Principles approach can help organizations develop more agile, adaptable management structures that are better suited to the rapidly evolving technological landscape.

b. **Addressing data privacy, security, and ethical concerns**: By examining the core principles underlying data protection and ethics, the First Principles approach can help organizations identify innovative strategies to safeguard data privacy and security, while ensuring that AI systems are designed and implemented ethically.

c. **Ensuring data quality and accuracy**: By breaking down data management processes into their fundamental components, the First Principles approach can help organizations identify areas where data quality and accuracy can be improved, leading to better AI outcomes.

d. **Facilitating talent acquisition and skill development**: By fostering a culture of continuous learning and interdisciplinary collaboration, the First Principles approach can help organizations attract and retain top talent, while equipping their workforce with the skills needed to succeed in the age of AI.

Examples of First Principles Methodology in Action

Chapters 2 and 3 will cover detailed examples of how to use First Principles methodology, both AI and non-AI projects. Probably the most known current example of the First Principles methodology in action is SpaceX's development of reusable rockets.[16] When SpaceX was founded, the prevailing wisdom in the aerospace industry was that rockets were disposable and that it was not cost-effective to try to reuse them. However, Elon Musk, the founder of SpaceX, used the First Principles methodology to break down the problem and identify the basic principles that governed it. Because of that, he was able to identify new solutions that were previously not considered.

Musk understood that the high cost of rockets was primarily due to their being disposable. He believed that by developing reusable rockets, the cost of space travel could be dramatically reduced. He used the First Principles methodology to identify the key components of a rocket and the basic principles that governed their behavior. By doing so, he was able to develop a completely new approach to rocket design that enabled SpaceX to successfully launch and land reusable rockets, a feat that was previously thought to be impossible.

Another example of the First Principles methodology in action is Tesla's development of electric cars.[17] When Tesla was founded, the prevailing wisdom in the automotive industry was that electric cars were not practical and that they would never be able to compete with gasoline-powered cars. However, Elon Musk again used the First Principles methodology to break down the problem and identify the basic principles that governed it.

Musk realized that the main obstacle to electric cars was the limitations of battery technology, which made it difficult to achieve the range and performance of gasoline-powered cars. He used the First Principles methodology to identify the basic principles

---

[16] https://d3.harvard.edu/platform-rctom/submission/spacex-a-first-principles-company/

[17] www.businessinsider.com/elon-musk-first-principles-2015-1?r=US&IR=T

of battery chemistry and to develop new approaches to battery design. By doing so, he was able to create a completely new category of electric cars that offered superior performance and range, and that have since disrupted the entire automotive industry.

The First Principles methodology is a powerful tool for problem-solving and innovation that can help companies to uncover deep issues and unlock breakthrough innovations. By breaking down complex problems into their fundamental components and using basic principles to develop innovative solutions, companies can develop solutions that are based on fundamental truths, rather than relying on assumptions or intuition. This approach has been used by some of the most successful companies in the world and can be a valuable tool for companies looking to grow their business with AI.

Humans and Technology

As we explained in an early section, up to 70% of all transformations in the enterprise will end up failing.[18] There are several reasons that explain this high rate of failure, but many are linked to the fact that the projects must be executed within a human organization. History is filled with examples where projects that were totally technically feasible did not manage to be launched. As a very recent example, Google invented the "Transformers"[19] back in 2017, the technology behind the latest Large Language Models. However, it failed to be the first to exploit that advantage commercially, while a competitor, OpenAI released both GPT4 and ChatGPT, with great commercial success. History will tell, but this could be the Kodak[20] moment for Google, as most of its revenues are based on Search, and future LLM's could replace their current models. No doubt many books will be written about this in the next decade or so!

As we move toward a future where technology and artificial intelligence (AI) play increasingly important roles in our lives, it is crucial that we understand the relationship between humans and technology. This relationship is complex and often misunderstood, but it is essential to the success of any AI project.

---

[18] www.mckinsey.com/capabilities/transformation/our-insights/
common-pitfalls-in-transformations-a-conversation-with-jon-garcia
[19] https://arxiv.org/abs/1706.03762
[20] www.weforum.org/agenda/2016/06/leading-innovation-through-the-chicanes/

Conway's Law

One important aspect of this relationship is Conway's Law, which states that the design of any system will reflect the communication structure of the organization that produces it. This means that if your organization is siloed, your technology will be siloed, and if your organization is collaborative, your technology will be collaborative.

For example, if your organization has separate teams for data collection, data analysis, and data visualization, your AI system will likely have separate modules for each of these functions. However, if your organization has cross-functional teams that work together on projects, your AI system will likely have integrated functions that work together seamlessly.

Understanding the impact of Conway's Law on your AI project can help you design a system that is tailored to your organization's communication structure, leading to more effective implementation and adoption.

I have seen many projects fail because of this principle. Technical teams, with the best intentions, tend to design the "best possible theoretical system" not taking into account where the system will be hosted and the operation. The First Principles approach will help to take this into account as we will see in future chapters.

The Innovator's Dilemma

Another important concept to consider is the Innovator's Dilemma, which is the idea that companies that are successful with their current products or services are often resistant to disruptive innovation. This is because they are focused on protecting their current business model and may not see the potential value of new technologies.

This is particularly relevant for AI projects, as AI has the potential to disrupt many industries and business models. However, companies that are successful with their current methods may be resistant to change and innovation. It is important to recognize this and actively work to overcome it.

Human Biases

All stakeholders in a company, including management, have human biases that can affect decision-making. These biases can lead to collective mistakes that are based on flawed assumptions and perspectives.

For example, a company that has traditionally relied on manual labor may be biased toward solutions that involve more manual labor, even if an AI solution would be more efficient and cost-effective. These biases can also be based on factors such as gender, race, or age, which can lead to exclusionary practices.

To overcome these biases, it is important to have a diverse team working on AI projects and to actively seek out input and perspectives from a range of stakeholders. This can help ensure that AI solutions are inclusive and effective.

Decision-Making in Corporate Environments

Finally, it is important to recognize that decision-making in corporate environments is often driven by those who have the power, rather than those who are right or have the knowledge. This can lead to decisions that are based on political considerations or personal agendas, rather than what is best for the company or the AI project.

To overcome this, it is important to establish clear decision-making processes and to ensure that all stakeholders have a voice in the decision-making process. This can help ensure that AI projects are driven by data and analysis, rather than politics and personal agendas.

Key Takeaways

In this chapter, we have explored the potential of AI to transform enterprises and society. We have also highlighted the challenges associated with implementing this technology and introduced the First Principles approach to overcome these challenges.

The key takeaways from this chapter can be summarized as follows:

- **Takeaway point 1**: Ensure you have **defined the problem to solve extremely well**. Defining the problem correctly is critical to the success of any AI project. Before embarking on an AI initiative, it is important to have a clear understanding of the problem to be solved and the potential impact of the solution. This will help to ensure that the right technology is chosen and that the project delivers real business value.

- **Takeaway point 2**: Be aware of the **key challenges to implementing AI and establish an action plan** to address and mitigate all the potential issues. Some of the challenges that companies face when implementing AI include the language barrier between data scientists/engineers and business stakeholders, the lack of a clear ROI, and the need for effective data management. To overcome these challenges, it is important to establish an action plan that includes a clear communication strategy, a well-defined ROI, and a robust data management framework.

- **Takeaway point 3**: AI, like all technologies, **will be implemented in organizations managed by humans**. Ensure the right governance and measurement processes are in place to be successful. Implementing AI requires a shift in organizational mindset and culture. It is important to establish the right governance and measurement processes to ensure that the technology is used effectively and responsibly. This will help to build trust among stakeholders and maximize the value of the technology.

In closing, AI has the potential to transform the way businesses operate and make decisions, but successful implementation requires effective communication and understanding between technical and businesspeople. The First Principles methodology can help address the challenges faced in implementing AI solutions, but it is also important to consider the impact of human biases and decision-making processes in corporate environments.

Following these strategies, organizations can successfully navigate the rapidly evolving technological landscape, leverage AI's potential, and drive innovation and value creation in a fast-moving world.

The next two chapters will go deeper into the First Principles methodology and how to apply them to build our future AI systems.

As we embark on this journey, let us remember that the future of AI, and by extension, our own future, is in our hands. It is up to us to ensure that this technology serves as a force for good, propelling humanity toward a brighter, more inclusive future.

CHAPTER 2

What Is First Principles Methodology

In the rapidly evolving world of technology and artificial intelligence, businesses are faced with a multitude of methodologies to implement AI solutions within their enterprise. Each approach offers its own set of advantages and challenges, but the First Principles methodology stands out as the most effective and **adaptable** for addressing complex issues in AI adoption. Rooted in a deep understanding of the underlying principles that govern AI, this method offers organizations a clear and logical framework to build custom solutions tailored to their unique needs, and more importantly, it allows enterprises to be constantly updated in the fast-changing AI landscape. By embracing the First Principles approach, businesses can harness the full potential of AI while avoiding the pitfalls of blindly applying pre-built models or relying on superficial assumptions. In this chapter, we will delve into the intricacies of the First Principles methodology and reveal how it can revolutionize the way AI is incorporated into the modern enterprise, resulting in increased efficiency, enhanced decision-making, and unprecedented business growth. First Principles methodology is a design approach that can be applied to create successful AI systems by starting with fundamental, underlying principles.

First Principles thinking is an essential approach to problem-solving and innovation that **involves breaking down complex challenges into their fundamental elements and building solutions from the ground up**. This approach has been used by some of history's greatest minds and entrepreneurs, such as Aristotle, Newton, Einstein, and Musk, to develop innovative ideas and disrupt industries. In the context of artificial intelligence (AI) implementation, applying First Principles thinking can help businesses overcome common limitations, foster innovation, and create more robust and adaptable AI systems to the ever-changing AI landscape.

© Francisco Javier Campos Zabala 2023
F. J. Campos Zabala, *Grow Your Business with AI*, https://doi.org/10.1007/978-1-4842-9669-1_2

First Principles thinking is a method of problem-solving that requires individuals to challenge existing assumptions, question traditional approaches, and develop new solutions based on fundamental truths. Instead of relying on analogies or established practices, first principle thinking focuses on identifying the core components of a problem and using them as building blocks to create innovative solutions. This approach encourages critical thinking and fosters creativity, which are essential qualities when developing and implementing AI systems.

The importance of First Principles thinking in AI implementation can be attributed to several factors:

1. **Enhances adaptability and scalability**: By focusing on fundamental components, First Principles thinking allows for the development of AI systems that are more adaptable to both changing business requirements and more importantly new AI algorithms that are being constantly developed. It can also scale more efficiently.

2. **Encourages innovative solutions**: By breaking down problems into their core components and questioning existing solutions, First Principles thinking fosters creativity and encourages the development of innovative AI systems that cater to unique business needs.

3. **Overcomes limitations of existing AI systems**: Traditional AI systems may suffer from issues such as bias and overfitting. By using First Principles thinking, companies can identify the root causes of these issues and develop solutions that mitigate their impact, leading to more robust and accurate AI systems.

4. **Ensures a strong foundation for AI system development**: First Principles thinking promotes a deep understanding of the problem at hand, which helps create a solid foundation for AI system development. This ensures that the resulting AI system is more likely to succeed in addressing the specific needs of the business.

Defining First Principles Thinking

First Principles thinking is a powerful problem-solving approach that helps individuals and organizations innovate by analyzing complex issues from their foundational elements. In this section, we will explore the origins of First Principles thinking and outline its core components that can be leveraged to create successful AI systems.

The best way to describe the concept is listening to one of the contemporary best examples of how to apply the methodology effectively. Elon Musk[1] has achieved incredible results, delivering innovative solutions in multiple challenging and competitive industries – aerospace, renewable energy, and transportation:

> *I think it's important to reason from First Principles rather than by analogy. So the normal way we conduct our lives is, we reason by analogy. We are doing this because it's like something else that was done, or it is like what other people are doing with slight iterations on a theme. And it's mentally easier to reason by analogy rather than from First Principles. First Principles is kind of a physics way of looking at the world, and what that really means is, you boil things down to the most fundamental truths and say, "okay, what are we sure is true?" and then reason up from there. That takes a lot more mental energy.*

Origin and Historical Context

The concept of First Principles thinking dates to ancient Greek philosophy, where the philosopher Aristotle introduced the notion of seeking fundamental truths as a basis for understanding complex concepts. In more recent times, notable figures like Elon Musk have popularized this approach, using it to disrupt industries and create groundbreaking solutions.

Throughout history, several key thinkers have used or contributed to the development of First Principles methodology. Here are some notable figures and examples, pictured in Figure 2-1:

- **Aristotle (384–322 BC):** Aristotle is often credited as one of the first philosophers to emphasize the importance of First Principles. In his work *Posterior Analytics*[2], he introduced the concept of "archai"

---

[1] Foundation 20 // Elon Musk - YouTube (min 23+)

[2] https://antilogicalism.com/wp-content/uploads/2016/12/aristotle_posterior.pdf

or starting points, from which knowledge and understanding could be derived. He believed that these First Principles were self-evident truths that could not be deduced further.

- **Plato (428/427–348/347 BC)**: Plato, a student of Socrates, also emphasized the importance of First Principles. In his "Theory of Forms," he proposed that understanding the abstract, unchanging concepts (or "Forms") that underlie reality was crucial to acquiring true knowledge. This notion is like the First Principles approach, as it involves breaking down complex issues into their most fundamental components.

- **René Descartes (1596–1650)**: Descartes, the French philosopher and mathematician, is known for his method of doubt, which he employed to systematically question everything he believed to be true. By doubting everything, Descartes aimed to arrive at foundational truths, or First Principles, that could not be doubted. His famous quote, "Cogito, ergo sum" (I think, therefore I am), is an example of a first principle derived from his method of doubt.

- **Isaac Newton (1643–1727)**: Newton's work in physics and mathematics is an excellent example of applying First Principles. His three laws of motion and law of universal gravitation were derived from First Principles and observations of natural phenomena, revolutionizing our understanding of the physical world.

- **Elon Musk (1971–present)**: The CEO of Tesla and SpaceX, Elon Musk, is known for applying First Principles thinking to various industries, including electric cars, space exploration, and renewable energy. For instance, instead of relying on existing battery technology, Musk challenged his team to examine the fundamental properties of batteries and come up with a more efficient, cost-effective solution. This approach led to significant breakthroughs in electric vehicle battery technology.

Figure 2-1. *Aristotle, Plato, Newton, and Musk all employed First Principles*

These examples from history demonstrate how the First Principles methodology has been employed by influential thinkers across various disciplines. These individuals have made significant contributions to human knowledge and understanding, following relentlessly First Principles and breaking down complex problems into their most fundamental components,

Core Components of First Principles Thinking

There are four major core components whenever approaching a problem using First Principles:

1. **Challenging assumptions and questioning existing solutions**: First Principles thinking encourages critical examination of existing solutions and the assumptions they are based on. This process helps to identify limitations and flaws that may hinder innovation. For example, questioning the assumption that AI models must rely on large amounts of data can lead to the development of more efficient algorithms that require less training data. This means asking questions like

   a. Are there any assumptions that I'm making about this problem?

   b. Are there any existing solutions that are flawed?

   c. Are there any new solutions that I can come up with?

2. **Breaking down complex problems into fundamental components**: In First Principles thinking, a complex problem is deconstructed into its most basic elements, allowing for a deeper understanding of the issue at hand. By doing this, individuals can identify the underlying principles that govern the problem and recognize patterns that may not be immediately apparent. For instance, in the context of AI, this might involve understanding the core concepts of machine learning, such as data preprocessing, feature extraction, and model training. We will explore these core AI components in Chapter 3.

3. **Identifying the basic principles that govern those components**: Once the fundamental components have been identified, the next step is to identify the basic principles that govern those components. For example, the basic principles that govern customer interactions might include communication, transparency, and responsiveness.

4. **Building new solutions from the ground up**: Once the fundamental components have been identified and existing solutions have been scrutinized, First Principles thinking guides the development of new solutions built upon these foundational elements. This approach encourages outside-the-box thinking and fosters innovation by avoiding the constraints of established practices. These solutions are designed to address the fundamental components and the basic principles that govern them. In AI development, this might involve creating a novel machine learning model specifically tailored to address the unique needs of a particular business problem.

An example of how First Principles design can be applied in an AI project is reducing customer churn by analyzing all the emails exchanged with customers. The first step would be to break down the problem into its fundamental components, which might include customer data, email content, and customer interactions. The next step would be to identify the basic principles that govern those components, such as communication style, product feedback, and customer sentiment. Finally, those principles would be used to develop new, innovative solutions to reduce customer churn, such as personalized email content, targeted product recommendations, and proactive customer support. We will cover multiple use cases later on in the book.

Why First Principles Methodology Is Important for AI Implementations

First Principles thinking is a powerful tool that can be used to solve complex problems and create new products and services. In the context of AI, First Principles thinking can be used to create more efficient, accurate, and robust AI systems while minimizing inherent limitations. By understanding the fundamental principles of AI, we can design systems that are more powerful and adaptable. This can lead to significant improvements in performance and cost.

In this section, we go deeper into some of the key reasons why First Principles methodology is important for AI implementation.

Encourages Innovative Solutions

First Principles thinking encourages us to think outside the box and come up with new and innovative solutions to problems. This is because it forces us to question our assumptions and challenge the status quo. When we do this, we are more likely to come up with new ideas that have the potential to revolutionize the way we do things.

1. **Overcoming legacy systems**: Many companies are burdened by legacy systems and outdated technologies, which often hinder innovation. First Principles thinking allows organizations to break free from traditional approaches by analyzing the core principles of a problem and developing novel solutions. For instance, OpenAI's GPT-3, a state-of-the-art language model, is built on the foundation of First Principles thinking, enabling the model to generate high-quality text outputs that surpass previous AI-driven language models.

2. **Fostering a culture of innovation**: By promoting First Principles thinking, companies can foster a culture of innovation that encourages employees to challenge existing solutions and explore new ideas. This mindset enables businesses to stay ahead of their competitors and remain agile in the rapidly changing world of AI. A notable example is Google's DeepMind, which uses First Principles thinking to develop groundbreaking AI technologies, such as AlphaGo, a program that defeated the world champion in the game of Go.

Avoiding Limitations of Existing AI Systems

Many AI systems are designed based on existing data and algorithms. However, these systems are often limited by the data they are trained on and the algorithms they are built with. First Principles thinking allows us to break free from these limitations and create systems that are more powerful and adaptable:

1. **Reducing bias and overfitting**: Traditional AI systems often suffer from issues like bias and overfitting, which compromise the effectiveness and fairness of AI solutions. By adopting First

Principles thinking, organizations can better understand the underlying causes of these problems and develop strategies to address them. For example, First Principles thinking can guide the development of AI algorithms that are more resistant to overfitting by employing techniques such as regularization and cross-validation. They can also encourage to look for additional datasets to ensure a more robust final model.

2. **Enhancing transparency and explainability**: The black-box nature of many AI systems poses challenges in understanding the reasoning behind their decisions. First Principles thinking encourages a deep understanding of AI models' inner workings, allowing developers to create more transparent and explainable solutions. This can lead to increased trust in AI systems and promote their adoption across various industries.

Ensuring a Strong Foundation for AI System Development

First Principles thinking ensures that AI systems are built on a strong foundation of knowledge and understanding. This is because it forces us to understand the fundamental principles of AI before we start designing systems. When we do this, we are more likely to create systems that are robust and reliable.

1. **Aligning AI with business goals**: First Principles thinking ensures that AI systems are built on a solid foundation by aligning them with the organization's strategic goals. By identifying the core principles of a problem and developing tailored solutions, companies can create AI systems that address specific business challenges and drive growth. For example, a retail company could use First Principles thinking to develop an AI-powered inventory management system that optimizes stock levels and reduces waste, directly contributing to the company's bottom line.

2. **Developing robust AI solutions**: A strong foundation is essential for developing robust AI solutions that can withstand real-world challenges. First Principles thinking promotes a deep understanding of the problem at hand, enabling developers to

create AI systems that can handle unforeseen situations and edge cases. This results in AI solutions that are more reliable and effective in real-world applications. For example, many AI systems are designed without a clear understanding of the underlying data. This can lead to systems that are unstable and prone to failure. First Principles thinking can help us to understand the data better, resulting in more stable and reliable systems.

Enhancing Adaptability and Scalability

First Principles thinking can help us to create more robust AI systems by enhancing their adaptability and scalability. This is because it forces us to design systems that are **not reliant on any particular data or algorithm**. When we do this, our systems are more likely to be able to adapt to new situations and scale to new levels of complexity:

1. **Adapting to changing business requirements**: AI systems developed using First Principles thinking are more adaptable to changing business requirements. By focusing on the fundamental elements of a problem, these systems can evolve as the business landscape changes, ensuring their continued relevance and utility. For instance, an AI system for fraud detection designed using First Principles thinking can be easily updated to accommodate new types of fraud or changes in regulatory requirements. Another example, many AI systems are designed to work with a specific dataset. If the dataset changes, the system may no longer work as well. First Principles thinking can help us to design systems that are not reliant on any particular dataset. When we do this, our systems are more likely to be able to adapt to changes in data.

2. **Scaling AI systems efficiently**: First Principles thinking also enables the efficient scaling of AI systems. By understanding the core principles and limitations of an AI model, developers can create solutions that can be easily expanded to accommodate growing data volumes and user demands. This approach ensures that AI systems remain effective and efficient as they scale, contributing to the long-term success of the organization. This is also very important when designing cloud-native systems, as we will see in Chapter 19.

Facilitating Cross-Domain Applications

When solutions are broken down into core components, it is far easier to facilitate re-use and collaboration of those components in different domains:

1. **Encouraging transfer of knowledge**: First Principles thinking fosters the transfer of knowledge across different domains, allowing companies to leverage existing AI solutions in new areas. By understanding the core principles underlying a specific AI model, organizations can adapt and apply the model to new industries or applications. For example, an AI system initially developed for medical image analysis could be modified and applied to quality control in manufacturing.

2. **Promoting interdisciplinary collaboration**: The First Principles methodology encourages interdisciplinary collaboration, as it requires input from experts in various fields to identify the fundamental components of complex problems. By bringing together diverse perspectives, organizations can create AI systems that are more holistic and robust, resulting in better overall performance and utility.

Developing Ethical AI Systems

The nature of the core components can help focusing on responsible and Ethical AI System, as we will cover in detailed in Chapter 20:

1. **Addressing ethical concerns**: As AI systems become more pervasive, addressing ethical concerns becomes increasingly important. First Principles thinking can guide the development of AI systems that adhere to ethical guidelines and consider the potential consequences of their deployment. By understanding the fundamental principles of a problem, developers can create AI solutions that minimize harm and promote fairness.

2. **Ensuring responsible AI development**: First Principles thinking also ensures responsible AI development by promoting transparency, accountability, and explainability.

By understanding the core principles and limitations of AI models, developers can create AI systems that are more understandable and controllable, fostering trust among users and stakeholders.

How to Apply First Principles Thinking in AI Development

Applying First Principles thinking in AI development involves a series of steps that promote innovation, ensure a strong foundation for AI systems, and ultimately lead to the creation of more robust and adaptable AI solutions. This section will outline the key steps in this process and provide guidance on how to effectively apply First Principles thinking in AI development. Figure 2-2 offers a snapshot of these principles.

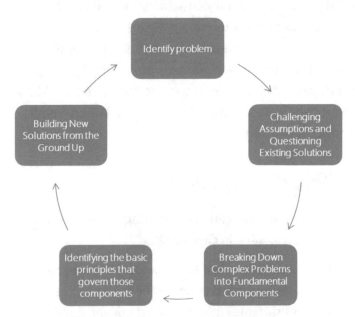

Figure 2-2. *First Principles process in AI development*

Identifying the Problem and Defining the Goal

The first step is to identify the problem that you want to solve. What are the specific goals that you want to achieve? Once you have a clear understanding of the problem and the goals, you can start to brainstorm solutions.

1. **Problem identification**: The first step in applying First Principles thinking is to identify the problem that needs to be addressed by the AI system. This involves understanding the business context, user requirements, and any constraints that may exist. To gain a comprehensive understanding of the problem, it is essential to involve stakeholders and domain experts, ensuring that their perspectives and insights are considered.

2. **Goal definition**: Once the problem has been identified, it is crucial to define a clear and measurable goal for the AI system. This goal should be aligned with the organization's overall strategy and objectives and should provide a specific target to guide the AI development process. By defining a clear goal, the development team can maintain focus and ensure that the AI system is designed to address the core problem effectively. It is also important to ensure the focus is to improve the current process, rather than having a perfect system.

Breaking Down the Problem into Fundamental Components

Once you have a good understanding of the problem, you can start to break it down into its fundamental components. This will help you to understand the problem at a deeper level and to identify the key factors that need to be considered in any solution:

1. **Analyzing the problem**: To apply First Principles thinking, it is essential to break down the problem into its fundamental components. This involves dissecting the problem into smaller, more manageable pieces, which can then be addressed individually. This process often requires collaboration with domain experts to ensure that the problem's key aspects are accurately identified and understood.

2. **Identifying key variables and relationships**: As part of the problem decomposition, it is important to identify the key variables and relationships that underpin the problem. This may involve identifying the relevant data sources, understanding the

dependencies between variables, and uncovering any hidden patterns or trends. By understanding these relationships, developers can make more informed decisions when designing AI systems and selecting appropriate algorithms.

Challenging Assumptions and Questioning Existing Solutions

Once you have a good understanding of the problem and its components, it's time to start challenging assumptions and questioning existing solutions. This is where First Principles thinking comes in. By starting from scratch and thinking about the problem from a new perspective, you can come up with innovative solutions that are not limited by the constraints of existing approaches.

1. **Challenging assumptions**: First Principles thinking requires challenging the assumptions that underlie existing solutions and approaches. This involves questioning conventional wisdom, reevaluating widely held beliefs, and considering alternative perspectives. By challenging these assumptions, developers can uncover new insights and identify innovative solutions that may have been overlooked. This is especially important in large organizations with complex regulations, as many would assume some constraints cannot be changed based on historical facts and existing regulations. However, when using First Principles and challenging assumptions, more often than not, this opens the door to new opportunities.

2. **Reviewing existing solutions**: In addition to challenging assumptions, it is essential to review existing solutions to the problem. This involves examining current AI systems, processes, and methodologies to identify any limitations, inefficiencies, or potential areas for improvement. By understanding the strengths and weaknesses of existing solutions, developers can design AI systems that build upon these insights and address the problem more effectively.

Building a New AI Solution from Scratch

Once you have a new solution in mind, it is time to start building it. This is where your knowledge of AI and your domain expertise will come in handy. You will need to select the right AI algorithms and techniques, and you will need to be able to implement them effectively:

1. **Selecting the right AI algorithms and techniques**: Once the problem has been broken down into its fundamental components, and assumptions have been challenged, it is necessary to select the appropriate AI algorithms and techniques to address the problem. This involves researching and evaluating various AI methods, considering their strengths and weaknesses, and selecting the best-fit approach based on the problem's specific requirements. It may also involve combining multiple algorithms or developing custom models to create a more tailored solution. We will go deep in later chapters in the best way to approach this for any problem.

2. **Iterative development and continuous improvement**: First Principles thinking promotes an iterative approach to AI development, with continuous improvement being a key focus. This involves developing prototypes, testing their performance, and refining the AI models based on feedback and results. By adopting an iterative approach, developers can identify and address any issues or limitations early in the development process, ensuring that the final AI system is robust and effective.

3. **Data-driven decision-making**: Data is a critical component of AI development, and First Principles thinking emphasizes the importance of data-driven decision-making. This involves collecting, analyzing, and leveraging data to inform the design, development, and optimization of AI systems. Data-driven decision-making enables developers to make more informed choices about the AI algorithms and techniques used, assess the performance of AI systems, and identify areas for improvement.

4. **Ensuring ethical considerations**: As AI systems become increasingly integrated into various aspects of business and society, ensuring ethical considerations are considered is of paramount importance. Applying First Principles thinking involves not only focusing on technical aspects but also considering the ethical implications of AI systems. This includes addressing issues such as fairness, transparency, accountability, privacy, and potential biases. By incorporating ethical considerations into the AI development process, organizations can create systems that are not only effective but also responsible and aligned with societal values. We will further expand on all these points in Chapter 22.

Applying First Principles thinking in AI development is a powerful approach that can lead to more innovative, effective, and responsible AI systems.

Real-World Examples of Applying First Principles Thinking in AI Development

In this section, we will explore three real-world case studies illustrating how First Principles thinking has been applied in AI-driven customer support, predictive maintenance in manufacturing, and personalized marketing campaigns:

1. **AI-driven customer support**: In the customer support domain, AI is being used to automate tasks that are currently performed by human agents. For example, AI chatbots can be used to answer frequently asked questions, resolve simple issues, and provide support for self-service tasks. This can free up human agents to focus on more complex issues, resulting in a better customer experience.

2. **Predictive maintenance in manufacturing**: In the manufacturing domain, AI is being used to predict when equipment is likely to fail. This information can be used to

schedule preventive maintenance, which can help to avoid costly downtime. For example, General Electric uses AI[3] to predict when its jet engines are likely to fail. This information is used to schedule preventive maintenance, which has helped to reduce the number of unexpected engine failures.

3. **Personalized marketing campaigns**: In the marketing domain, AI is being used to personalize marketing campaigns. This can be done by using AI to segment customers based on their interests and demographics. Once customers are segmented, AI can be used to create targeted marketing campaigns that are more likely to be successful. For example, Netflix[4] uses AI to recommend movies and TV shows to its users. This helps to ensure that users are always seeing content that they are interested in, which can lead to increased engagement and retention. By challenging existing assumptions about marketing strategies and exploring novel AI techniques like recommendation systems and clustering algorithms, the team could create a more targeted and personalized marketing approach that drives better results.

Case Study 1: AI-Driven Customer Support

Introduction to the Problem

A large e-commerce company was experiencing high customer support call volumes and long wait times, leading to customer dissatisfaction and an increase in negative reviews. The company's existing customer support system was unable to scale efficiently, as it relied heavily on human agents who had limited bandwidth to handle the growing number of customer inquiries.

---

[3] www.sps-aviation.com/story/?id=2646&h=GE-brings-AI-into-preventive-maintenance-to-reduce-jet-engine-failure-by-one-third
[4] https://research.netflix.com/research-area/machine-learning

Applying First Principles Thinking

The company decided to adopt a First Principles approach to redesign its customer support system using AI. The development team started by breaking down the problem into fundamental core components:

- Understanding customer queries

- Categorizing them

- Providing accurate and timely responses

Challenging Assumptions and Questioning Existing Solutions

The team questioned the assumption that human agents were the most effective solution for handling customer inquiries. They considered alternative AI techniques, such as natural language processing (NLP), sentiment analysis, and machine learning algorithms, to create an intelligent customer support system that could efficiently handle customer inquiries without sacrificing quality.

Building the AI Solution from Scratch

The development team selected the most appropriate AI algorithms and techniques to create a chatbot that could understand and respond to customer queries in real-time. They used NLP to analyze customer questions and extract relevant information, sentiment analysis to gauge customer emotions, and machine learning algorithms to continuously improve the chatbot's performance over time.

Results and Impact

The AI-driven customer support system significantly reduced wait times, improved customer satisfaction, and allowed the company to scale its customer support operations more efficiently. The chatbot was able to handle most routine inquiries, freeing up human agents to focus on more complex issues that required human intervention. This is a good example of how AI does not necessarily replace humans, but helps in improving the quality of work of the customer support teams, for example, the easy and repetitive tasks are done now by AI and humans can focus on only the most complex ones. This is a truly win-win-win scenario, where the end consumer gets a better and quicker treatment, the overall business outcome for the company is better by reducing cost and improving customer satisfaction which translates into more future revenues, and the customer support teams get more challenging and fulfilling jobs.

Case Study 2: Predictive Maintenance in Manufacturing

Introduction to the Problem

A global manufacturing company faced challenges in maintaining its production equipment, resulting in unplanned downtime and lost productivity. The company's reactive maintenance approach was proving to be costly and inefficient, as it relied on manual inspections and scheduled maintenance, often leading to equipment failures between maintenance intervals.

Applying First Principles Thinking

The company decided to implement a predictive maintenance system using AI to minimize equipment downtime and improve overall production efficiency. The development team began by breaking down the problem into its core components:

- Understanding the factors that contribute to equipment failure
- Identifying early warning signs of potential issues

Challenging Assumptions and Questioning Existing Solutions

The team challenged the assumption that scheduled maintenance was the most effective way to maintain production equipment. They explored alternative AI techniques, such as machine learning algorithms and sensor data analysis, to create a predictive maintenance system that could proactively identify potential equipment failures before they occurred.

Building the AI Solution from Scratch

The development team designed an AI system that used machine learning algorithms to analyze sensor data collected from production equipment, such as temperature, vibration, and pressure readings. By analyzing this data, the AI system was able to predict equipment failures and recommend proactive maintenance actions to prevent downtime.

Results and Impact

The predictive maintenance system significantly reduced unplanned downtime, improved overall equipment effectiveness (OEE), and increased the company's production efficiency. The AI-driven system allowed the company to transition from a reactive maintenance approach to a proactive, data-driven strategy, resulting in substantial cost savings and improved productivity.

Case Study 3: Personalized Marketing Campaigns

Introduction to the Problem

A retail company was struggling to engage its customers through traditional marketing campaigns, which relied on broad customer segments and one-size-fits-all messaging. The company sought to increase customer engagement and drive sales by delivering more personalized and relevant marketing messages to its customers.

Applying First Principles Thinking

The company decided to adopt a First Principles approach to redesign its marketing strategy using AI-driven personalization. The development team started by breaking down the problem into fundamental components, such as

- Understanding individual customer preferences

- Analyzing customer behavior

- Creating targeted marketing messages

Challenging Assumptions and Questioning Existing Solutions

The team questioned the assumption that traditional marketing segmentation was the most effective way to engage customers. They explored alternative AI techniques, such as customer clustering, collaborative filtering, and machine learning algorithms, to create a personalized marketing system that could tailor messages to individual customers based on their preferences and behavior.

Building the AI Solution from Scratch

The development team selected the most appropriate AI algorithms and techniques to create a personalized marketing platform. They used machine learning algorithms to analyze customer data, such as purchase history, browsing behavior, and demographic information, to identify patterns and preferences. The platform then used these insights to generate personalized marketing messages, offers, and product recommendations for each customer.

Results and Impact

The AI-driven personalized marketing campaigns significantly increased customer engagement, conversion rates, and average order value. By delivering more relevant and targeted messages, the company was able to establish stronger connections with its customers, resulting in higher customer lifetime value and improved brand loyalty.

These three case studies demonstrate the power of First Principles thinking in the development and implementation of AI systems. By breaking down complex problems into fundamental components, challenging assumptions, and building new solutions from the ground up, companies can create innovative and effective AI solutions that drive growth and enhance their competitive advantage. As more businesses recognize the potential of AI, the adoption of First Principles thinking will become increasingly important to ensure the successful development and deployment of AI systems that address real-world challenges and deliver tangible results.

Challenges and Limitations of Applying First Principles Methodology

While First Principles thinking has proven to be a powerful methodology for AI implementation, it does come with its share of challenges and limitations. In this section, we will explore the key challenges, including the time-consuming nature of the process, the requirement for expertise and domain knowledge, and the need to balance First Principles thinking with practical constraints.

Time-Consuming Process

One of the primary challenges of applying First Principles thinking is the time it takes to break down complex problems into their fundamental components, challenge assumptions, and build new solutions from scratch. This process can be significantly more time-consuming than adopting existing solutions or following conventional approaches. In a rapidly evolving field like AI, this can sometimes put companies at a disadvantage, as they may be slower to market compared to competitors who rely on established methods.

However, it is crucial to remember that the investment of time and effort in First Principles thinking can yield significant long-term benefits, such as the development of innovative and robust AI systems that outperform existing solutions. The key is to strike a balance between the time spent on First Principles thinking and the need for rapid development and deployment of AI systems.

Requires Expertise and Domain Knowledge

Applying First Principles thinking in AI development demands a deep understanding of both AI technologies and the specific domain in which the AI system will operate. This requires a team of experts with a diverse range of skills and knowledge, including AI algorithms, data science, domain-specific knowledge, and ethics.

Assembling such a team can be challenging, particularly for smaller organizations with limited resources. Additionally, training and retaining skilled personnel can be both time-consuming and expensive. Despite these challenges, having a team with the right expertise is crucial for the successful implementation of First Principles thinking and the development of effective AI solutions.

Balancing First Principles Thinking with Practical Constraints

When applying First Principles thinking, it is essential to strike a balance between the pursuit of innovative and groundbreaking solutions and the practical constraints faced by organizations. These constraints may include limited resources, tight deadlines, or the need to comply with industry-specific regulations.

In some cases, practical constraints may necessitate a hybrid approach that combines First Principles thinking with the adoption of existing solutions or the use of off-the-shelf AI tools. The key is to be flexible and adaptable, recognizing when it is appropriate to apply First Principles thinking and when it is more effective to leverage existing solutions or tools.

For example, a company may decide to use First Principles thinking to develop a novel AI algorithm for a specific problem while relying on existing data processing tools or infrastructure to support the implementation of the algorithm. This hybrid approach can help organizations strike the right balance between innovation and practicality.

Ensuring Ethical Considerations

As AI systems become more pervasive and powerful, ethical considerations become increasingly important. First Principles thinking provides an opportunity to incorporate ethical considerations from the ground up in the design of AI systems. However, navigating the complex ethical landscape can be challenging, particularly when developing AI solutions that have wide-ranging societal implications.

Organizations need to carefully consider the ethical implications of their AI systems, such as potential biases, fairness, transparency, and privacy concerns. This may require engaging with external stakeholders, such as regulators, ethicists, or community representatives, to ensure a comprehensive understanding of the potential ethical impacts of the AI solution and to develop strategies to mitigate any negative consequences.

Key Takeaways

Throughout this chapter, we have explored the importance of First Principles methodology and its crucial role in AI implementation. As organizations increasingly rely on AI-driven solutions to enhance their operations, the need for innovative and robust AI systems has never been more critical. By adopting a First Principles approach, businesses can create AI systems that address their unique challenges and provide lasting value.

First Principles thinking, a problem-solving approach used by notable figures like Aristotle and Elon Musk, is integral to the successful implementation of AI systems in businesses. This methodology breaks down complex problems into fundamental components, challenges assumptions, and questions existing solutions, fostering innovation. As AI becomes increasingly integrated into everyday life, First Principles can help organizations develop robust, scalable, and adaptable AI systems that stand out in a competitive landscape.

Incorporating First Principles methodology into AI development processes is not just a wise business decision but a step toward a sustainable future. It encourages a culture of innovation and problem-solving, allowing companies to create AI solutions tailored to their unique challenges, thereby providing lasting value. Thus, as organizations increasingly rely on AI-driven solutions, the need for this innovative approach becomes more critical than ever.

Here are three takeaways from this chapter:

1. **Takeaway 1**: First Principles thinking is a **powerful tool for solving complex problems**. By starting from the fundamental principles of a problem, you can come up with new and innovative solutions that are not limited by the constraints of existing approaches.

2. **Takeaway 2**: First Principles thinking requires **expertise and domain knowledge**. To successfully apply First Principles thinking, you need to have a deep understanding of the problem that you are trying to solve. This can be difficult if you are not familiar with the domain in which the problem exists.

3. **Takeaway 3**: First Principles thinking can be difficult to **balance with practical constraints**. In the real world, we often must make decisions based on limited resources and time. First Principles thinking can sometimes lead to solutions that are not feasible or practical.

Here are some Dos and Don'ts for best practices when applying First Principles thinking:

- Dos:

  a. **Focus on the problem and define clear goals**: A successful First Principles approach starts with identifying the problem and defining the goals. Be specific about the challenges you aim to address and the outcomes you want to achieve. By clearly defining the problem and the desired results, you can better focus your efforts and resources, ensuring that your AI solutions align with your organization's objectives.

b. **Break down problems into fundamental components**: When tackling complex problems, it's essential to break them down into their most basic parts. This process allows you to understand the problem more deeply and identify underlying issues that may not be immediately apparent. By focusing on the fundamentals, you can create AI solutions that address the root causes of the problem rather than just treating the symptoms.

c. **Embrace iterative development and continuous improvement**: Incorporating First Principles thinking into your AI development process does not mean you will develop the perfect solution right away. It is essential to embrace iterative development and continuous improvement. By regularly evaluating your AI system's performance and refining your approach based on feedback and data, you can ensure that your AI solutions continue to meet your organization's needs and adapt to changing circumstances. Be patient. First Principles thinking is a time-consuming process, but it can be worth it in the end.

- Don'ts:

a. **Rely solely on existing solutions or industry trends**: While it can be helpful to consider existing solutions and industry trends, First Principles thinking requires that you challenge assumptions and question the status quo. Don't be afraid to explore new ideas, even if they diverge from conventional wisdom. By questioning existing solutions, you can uncover unique insights and create innovative AI systems that set you apart from the competition. One of the key benefits of First Principles thinking is that it forces you to question the status quo. Don't be afraid to challenge assumptions and to come up with new solutions.

b.   **Overlook the importance of domain knowledge and expertise**: While First Principles thinking can help you challenge assumptions and develop innovative solutions, it's essential not to underestimate the value of domain knowledge and expertise. Engage experts in the relevant field to ensure that your AI systems are based on a solid understanding of the problem domain and incorporate the latest research and best practices.

c.   **Neglect ethical considerations and potential unintended consequences**: As you apply First Principles thinking to AI development, it's crucial to remain aware of ethical considerations and potential unintended consequences. Consider the impact of your AI systems on various stakeholders, including users, employees, and society at large. Ensure that your AI solutions are designed to minimize bias, protect privacy, and promote fairness. By addressing ethical concerns proactively, you can build trust in your AI systems and reduce the risk of reputational damage or regulatory backlash.

First Principles methodology offers a powerful framework for AI implementation that can lead to innovative and robust solutions. By focusing on the problem, breaking it down into fundamental components, and challenging assumptions, organizations can create AI systems that provide lasting value and set them apart from the competition. By embracing First Principles thinking, businesses can better position themselves for success in an increasingly competitive and AI-driven world.

As you embark on your journey to grow your company with AI, we encourage you to adopt a First Principles mindset and apply the best practices outlined in this chapter.

Next chapter, we will go deeper into applying First Principles for AI implementations.

CHAPTER 3

First Principles for Key Areas Needed for AI

This is probably one of the most challenging chapters in the book. Each of the topics I describe here has attracted hundreds of books, so it is a tall order to try to cover all these areas in a single chapter. However, following years of industry experience, I strongly believe the reader would benefit greatly to be introduced to all these principles, and many are very important to the success of implementing AI. While the book contains all the basis to apply these principles to implement AI, I would strongly recommend the reader to continue to expand their knowledge on all these methodologies following the resources listed at the end of the book.

As we have seen in the previous chapters, artificial intelligence (AI) is rapidly changing the world, and businesses are increasingly looking to AI to improve their operations and gain a competitive edge. However, successfully implementing AI in an enterprise setting can be challenging. There are several factors that need to be considered, which are very contextual to each enterprise such as company size, culture, regulatory landscape, and competitive marketplace. This is the reason why there is not a "silver bullet" to implement AI, and the same project that works very well in one company could be a total disaster in a similar company. This chapter will provide an overview of the First Principles approach for each of these key areas which should be explored to different levels depending on each unique enterprise's context. The key areas to be considered are the need for innovation, the ability to implement change, the importance of design and systems thinking, and the need for a strong foundation in data and AI.

As explained in Chapter 2, First Principles thinking is a problem-solving approach that involves breaking down complex problems into their most basic components, questioning assumptions, and building solutions from the ground up. This approach can be used to solve complex problems that are not easily solved using traditional methods.

F. J. Campos Zabala, *Grow Your Business with AI*, https://doi.org/10.1007/978-1-4842-9669-1_3

This approach encourages businesses to think critically about their AI initiatives and develop solutions that are tailored to their specific challenges, rather than merely adopting off-the-shelf technologies, or following industry trends. Table 3-1 explains what First Principles will focus to address each of the main challenges to implement AI, and how depending on your specific enterprise context you will have to spend different amounts of time in each area to ensure overall success for the project.

Table 3-1. *Main challenges to implement AI and what First Principles to use*

AI challenge	Type	First Principles
Resistance to change	Generic to all tech	Innovation Change management
Lack of understanding and expertise	Generic to all tech	Change management Data and AI
Business and tech alignment	Generic to all tech	Innovation Design and system thinking Data and AI
Change management best practices	Generic to all tech	Change management
Outdated management practices	Specific to AI	Change management Design and system thinking
Language barrier	Specific to AI	Design and system thinking Data and AI
Data and infrastructure	Specific to AI	Design and system thinking Data and AI
Governance and regulation	Specific to AI	Design and system thinking Data and AI
Metrics and measurement	Specific to AI	Design and system thinking Data and AI

Embracing a First Principles approach to AI implementation in an enterprise setting is crucial for several reasons. First, it encourages organizations to think beyond traditional methods and assumptions, fostering a culture of innovation that can lead to breakthrough solutions. Second, by focusing on the fundamental aspects of each key area, organizations can create more robust and adaptable AI systems that can evolve alongside changing business needs and market conditions. Finally, a First Principles approach can help organizations better align their AI initiatives with their overall business goals and objectives, ensuring that these technologies are effectively integrated into the fabric of the enterprise.

We will cover the following areas:

– **Innovation First Principles**: Innovation is essential for any business that wants to stay ahead of the competition. AI can be a powerful tool for innovation, but it is important to use AI in a way that is aligned with the company's goals and objectives. There are several First Principles that can be applied to innovation with AI. One of the most important is to start with the end user. What are the user's needs and wants? What problems are they facing? Once you understand the user, you can start to brainstorm solutions that use AI to address their needs. Another important first principle is to be iterative. Do not be afraid to experiment and make changes. AI is a complex technology, and it takes time to find the right solutions. Be patient and be willing to learn from your mistakes. Finally, it is important to be creative. Do not be afraid to think outside the box. AI can be used to solve problems in new and innovative ways. We will expand all these points in this chapter.

– **Implementing change in organizations First Principles**: Implementing change is never easy, but it is especially challenging when it comes to AI. AI is a complex technology, and it can be disruptive to existing processes and workflows. There are several First Principles that can be applied to implementing change with AI. One of the most important is to *establish a clear vision for change*. What do you want to achieve with AI? Once you have a clear vision, you can start to build a coalition of support and create a roadmap for change. Another important first principle is to communicate effectively. Keep everyone informed of your progress and be transparent about challenges. This will help to build trust and support for change. Finally, it is important to celebrate successes. This will help to keep people motivated and engaged.

– **Design and system thinking First Principles**: Design and systems thinking are two important approaches for creating successful AI systems. Design thinking focuses on the user and the user experience. Systems thinking focuses on the entire system, not just individual parts. When designing AI systems, it is important to keep the user in mind. What are the user's needs and wants? How can the system be designed to make the user's life easier? It is also important to think about the entire system. How does the AI system interact with other systems? How does it fit into the overall business process? By applying design and systems thinking, you can create AI systems that are user-friendly and effective.

– **Data and AI First Principles:** Data is the foundation of AI. Without high-quality data, AI systems will not be able to learn and perform effectively. There are several First Principles that can be applied to data collection and preparation. One of the most important is to ensure that the data is accurate and complete. This will help to ensure that the AI system learns from the data and does not make mistakes. Another important first principle is to label the data carefully. This will help the AI system to understand the meaning of the data and to learn more accurately. Finally, it is important to use the right tools. There are a variety of tools available to help you with data collection, preparation, and analysis.

A First Principles approach to AI means starting with the fundamental principles of AI and working from there. This approach can help businesses to avoid making common mistakes, such as

- **Not considering the user's needs**: AI systems should be designed with the user in mind. What are the user's needs and wants? How can AI be used to improve the user experience?

- **Not thinking holistically**: AI systems are not just individual components. They are part of a larger system, and it's important to consider the entire system when designing and implementing AI systems.

- **Not being iterative**: AI systems are not perfect. They need to be tested and refined over time. It's important to be iterative and to be willing to make changes based on feedback.

In the following sections, we will delve deeper into the First Principles approach for each of the key areas necessary for successful AI implementation, providing practical guidance and real-world examples to help organizations navigate the complexities of AI adoption.

Innovation First Principles

In the rapidly evolving landscape of artificial intelligence, the successful implementation of AI within the enterprise relies on a solid foundation of First Principles. These guiding tenets ensure that AI projects are driven by clear objectives, informed by the latest research, and aligned with the company's long-term goals. However, as history has shown, achieving true innovation remains a daunting challenge for even the most established organizations. A striking example of this struggle can be observed in the frequent turnover of the top ten companies every decade or so. This phenomenon can largely be attributed to the "**innovator's dilemma,**" which posits that successful companies often struggle to adapt to disruptive changes in the market due to their entrenched business models, established processes, and prioritization of existing customers' needs over the exploration of new opportunities. Consequently, they are often eclipsed by more agile, forward-thinking competitors who are unencumbered by the weight of previous success.

In this section, we will explore the core components of innovation First Principles, including organizational setup, culture and mindset shift, employee skill development, and the innovation process itself.

Doing the Right Things: Organization Foundational Setup

When it comes to innovation, the way the organization is set up is undoubtedly one of the most important points to get right. While everyone will say they want to innovate, the reality is that very few are set up to achieve innovation efficiently. The main reason is that in most organizations there is a separation between "the WHAT" and "the HOW" teams, and neither can be fully successful on their own. There are three main areas that need to be addressed to set for success:

1. **Define common language**: To collaborate effectively, it's essential to create a common language that allows people to work together across functions and disciplines. **Business capabilities** can serve as this common language, bridging the gap between senior management, business, and technical teams. This common language facilitates better communication and understanding, leading to more successful AI initiatives. For example, consider using the AI Canvas to align team members on AI projects. We will expand on the language barrier and how to overcome it in later chapters.

2. **Organizational culture and mindset shift**: A successful AI implementation requires an organizational culture that embraces change, encourages experimentation, and fosters a growth mindset. This involves promoting a culture of continuous learning, embracing failure as an opportunity to learn, and empowering employees to take risks. Companies like Google, with their famous "20% time for R&D" policy, demonstrate the value of nurturing a culture of innovation.

3. **Employee skill development and training**: As AI continues to advance, it's crucial to invest in employee skill development and training. Organizations should provide resources and opportunities for employees to learn about AI, data science, and related fields. This can include workshops, online courses, and mentorship programs. For instance, Amazon offers its employees the Machine Learning University[1] to help them develop AI skills.

Doing Things Right: Create an Innovation Process

As well as having the right organization with the right culture, it is important to create a process to (1) generate innovative solutions and (2) scale them across the enterprise. The following steps will maximize changes of success; each enterprise should adapt these to their specific context:

1. **Define the problem space**: The first step in the innovation process is defining the problem you aim to solve with AI. This involves understanding the user experience and *adopting a customer-centric design approac*h. Techniques like the "jobs-to-be-done" framework can help identify unmet needs and opportunities for AI-driven solutions.

2. **Brainstorm solutions**: Encourage your team to think outside the box and generate a wide range of potential solutions. Techniques like design thinking and brainstorming sessions can help drive creative problem-solving.

---

[1] https://press.aboutamazon.com/2019/7/amazon-pledges-to-upskill-100-000-u-s-employees-for-in-demand-jobs-by-2025

3. **Prioritize solutions**: Evaluate and prioritize the generated ideas based on their potential impact, feasibility, and alignment with business objectives. Tools like the Eisenhower Matrix[2] can be useful for prioritizing tasks and projects.

4. **Build a prototype**: Develop a minimum viable product (MVP) or prototype to test your solution's core functionality. This allows you to gather valuable feedback and iterate quickly, without waiting for perfection.

5. **Test and iterate**: Gather feedback from users and stakeholders and make changes based on their input. This iterative approach ensures that your AI solution addresses real user needs and continuously improves over time. The Lean Startup[3] methodology provides a framework for rapid testing and iteration.

6. **Launch and measure success**: Once you have a working solution, launch it and measure its success using key performance indicators (KPIs) and other relevant metrics. This will help you understand the effectiveness of your AI implementation, and identify areas for further improvement. Tools like Microsoft PowerBI, Google Analytics, and Tableau can help track and visualize your success metrics.

Applying innovation First Principles to your AI initiatives involves creating a strong organizational foundation, fostering a culture of innovation, and adopting a structured innovation process.

---

[2] www.hubspot.com/business-templates/eisenhower-matrix
[3] https://hbr.org/2013/05/why-the-lean-start-up-changes-everything

Implementing Change in Organizations First Principles

This topic is more important the bigger and the longer an organization has been established. Implementing change in organizations is a complex and challenging task. It requires a deep understanding of the organization's culture, values, and goals. It also requires a clear vision for the future and a plan for how to achieve that vision.

The successful implementation of AI initiatives in an organization requires more than just technical expertise. It involves organizational change management that incorporates a First Principles approach to understand and address the challenges, barriers, and opportunities that arise during the AI adoption process. This section will discuss the core components of implementing change in organizations using First Principles thinking.

Establish a Clear Vision for Change and Identify Root Causes

To effectively implement AI in an organization, it is essential to have a clear vision of what you want to achieve with AI. This vision should be aligned with the organization's broader strategic goals and objectives. By establishing a clear vision for change, you can create a sense of purpose and direction that guides the AI implementation process.

In addition to having a clear vision, it is also important to identify the root causes of the problems you want to address with AI. This involves conducting a thorough analysis of your organization's current situation, identifying gaps and inefficiencies, and understanding the underlying issues that need to be resolved. Using a First Principles approach, you can break down complex problems into their fundamental components and identify the root causes that must be addressed for successful AI adoption.

Assessing organizational readiness for AI adoption is a critical step in the process. This involves evaluating your organization's existing infrastructure, resources, and capabilities to determine its capacity to support AI initiatives. It may also include identifying any barriers or resistance to change that may hinder AI adoption. We will explore the AI maturity models in Chapter 21, scaling AI.

Create a Roadmap for Change

Once you have established a clear vision for change and identified the root causes of the problems you want to address, the next step is to create a roadmap for change. This roadmap should outline the key milestones, timelines, and resources required for successful AI implementation.

A First Principles approach to creating a roadmap for change involves breaking down the AI implementation process into manageable steps and aligning these steps with the organization's strategic goals and objectives. This ensures that AI initiatives are integrated into the broader organizational strategy and are supported by a clear and coherent plan of action.

Build a Coalition of Support

Implementing change in an organization, particularly when it involves the adoption of new and potentially disruptive technologies like AI, requires the support and buy-in of key stakeholders. Building a coalition of support involves identifying and engaging individuals who are willing to help champion and drive the AI implementation process.

This coalition of support may include senior management, IT professionals, data scientists, and other subject matter experts within the organization. By involving these stakeholders early in the AI implementation process, you can leverage their expertise and insights to help shape the direction of your AI initiatives and address potential challenges and resistance to change.

Empowering people and teams within the organization is a critical aspect of building a coalition of support. This involves providing the necessary resources, training, and opportunities for skill development to enable individuals and teams to effectively contribute to the AI implementation process.

Build Trust and Transparency

As with any organizational change, implementing AI initiatives can be met with resistance and skepticism from employees and stakeholders. Building trust and transparency is essential for overcoming these challenges and ensuring the successful adoption of AI.

Communication plays a crucial role in building trust and transparency. It is important to keep everyone informed about the progress of AI initiatives and be transparent about the challenges, setbacks, and successes experienced along the way. This includes sharing information about the rationale behind AI initiatives, the expected benefits, and the potential risks and implications for the organization and its employees.

By fostering open and transparent communication, you can help to alleviate concerns and misconceptions about AI and its impact on the organization, while also encouraging employees to actively engage in the AI implementation process.

Recognize and Reward Progress

Recognizing and rewarding progress is an important aspect of change management that helps to keep people motivated and engaged during the AI implementation process. Celebrating successes, both big and small, can reinforce the value of AI initiatives and demonstrate their positive impact on the organization.

To recognize and reward progress, organizations can

a. **Regularly share success stories and case studies** that highlight the benefits and achievements of AI initiatives.

b. **Offer incentives and rewards to individuals and teams** who have contributed significantly to the success of AI projects.

c. **Encourage peer recognition** and support by fostering a culture of collaboration and shared learning.

By recognizing and rewarding progress, organizations can help to build momentum and enthusiasm for AI adoption, while also reinforcing the importance of continuous learning, improvement, and innovation.

Design and System Thinking First Principles

Design thinking is a human-centered approach to problem-solving. It is a process that involves understanding the needs of users, brainstorming solutions, and testing prototypes. Design thinking can be used to solve any type of problem, including those that involve AI.

Systems thinking is a way of looking at the world as a complex system of interrelated parts. It is a helpful tool for understanding how AI systems work and how they can be used to solve problems. One of the key elements in the process is to ensure you balance technical feasibility with both a user-desirability and financial viability, as Figure 3-1 illustrates.

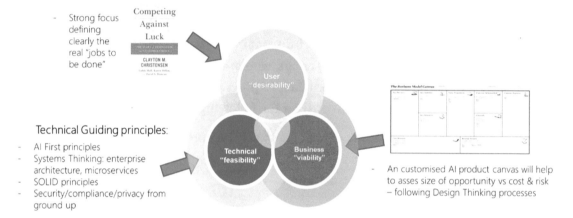

Figure 3-1. *Design and systems thinking methodology*

When designing AI systems, it is important to consider the following First Principles:

- Start with the user. What are the user's needs and wants? What problems are they trying to solve?

- Think holistically. Consider the entire system, not just individual parts. How will the AI system interact with other systems? Specifically, look at how data will flow from different parts of your enterprise and the external world.

- Be iterative. Don't be afraid to experiment and make changes. AI systems are complex, and it may take time to find the right solution.

- Be adaptable. Things change, so be prepared to adapt your designs accordingly.

- Be creative. Don't be afraid to think outside the box. There are many ways to use AI to solve problems.

In this subsection, we will explore the First Principles approach to design and system thinking in the context of AI implementation. By understanding and applying these principles, organizations can create AI solutions that are user-centered, effective, and adaptable to the ever-changing business environment.

Start with the User: Human-Centered AI Solutions

The first step in creating AI solutions that bring real value to an organization is to start with the user. Understanding the user's needs, wants, and pain points is essential to developing AI systems that truly address their requirements. To apply First Principles in creating user-centered AI solutions, consider the following:

a. **Conduct user research**: Gather insights from potential users through interviews, surveys, and observation. Understand their needs, preferences, and frustrations.

b. **Develop user personas**: Create detailed representations of different user segments to help guide the design process and ensure that AI solutions are tailored to meet their specific needs.

c. **Map user journeys**: Identify the key touchpoints and interactions users have with your product or service and use these insights to inform the design of AI systems that improve user experience.

Problem Framing and Ideation

Effective problem framing and ideation are essential to the development of AI solutions that truly address user needs. By applying First Principles thinking to this process, organizations can ensure that their AI initiatives are focused on solving the right problems and delivering meaningful results. Key steps in problem framing and ideation include the following:

a. **Define the problem**: Clearly articulate the problem you are trying to solve with AI. Ensure that the problem is well defined and specific enough to be actionable.

b. **Generate ideas**: Encourage brainstorming and the generation of diverse ideas to address the problem. Promote a culture of creativity and open-mindedness.

c. **Evaluate and refine ideas**: Assess the feasibility, impact, and relevance of the generated ideas. Iterate and refine the concepts to develop the most promising solutions.

Systems Thinking: Balancing Simplicity and Complexity in AI System Design

Applying systems thinking to AI design involves considering the entire system, not just individual components. By taking a holistic approach, organizations can create AI solutions that are more robust, resilient, and adaptable to changing conditions. Key principles of systems thinking include the following:

a) **Understand interdependencies**: Recognize the relationships and connections between different elements of the system, and consider how they interact and influence each other.

b) **Identify feedback loops**: Determine how actions and decisions within the system can create reinforcing or balancing feedback loops, and use this understanding to inform the design of AI solutions.

c) **Balance simplicity and complexity**: Strive to create AI systems that are as simple as possible, but not simpler. Recognize the inherent complexity of real-world problems and design AI solutions that can effectively navigate and manage this complexity.

d) **Be iterative**: Experimentation and continuous improvement.

In the rapidly evolving world of AI, iteration is crucial. By embracing experimentation and continuous improvement, organizations can ensure that their AI solutions remain relevant, effective, and aligned with user needs. Key principles of iteration include:

a. **Prototype and test**: Develop early-stage prototypes of AI solutions and test them with users to gather feedback and insights. Use this feedback to make improvements and refinements.

b.   **Fail fast and learn**: Recognize that failure is an opportunity for learning and growth. Encourage a culture of experimentation and risk-taking and learn from mistakes to drive continuous improvement.

c.   **Measure success**: Establish clear metrics and KPIs to measure the performance of AI solutions and use this data to inform ongoing iteration and improvement.

Be Adaptable: Preparing for Change and Uncertainty

In a rapidly changing business environment, adaptability is crucial. By designing AI solutions that are flexible and responsive to change, organizations can ensure that their systems remain effective and aligned with evolving user needs and market conditions. Key principles of adaptability include the following:

a.   **Design for flexibility**: Create AI systems that can be easily updated, modified, or extended as needed. Emphasize modularity and scalability in the design process to facilitate future adaptation.

b.   **Monitor trends and emerging technologies**: Stay informed about new developments and trends in the AI field, and be prepared to incorporate relevant innovations into your AI solutions. There is a list of sources in the appendix; some good sources are industry analysts Gartner, Forrester, or IDC or Tech consulting regular reports such as TW Tech Radar.[4]

c.   **Encourage a culture of learning and adaptability**: Promote a mindset of continuous learning and improvement within the organization and empower team members to embrace change and adapt to new challenges.

---

[4] www.thoughtworks.com/radar

Be Creative: Encouraging Innovation and Out-of-the-Box Thinking

Creativity is essential to the successful implementation of AI in an enterprise setting. By fostering a culture of innovation and out-of-the-box thinking, organizations can develop AI solutions that deliver real value and set them apart from competitors. Key principles of creativity include:

a. **Encourage diverse perspectives**: Foster a culture that values diversity and inclusion, recognizing that diverse perspectives lead to more innovative and effective solutions.

b. **Promote cross-functional collaboration**: Encourage collaboration and knowledge-sharing between different departments and teams, as this can lead to more creative problem-solving and the development of more holistic AI solutions.

c. **Provide time and space for creativity**: Allow team members the freedom to explore new ideas and experiment with innovative approaches, without the pressure of immediate results or rigid deadlines.

Data and AI First Principles

Data is the foundation of AI. Without high-quality data, AI models cannot learn and perform well. Applying a First Principles approach to data and AI is essential for successfully implementing AI solutions in an enterprise setting. By focusing on core components such as problem definition, data collection, model selection, training, evaluation, deployment, and monitoring, organizations can create AI systems that deliver real value and drive growth. This subsection will delve into each of these core components and provide guidance on how to apply First Principles to each step. Later chapters in the book will go deeper into the key areas explained here.

1. Problem Definition

The first step in the AI process is to define the problem that needs to be solved. This involves identifying the specific business challenges or opportunities that AI can address and determining the desired outcomes. To do this effectively, it is essential to

a. **Clearly articulate the problem**: Ensure that the problem statement is concise, specific, and understandable to all stakeholders.

b. **Align with business objectives**: Ensure that the AI solution is aligned with the organization's overall goals and objectives, and that it supports the strategic vision.

c. **Involve relevant stakeholders**: Engage with key stakeholders from different departments and functions to ensure that their perspectives and needs are considered in the problem definition process.

2. Determine Data Requirements and Data Collection

Once the problem has been defined, the next step is to determine the data requirements and collect the necessary data for training AI models. Key principles for effective data collection include

a. **Ensuring data quality, integrity, and privacy**: Data quality is crucial for effective AI models. Ensure that the data is accurate, complete, and up-to-date, while also maintaining data privacy and security.

b. **Collecting high-quality data**: Collect diverse and representative samples of data that capture the full range of relevant scenarios and use cases.

c. **Labeling data carefully**: Properly label data to ensure that AI models can learn from it accurately. This may involve manual labeling or using automated labeling tools.

d. **Data preprocessing**: Clean and preprocess data to eliminate errors, inconsistencies, and redundancies, and to ensure that it is in a format suitable for AI model training.

e. **Using the right tools**: Leverage a variety of tools and technologies to facilitate data collection, labeling, and analysis.

3. Model Selection

Selecting the appropriate AI algorithms and models is a critical step in the AI process. To do this effectively, it is essential to

a. **Understand the strengths and weaknesses of different AI algorithms**: Be familiar with the various AI algorithms available and their respective advantages and disadvantages.

b. **Match the algorithm to the problem**: Choose an AI algorithm that is well suited to the specific problem and data characteristics.

c. **Experiment and iterate**: Don't be afraid to try different algorithms and models to determine which one works best for the given problem.

4. Model Training

Training AI models requires patience and persistence, as it can be a time-consuming process. Key principles for effective model training include

a. **Splitting data into training and validation sets**: Divide the data into separate sets for training the model and validating its performance, ensuring that the model does not overfit the training data.

b. **Regularly evaluating model performance**: Monitor the performance of the AI model during training and make adjustments as necessary to improve its accuracy and efficiency.

c. **Leveraging computational resources**: Utilize appropriate hardware and software resources, such as GPUs and parallel processing, to expedite model training.

5. Model Evaluation

Evaluating the performance of AI models is critical to ensure that they are accurate and effective in solving the defined problem. Key principles for model evaluation include

a. **Using appropriate evaluation metrics**: Select evaluation metrics that accurately reflect the desired outcomes and the specific characteristics of the problem and data.

b. **Performing cross-validation**: Use cross-validation techniques to estimate the model's performance on unseen data and to reduce the risk of overfitting.

c. **Comparing models**: Compare the performance of different models and algorithms to identify the most suitable one for the given problem.

6. Deployment

Deploying AI models involves integrating them into the organization's existing systems and processes. To ensure successful deployment, it is important to

a. **Plan for scalability**: Design AI models and systems with scalability in mind, considering factors such as computational resources, data storage, and system architecture.

b. **Ensure seamless integration**: Ensure that the AI model can be easily integrated with existing systems, processes, and workflows, minimizing disruptions and maximizing value.

c. **Establish monitoring and maintenance procedures**: Set up processes for ongoing monitoring, maintenance, and updating of AI models to ensure that they continue to perform optimally over time.

7. Monitoring and Maintenance

Continuous monitoring and improvement of AI systems are crucial for maintaining their effectiveness and ensuring that they continue to deliver value. Key principles for effective monitoring and maintenance include

a. **Setting up monitoring systems**: Establish monitoring systems to track the performance of AI models in real-time and to identify potential issues or areas for improvement.

b. **Regularly evaluating model performance**: Periodically review the performance of AI models against predefined benchmarks and metrics to ensure that they continue to deliver the desired outcomes.

c. **Updating models as necessary**: Make adjustments to AI models as needed, based on changes in the data, the problem, or the desired outcomes.

8. Ethical and Safety Considerations

Ethical and safety considerations should be an integral part of the AI development process, ensuring that AI models and systems are designed and implemented responsibly. Key principles for ethical and safe AI include

a. **Ensuring fairness and transparency**: Design AI models to be fair and transparent, avoiding biases and discriminatory outcomes.

b. **Protecting data privacy and security**: Ensure that data is collected, stored, and processed in a manner that respects privacy rights and safeguards against unauthorized access or misuse.

c. **Implementing robust safety measures**: Develop safety mechanisms to prevent unintended or harmful consequences arising from the use of AI systems.

Integrating First Principles Across Key Areas

In the previous sections, we have discussed the First Principles for each of the key areas that are necessary for successfully implementing AI in an enterprise setting. In this section, we will discuss how to integrate these First Principles across key areas (see Figure 3-2).

Figure 3-2. *Putting it all together*

The first step is to create a common understanding of the First Principles within the organization. This can be done through training, workshops, and other educational initiatives. Once there is a common understanding of the First Principles, the next step is to develop a plan for integrating them across key areas. This plan should identify the key areas where integration is needed, and it should outline the steps that need to be taken to achieve integration.

Integrating First Principles thinking across the key areas of AI implementation is crucial for creating a cohesive and effective approach to AI adoption and growth within an organization. In this section, we will discuss how to establish a unified First Principles approach, leverage synergies between innovation, change management, design thinking, and data-driven strategies, and build a sustainable AI ecosystem within the enterprise.

Establishing a Cohesive First Principles Approach Throughout the Organization

To establish a cohesive First Principles approach, it is important to create a shared understanding of the underlying principles and values that guide AI implementation across all levels and functions of the organization. This can be achieved through

a. **Establishing a common language**: Ensure that all stakeholders, including senior management, business, and technical teams, share a common understanding of AI concepts, technologies, and goals. This will facilitate effective collaboration and decision-making across disciplines.

b. **Promoting a culture of learning and experimentation**: Encourage a mindset of continuous learning, curiosity, and experimentation within the organization. This will enable employees to embrace AI technologies and adapt to new ways of working.

c. **Aligning organizational structure and processes**: Adapt organizational structures and processes to support the implementation of AI, including the creation of cross-functional teams, the establishment of clear roles and responsibilities, and the adoption of agile methodologies for AI project management.

Leveraging Synergies Between Innovation, Change Management, Design Thinking, and Data-Driven Strategies

A successful AI implementation requires the seamless integration of innovation, change management, design thinking, and data-driven strategies. To leverage synergies between these key areas, organizations can

a. **Foster cross-functional collaboration**: Encourage collaboration and knowledge sharing between teams focused on innovation, change management, design thinking, and data-driven strategies. This will lead to the development of more effective and holistic AI solutions.

b. **Align AI initiatives with business goals and objectives**: Ensure that AI projects are aligned with the organization's overall strategic goals and objectives, and that they address real business challenges and opportunities.

c. **Apply a user-centered approach**: Apply design thinking and user-centered methodologies to the development of AI solutions, ensuring that they meet the needs and expectations of end users and deliver real value.

d. **Adopt a data-driven mindset**: Encourage a data-driven culture within the organization, where decisions are informed by insights derived from data analysis and AI models.

Building a Sustainable AI Ecosystem Within the Enterprise

Creating a sustainable AI ecosystem within an organization involves establishing the necessary infrastructure, processes, and resources to support the ongoing development, deployment, and maintenance of AI solutions. Key steps for building a sustainable AI ecosystem include

a. **Developing an AI strategy**: Create a comprehensive AI strategy that outlines the organization's vision for AI, identifies key focus areas, and sets targets and milestones for AI implementation.

b. **Investing in AI infrastructure**: Invest in the necessary hardware, software, and network infrastructure to support AI development and deployment, including cloud computing resources, data storage and processing capabilities, and AI development platforms and tools.

c. **Building AI capabilities**: Develop the necessary AI capabilities within the organization, including technical expertise in AI development and deployment, as well as business and domain knowledge to identify and prioritize AI opportunities.

d. **Establishing AI governance and ethics frameworks**: Implement AI governance and ethics frameworks that ensure the responsible and ethical development and use of AI technologies, including guidelines for data privacy and security, transparency, fairness, and safety.

e. **Fostering partnerships and collaborations**: Build relationships with external partners, including technology providers, academic institutions, and industry networks, to access knowledge, resources, and expertise that can support the organization's AI journey.

By integrating First Principles thinking across innovation, change management, design thinking, and data-driven strategies, organizations can establish a cohesive approach to AI implementation that maximizes the potential for success and growth. By building a sustainable AI ecosystem within the enterprise, organizations can create an environment that supports the ongoing development, deployment, and maintenance of AI solutions, ensuring that they continue to deliver value and drive competitive advantage.

Here are some additional tips for using the First Principles approach with AI:

- **Be patient**: It takes time to learn and apply the First Principles approach. Don't expect to see results overnight.

- **Be persistent**: Don't give up if you don't see results immediately. Keep trying, and you will eventually succeed.

- **Be open to feedback**: Be willing to listen to feedback from others. They may be able to help you to improve your approach.

- **Be humble**: Don't be afraid to admit when you don't know something. There is always more to learn.

Case Studies: Success Stories of First Principles in AI Implementation

The First Principles approach has been used successfully by several companies to implement AI. In this section, we will analyze real-world examples of companies that have successfully adopted First Principles for AI implementation. These case studies demonstrate the impact of First Principles thinking on AI initiatives and provide valuable lessons learned and best practices that can be applied by other organizations seeking to grow their business with AI.

Case Study 1: Tesla – Innovating in Autonomous Driving

Tesla, the American electric vehicle and clean energy company, has been a pioneer in the field of AI and autonomous driving. The company's approach to AI implementation reflects a strong commitment to First Principles thinking, particularly in the areas of innovation, design, and data-driven strategies.

Tesla's innovation process begins with a clear problem statement: developing sustainable energy solutions and reducing dependence on fossil fuels. To achieve this, Tesla has focused on creating electric vehicles with advanced autonomous driving capabilities. They have invested heavily in AI research and development, building a team of world-class AI experts and fostering a culture of learning and experimentation.

Tesla's design and systems thinking is evident in the development of their Autopilot system, which is designed to be user-centric and adaptable. By continuously collecting data from the fleet of Tesla vehicles on the road, the company is able to train and improve its AI algorithms, resulting in a safer and more efficient driving experience for users. This data-driven approach, combined with a relentless focus on iteration and improvement, has allowed Tesla to maintain a competitive edge in the rapidly evolving field of autonomous driving.

Lessons learned:

- Begin with a clear problem statement and align AI initiatives with broader business goals.

- Foster a culture of learning and experimentation.

- Focus on user-centric design and adaptability.

- Embrace a data-driven approach to AI development and improvement.

Case Study 2: Netflix – Transforming Entertainment with AI

Netflix, the streaming entertainment giant, has revolutionized the way people consume content through its use of AI and machine learning algorithms. The company's success in implementing AI is rooted in its commitment to First Principles thinking, particularly in the areas of innovation, design, and data-driven strategies.

Netflix's innovation process is centered around delivering a personalized and engaging user experience. By using AI to analyze user preferences, viewing habits, and content metadata, Netflix is able to deliver highly targeted content recommendations that keep users engaged and coming back for more.

Design and systems thinking play a crucial role in Netflix's AI implementation, with a strong focus on user-centric design and adaptability. The company continuously experiments with new AI models and algorithms, iterating and improving its recommendation engine based on user feedback and performance metrics.

Netflix's data-driven strategy is key to its AI success, as the company collects and processes vast amounts of user data to inform its AI models. By maintaining high standards for data quality, integrity, and privacy, Netflix ensures that its AI-driven recommendations are accurate, relevant, and respectful of user privacy.

Lessons learned:

- Focus on delivering a personalized and engaging user experience.

- Embrace user-centric design and adaptability.

- Iterate and improve AI models based on user feedback and performance metrics.

- Prioritize data quality, integrity, and privacy.

Case Study 3: Zipline – Revolutionizing Healthcare Delivery with AI-Powered Drones

Zipline, a startup specializing in drone delivery of medical supplies, has successfully implemented AI to revolutionize healthcare delivery in remote and underserved areas. The company's approach to AI implementation is grounded in First Principles thinking, particularly in the areas of innovation, design, and data-driven strategies.

Zipline's innovation process began with a clear problem statement: improving access to lifesaving medical supplies in areas with limited infrastructure and resources. The company developed an AI-powered drone delivery system to address this problem, creating a fast and reliable solution for delivering medical supplies to remote locations.

Zipline's design and systems thinking are evident in the development of its drone delivery system, which is centered around user needs and adaptability. The company has taken a holistic approach to system design, considering not only the drones themselves but also the logistical and operational aspects of the delivery process.

This focus on systems thinking has allowed Zipline to create a scalable and efficient solution that can be adapted to different geographical regions and healthcare delivery challenges.

Data-driven strategies play a key role in Zipline's AI implementation, as the company collects and analyzes data on flight patterns, weather conditions, and delivery performance to optimize its drone operations. By leveraging AI algorithms and models, Zipline is able to continually improve the efficiency and reliability of its delivery system, ensuring that medical supplies reach their destinations quickly and safely.

Lessons learned:

- Start with a clear problem statement and focus on addressing user needs.

- Apply systems thinking to create scalable and adaptable solutions.

- Leverage data-driven strategies to optimize AI-driven operations and improve performance.

These case studies illustrate the power of First Principles thinking in AI implementation across various industries. As organizations continue to adopt AI, the lessons learned and best practices from these case studies can serve as valuable guidance for successful AI implementation. By embracing First Principles thinking and applying these principles across innovation, change management, design and systems thinking, and data and AI strategies, businesses can harness the transformative power of AI to drive growth and success in an increasingly competitive landscape.

Challenges and Limitations of Applying First Principles in AI

The First Principles approach is a powerful tool for AI, but it is not without its challenges and limitations. In this section, we will explore the challenges and limitations organizations may face when applying First Principles in AI. By understanding these challenges and limitations, businesses can better navigate the complexities of AI implementation and maximize their chances of success.

Addressing Potential Obstacles and Constraints in Adopting First Principles

While the First Principles approach is very powerful, there are a few challenges to consider before fully adopting the methodology, specially for smaller and non-strategic projects:

a. **Resource constraints**: Implementing AI solutions can be resource-intensive, requiring significant investments in time, money, and expertise. Organizations may face challenges in allocating sufficient resources to fully leverage the First Principles approach in AI initiatives. This can limit the scope and effectiveness of AI projects and hinder the organization's ability to derive maximum value from AI adoption.

b. **Resistance to change**: Adopting a First Principles mindset often requires a significant shift in organizational culture and mindset. Employees and stakeholders may resist this change, making it difficult to gain buy-in and support for AI initiatives. Overcoming this resistance requires strong leadership and effective communication to demonstrate the value of First Principles thinking and its relevance to AI implementation.

c. **Organizational silos**: First Principles thinking requires collaboration across multiple departments and functions. However, many organizations are structured in silos, making it difficult for teams to work together and share insights. Breaking down these silos is crucial for fostering collaboration and ensuring that AI projects are aligned with organizational goals and objectives.

Balancing First Principles Thinking with Practical Considerations

Enterprises embarking on new projects should also focus on the business value generated; this is why there are some situations where First Principles might not be the most suitable one – even if technically it might deliver the best results.

a. **Striking the right balance**: While First Principles thinking can help organizations uncover novel insights and solutions, it can also lead to over-analysis and paralysis. Striking the right balance between First Principles thinking and practical considerations is essential to ensure that AI projects move forward in a timely and efficient manner.

b. **Managing complexity**: AI systems can be complex, and the First Principles approach requires organizations to grapple with this complexity head-on. However, managing complexity can be challenging, particularly for organizations with limited experience in AI. Balancing simplicity and complexity in AI system design is crucial to ensure that AI solutions are effective and user-friendly.

c. **Ensuring timeliness**: First Principles thinking can be a time-consuming process, as it requires a thorough examination of assumptions and constraints. In the fast-paced world of technology and business, organizations must balance the need for thorough analysis with the need to move quickly and seize market opportunities.

Ensuring the Scalability and Adaptability of AI Solutions

First principles guidelines have to be balanced across the short-term needs of the enterprise.

a. **Scalability**: A key challenge in applying First Principles to AI is ensuring that AI solutions can scale effectively to meet the needs of the organization. This requires a deep understanding of the underlying technology, infrastructure, and data requirements, as well as the ability to anticipate future needs and growth. Organizations must invest in scalable AI solutions to maximize the value of their AI initiatives.

b. **Adaptability**: AI systems must be adaptable to changing circumstances, whether in the form of new data, evolving user needs, or shifting market conditions. First Principles thinking can help organizations design adaptable AI systems, but it can also be a challenge to maintain this adaptability in the face of real-world constraints and pressures. Balancing adaptability and stability in AI systems is essential for long-term success.

Ethical and Safety Considerations

Finally, First Principles on AI projects need to be balanced with the different overall AI safety frameworks, especially when short-term objectives might be different from long-term ones.

   a. **Ethical concerns**: AI systems have the potential to raise a host of ethical concerns, from data privacy to algorithmic bias. Applying First Principles thinking to AI requires organizations to carefully consider these ethical implications and develop strategies to address them. Balancing the benefits of AI with the need for ethical and responsible use is a critical challenge for organizations implementing AI solutions.

   b. **Safety and reliability**: Ensuring the safety and reliability of AI systems is paramount, particularly in industries where mistakes can have significant consequences. The First Principles approach can help organizations identify potential risks and vulnerabilities in AI systems, but it also requires a thorough understanding of the technology and its potential impact. Developing robust safety and reliability measures is essential to minimize risks and ensure that AI solutions operate as intended.

In conclusion, while applying First Principles thinking to AI can yield significant benefits, organizations must also be mindful of the challenges and limitations that can arise during implementation. By addressing potential obstacles, striking the right balance between First Principles thinking and practical considerations, and ensuring the scalability, adaptability, and ethical considerations of AI solutions, organizations can better position themselves for success in AI adoption.

To navigate these challenges and limitations effectively, organizations should consider the following strategies:

1. **Invest in education and training**: Equip employees with the knowledge and skills necessary to understand and implement First Principles thinking in AI. This includes training in data science, machine learning, and systems thinking, as well as courses on ethics and safety in AI.

2. **Foster a culture of collaboration and open communication**: Encourage cross-functional collaboration and open communication to break down organizational silos and foster a shared understanding of First Principles thinking and its applications in AI.

3. **Leverage external expertise**: Collaborate with external partners, consultants, and experts to gain insights and guidance on the application of First Principles thinking in AI. This can help organizations overcome resource constraints and build a deeper understanding of AI technology and its potential impact.

4. **Develop a clear roadmap for AI implementation**: Create a strategic roadmap that outlines the organization's vision for AI adoption, as well as the steps and resources required to achieve this vision. This roadmap should be informed by First Principles thinking and should be regularly reviewed and updated to ensure alignment with organizational goals and objectives.

5. **Monitor and measure progress**: Establish metrics and performance indicators to monitor the progress and effectiveness of AI initiatives. This can help organizations identify areas for improvement and ensure that AI projects are delivering the expected value and impact.

Key Takeaways

In this chapter, we delved into the application of First Principles thinking for successful enterprise AI implementation. This approach, which involves dissecting complex problems into their basic elements, fosters innovative solutions and promotes effective AI adoption.

Innovation First Principles focus on organizational culture, mindset changes, and skill development. For successful innovation, organizations need a common language to facilitate team collaboration and a strong focus on user experience in AI solution development. Change implementation requires a clear vision, progress roadmap, and support coalition. Communication, trust, and transparency are key to overcoming resistance to change and enhancing AI acceptance.

Design and system thinking First Principles advocate for a user-centric approach, viewing systems as a whole, and nurturing adaptability and creativity. This leads to AI solutions that balance simplicity and complexity. Data and AI First Principles highlight the need for clear problem definition, data quality, privacy, as well as careful AI model selection and training. Ethical and safety measures are vital to responsible AI deployment and maintenance.

Creating a cohesive approach that integrates First Principles thinking across innovation, change management, design thinking, and data-driven strategies is crucial for a sustainable AI ecosystem. Real-world case studies exemplify the effect of First Principles thinking on AI projects, providing valuable lessons and best practices. Despite challenges in balancing First Principles thinking with practical concerns and ensuring AI solution scalability, this approach remains invaluable for organizations on their AI journey.

The following are the three key takeaways:

- **Takeaway point 1**: The successful implementation of AI initiatives in an organization requires **more than just technical expertise**; you need to consider innovation, the ability to implement change, the importance of design and systems thinking, and the need for a strong foundation in data and AI. The specific situation of your enterprise will dictate how much effort to put into each area. Ensure you consider all dimensions of a project from a First Principles perspective, and do not skip any steps, regardless of how "trivial" they might look.

- Following a systematic approach and addressing every aspect of AI implementation, from problem definition to ethical considerations, ensures a solid foundation for success. Do not overlook or undervalue any step in the process, as each plays a crucial role in the overall outcome.

- **Takeaway point 2**: AI is progressing at an astonishing pace; the tools and models are being improved all the time, but the fundamental First Principles are stable.

  - Although AI technology is constantly evolving, the core First Principles remain consistent. By grounding your AI projects in these foundational concepts, you can achieve long-lasting success and adapt to changing circumstances more effectively.

- **Takeaway point 3**: Key lessons learned from chapter examples and samples:

  - **Innovation First Principles**: Invest in employee skill development and training, promote a culture of collaboration, and focus on user experience and customer-centric design.

  - **Implementing change First Principles**: Identify root causes, develop a shared vision, build trust and transparency, empower teams, provide continuous feedback, and recognize progress.

  - **Data-driven projects First Principles**: Clearly define problem statements and objectives, gather relevant data, formulate hypotheses, design experiments, build MVPs, and integrate with business processes.

  - **Design thinking/system thinking First Principles**: Apply empathy, observation, problem framing, ideation, prototyping, systems thinking, iteration, collaboration, human-centered design, and ethical considerations.

Here are some Dos and Don'ts for best practices when applying First Principles thinking in AI development:

a. **Dos**:

   a. Invest in employee training and skill development to foster a culture of innovation and collaboration.

   b. Prioritize user experience and customer-centric design when developing AI solutions.

   c. Communicate effectively and transparently when implementing change.

   d. Consider the entire system when designing AI solutions.

   e. Prioritize data quality, integrity, and privacy when working with AI models.

b. **Don'ts:**

   a. Overlook the importance of continuous learning and growth.

   b. Focus solely on technology without considering the end user's needs.

   c. Underestimate the power of trust and transparency in overcoming resistance to change.

   d. Get bogged down in the details of individual components without considering the big picture.

   e. Neglect the ethical and safety implications of AI technology.

By applying First Principles thinking across innovation, change management, design and systems thinking, and data and AI strategies, organizations can unlock the transformative potential of AI technology and position themselves for long-term success in an increasingly competitive and rapidly evolving landscape.

The next chapter (Chapter 4) is the last one of Part 1, "Introduction and First Principles," of this book. We will explore in detail all the key barriers when implementing AI, so we can effectively plan for them.

The Barriers for Implementing AI

This is the last chapter from Part I, "Introduction and First Principles." We have focused so far, first, on understanding both the incredible potential but also some of the important risks of AI, and then drilling down on First Principles and potential challenges to implement AI. One of the main objectives of the book is to help people from all types of enterprises to be successful with their AI initiatives. You might have probably noticed I have not gone very deep into AI yet; indeed, there is a strong reason for this approach. While there are plenty of books which only focus on the technical aspects of AI projects, I strongly believe you need to really understand the reasons behind how it is so hard to implement AI, so you can then target a specific action plan for your enterprise. We spent Chapter 1 describing the core underlying issue, achieving effective communication across the ecosystem, which is sometimes referred as "the two cultures"[1], how a separation of the scientific and humanities communities creates a gap in understanding across all society, which naturally includes the business world. In this chapter, we will go deeper into the most common challenges, and following the First Principles methodology, we will separate the issues that anyone implementing a new technology will encounter from the issues specific to artificial intelligence. This chapter will also show some techniques to overcome those barriers; however, as you will see, there is a strong dependency in the type and culture of the organization.

---

[1] https://sciencepolicy.colorado.edu/students/envs_5110/snow_1959.pdf

© Francisco Javier Campos Zabala 2023
F. J. Campos Zabala, *Grow Your Business with AI*, https://doi.org/10.1007/978-1-4842-9669-1_4

Common Barriers Associated with Implementing Any New Technology

Implementing new technology is always challenging, regardless of the specific type of technology being implemented. The following barriers are common to any technology implementation and must be considered when implementing AI:

1. **Resistance to change**: Employees and stakeholders may resist new technology, fearing job displacement or disruptions to existing processes. To overcome resistance, organizations should communicate the benefits of AI, involve employees in the implementation process, and provide training and resources to help them adapt.

2. **Lack of understanding/skills and expertise**: Successfully implementing new technology requires knowledge and expertise. Organizations can address this barrier by investing in upskilling their workforce, partnering with external experts, and fostering a culture of continuous learning.

3. **Business and strategy alignment**: Ensuring new technology aligns with an organization's overall goals and strategies is crucial. To achieve alignment, organizations should develop a comprehensive strategy that outlines how AI can support their objectives and facilitate regular communication between business and technical stakeholders.

4. **Change management best practices**: Effective change management is essential for successful technology implementation. Organizations should develop a change management plan that outlines objectives, timelines, and key activities, and ensure stakeholder engagement and cultural alignment throughout the process.

Barriers Specific to Artificial Intelligence

In addition to the common barriers associated with implementing new technology, AI initiatives face specific challenges due to the nature of the technology. The following are the key barriers specific to AI implementation:

1. **Outdated management guidelines**: Many management guidelines in use today were established in the 1950s and 1970s, and they do not fully account for the rapid advancements in technology and data processing capabilities. As a result, organizations might struggle to adapt to the changes brought about by AI adoption. Business leaders need to update their management approaches to align with the evolving technological landscape and take advantage of the opportunities AI offers.

2. **Language barrier**: Bridging the gap between business-minded and technical-minded stakeholders is critical for AI projects. Establishing a common language and understanding can be achieved through regular meetings, workshops, and cross-functional collaboration. We will also discuss "the two cultures" by C.P. Snow, where the miscommunication gap between the scientific and humanity community is having a profound impact in society, including business.

3. **Data and infrastructure**: AI technologies rely on data quality, storage, and processing power. Organizations may face challenges related to data management and infrastructure. To address these issues, businesses should invest in modernizing their data infrastructure, implementing robust data governance policies, and utilizing cloud-based solutions.

4. **Governance and regulation**: AI adoption brings legal and regulatory considerations, such as data privacy, security, and compliance. Organizations must ensure they meet these requirements by conducting regular audits, establishing a dedicated AI ethics committee, and staying informed about the latest regulatory developments.

5. **Metrics and measurement**: Establishing clear key performance indicators (KPIs) and metrics is vital for measuring the success of AI initiatives. Organizations should develop a set of quantitative and qualitative metrics to track progress and evaluate AI's impact on the business.

Organizations can maximize the benefits of AI and drive significant value, once they have a deep understanding of these barriers, so they can produce a specific plan addressing these barriers to their success. The larger the organization, the most important the people/culture elements are, versus in smaller organization the technical barriers can have a larger impact. In the rest of the chapter, we will go deep into each of these nine barriers.

Barrier 1: Resistance to Change

One of the most significant barriers to implementing AI (and pretty much any new technology/process) in a company is resistance to change. Employees and stakeholders may resist the implementation of AI for a variety of reasons, including fear of job loss, lack of understanding, and concerns about the impact on company culture. In this section, we will explore these reasons in more detail and discuss strategies to address this barrier. Using a First Principles approach, we can break down the core components of this resistance and explore strategies to address them effectively.

Core components of resistance to change:

1. **Fear of job loss**: Employees may be concerned that AI will automate their tasks, rendering their roles obsolete.

2. **Lack of understanding**: Some employees might not comprehend the full potential of AI and how it can benefit the organization, leading to resistance.

3. Employees may worry that the introduction of AI will result in a **significant shift in the company's values and culture**, impacting their work environment.

The following are some typical strategies to address resistance to change:

1. **Clear communication**: Ensure open and transparent communication about the purpose and benefits of AI implementation. Educate employees on how AI can enhance their roles and contribute to the company's growth. Address concerns and misconceptions to help build understanding and trust.

2. **Employee involvement**: Involve employees in the decision-making and implementation process. Encourage their input and feedback, and actively listen to their concerns. This sense of ownership and participation can help reduce resistance.

3. **Training and reskilling**: Invest in employee training to help them acquire the necessary skills to work with AI technologies. This can alleviate fears of job loss and create a more adaptable workforce.

4. **Showcase success stories**: Share examples of how AI has benefited other organizations, both internally and externally. Demonstrating the positive impact of AI can help employees understand its potential and foster acceptance.

5. **Address cultural concerns**: Reinforce the organization's commitment to its core values and culture. Emphasize that AI is a tool to enhance human capabilities, not replace them. Support a culture that embraces innovation while preserving the organization's unique identity.

6. **Establish AI champions**: Identify and empower key individuals within the organization to advocate for AI adoption. These champions can help drive change by sharing their knowledge, expertise, and enthusiasm with their colleagues.

This barrier will be present in all organizations, so it is important to address it adequately, and the action plan is adapted to each enterprise's specific characteristics such as size and culture. When organizations fully understand the core components of resistance to change, they can create a unique environment that is more receptive to AI adoption. Incorporating relevant examples, data, and visual aids can further illustrate the benefits of embracing AI, fostering a culture of innovation and growth. Companies should prioritize education, governance, communication, involvement, and upskilling to help address resistance and promote a smooth transition to AI-powered workflows.

Barrier 2: Lack of Understanding and Expertise

One key barrier to implementing AI in organizations is the lack of understanding and expertise. To successfully adopt AI, it is crucial for organizations to develop the necessary skills and knowledge in their workforce. This subsection will provide an overview of the essential skills and knowledge for AI implementation and strategies to build and develop expertise within an organization.

The following are essential skills and knowledge for AI implementation:

1. **Data literacy**: Employees should be able to interpret and analyze data, as well as understand the importance of data quality and integrity. This point is often underestimated by organizations, as the overall data literacy levels of the population of most countries are quite low. In the USA, it is estimated that the lack of data literacy, when it comes to finance, costed each American $1,819 in 2022.[2] The survey is quite revealing, as most people will fail to grasp basic math's concepts. AI requires quite a bit of background on Statistics and Advanced Math; hence there is a very large gap, and many training courses fail because they assume a basic level which is simply not there.

2. **AI/ML techniques**: Familiarity with various AI and machine learning algorithms, their applications, and the ability to choose the appropriate technique for a given problem. It is important there is an orchestrated training program, as the worse situation is to let teams to just listen to the myths from the media, which by design focus on the negative and rarely offer an overall unbiased view of each situation.

3. **Programming and software skills**: Knowledge of programming languages (e.g., Python, R) and tools commonly used in AI development, such as TensorFlow or PyTorch. We will list these in later chapters.

---

[2] www.financialeducatorscouncil.org/financial-illiteracy-costs-2/

4. **Domain expertise**: Understanding the specific industry or business context in which AI will be applied, enabling more effective solutions.

5. **Ethical considerations**: Awareness of ethical implications, including data privacy, security, and fairness, is crucial for responsible AI implementation.

The following strategies can be used to address the lack of understanding and expertise:

1. **Training programs**: Implement comprehensive training programs to develop the necessary AI skills among existing employees. This could include workshops, online courses, or partnering with educational institutions. It is also recommended to target specific courses for specific audiences – for instance, one set for senior management, one for middle management, and a wider course for all the workforce. A good example of online resources is the NLP "TutorialBank," a collections of learning resources to learn NLP.[3]

2. **Hire AI talent**: Recruit skilled AI professionals, such as data scientists, machine learning engineers, and AI strategists, to build a dedicated AI team.

3. **Collaboration and knowledge sharing**: Encourage collaboration between technical and non-technical teams to facilitate knowledge sharing and improve overall AI understanding within the organization.

4. **External partnerships**: Collaborate with external AI experts, consultancies, or research institutions to access specialized knowledge and accelerate AI implementation. Most governments have set up national AI plans to accelerate AI as a competitive advantage, and as part of those roadmap government-backed groups and agencies are created to promote AI. For instance, in

---

[3] https://arxiv.org/pdf/1805.04617.pdf

the UK, "The Alan Turing institute" [4] provides plenty of thought AI leadership and industry collaboration programs that enterprises can take advantage of.

5. **Continuous learning**: Foster a culture of continuous learning and professional development to ensure that employees stay up-to-date with the latest AI advancements and techniques. The good news is that there are plenty of resources online, many free for people to learn. We will explore some of these resources later in the book.

6. **Mentoring and coaching**: Establish mentorship programs where experienced AI practitioners guide and support less experienced employees in developing their AI skills.

Barrier 3: Business and Strategy Alignment

Another barrier to AI implementation is ensuring that new technology aligns with an organization's overall goals and strategies. This is a very important barrier which very few businesses managed to get it right. Achieving alignment is critical to realizing the full potential of AI in driving business growth and innovation. This subsection will outline strategies for aligning AI initiatives with business objectives and facilitating regular communication between business and technical stakeholders.

In the journey of growing your enterprise with AI, it is crucial to ensure that the overall business strategy encompasses the strategic capabilities of AI. This requires a thorough understanding of the technology, its potential, and the best way to leverage it for business growth. However, one of the most prominent barriers to achieving this harmony is the lack of communication between management and AI tech teams. This communication barrier is reminiscent of the divide between the "two cultures" as described by C.P. Snow. In his seminal work, *The Two Cultures*, C.P. Snow outlines the cultural chasm between the scientific and social science worlds, where professionals from each realm struggle to communicate effectively with one another. This division often leads to misunderstandings and missed opportunities for collaboration, and the same is true for the AI business landscape.

---

[4] www.turing.ac.uk/

To overcome this barrier and ensure that the overall business strategy is infused with AI's strategic capabilities, both management and AI tech teams must strive to bridge the communication gap. Here are typical strategies to address the business and strategy alignment barrier:

1. **Foster mutual understanding; engage executive leadership**: Secure commitment from top-level executives by demonstrating the potential value of AI and its alignment with the organization's strategic vision. Executive sponsorship can help drive AI adoption and facilitate cross-functional collaboration. Encourage cross-functional training and workshops for both management and AI tech teams. This will allow both sides to understand each other's language, objectives, and constraints, fostering empathy and easing communication.

2. **Develop a comprehensive AI strategy; establish clear goals**: Create a clear and well-defined AI strategy that outlines how AI can support the organization's objectives. This should include identifying specific use cases, setting measurable goals, and determining the resources required for AI implementation. Align your AI initiatives with your overall business objectives. Ensure that the AI tech teams understand the business goals and that management is aware of the technical possibilities and limitations of AI.

3. **Establish a cross-functional AI team**: Create a team comprising members from various departments, including IT, data science, and relevant business units. Ensure the right governance is in place – where all team members have aligned incentives and/or objectives. This diverse team can help ensure that AI initiatives are aligned with business goals and that stakeholders' concerns are addressed.

4. **Regular communication and collaboration**: Facilitate open and transparent communication between technical and non-technical stakeholders. Regular meetings, workshops, and updates can help keep everyone informed about AI initiatives and their progress, ensuring alignment with business objectives. Create

opportunities for interdisciplinary teamwork, where management
and AI tech teams can work together on projects, share ideas,
and solve problems collectively. This will not only bridge the
communication gap but also bring about innovative solutions that
leverage AI's capabilities to drive business growth.

5. **Designate AI ambassadors**: Identify individuals who can act
   as liaisons between management and AI tech teams. These
   ambassadors should be skilled in both business and technology
   and can help translate objectives, requirements, and progress
   updates between the two groups

6. **Prioritize AI projects based on value and feasibility**: Evaluate AI
   initiatives based on their potential impact on business objectives
   and their feasibility in terms of resources and technology. Focus
   on projects that provide the most significant value while being
   achievable within the organization's constraints.

7. **Monitor and adjust AI initiatives and emphasize
   communication**: Regularly assess the progress of AI projects
   and their alignment with business goals. Be prepared to adjust
   or change direction based on feedback, performance metrics,
   or changes in business priorities. Encourage continuous
   open and transparent communication across all levels of the
   organization. This includes regular updates, feedback sessions,
   and brainstorming meetings where both management and AI
   tech teams can discuss challenges, opportunities, and AI-related
   developments.

8. **Develop success stories**: Demonstrate the value of AI by
   showcasing successful implementations and their impact on the
   organization's goals. These success stories can serve as examples
   to reinforce the alignment between AI initiatives and business
   strategies.

By incorporating these strategies, organizations can break down the barriers
between the two cultures and create a unified, AI-driven business strategy. This will
not only ensure that AI's strategic capabilities are fully leveraged but will also empower

the organization to adapt and innovate in the rapidly evolving landscape of artificial intelligence. Table 4-1 is a comparison table which highlights the key differences between traditional business strategy approaches and AI-enabled strategy approaches.

Table 4-1. *The key differences between traditional business strategy approaches and AI-enabled strategy approaches*

Aspect	Traditional business strategy approaches	AI-enabled strategy approaches
Goal-setting	Based on historical performance, market trends, and human intuition	Utilizes AI-generated insights, simulations, and predictive analytics to inform and refine goals
Data-driven decision-making	Decisions are made using limited datasets, often based on past experiences and intuition	Harnesses vast amounts of data from multiple sources, enabling real-time decision-making and continuous optimization
Adaptability	Reactive to change, requiring manual adjustment to strategy and a longer time to adapt	Proactive and self-learning, capable of adapting in real-time based on new data and market conditions
Resource allocation	Primarily based on budgeting and forecasting using historical data and trends	AI-powered algorithms dynamically allocate resources based on current data and performance metrics
Market analysis	Periodic and manual analysis of market trends, competitors, and customer needs	Continuous, automated analysis of market conditions, competitive landscape, and customer preferences using AI tools
Risk management	Risk assessment and mitigation is often subjective and based on past experiences	AI-driven predictive analytics help identify potential risks and suggest mitigation strategies in real-time
Innovation and competitive advantage	Incremental innovation based on known business models and technologies	Breakthrough innovation by leveraging AI's capabilities to identify new opportunities and create unique value propositions

(continued)

Table 4-1. (*continued*)

Aspect	Traditional business strategy approaches	AI-enabled strategy approaches
Customer understanding and personalization	Segmentation and targeting based on demographic data and broad customer profiles	Granular understanding of individual customer preferences and behavior, enabling hyper-personalized experiences
Performance measurement and evaluation	Manual tracking of KPIs, often with a focus on short-term results	Automated, real-time tracking of KPIs, allowing for a more holistic view of performance and long-term outcomes

Barrier 4: Change Management

Effective change management is essential for successful technology implementation, including AI adoption. Organizations should develop a change management plan that outlines objectives, timelines, and key activities, and ensures stakeholder engagement and cultural alignment throughout the process. This subsection will highlight strategies for managing change and overcoming potential challenges during AI implementation.

The following are typical strategies to address change management barriers:

1. **Develop a change management plan**: Create a structured plan that includes clear objectives, timelines, and key activities to guide the organization through the AI implementation process. This plan should outline the desired outcomes and establish a framework for managing change.

2. **Identify key stakeholders**: Determine the individuals and groups within the organization who will be directly or indirectly affected by the AI implementation. Engage these stakeholders early in the process to understand their needs, concerns, and expectations.

3. **Communicate the vision and benefits**: Clearly communicate the purpose of the AI initiative, its expected benefits, and how it aligns with the organization's strategic objectives. This communication should be ongoing and tailored to different stakeholder groups to ensure understanding and buy-in.

4. **Provide training and support**: Offer comprehensive training and support for employees affected by the AI implementation. This includes technical training for new tools and systems, as well as support for adapting to new processes and workflows.

5. **Establish a feedback loop**: Create channels for stakeholders to provide feedback and voice concerns throughout the AI implementation process. This feedback loop allows for adjustments and improvements to be made as needed, ensuring a smoother transition.

6. **Foster a culture of innovation and adaptability**: Encourage a culture that embraces change, innovation, and continuous learning. This will help employees to be more open and adaptable to new technologies such as AI.

7. **Celebrate successes and learn from failures**: Recognize and celebrate the milestones and successes achieved during the AI implementation process. Additionally, analyze and learn from any setbacks or challenges encountered along the way to inform future initiatives.

Lastly, there are several change management frameworks; Figure 4-1 describes the popular Kotter's 8-step model.[5]

---

[5]www.kotterinc.com/methodology/8-steps/

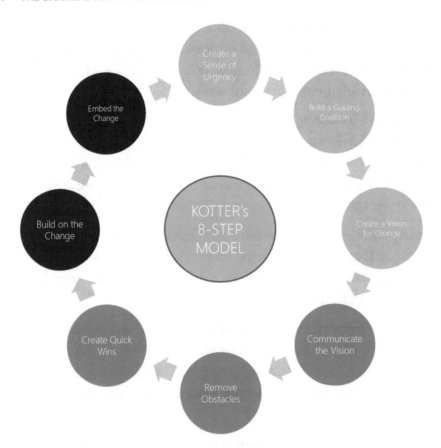

Figure 4-1. *Kotter's model for change management*

Barrier 5: Outdated Management Practices

The foundation of most MBA programs is influenced by a few management gurus such as **Michael Porter** and its five forces framework, **Tom Peters**, **W. Edwards Deming**, **Clayton Christensen** and his "jobs-to-be-done," and many others. Among all of them, **Peter Drucker** is widely considered the father of modern management theory. Therefore, most companies today are managed following these principles developed in the 1950s and 1970s. Nevertheless, in the 2020+, the era of data and AI, Peter Drucker's key principle of enterprise management, which states that "Marketing and innovation produce results; all the rest are costs," may no longer fully encompass the breadth of value creation opportunities that modern organizations have at their disposal. While marketing and innovation remain essential components of business success, the rapid rise of data and AI has introduced new dimensions to the value generation process that traditional management techniques may not adequately address.

Traditional management techniques often emphasize top-down decision-making, rigid hierarchies, and well-defined roles and responsibilities. However, the dynamic nature of data and AI requires organizations to adopt more agile, collaborative, and adaptive approaches to remain competitive. By leveraging data and AI effectively, organizations can generate insights, optimize processes, enhance customer experiences, and create new business models that were previously unattainable.

The Need for Evolving Management Practices for AI

Traditional management techniques may miss the point about leveraging data and AI in several ways:

- **Limited focus on data-driven decision-making**: Traditional management may prioritize experience and intuition over data-driven insights. However, in the era of data and AI, harnessing the power of data analytics and machine learning can lead to more accurate, timely, and informed decisions, ultimately driving better business outcomes.

- **Inadequate investment in data infrastructure and talent**: Traditional management may not recognize the importance of investing in robust data infrastructure, AI technologies, and skilled talent to capitalize on the value of data. The lack of investment in these areas can hinder an organization's ability to fully harness the potential of data and AI. Organizations must strategically invest in upskilling their workforce and identifying the right talent for AI projects.

- **Resistance to change and innovation**: Traditional management techniques may foster resistance to change and innovation, particularly when it comes to adopting new technologies like AI. Embracing a culture of continuous learning and experimentation is essential for organizations to stay competitive in the rapidly evolving AI landscape.

- **Organizational structure – insufficient cross-functional collaboration**: Traditional management structures often emphasize departmental silos, which can impede effective collaboration between technical and non-technical teams. Leveraging data and AI often requires a diverse set of skills and perspectives, necessitating cross-functional collaboration for successful implementation. AI-driven organizations may need to adopt more agile, cross-functional team structures that enable collaboration between technical and non-technical stakeholders.

- **Performance management**: Traditional performance evaluation methods may not be suitable for AI projects, which often require a different set of success metrics and evaluation criteria, both in technical performance but also financially, as the economics of AI projects is different from classical technologies.

- **Lack of emphasis on ethical AI**: Traditional management techniques may not fully address the ethical implications of AI and data-driven decision-making. As AI becomes increasingly integrated into business operations, it is crucial for organizations to prioritize ethical considerations and develop robust governance frameworks that ensure responsible AI adoption.

By recognizing and addressing the limitations of traditional management techniques in the era of data and AI, organizations can unlock new opportunities for value creation and drive transformative growth. This requires embracing a culture of data-driven decision-making, investing in the necessary infrastructure and talent, fostering innovation, promoting cross-functional collaboration, and prioritizing ethical AI adoption. With these shifts in management practices, businesses can fully harness the power of data and AI to revolutionize their industries and create lasting competitive advantages.

Strategies for Updating Management Guidelines to Accommodate AI

To keep pace with AI's rapid advancements, organizations need to update their management guidelines to support AI implementation effectively. Here are several strategies that can help organizations update their management practices to accommodate AI:

- **Encourage a data-driven culture**: A data-driven culture values evidence-based decision-making and embraces AI-generated insights. Encouraging data-driven decision-making can help organizations make better use of AI capabilities.

- **Adopt agile methodologies**: Agile methodologies, such as Scrum and Kanban, promote iterative development and continuous improvement. By adopting agile methodologies, organizations can ensure their management practices can respond more quickly to the dynamic nature of AI projects.

- **Foster cross-functional collaboration**: AI projects often require a diverse set of skills, including data scientists, engineers, and business experts. Encouraging cross-functional collaboration can ensure that all necessary skills are available and that different perspectives are considered during the AI implementation process. Some large enterprises are making mandatory for all new projects before obtaining funding, to present a section on how Data Science (AI/ML) will be applied.

- **Develop new performance evaluation criteria**: Traditional performance evaluation methods may not accurately capture the success of AI projects. Organizations should develop new performance evaluation criteria that focus on AI-specific metrics, such as model accuracy, data quality, and business impact. Table 4-2 is a comparison table that highlights the differences between traditional performance evaluation criteria and AI-specific performance evaluation criteria for projects within the enterprise. As AI projects become more prevalent, organizations must adapt their performance evaluation methods to ensure that they are accurately measuring the success of AI-driven initiatives and making well-informed decisions.

Table 4-2. *Evaluation criteria for projects: traditional vs AI-based ones*

Aspect	Traditional performance evaluation criteria	AI-specific performance evaluation criteria
Metrics	Financial (ROI, NPV, etc.), project schedule, resource utilization, scope adherence	Financial, model accuracy, precision, recall, F1 score, area under the curve (AUC), training and validation loss
Data source	Historical financial data, project management systems, manual reporting	Raw datasets, structured/unstructured data, real-time data streams, API integrations
Time horizon	Fixed, periodic evaluations (quarterly, annually)	Continuous, real-time monitoring and evaluation
Scalability	Limited by manual processes and data availability	Highly scalable due to automation and data-driven nature
Adaptability	Rigid and focused on predefined goals, slower to adjust	Dynamic and capable of adjusting based on data and evolving project requirements
Risk management	Qualitative assessment, reliant on human judgment and experience	Quantitative risk assessment based on data, predictive analytics, and algorithmic evaluation
Interpretability and explainability	Relatively straightforward, based on established metrics	Complex, requiring model interpretability and explainability for non-technical stakeholders
Bias and fairness	Limited consideration, dependent on human awareness of potential biases	Systematic identification and mitigation of biases in data and model outputs, ensuring fairness in AI applications
Data quality and integrity	Assumes accurate and reliable data sources	Requires extensive data preprocessing, validation, and cleaning to ensure high-quality inputs and outputs

- **Invest in talent development**: Organizations must invest in developing the skills needed for AI implementation, such as data science, machine learning, and AI ethics. This investment can include training programs, workshops, and partnerships with educational institutions.

- **Emphasize ethical AI**: As AI's impact on society grows, ethical considerations become increasingly important. Organizations should integrate ethical AI principles into their management guidelines, ensuring that AI projects align with the company's values and comply with relevant regulations.

Adapting management practices to accommodate AI is crucial for organizations seeking to leverage the technology's full potential. Embracing data-driven decision-making, adopting agile methodologies, fostering cross-functional collaboration, developing new performance evaluation criteria, investing in talent development, and emphasizing ethical AI can help organizations successfully navigate the AI-driven landscape and unlock its transformative potential.

As AI continues to evolve, organizations must remain vigilant and adaptable, continuously reviewing and refining their management practices to stay ahead of the curve. By doing so, companies can not only overcome the barriers associated with AI implementation but also harness the technology's power to drive business growth and innovation.

Barrier 6: Language Barrier

Bridging the gap between business-minded and technical-minded stakeholders is critical for AI projects. Different backgrounds and areas of expertise can lead to misunderstandings and miscommunication. Establishing a common language and understanding can be achieved through regular meetings, workshops, and cross-functional collaboration. This subsection will explore strategies to overcome language barriers between stakeholders in AI projects.

Strategies to address language barriers are the following:

1. **Encourage cross-functional collaboration**: Bring together teams from various departments, such as IT, business, and data science, to work on AI projects. This collaboration helps to establish a shared understanding of the goals, challenges, and potential solutions.

2. **Hold regular meetings and workshops**: Conduct meetings and workshops that involve both business and technical stakeholders to discuss AI projects, objectives, and progress. These sessions create opportunities for open communication and help bridge the language gap.

3. **Develop a common vocabulary**: Create a glossary of key terms and concepts that are relevant to AI projects, and ensure all stakeholders have access to it. This common vocabulary will facilitate clearer communication between different parties.

4. **Assign liaisons or "translators"**: Identify individuals who possess both business and technical expertise and can effectively communicate with both groups. These liaisons or translators can help bridge the communication gap and ensure that everyone is on the same page.

5. **Provide training and education**: Offer training sessions and educational materials for all stakeholders to develop a better understanding of AI technologies, their potential applications, and the specific terminology used in AI projects.

6. **Foster a culture of open communication**: Encourage an organizational culture that values open communication, active listening, and empathy. This will help break down language barriers and promote a more collaborative environment for AI projects.

Barrier 7: Data and Infrastructure

AI technologies rely on data quality, storage, and processing power. Organizations may face challenges related to data management and infrastructure. To address these issues, businesses should invest in modernizing their data infrastructure, implementing robust data governance policies, and utilizing cloud-based solutions whenever appropriated. This subsection will explore the key data and infrastructure challenges and propose strategies to overcome these barriers.

The following are some typical strategies to address data and infrastructure barriers:

1. **Modernize data infrastructure**: Invest in upgrading existing data infrastructure to support the increased demands of AI technologies. This may involve upgrading hardware, implementing high-performance computing resources, and using scalable storage solutions.

2. **Implement robust data governance policies**: Develop and enforce data governance policies that ensure data quality, consistency, and security. These policies should cover data collection, storage, processing, and sharing and should be regularly reviewed and updated.

3. **Utilize cloud-based solutions**: Leverage cloud-based infrastructure and services to store, process, and manage large volumes of data. Cloud solutions can offer scalability, flexibility, and cost savings compared to traditional on-premises infrastructure. Here, a note of caution, please make sure you use First Principles in your business case for the cloud; in some instances it might be better to have some of your own data centers for some specific workloads.

4. **Establish a data management team**: Create a dedicated team responsible for data management, including data quality, storage, and processing. This team should work closely with AI project teams to ensure that data requirements are met and that data is readily available for analysis and modeling.

5. **Invest in data integration and ETL tools**: Use data integration and ETL (extract, transform, load) tools to automate the process of collecting, transforming, and loading data from multiple sources into a centralized repository. This will improve data quality and consistency and reduce the time and effort required to prepare data for AI projects.

6. **Develop a data strategy**: Create a comprehensive data strategy that aligns with the organization's overall business objectives and AI initiatives. This strategy should outline the data sources, storage solutions, data processing requirements, and governance policies needed to support AI projects.

Barrier 8: Governance and Regulation

AI adoption brings legal and regulatory considerations, such as data privacy, security, and compliance. Organizations must ensure they meet these requirements by conducting regular audits, establishing a dedicated AI ethics committee, and staying informed about the latest regulatory developments. This subsection will explore the key governance and regulation challenges and propose comprehensive strategies to overcome these barriers.

There are several chapters later in the book to address governance, ethics, and regulation. In the meantime, the following are some strategies to address governance and regulation barriers:

1. **Conduct regular audits**: Perform periodic audits to assess compliance with relevant regulations and identify any potential areas of non-compliance. Regular audits help organizations stay compliant, avoid potential fines, and maintain a positive reputation.

2. **Establish a dedicated AI ethics committee**: Create an AI ethics committee composed of cross-functional stakeholders, including legal, compliance, and technology experts. This committee should be responsible for developing and enforcing ethical guidelines for AI projects, ensuring compliance with regulations, and addressing any ethical dilemmas that may arise during the AI implementation process.

3. **Stay informed about regulatory developments**: Keep abreast of the latest regulatory developments in the AI space, both domestically and internationally. This will help your organization proactively adjust its policies and practices to remain compliant with evolving regulations.

4. **Develop and implement AI-specific policies**: Draft and enforce AI-specific policies that cover areas such as data usage, algorithmic transparency, and fairness. These policies should be aligned with the organization's overall governance framework and regularly reviewed and updated to ensure ongoing compliance.

5. **Educate employees and stakeholders**: Provide regular training and education sessions for employees and stakeholders on AI-related regulations, policies, and ethical considerations. This will help foster a culture of compliance and ensure that all team members understand their responsibilities in the context of AI implementation.

6. **Collaborate with regulators and industry associations**: Engage with regulators and industry associations to contribute to the development of AI-related regulations and standards. This collaboration can help your organization stay informed about upcoming regulatory changes and ensure that its voice is heard in the policymaking process.

Barrier 9: Metrics and Measurements

Establishing clear key performance indicators (KPIs) and metrics is vital for measuring the success of AI initiatives. Organizations should develop a set of quantitative and qualitative metrics to track progress and evaluate AI's impact on the business. This subsection will discuss the importance of metrics and measurement and provide comprehensive strategies to address this barrier.

Strategies to address metrics and measurement barriers are the following:

1. **Define clear KPIs and objectives**: Align AI projects with specific business goals and establish clear KPIs that reflect the desired outcomes. This will help organizations evaluate AI initiatives' success and ensure their alignment with overall business objectives.

2. **Develop a balanced set of metrics**: Use both quantitative (e.g., accuracy, precision, recall) and qualitative (e.g., user satisfaction, fairness, transparency) metrics to evaluate AI systems. A balanced set of metrics can provide a more comprehensive understanding of the AI system's performance and its impact on the business.

3. **Track metrics throughout the AI project lifecycle**: Continuously monitor and track relevant metrics during the development, deployment, and maintenance of AI systems. This allows for

timely identification of potential issues and enables organizations
to make data-driven decisions to optimize the AI system's
performance.

4. **Utilize data visualization tools**: Employ data visualization tools
   to display AI project metrics in a user-friendly and accessible
   format. This can help stakeholders quickly understand the AI
   system's performance and make informed decisions based
   on data.

5. **Establish benchmarking standards**: Compare the AI system's
   performance against industry benchmarks or internal standards
   to determine its relative success. Benchmarking can help identify
   areas for improvement and promote best practices within the
   organization.

6. **Conduct regular reviews and evaluations**: Periodically review
   and evaluate AI projects' performance using the defined
   metrics. These reviews can help organizations identify areas for
   improvement, adjust strategies, and ensure ongoing alignment
   with business objectives.

Key Takeaways

Overcoming the barriers to AI implementation requires a thorough understanding
of both the common challenges faced by new technologies and the unique barriers
specific to AI. By addressing these barriers through effective change management, cross-
disciplinary collaboration, and a comprehensive plan, organizations can successfully
integrate AI into their operations and drive growth and innovation.

- **Takeaway point 1**: **Common barriers to new technologies** – the
  human change management factor

  - Like any new technology, AI faces barriers related to
    human change management. Resistance to change, lack of
    understanding, and fear of job loss are common issues that
    organizations face when adopting AI.

- To overcome these barriers, organizations must foster a culture of learning and adaptability. This can be achieved through effective communication, comprehensive training programs, and highlighting the benefits of AI to employees.

- Encouraging collaboration between technical and non-technical teams, as well as promoting transparency in AI development and deployment, will help address these common barriers and ensure a smoother integration of AI into the organization. Organizations should provide ample training and education to employees, communicate the benefits of the AI initiative, and solicit feedback from stakeholders.

- **Takeaway point 2**: **AI-specific barriers** – foundational technology and language barriers

  - AI has unique barriers due to its status as a foundational technology, which requires a strong understanding of both the technical and business aspects of its application.

  - A key challenge is the language barrier that exists between business and data science teams. This can result in miscommunication, misaligned goals, and ineffective AI implementation. Organizations should appoint a designated liaison to bridge the gap between these two groups, translate technical concepts into layman's terms, and ensure that everyone is on the same page.

  - Addressing this barrier requires fostering a culture of cross-disciplinary collaboration and ensuring that both technical and non-technical team members have a basic understanding of AI concepts and applications.

- **Takeaway point 3: the importance of a comprehensive plan to address barriers**

  - To ensure the successful implementation of AI, organizations must have a comprehensive plan in place to address both the common barriers to new technologies and the AI-specific challenges.

- This plan should include effective communication strategies, ongoing training and support, and a focus on fostering a culture of collaboration and understanding across teams.

- By addressing the human implementation factor, organizations can unlock the full potential of AI and drive significant value for their business.

As this chapter marks the end of Part I, "Introduction and First Principles," we will move into the next part of the book, Part II, "The WHY." Here we will explore the reasons why companies should invest in AI. This is an area where, like other new technologies, I have seen many organizations jumping right into the solution and implementation ("the WHAT" and "the HOW") without fully understanding both the foundations and the business rationale and more importantly whether they should do it or not. Over the next three chapters, we will go a bit deeper into what is exactly AI and its role in the enterprise, current AI trends, and how to achieve an effective data monetization with AI across the enterprise.

PART II

The WHY

CHAPTER 5

Introduction to AI and Its Role in Business

This chapter is the first one in the second part of the book, "The WHY." Over the next three chapters, we will explore in detail the underlying reasons why most companies should fully embrace AI. I will provide the reader with an overview of AI, its history, and how AI can be integrated within the business fabric of enterprises, all from a First Principles point of view. This will help business and tech executives develop a solid foundation to incorporate AI into their strategies and drive sustainable growth.

You will see why we have waited until this chapter for an in-depth definition of AI: it is complicated. On the one hand, at a high level, there is some agreement in the field that AI refers to the development of **computer systems capable of performing tasks that usually require human intelligence**, such as visual perception, speech recognition, decision-making, and natural language understanding. On the other hand, when you go deep down to define what is exactly AI and how it is different from other technologies, we see it is quite complicated, and for some advanced concepts (what is intelligence, consciousness, or what is exactly a "super-intelligence"), there are many opinions in the field, some opposing ones. One recent example is when the European Union started legislation on AI; they really struggled on the exact definition of what an AI system is. The EU regulation[1] tries to be very specific on the type of algorithms, which is an issue due to two key reasons, as follows:

    a.   Listing exactly what AI algorithms are in use now will miss the new ones being continually being developed.

---

[1] https://digital-strategy.ec.europa.eu/en/policies/regulatory-framework-ai

© Francisco Javier Campos Zabala 2023
F. J. Campos Zabala, *Grow Your Business with AI*, https://doi.org/10.1007/978-1-4842-9669-1_5

b. It also extended to some rules-based algorithms that, technically speaking, it is not really AI but "traditional" math/statistics algorithms, such as an algorithm programmed with a well-defined sequence of rules to decide, prediction, or recommendation, for example, the amount an individual should receive in their social security payment, their grades on a particular exam, etc.

Definition of AI used throughout the book.

I have used the International Organization for Standardization (ISO) definition of AI[2],() which is "an interdisciplinary field, usually regarded as a branch of computer science, dealing with models and systems for the performance of functions generally associated with human intelligence, such as reasoning and learning."

We will provide the core components from a First Principles point of view to go deeper in the different definitions and to also explain the historical evolution. The reason why it is very important to have a good intuition about how AI has evolved is to predict how AI will evolve over the next few decades.

The core components of AI are as follows:

a. Machine learning algorithms

b. Data (structured and unstructured)

c. Computational power and hardware

d. Software and programming languages

e. Human-computer interaction

What Is AI and How Does It Differ from Other Technologies?

It is very helpful to understand how an AI program differs from a traditional software program. As we have seen in the introduction, artificial intelligence (AI) encompasses the study and creation of computer systems capable of executing tasks that previously demanded human intellect. AI is an extensive domain, with machine learning (ML) as a subfield.

---

[2] ISO/IEC 22989:2022(en), Information technology — Artificial intelligence — Artificial intelligence concepts and terminology

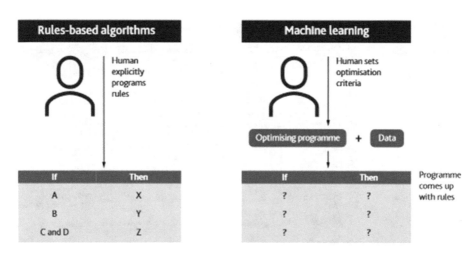

Figure 5-1. *ML algorithms make decisions without being explicitly programmed[3]*

Machine learning involves computer programs that can adapt models or identify patterns from data without explicit programming and with minimal to no human intervention (Figure 5-1). This contrasts with "rules-based algorithms," where human programmers explicitly dictate the decisions made under specific world states.

In addition to defining AI, it is crucial to examine the attributes of AI applications and how they distinguish themselves from non-AI applications that achieve similar outcomes.

---

[3] www.fca.org.uk/publication/research/research-note-on-machine-learning-in-uk-financial-services.pdf

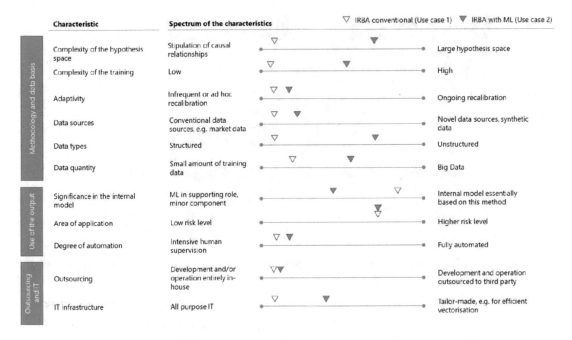

Figure 5-2. *AI systems characteristic*

These attributes can encompass AI's complexity, its iterative methodology, the employment of hyperparameters, and the utilization of unstructured datasets. For instance, the **Bundesbank and BaFin**[4] adopted this strategy in a recent publication (refer to Figure 5-2). Instead of relying on a specific definition of machine learning, the document outlines various machine learning characteristics that establish a demarcation between what could be considered in and out of scope. Given the absence of a universally accepted definition of AI, this approach might prove beneficial for the industry.

Intuition About Models and Algorithms

All models are wrong, but some are useful.

—George Box

---

[4] Consultation paper: Machine learning in risk models – Characteristics and supervisory priorities (bundesbank.de)

Intelligence in AI refers to the ability of an algorithm to autonomously learn, adapt, and make decisions or predictions based on data. It encompasses the system's capacity to recognize patterns, identify relationships, and reason in ways that mimic or surpass human cognitive abilities.

At a fundamental level, the objective of AI is to establish a model or algorithm capable of predicting the right outcome for any given input, even if the system has never encountered that specific input before. This is achieved by developing algorithms that can generalize from the patterns and relationships they learn from the training data. The goal is to create systems that can adapt and make accurate predictions or decisions in novel, unseen situations.

Achieving this level of intelligence in AI allows for the creation of more robust and versatile solutions that can handle a wide range of problems and adapt to new information or changing environments. This is crucial for real-world applications, where the data is often dynamic, and the systems must be capable of adjusting to new circumstances and making informed decisions without requiring constant human intervention.

It is important to keep in mind that what we are trying to do at its fundamental level is to find the best model that, fitting whatever data we have seen so far (training dataset), will be able to predict the right outcome in new circumstances.

An interesting fact is the so-called **no free lunch principle**: there is no single algorithm that works best for every problem or dataset. In simpler terms, it means that each algorithm has its strengths and weaknesses, and its performance is dependent on the specific problem it is trying to solve. Consequently, selecting the optimal algorithm requires understanding the characteristics of the problem and tailoring the approach to the unique requirements of that problem.

The first step in using AI to solve a problem is to select the appropriate algorithm. There are many different algorithms available, each with its own strengths and weaknesses. The choice of algorithm will depend on the specific problem being solved.

For example, if the problem is to classify images, a convolutional neural network (CNN) would be a good choice. CNNs are a type of neural network that are well-suited for image classification. They can learn the spatial relationships between pixels in an image, which is important for identifying objects.

Selecting the right algorithm for a specific problem is a critical aspect of the AI implementation process. As we described AI in the last section, in ML, the humans specify an optimization criterion (or sometimes called "objective function"), and the machine will follow it when seeing new data. This subsection aims to provide a basic understanding of the intuition behind algorithm selection, the overall process, and key factors to consider. By grasping these fundamental concepts, business executives can better comprehend AI applications and make informed decisions for their organizations.

It is worth noticing that you do not need to understand all the details to take advantage of the AI/ML algorithms; however, understanding the fundamentals will provide the reader a better grasp of the concepts and where certain algorithms can work better than others.

The overall process of algorithm selection involves the following steps:

1. **Analyze the training dataset**: Start by examining the available training data, which contains input-output pairs. The goal is to understand the data's structure, identify patterns, and determine the type of problem at hand (classification, regression, etc.).

2. **Choose a loss function**: The loss function quantifies the difference between the algorithm's predictions and the actual output. Common loss functions include the sum of squares (used in regression problems) and the sum of absolute values. The choice of loss function depends on the problem type and the desired properties of the model, such as robustness to outliers or sensitivity to small errors.

3. **Determine the optimization method**: To minimize the loss function, various optimization methods can be employed, such as gradient descent or stochastic gradient descent. These methods dictate how far to move in the weight space at each step to find the optimal solution. The choice of optimization method depends on factors like the size of the dataset and the complexity of the problem.

4. **Select the batch size**: During the optimization process, the dataset can be divided into smaller subsets, or "batches," to speed up computation and improve convergence. The choice of batch size can impact the algorithm's performance and should be chosen based on factors like the available computational resources and the desired balance between speed and accuracy.

5. **Tune hyperparameters**: Hyperparameters are parameters that control the learning process and are not learned by the algorithm itself. They include factors like the learning rate, the number of hidden layers in a neural network, and the amount of regularization. Hyperparameter tuning involves finding the optimal values for these parameters to maximize the algorithm's performance on out-of-sample predictions.

We will go into the details of this process in later chapters (the WHAT and the HOW) or how one picks the right algorithm, and more importantly, the tools and methodologies to implement it successfully within enterprise.

Different Types of Algorithms

While Chapters 8, 9, and 10 will go in detail of the algorithms themselves, here we will present here a few popular classifications of AI/ML algorithms. There are few different classifications, or "taxonomies."

We will start with the most popular one, machine learning. ML is a subset of AI that focuses on creating algorithms that can learn and improve from experience. ML algorithms can be broadly categorized into three main types: supervised learning, unsupervised learning, and reinforcement learning. These types of ML differ in their approach to learning and the kind of data they use.

Supervised Learning

Supervised learning is the most common form of ML. In this approach, algorithms are trained on labeled data, which consists of input-output pairs. The goal is to learn a mapping from input data to the correct output. Supervised learning is commonly used for tasks such as classification and regression.

Unsupervised Learning

Unsupervised learning involves training algorithms on data without labels. The goal is to find patterns or structures within the data, such as grouping similar data points together (clustering) or reducing the dimensionality of the data (dimensionality reduction). Unsupervised learning is often used for tasks like anomaly detection or data compression. Figure 5-3 shows both algorithms applied to the same dataset. Supervised learning focuses on making predictions based on labeled data, while unsupervised learning aims to identify underlying patterns in the data without relying on labels, and both can offer complementary insights when applied to the same dataset.

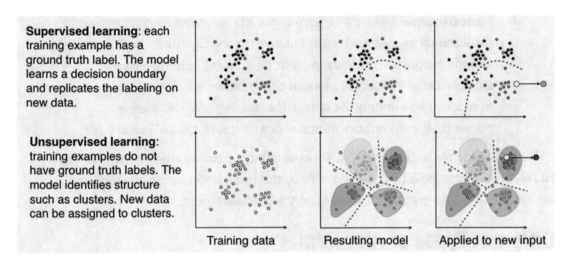

Figure 5-3. *Supervised vs unsupervised learning[5]*

Reinforcement Learning

Reinforcement learning is a type of ML where an algorithm learns to make decisions by interacting with an environment. The learning agent receives feedback in the form of rewards or penalties and adjusts its behavior to maximize the cumulative reward over time. Reinforcement learning is particularly useful in scenarios where the optimal solution is not known beforehand, such as game playing or robotics.

Table 5-1 shows these three main popular ML types and their typical use cases.

Table 5-1. *Taxonomy of machine learning types and their goals and use cases*

Type of ML	Goal	Example use case
Supervised learning	Learn a mapping from input data to output	Image classification
Unsupervised learning	Find patterns or structures within data	Anomaly detection
Reinforcement learning	Maximize cumulative reward over time	Game playing, robotics

---

[5] www.researchgate.net/figure/Supervised-and-unsupervised-machine-learning_fig2_325867536

As well as the above most current popular taxonomy for the most used models, it is worth mentioning there are many others. A good wide definition is given in the book *The Master Algorithm*[6] by Pedro Domingos – see Table 5-2. He describes five "tribes" of AI algorithms, each with its unique approach to learning from data. The five tribes are as follows:

- **Symbolists**: Symbolists focus on manipulating symbols and logic to form rules and representations of knowledge. They primarily use techniques like inverse deduction and inductive logic programming. While symbolist methods were popular in early AI research, they have been overshadowed by other approaches due to their limitations in handling uncertainty and processing large datasets.

- **Connectionists**: Connectionists model learning based on neural networks, inspired by the human brain's structure and function. They have gained significant popularity due to the success of deep learning in various applications such as image recognition, natural language processing, and speech recognition. Connectionist methods currently dominate the field of AI research and commercial applications.

- **Evolutionaries**: Evolutionaries take inspiration from the natural process of evolution, using techniques like genetic algorithms and genetic programming to optimize solutions. While these methods have been successful in certain optimization problems, they tend to be less popular than other approaches due to their computational complexity and slower convergence.

- **Bayesians**: Bayesians focus on probabilistic inference and reasoning under uncertainty, using Bayesian networks and graphical models. These methods have been particularly useful in applications where uncertainty is inherent, such as medical diagnosis and natural language understanding. However, Bayesian methods can be computationally intensive, limiting their widespread adoption in some cases.

---

[6]www.amazon.co.uk/Master-Algorithm-Ultimate-Learning-Machine/dp/0241004543

- **Analogizers**: Analogizers learn from data by identifying and extrapolating similarities and relationships between instances. Techniques like Support Vector Machines (SVM) and k Nearest Neighbor(kNN) algorithms fall under this category. While these methods have proven effective in various applications, they tend to be less popular than connectionist approaches, particularly in large-scale data-driven problems.

Connectionist methods are currently the most popular among the five tribes due to their success in handling large datasets and complex problems. However, each tribe has its strengths and weaknesses, and understanding these different approaches can help researchers and practitioners choose the most suitable techniques for their specific AI challenges.

Table 5-2. *Different families of algorithms – as per Pedro Domingo's book*

Family type/"tribe"	Strength	Example algorithms
Symbolists	Structure inference	Inverse deduction, decision trees
Connectionists	Estimating parameters	Backpropagation, deep neural networks, perceptrons
Evolutionaries	Structure discovery	Genetic programming
Bayesians	Uncertainty reduction	Probabilistic inference, Naïve Bayes, LDA
Analogizers	Mapping to novelty	Kernel machines: SVM, kNN

AI vs ML vs Deep Learning?

There is also a bit of confusion about how AI relates to ML or deep learning.

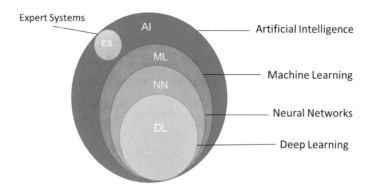

Figure 5-4. *AI definitions*

The differences between these terms can be visualized using concentric circles (Figure 5-4), with deep learning at the center and AI as the outermost circle.

- **AI (artificial intelligence)**: AI is the broadest concept, referring to the development of computer systems that can perform tasks typically requiring human intelligence. This includes expert systems, problem-solving, pattern recognition, decision-making, and natural language understanding. AI encompasses various techniques and approaches to achieve these intelligent behaviors.

- **ML (machine learning)**: As a subfield of AI, ML focuses on developing algorithms that enable computers to learn from and make predictions or decisions based on data. Rather than being explicitly programmed for specific tasks, ML models can "learn" from examples and improve their performance over time. ML covers a wide range of algorithms, including decision trees, support vector machines, and clustering algorithms.

- **Neural networks**: Neural networks are a specific type of machine learning model inspired by the structure and function of the human brain. They consist of interconnected nodes (neurons) that process and transmit information. Neural networks can be used for various tasks, such as image recognition, natural language processing, and game playing. They can learn complex patterns and generalize from training data to make predictions or decisions.

- **Deep learning**: At the center of the concentric circles, deep learning is a subset of neural networks that involves using multi-layered neural networks with many hidden layers. These deep architectures allow the model to learn hierarchical representations of data, enabling the extraction of high-level features and abstractions. Deep learning has been responsible for significant breakthroughs in AI, particularly in areas like computer vision, natural language processing, and speech recognition. Most current large language models such as ChatGPT or Bard use deep learning.

Artificial General Intelligence

One of the main challenges in the field is the usage of the same terms to mean very different things. Indeed, whenever people use the term "AI," they could be referring to very different concepts.

Across the book, whenever I refer to AI, I am talking about the current generation, or "narrow AI," also known as weak AI or artificial specific intelligence, refers to AI systems that excel at specific tasks or domains but lack the versatility and adaptability of human intelligence.

AGI (artificial general intelligence) represents the next level, where AI systems can understand, learn, and apply knowledge across a wide range of tasks, like human intelligence.

In contrast, **superintelligence** describes an AI that has undergone rapid self-improvement after reaching "*the Singularity*," resulting in an entity with intellectual capabilities far surpassing any humans.

Consciousness, on the other hand, is a complex and elusive concept, often associated with self-awareness, perception, and subjective experience. Although researchers and philosophers have debated the nature of consciousness for centuries, a clear and universally agreed-upon definition remains elusive. This lack of consensus makes it challenging to determine if and how AI systems could achieve consciousness and raises questions about the ethical implications of developing such advanced technologies.

We will go deeper through all these fascinating concepts and potential future developments – at least inasmuch as it is possible at the moment! – in Chapter 23, but for the time being it is good to be aware of these different concepts, so whenever in conversation you can frame an informed point of view.

The History of AI: Its Evolution over Time

The story of AI would surprise the reader in many aspects. The AI field traces its roots to the **Dartmouth Conference**[7] held in the summer of 1956. This conference was organized by John McCarthy, Marvin Minsky, Nathaniel Rochester, and Claude Shannon, who are considered the founding fathers of AI. The Dartmouth Conference aimed to explore the potential of machines to simulate human intelligence and problem-solving abilities.

In the original proposal for the conference, the organizers stated:

> *We propose that a 2-month, 10-man study of artificial intelligence be carried out during the summer of 1956 at Dartmouth College in Hanover, New Hampshire. The study is to proceed on the basis of the conjecture that every aspect of learning or any other feature of intelligence can in principle be so precisely described that a machine can be made to simulate it.*

This quote highlights the optimism of the early AI pioneers, who believed that creating artificial general intelligence (AGI) could be accomplished within a single summer with a small group of researchers. While this ambitious goal was not realized during the conference, the event marked the beginning of formal AI research, setting the stage for decades of advancements and innovations in the field.

As you can see in Figure 5-5, AI history has been marked by alternating periods of optimism and pessimism, often referred to as "AI summers" and "AI winters." These fluctuations in the field have been influenced by various factors, including technological breakthroughs, funding availability, and public perception:

- **First AI Summer (late 1950s–1960s)**: The Dartmouth Conference in 1956 marked the beginning of AI research. This period saw early optimism and significant funding for AI projects, leading to the development of early AI systems, such as symbolic reasoning systems and rule-based expert systems.

- **First AI Winter (1970s)**: During this period, optimism faded due to the limitations of early AI systems and their inability to fulfill the initial high expectations. This led to reduced funding and a slowdown in AI research. The Lighthill Report in the UK[8] and the Mansfield Amendment[9] in the USA were key factors contributing to this decline.

---

[7] https://home.dartmouth.edu/about/artificial-intelligence-ai-coined-dartmouth
[8] https://publications.parliament.uk/pa/ld201719/ldselect/ldai/100/10018.htm
[9] www.nsf.gov/nsb/documents/2000/nsb00215/nsb50/1970/mansfield.html

– **Second AI Summer (1980s)**: AI regained momentum with the emergence of expert systems, which were commercialized and adopted by various industries. This period also saw the rise of funding for AI research, primarily driven by the Japanese Fifth Generation Computer Systems project, which aimed to develop advanced AI systems.

– **Second AI Winter (late 1980s–1990s)**: This winter occurred due to the limitations of expert systems, which were brittle, difficult to maintain, and costly. Additionally, the Japanese project[10] failed to meet its ambitious goals, leading to a decline in funding and public interest in AI.

– **Third AI Summer (late 1990s–present)**: The current AI summer began with the advent of the Internet, big data, and advances in computational power. This period has seen the development of machine learning and deep learning techniques that have led to breakthroughs in various AI applications, such as computer vision, natural language processing, and speech recognition. The success of these techniques has attracted substantial investment and interest in AI research and development.

I personally experienced the second AI winter. I started my Industrial Engineering degree in early 1990s, and when I asked my professor to do the AI specialization (or as it was called, "Automation and Robotics"), his honest advice was "don't do it, really think about your future, do you want to end up in the middle of nowhere, in charge of an automated factory to produce obscure industrial equipment?" I do believe the professor had my interest at heart as AI funding at the time was limited and hence career opportunities; however, I decided to do the specialization and time proved me right!

---

[10] www.nytimes.com/1992/06/05/business/fifth-generation-became-japan-s-lost-generation.html

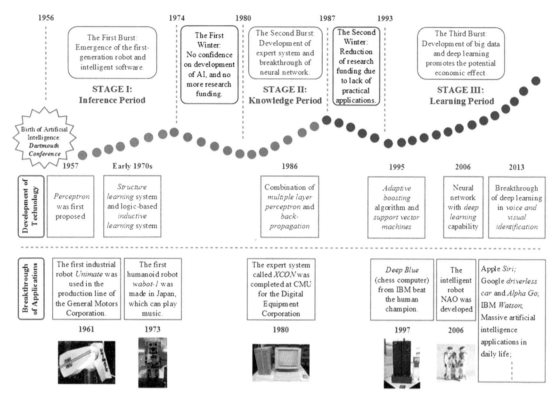

Figure 5-5. *A not-so-brief story of AI*[11]

We will now go through the development of AI core components over time. They all developed at different speeds, but they are also interdependent on each other. For instance, some algorithms that were known decades ago only became popular once the hardware or the data was available. One of the most recent AI successes, deep learning, is based on neural networks. While the basic neural network math was developed in the 1950s and some even before (the chain rule was discovered in the 17th century), the backpropagation algorithm is probably the most fundamental building block. It was first introduced in the 1960s and almost 30 years later (1989) popularized by Rumelhart, Hinton, and Williams in a paper called "Learning representations by back-propagating errors." But it was not until around 2010, where some tweaks to the original algorithm, a combination of higher computer speed, lower cost, and the large amount of data availability, made them very popular and hence started to get real traction in industry.

---

[11] www.researchgate.net/figure/Development-history-of-artificial-intelligence-AI_
fig8_323591839

Machine Learning Algorithms

AI research began in the mid-20th century, focusing on developing algorithms that could learn from data and improve their performance over time. Key milestones include the following:

- **1950s**: Early AI research focused on symbolic reasoning and rule-based systems (e.g., Samuel's Checkers-playing program).

- **1980s**: The advent of connectionism and the development of artificial neural networks (e.g., Rumelhart, Hinton, and Williams' backpropagation algorithm).

- **1990s**: The rise of statistical learning methods, such as support vector machines and Bayesian networks.

- **2010s**: The resurgence of deep learning and the development of more advanced neural network architectures (e.g., CNNs, RNNs, LSTMs, and Transformers).

Data (Structured and Unstructured)

As AI evolved, the availability and importance of data grew significantly. Advances in data storage and retrieval, as well as the growth of the Internet, facilitated access to massive amounts of data, enabling the development of more sophisticated AI models.

- **1950s–1960s**: Early days of computing and data storage. Data storage was limited and costly, often relying on magnetic tapes or punch cards for input and output.

- **1970s–1980s**: Rise of relational databases and structured data. The use of relational databases and Structured Query Language (SQL) became the standard for organizing and querying structured data.

- **1990s**: Data warehousing and the growth of unstructured data. With the advent of the Internet, there was an explosion in the volume and variety of data available, including unstructured data such as text, images, and multimedia. Data warehousing emerged as a solution for consolidating, storing, and analyzing large volumes of structured data from different sources.

- **2000s**: Big data and the rise of machine learning. As the volume, variety, and velocity of data continued to grow, the concept of "big data" emerged, along with new technologies for processing and analyzing massive datasets. This period saw the rise of distributed computing frameworks like Hadoop and NoSQL databases for handling unstructured data.

- **2010s**: Cloud computing, data lakes, and deep learning. Cloud computing revolutionized the way data is stored and processed, making it more accessible and scalable. Data lakes emerged as a solution for storing and processing vast amounts of raw, unstructured data in its native format.

- **2020s**: Data lakehouses and the fusion of structured and unstructured data. Data lakehouses combine the best aspects of data lakes and data warehouses, enabling organizations to store and analyze both structured and unstructured data in a unified platform.

Computational Power and Hardware

The growth of AI has been closely tied to advances in computational power. Key milestones include the following:

- **1940s–1960s**: The development of early digital computers, such as the Electronic Numerical Integrator and Computer (ENIAC).

- **1970s–1980s**: The invention of microprocessors and the rise of personal computers.

- **1990s–2000s**: The growth of parallel processing and the development of Graphics Processing Units (GPUs), which greatly accelerated AI computations.

- **2010s**: The rise of specialized hardware for AI, such as Tensor Processing Units (TPUs) and neuromorphic chips.

Software and Programming Languages

AI research and development have relied on various programming languages and software frameworks. Some key milestones include the following:

- **1950s–1960s**: Early AI languages such as Lisp and Prolog.

- **1980s–1990s**: The rise of object-oriented programming languages, such as C++ and Java.

- **2000s–2010s**: The development of Python as a dominant language for AI research, and the emergence of machine learning frameworks like TensorFlow, PyTorch, and Keras.

Human-Computer Interaction

AI systems have become increasingly integrated with human lives, leading to advancements in human-computer interaction. Key milestones include the following:

- **1960s–1970s**: The development of early graphical user interfaces (GUIs) and natural language processing (NLP) techniques.

- **1980s–1990s**: The rise of personal computers, the Internet, and the World Wide Web, enabling more accessible and user-friendly AI applications.

- **2000s–2010s**: The growth of mobile devices, voice assistants, and AI-powered recommendation systems, further integrating AI into daily life.

The interesting fact of looking at the evolution of AI through the lenses of their core components is how breakthrough moments happen when different small increments from different components converge to create something more powerful that the individual parts. Similarly, and looking at the future – more in later chapters – but just imagine for a moment what will happen when the current Hardware meets the Quantum Computing developments, when, as the Metaverse (both Augmented Reality and Virtual

Reality) continues to evolve and humans spend more time on it, the data that will be available or finally, as more and more genetic data is uncovered, together with the processes to manipulate genetic material (e.g., CRISPR[12]), what AI could accomplish to help humanity (end diseases, extend human lifespan, etc.).

AI in Business: Opportunities and Applications

As per the early sections, we have seen how *AI technologies can automate "human-like" decisions at a local level at massive scale*. Taking these capabilities to the enterprise means that every business process that currently relies on human involvement can either be optimized or completely replaced by the machines.

Artificial intelligence has already been transforming the way businesses operate and compete in today's rapidly evolving market landscape. By adopting AI in their strategic plans, companies can unlock unprecedented opportunities to enhance decision-making, improve customer experience, streamline operations, and enable innovation. This subsection will delve into the various ways AI can be integrated into business strategy, with each key point substantiated by relevant examples and data.

Enhancing Decision-Making

The growing volume of data generated by businesses and consumers provides a wealth of information that can be harnessed using AI algorithms. AI-powered analytics enable businesses to derive actionable insights and make data-driven decisions. Key applications include the following:

- **Data-driven insights**: AI-powered analytics tools can process vast amounts of structured and unstructured data, extracting valuable insights that help businesses make more informed decisions. For example, advanced data analysis can identify patterns and trends that might be overlooked by traditional methods, enabling companies to better understand customer behavior, optimize pricing strategies, and forecast demand.

---

[12] https://sitn.hms.harvard.edu/flash/2014/crispr-a-game-changing-genetic-engineering-technique/

- **Predictive analytics**: Predictive analytics, a key application of AI, involves using historical data to forecast future outcomes. Businesses can leverage predictive analytics to anticipate customer preferences, identify potential market shifts, and proactively mitigate risks. For instance, AI-powered algorithms can predict equipment failures, enabling companies to schedule maintenance and avoid costly downtime.

Improving Customer Experience

AI-driven personalization and customer experience enhancements can help businesses foster customer loyalty and increase revenue. Key applications include the following:

- **Personalization**: AI can enable hyper-personalization by analyzing individual customer behavior, preferences, and demographics. This granular understanding allows companies to tailor marketing messages, product recommendations, and user experiences for each customer. For example, e-commerce platforms like Amazon use AI to recommend relevant products, resulting in increased customer satisfaction and higher conversion rates.

- **Chatbots and virtual assistants**: AI-powered chatbots and virtual assistants can handle routine customer inquiries, reducing response times and freeing up human agents to focus on more complex tasks. With natural language processing capabilities, these tools can understand and respond to customer queries, providing efficient and personalized support.

Streamlining Operations

AI-powered automation can significantly enhance a company's productivity by streamlining processes, reducing manual tasks, and minimizing errors. Some key applications of AI in automation include the following:

- **Automation**: AI can automate repetitive tasks and processes, increasing efficiency and reducing human error. Robotic process automation (RPA) tools can handle tasks such as data entry, invoice processing, and payroll management, allowing employees to focus on more strategic responsibilities. For some industries, *Industrial Automation*, AI-powered robots can perform tasks in manufacturing and assembly lines with high precision and speed, resulting in improved production efficiency and reduced operational costs.

- **Process optimization**: AI-driven analytics can identify inefficiencies and bottlenecks in existing processes, enabling businesses to optimize workflows, reduce costs, and improve overall performance. For example, AI can optimize supply chain management by predicting demand fluctuations and adjusting inventory levels accordingly.

Enabling Innovation

AI can accelerate the innovation process and drive new product development by identifying emerging trends, generating novel ideas, and optimizing design and manufacturing processes. Key applications include:

- **New product development**: AI can accelerate new product development by identifying market gaps, predicting customer preferences, and simulating product performance. By leveraging AI in the design phase, companies can optimize product features, reduce development time, and minimize costs. This includes Generative *Design*, where AI algorithms can explore a vast design space to generate innovative product concepts that meet specific requirements and constraints, such as weight reduction, cost optimization, and performance improvement.

- **Identifying untapped markets**: AI algorithms can analyze market data, competitor performance, and customer preferences to identify new growth opportunities and untapped markets. This strategic use of AI can provide businesses with a competitive edge, enabling them to seize opportunities before their rivals.

As we have seen, the opportunities and applications of AI in business are vast and transformative. We will go into the details of how to identify specific areas to implement AI in your enterprise in later chapters. From automating mundane tasks to driving strategic decision-making, AI has the potential to significantly improve efficiency, competitiveness, and innovation across various industries. Businesses can successfully integrate AI into their operations, ensuring sustainable growth and long-term success using First Principles to unlock this business potential. Table 5-3 provides some examples.

Table 5-3. Examples of AI applications and their benefits in business strategy

Application	Benefit	Example
Data-driven insights	Informed decision-making	Optimizing pricing strategies
Predictive analytics	Anticipating future outcomes	Predicting equipment failures
Personalization	Enhanced customer experience	Tailored product recommendations
Chatbots	Efficient customer support	AI-powered virtual assistants
Automation	Increased efficiency	Robotic process automation
Process optimization	Improved performance	Optimizing supply chain management
New product development	Accelerated innovation	AI-assisted design
Data-driven insights	Informed decision-making	Optimizing pricing strategies
Identifying untapped markets	Market expansion opportunities	Discovering new growth segments

Key Takeaways

In this chapter, we explored the foundations of AI, its history, and the opportunities and applications it presents for businesses. Here are the three key takeaways to remember from this chapter:

- **Takeaway point 1: Understanding AI fundamentals**
    - It is essential for business executives to have a firm grasp of AI concepts, including their definition, types, and core components. This understanding enables informed decision-making and allows organizations to leverage AI's full potential effectively.

- **Do**: Invest time and resources in learning the basics of AI, ML, neural networks, and deep learning. Encourage continuous learning and training within the organization to stay updated on the latest AI developments.

- **Don't**: Overlook the importance of understanding AI fundamentals, as this knowledge gap can lead to unrealistic expectations and poor implementation of AI technologies.

- **Takeaway point 2: Learning from AI history**

  - *AI is a rapidly developing field, and there are several best practices that businesses should follow when using AI.* The history of AI, marked by alternating periods of optimism and pessimism, provides valuable lessons for businesses venturing into AI adoption. Understanding the factors that led to AI winters and summers can help organizations navigate potential challenges and capitalize on emerging opportunities.

  - **Do**: Study past successes and failures in AI to identify best practices and avoid repeating past mistakes. Recognize the importance of setting realistic expectations and goals when implementing AI solutions.

  - **Don't**: Ignore the lessons from AI history, as they can provide invaluable insights into managing expectations, securing funding and overcoming technological barriers.

- **Takeaway point 3: Leveraging AI in business**

  - *AI is a powerful tool that can be used to improve business performance.* AI presents a wide range of opportunities and applications for businesses, including enhancing decision-making, improving customer experience, streamlining operations, and enabling innovation. Companies must identify the most relevant AI applications for their specific needs and goals to maximize the benefits of AI adoption.

- **Do**: Conduct a thorough analysis of your business processes and identify areas where AI can provide the most significant impact. Prioritize AI initiatives that align with your company's strategic objectives and carefully monitor the implementation and outcomes.

- **Don't**: Adopt AI technologies without a clear understanding of their purpose and potential benefits. Avoid implementing AI solutions merely for the sake of following trends or competing with rivals, as this can result in wasted resources and disappointing outcomes.

As we have seen in the brief history of AI, it is still early days, especially compared to other sciences or technology fields. In the next chapter, we will explore the current trends on AI.

CHAPTER 6

Key Trends in AI

In the ever-evolving landscape of artificial intelligence (AI), businesses must stay informed about the latest trends, challenges, and opportunities to remain competitive and drive growth. This chapter aims to provide a comprehensive overview of the current trends in AI, using a First Principles approach to analyze their potential impact on businesses and the future of AI technology.

As we saw on earlier chapters, the core components of AI from First Principles point of view are:

a. Machine learning algorithms

b. Data (structured and unstructured)

c. Computational power and hardware

d. Software and programming languages

e. Human-computer interaction

We begin by examining the latest advances in machine learning algorithms, including generative AI, foundational models, reinforcement learning, robotics, computer vision, and image recognition. We will discuss the implications of these breakthroughs for businesses and AI-driven innovation.

Next, we explore the increasing importance of data in AI development, highlighting the significance of data quality, quantity, diversity, and ethical data handling. We will provide best practices for effective data management and utilization, tailored for business needs and potential benefits.

We then delve into AI hardware and infrastructure, discussing progress in specialized AI hardware, cloud-based platforms, and edge computing. We also look at the future trends in quantum computing and their potential impact on AI.

In the software and programming languages section, we cover popular AI programming languages, libraries, open-source tools, and frameworks.

F. J. Campos Zabala, *Grow Your Business with AI*, https://doi.org/10.1007/978-1-4842-9669-1_6

The human-computer interaction section focuses on improvements in AI-driven user interfaces, experiences, augmented and virtual reality, and the role of AI in accessibility and inclusivity.

Lastly, we address AI ethics, fairness, and transparency, emphasizing the importance of ethical considerations in AI applications, approaches to ensure fairness and transparency, regulatory frameworks, guidelines, and strategies for addressing bias and ensuring accountability.

By the end of this chapter, you will have gained valuable insights into the key trends shaping the AI landscape, empowering you to make informed decisions and leverage AI for better business outcomes responsibly. The First Principles framework will also allow us to follow all the new developments and to get an intuition of both the importance of every new advancement but also how to apply it to your enterprise.

Advances in Machine Learning Algorithms

In this subsection, we will explore the significant advances in machine learning algorithms and their implications for businesses and AI-driven innovation. Using a First Principles approach, we will discuss breakthroughs in various areas, such as generative AI, foundational models, reinforcement learning, robotics, computer vision, and image recognition. We will also touch on the evolution of deep learning architectures and emerging trends in transfer learning and meta-learning.

Generative AI

Generative AI models, such as Generative Adversarial Networks (GANs) and Variational Autoencoders (VAEs), have shown remarkable progress in recent years. These models can generate high-quality, realistic data, such as images, music, and text. Businesses can leverage generative AI for applications like content creation, data augmentation, and product design.

Generative AI refers to a class of machine learning models that can generate new data samples based on patterns learned from existing data. This ability has opened a wide range of applications across various industries. Among the most popular generative models are (Table 6-1).

a. **Variational Autoencoders (VAEs)**: VAEs are a type of unsupervised learning model that can generate new data samples by learning the underlying structure and distribution of the input data. VAEs consist of an encoder and a decoder, which work together to compress and reconstruct the input data while maintaining its essential characteristics.

b. **Generative Adversarial Networks (GANs)**: GANs consist of two neural networks, the generator and the discriminator, that are trained together in a process of competition. The generator creates fake data samples, while the discriminator evaluates the authenticity of the generated samples. This process results in the generator improving its ability to create realistic data samples. They were released in the famous 2014 paper.[1]

c. **Stable Diffusion**: Stable Diffusion is a recent advancement in generative modeling that combines aspects of both GANs and VAEs. It utilizes a diffusion process to model the data distribution, enabling the generation of high-quality samples with improved stability and training efficiency.

---

[1] https://arxiv.org/abs/1406.2661

Table 6-1. *Table comparison of most common generative AI models*

Generative AI model	Key features	Pros	Cons
GANs (Generative Adversarial Networks)	Two neural networks (generator and discriminator) compete to generate realistic data	High-quality, realistic output; continual improvement through competition between networks	Difficult to train; model collapse; can be sensitive to hyperparameters
VAEs (Variational Autoencoders)	Neural networks learn a probabilistic mapping between input data and latent space	Easier to train than GANs; stochastic nature allows diverse outputs; can handle missing data	Lower quality output compared to GANs; less control over generated output
Stable Diffusion	Diffusion process to generate data by denoising a noise distribution	Stable training process; allows more control over the generated output	Slower sampling process compared to GANs and VAEs; requires more computation resources

Generative AI models have a wide range of applications across various industries, including the following:

- **Art and design**: GANs and VAEs can be used to generate unique artwork, design elements, or even entire scenes for video games and virtual reality experiences.

- **Drug discovery**: Generative AI models can accelerate the drug discovery process by generating novel chemical compounds with desirable properties, reducing the time and cost associated with traditional methods.

- **Retail and e-commerce**: GANs can be employed to create realistic product images or simulate different environments, allowing businesses to enhance their product offerings and improve customer experience.

- **Media and entertainment**: Generative AI can be used to create realistic deepfakes, synthesize voices, or generate new music, transforming the way content is produced and consumed.

However, there are challenges associated with implementing generative models, including the following:

- **Ethical concerns**: The creation of deepfakes and the potential misuse of generative AI technologies raise ethical and legal concerns that need to be addressed.

- **Computational resources**: Training generative models often requires significant computational power, which can be a barrier for smaller businesses.

- **Model complexity**: Generative models can be complex and difficult to understand, posing challenges for businesses to implement and optimize them effectively.

I have included some actual prompting exercises for some popular generative AI engines at the end of the chapter, so the reader can see for themselves how to create all different kinds of content.

Foundational Models and Large-Scale Language Models

Large-scale language models like GPT-4 and BERT have revolutionized the field of natural language processing (NLP). These models can "understand" and generate human-like text, enabling applications such as chatbots, sentiment analysis, and text summarization. Businesses can use these models to automate customer service, gain insights from user-generated data, and improve content creation.

The key innovation behind these models is *the self-attention mechanism*[2], which allows them to process and contextualize vast amounts of textual information, enabling them to generate coherent and contextually relevant responses. With the increasing scale and sophistication of these models, researchers have been able to create even more powerful versions, such as GPT-4 and beyond, which have demonstrated remarkable capabilities in various NLP tasks.

---

[2] https://arxiv.org/abs/1706.03762

Large language models like ChatGPT have shown great promise in a wide range of applications, primarily due to their ability to understand and generate contextually relevant text. Some of the most notable capabilities and applications of ChatGPT and other conversational AI models include

- **Customer support**: ChatGPT can be used to create AI-powered chatbots that can understand and respond to customer queries in real-time, offering faster and more efficient customer support.

- **Content generation**: These models can generate high-quality, human-like text for various purposes, such as blog posts, social media updates, and marketing materials, enabling businesses to streamline their content creation process and reduce the need for manual input. There are also code generators such as GitHub Copilot, Amazon Code Whisperer, and Google's Bard.

- **Virtual assistants**: Large language models can be integrated into virtual assistants to provide more accurate and context-aware responses, enhancing their utility and effectiveness for users.

- **Data analysis and summarization**: ChatGPT can be employed to analyze large volumes of textual data and generate concise summaries, enabling businesses to make better-informed decisions based on the information at hand.

- **Language translation**: With their advanced understanding of natural language, these models can be used for accurate and efficient language translation, facilitating global communication and collaboration.

This is one of the areas with more potential and more research and industry focus in summer 2023; the next Open Source Large Scale language models have incredible potential. We will explain in detail these models in Chapter 10.

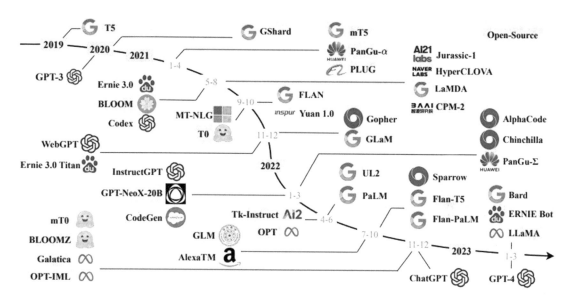

Figure 6-1. *Timeline of LLM[3]*

Reinforcement Learning and Robotics

Reinforcement learning (RL) algorithms have shown significant progress, enabling autonomous decision-making and control in complex environments. Applications include robotics, autonomous vehicles, and game playing. Businesses can benefit from RL algorithms to optimize supply chain management, automate warehouse operations, and enhance customer experiences. One of the companies that has done a lot of research in this area is DeepMind (Google), and their RL-based models got a lot of press attention in the last few years; first defeating for the first time the human champion playing Go[4] and latest for solving the protein folding problem.[5]

---

[3] [2303.18223] A Survey of Large Language Models (arxiv.org) – Page 5
[4] www.deepmind.com/research/highlighted-research/alphago
[5] www.deepmind.com/blog/alphafold-reveals-the-structure-of-the-protein-universe

Computer Vision and Image Recognition

Advancements in computer vision and image recognition have enabled machines to accurately identify and classify objects in images and videos. These capabilities have applications in industries like healthcare, retail, manufacturing, and security. Businesses can leverage computer vision to automate quality control, enhance security systems, and create personalized shopping experiences.

Evolution of Deep Learning Architectures and Techniques

Deep learning architectures have evolved significantly, with new techniques like transformer models, capsule networks, and self-attention mechanisms. These advancements have improved model performance and efficiency, enabling more complex AI applications. Businesses can use these state-of-the-art models to drive innovation and gain a competitive edge. We will explore all of those in later chapters.

Emerging Trends in Transfer Learning and Meta-learning

Transfer learning and meta-learning techniques allow AI models to learn more efficiently from limited data by leveraging knowledge gained from related tasks. These approaches have gained popularity in recent years, reducing training time and resources while improving model performance. Businesses can utilize transfer learning and meta-learning to accelerate AI development and adapt models to specific use cases.

Implications for Businesses and AI-Driven Innovation

The advances in machine learning algorithms have opened new opportunities for businesses to leverage AI for innovation and growth. By understanding and embracing these trends, businesses can unlock the potential of AI to drive efficiency, enhance customer experiences, and create new revenue streams.

The Increasing Importance of Data

Data is the lifeblood of artificial intelligence (AI) systems, powering the development and success of advanced machine learning algorithms. In today's increasingly digitized business landscape, data has emerged as a critical asset for organizations seeking to harness the transformative power of AI to drive growth and innovation.

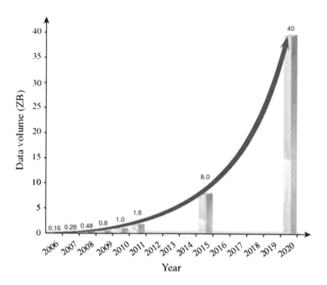

Figure 6-2. *Growth of global data volume[6]*

AI systems rely on vast amounts of data to learn, adapt, and make informed decisions. The quality and quantity of data used to train AI models directly influence their accuracy and effectiveness. As the volume of data generated by businesses, consumers, and connected devices continues to grow exponentially (Figure 6-2), companies must prioritize data management and utilization to fully capitalize on the opportunities offered by AI.

---

[6]www.researchgate.net/figure/Global-growth-trend-of-data-volume-2006-2020-based-on-The-digital-universe-in-2020_fig1_274233315

The growing significance of data in the business landscape is evident in the following key trends:

- **The shift toward data-driven decision-making**: Companies are increasingly leveraging AI-driven insights to make more informed decisions, streamline operations, and enhance customer experiences. Data-driven approaches have been shown to improve decision-making processes, resulting in better outcomes and higher returns on investment (ROI).

- **The rise of big data and advanced analytics**: The advent of big data technologies has enabled organizations to collect, store, and process vast quantities of data from diverse sources. Advanced analytics tools, powered by AI and machine learning, can uncover hidden patterns and insights within these large datasets, enabling businesses to make more informed decisions and optimize their operations.

- **The democratization of AI**: The widespread availability of cloud-based AI platforms, open-source tools, and pre-trained AI models has made it easier for businesses of all sizes to access and implement AI technologies. These developments have lowered the barriers to entry for AI adoption, allowing companies to harness the power of data-driven insights without the need for extensive in-house expertise or resources.

To ensure the effectiveness of AI-driven initiatives, businesses must prioritize data quality, quantity, and diversity. ***High-quality data*** refers to accurate, complete, and consistent information that accurately represents real-world phenomena. ***The quantity of data*** is essential for training robust AI models, as larger datasets enable AI systems to learn more effectively and generalize their findings to new situations. ***Data diversity***, or the inclusion of data from various sources and domains, ensures that AI models are exposed to a wide range of scenarios and contexts, reducing the likelihood of biases and enhancing overall performance.

Ethical data handling and privacy concerns are also paramount in the age of AI. Businesses must ensure that their data collection, storage, and processing practices adhere to relevant data protection regulations and ethical guidelines. This includes obtaining informed consent from users, anonymizing personal information, and implementing robust data security measures to prevent unauthorized access and data breaches.

The following are some of the key trends in data which will impact their usage within AI:

- **Move to cloud**: As the volume and complexity of data grows, businesses are increasingly turning to cloud-based solutions for data storage, processing, and analysis. Cloud-based AI platforms offer scalable and cost-effective infrastructure, allowing organizations to access advanced AI capabilities without the need for significant upfront investments. This shift to the cloud has accelerated AI adoption and innovation, enabling businesses to leverage AI-driven insights at scale.

- **Growth of data (including edge data)**: The exponential growth of data generated by connected devices, sensors, and IoT systems has given rise to edge data, or data generated and processed at the edge of the network, close to its source. Edge data offers real-time insights and enables businesses to make more informed decisions, optimize operations, and enhance customer experiences. The proliferation of edge computing and on-device AI has further fueled the growth of edge data, driving the development of more responsive and efficient AI systems.

- **Lakehouses**: The emergence of lakehouses, which combine the benefits of traditional data warehouses and data lakes, has revolutionized data management for AI. Lakehouses enable businesses to store both structured and unstructured data in a single, unified platform, simplifying data ingestion, processing, and analysis. This approach facilitates seamless integration between AI tools and data sources, accelerating the development and deployment of AI-driven solutions.

Adopting a First Principles approach, businesses should identify their specific data needs and potential benefits, then design data management and utilization strategies that align with their overarching business objectives. By doing so, organizations can ensure they are well positioned to leverage the transformative power of AI and data in the pursuit of growth and innovation.

AI Hardware and Infrastructure

Hardware has been no doubt one of the fundamental core component drivers in advancing AI. Comparing hardware capability to when AI started back in the 1950s to hardware 2020s is extremely more powerful and cheaper. As popular science author Michio Kaku[7] put it:

> *Today, your cell phone has more computer power than all of NASA back in 1969, when it placed two astronauts on the moon.*

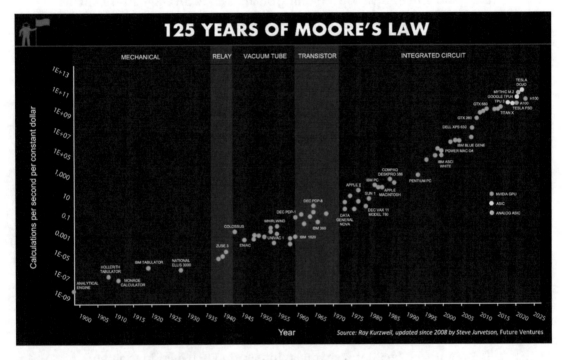

Figure 6-3. 125 years of Moore's law (still ongoing)

---

[7] www.goodreads.com/book/show/8492907-physics-of-the-future

Behind this incredible progress, we have Moore's Law[8], first proposed by Gordon Moore in 1965 (Figure 6-3). It is an empirical observation that the number of transistors on a microchip doubles approximately every 2 years, leading to a corresponding increase in processing power. This trend has been a driving force behind the rapid advancements in computing and technology over the past several decades. However, as we approach the physical limits of silicon-based chip manufacturing, Moore's Law is expected to slow down. Researchers and engineers are exploring alternative materials and innovative chip architectures, such as 3D stacking and neuromorphic computing, to continue the progress. Although it is unclear how much further Moore's Law can be sustained, ongoing innovations in the field suggest that the growth of computing power will continue, albeit at a potentially slower pace.

Another important point to consider about the future evolution of computers, looking at First Principles, is the efficiency of current computers and how they compare to biological brains.

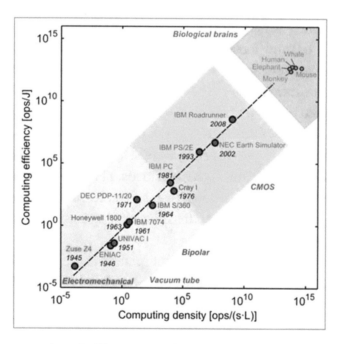

Figure 6-4. *Computational efficiency and computational density of computers compared with mammalian brains*

---

[8] www.britannica.com/technology/Moores-law

Figure 6-4[9] shows that current computer architecture requires quite a bit of power per computing unit, and when compared to biological brains, there is a large gap in efficiency. Indeed, the human brain is an impressive biological machine, capable of storing vast amounts of information and processing it at incredible speeds. It does this while maintaining a relatively small size and consuming minimal power. In comparison, modern supercomputers, though powerful, still fall short in terms of size and power consumption efficiency. The race for the world's fastest and most power-efficient supercomputer is on, but the industry is facing new bottlenecks as transistor density reaches its limit on 2D chips.

One of the areas that the computer industry is exploring to improve its efficiency is to turn to the human brain for inspiration. The brain's efficiency is unmatched, ***achieving five to six orders of magnitude more computing per unit of energy consumed***. This incredible efficiency is achieved while simultaneously supporting the brain's cellular activities.

It is also important to point out that as well as generic computing components, there have also been notable advancements in specialized AI hardware, such as Graphics Processing Units (GPUs) and Tensor Processing Units (TPUs), which have significantly accelerated the development and deployment of AI systems. GPUs, originally designed for rendering graphics, have proven to be highly efficient in handling the parallel computations required for deep learning. Their parallel processing capabilities have made them the go-to choice for training large neural networks.

On the other hand, TPUs, developed by Google specifically for machine learning tasks, offer a more tailored solution for AI workloads. TPUs are designed to accelerate tensor operations, the core computations used in deep learning algorithms. They offer greater performance per watt compared to GPUs, making them more energy-efficient for AI processing.

Together, these specialized AI hardware components have dramatically reduced the time and cost associated with training and deploying AI models, enabling businesses to leverage AI-driven solutions more efficiently.

---

[9]www.zurich.ibm.com/pdf/news/Towards_5D_Scaling.pdf

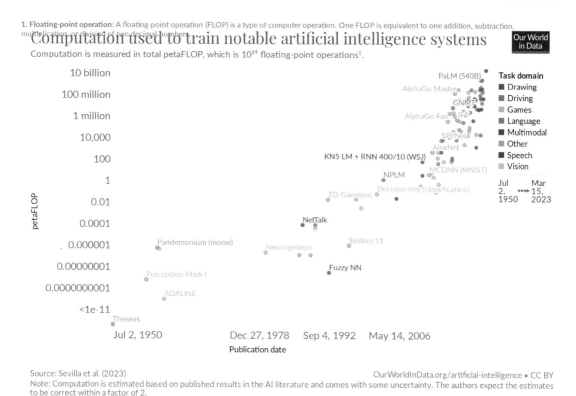

Figure 6-5. *Computation used to train notable AI systems*

Figure 6-5 shows the growth on computing power, with the latest known AI system (GPT4) needed more than 10 billion PetaFLOPs.

In terms of infrastructure, the advent of cloud-based AI platforms and infrastructure has democratized access to AI capabilities and resources. Cloud providers, such as AWS, Google Cloud, and Microsoft Azure, offer comprehensive AI services and tools that cater to various AI workloads, from training and inference to deployment and management. Businesses can leverage these platforms to scale AI applications without the need for significant upfront investments in hardware and infrastructure.

Furthermore, cloud-based AI platforms offer seamless integration with other cloud services, such as data storage and analytics, facilitating a more cohesive and efficient AI development pipeline. This enables businesses to focus on their core competencies and innovate faster with AI-driven solutions. We will go into all these details later in the HOW part of the book.

Another interesting trend is edge computing and on-device AI. Both have emerged as key trends in AI hardware and infrastructure, driven by the need for real-time processing, reduced latency, and improved privacy. By bringing AI processing closer to the data source, edge computing enables faster decision-making and minimizes the need to transmit data to centralized data centers, thereby reducing bandwidth requirements and associated costs.

On-device AI, powered by specialized chips like Apple's Neural Engine and Google's Edge TPU, allows for local AI processing on smartphones, IoT devices, and other edge devices. This facilitates real-time, context-aware AI applications, such as autonomous vehicles, smart home systems, and wearable health monitors.

As a final trend, Quantum Computing, an emerging field of study that leverages the principles of quantum mechanics, holds immense potential for revolutionizing AI hardware and infrastructure. Quantum computers are designed to solve certain types of complex problems exponentially faster than classical computers, making them an ideal candidate for solving some optimization problems and accelerating AI model training. We will also go into detail at the end of the book.

Although quantum computing is still in its early stages of development, its potential impact on AI is substantial. Companies like IBM, Google, and Microsoft are actively researching and developing quantum computing technologies, which, if successful, could drastically change the AI landscape, enabling more efficient and powerful AI systems.

Software and Programming Languages

In this subsection, we will explore the critical role of software and programming languages in the development and deployment of AI systems. We will discuss popular programming languages and libraries used for AI, open-source tools and frameworks, emerging AI-first software paradigms, and strategies for integrating AI into existing software systems.

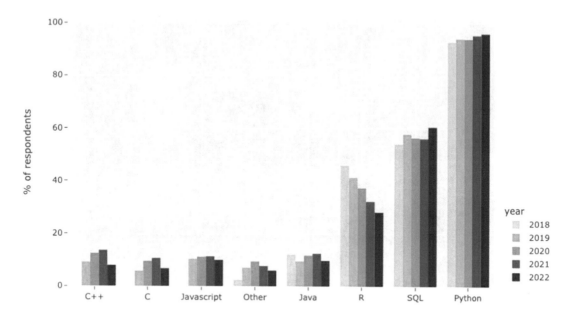

Figure 6-6. *Popularity of programming languages in AI development[10]*

The choice of programming languages and libraries plays a crucial role in the development of AI solutions. Some of the most popular programming languages for AI include Python, R, Java, and C++ (Figure 6-6). Python, in particular, has gained widespread adoption due to its simplicity, readability, and extensive library support.

---

[10] State of Data Science and Machine Learning 2022 | Kaggle

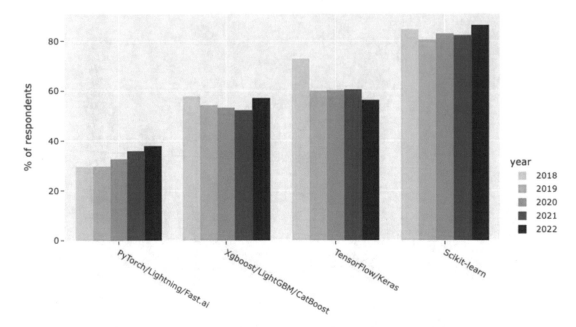

Figure 6-7. *AI libraries and their respective programming languages[11]*

Python libraries such as TensorFlow, PyTorch, and Keras have become indispensable tools for building deep learning models. Scikit-learn is widely used for traditional machine learning tasks, while NLP libraries like spaCy and NLTK have made natural language processing more accessible (Figure 6-7).

The AI landscape has been significantly shaped by the proliferation of open-source tools and frameworks. Open-source software promotes collaboration, accelerates innovation, and lowers the barriers to entry for organizations looking to adopt AI. Some popular open-source AI frameworks include TensorFlow and PyTorch.

These frameworks provide a foundation for developing, training, and deploying AI models across various domains, including computer vision, natural language processing, and reinforcement learning.

As AI becomes more advanced, we are witnessing the emergence of AI-first software paradigms. These paradigms prioritize AI capabilities from the ground up, rather than treating them as supplementary components. For example, AI-driven development (AID) tools are designed to support and enhance the work of developers by offering AI-powered code generation, bug detection, and optimization.

---

[11] State of Data Science and Machine Learning 2022 | Kaggle

Another AI-first paradigm is conversational AI, which centers around natural language interfaces for interacting with software systems. These interfaces, powered by advanced NLP algorithms, enable more intuitive and human-like communication between users and software applications.

Human-Computer Interaction and AI

In this subsection, we will explore the significant advancements in human-computer interaction (HCI) driven by AI, including improvements in user interfaces and experiences, the role of augmented and virtual reality, AI's impact on accessibility and inclusivity, and ethical considerations in AI-human interactions.

AI has transformed user interfaces and experiences by enabling more personalized, intuitive, and efficient interactions between humans and computers. Examples of AI-driven improvements include

- **Conversational AI**: Chatbots and virtual assistants, such as Apple's Siri, Amazon's Alexa, and Google Assistant, provide natural language interfaces that allow users to communicate with devices using voice or text.

- **Recommendation systems**: AI-powered algorithms offer personalized content, product, and service recommendations, enhancing user experiences on platforms like Netflix, Amazon, and Spotify.

Augmented reality (AR) and virtual reality (VR) technologies have evolved significantly, thanks to AI's capabilities. These immersive platforms provide novel ways for users to interact with digital content and experiences. For instance, AI-powered object recognition and tracking enable seamless integration of digital content into real-world environments in AR applications, while AI-driven avatars in VR environments enhance social interactions and user engagement.

AI plays a critical role in promoting accessibility and inclusivity by developing technologies that cater to users with diverse abilities and needs. Examples of AI-driven accessibility tools include

- **Voice recognition**: AI-powered speech-to-text systems enable users with mobility impairments to control devices and access services.

- **Computer vision**: AI-driven image recognition and scene understanding help visually impaired users navigate their environments and access visual content.

- **Sign language recognition**: AI can interpret sign language, allowing deaf or hard-of-hearing individuals to communicate more effectively with others.

AI Ethics, Fairness, and Transparency

In this subsection, we will discuss the importance of ethical considerations in AI applications, approaches to ensure fairness and transparency in AI systems, and regulatory frameworks and guidelines for AI development.

This is an area that has attracted considerable interest recently; the number of research papers went from hardly anything to thousands per year after 2017. There were a few high-profile cases that attracted a lot of public and press interest, such as the US criminal system using a system to grant Bail[12]. We will explore this issue in detail in later chapters, and why it is not always possible to have an absolute answer.

Ethical considerations are crucial in AI applications to ensure responsible development and deployment, as well as maintain public trust. Key ethical concerns include data privacy, algorithmic bias, and accountability. By addressing these issues, companies can develop AI solutions that benefit society while minimizing potential harms.

To ensure fairness and transparency in AI systems, several approaches can be employed:

- **Bias detection and mitigation**: Identifying and addressing biases in training data and algorithms can help create AI systems that treat different user groups equitably.

---

[12] www.washingtonpost.com/news/monkey-cage/wp/2016/10/17/can-an-algorithm-be-racist-our-analysis-is-more-cautious-than-propublicas/

- **Explainability**: Developing AI models that provide understandable explanations for their decisions allows users to trust and effectively interact with AI systems. While an explainable system does not necessarily equal a fair system necessarily, it can really help to ensure the system is fair.

- **Transparency in data usage**: Clearly communicating how data is collected, stored, and used can help address privacy concerns and ensure users are informed about how their information is utilized.

Regulatory frameworks and guidelines play an essential role in shaping the ethical development and deployment of AI technologies. Some examples include

- **The European Union's AI Regulation**: This proposal outlines requirements for transparency, accountability, and human oversight in AI systems, with a focus on high-risk applications.

- **The OECD Principles on AI**: These principles, endorsed by 42 countries, promote human-centered AI development, including fairness, transparency, and robustness.

- **Industry-specific guidelines**: Organizations within specific industries, such as healthcare and finance, have developed guidelines for the responsible use of AI in their respective sectors.

PROMPT EXERCISES

In our first tests, we will use ChatGPT[13] to create the main bullet points for an upcoming strategy presentation to your business senior management on you plans for AI. There are many manuals on how to create an effective prompt; we will explain how in the appendix. Please note, that due to the way the Transformers work, you will likely get different answers – the machine injects some randomness, and by the time the book is published, there will be newer versions of the APIs. Figures 6-8 and 6-9 show examples of both prompts and the answers by the machine.

---

[13] Version: ChatGPT May 3 Version – Model GPT4

```
<Begin Prompt>
    Act as an Expert Business leader in AI. You need to prepare a presentation
    to the Board about the company AI strategy. Create the bullet points and
    suggested images for 3 slides
</End Prompt>
```

Output:

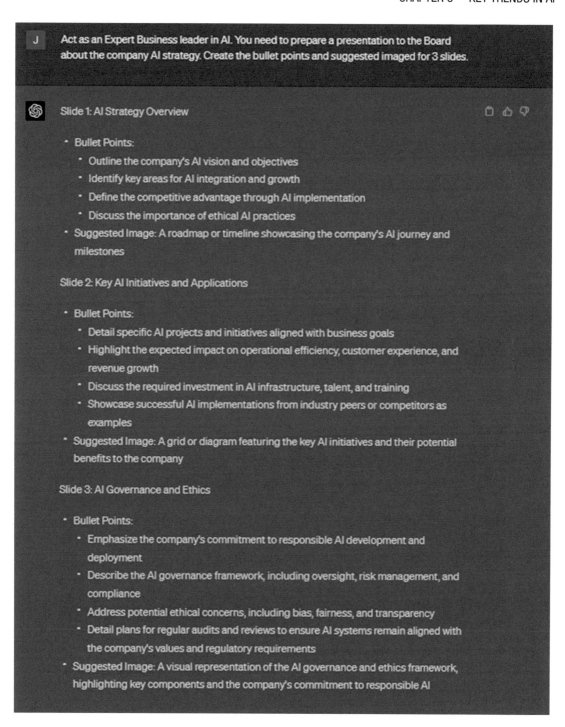

Figure 6-8. *Generative AI text – using OpenAI's ChatGPT*

Our next test, we will use DALL-E to create a new picture to put in the first page of the presentation you created before.

```
<Begin Prompt>
    an abstract visual of the future of artificial intelligence
</End Prompt>
```

Output:

Figure 6-9. *Generative AI picture – using OpenAI's DALL-E[14]*

---

[14] https://labs.openai.com/

Key Takeaways

In this chapter, we have examined key trends in AI and their potential impact on businesses. Now, let's recap three AI trends and their implications for businesses.

- **Advances in machine learning algorithms**: Breakthroughs in algorithms have enabled companies to leverage AI for various applications, including natural language processing, computer vision, and generative models. This has led to new business opportunities and improved efficiency across industries.

  - **Do**: Invest in AI research and development to stay ahead of the competition and capitalize on emerging trends.

  - **Don't**: Neglect to understand the limitations and risks associated with the AI algorithms you employ, as this could lead to unintended consequences.

- **AI hardware and infrastructure**: Developments in specialized AI hardware, cloud-based AI platforms, and edge computing have made it easier for companies to deploy AI solutions, thereby accelerating innovation and growth.

  - **Do**: Evaluate the specific needs of your business to determine the most suitable AI hardware and infrastructure solutions.

  - **Don't**: Assume that the most expensive or cutting-edge hardware will automatically yield the best results for your organization.

- **AI ethics, fairness, and transparency**: Ensuring ethical AI development and deployment is critical for maintaining public trust and mitigating potential harms. Companies need to focus on fairness, transparency, and adherence to regulatory frameworks to achieve responsible AI usage.

  - **Do**: Develop an AI ethics framework to guide your company's AI development and deployment, ensuring fairness and transparency.

  - **Don't**: Ignore the potential ethical issues surrounding AI, as this could result in reputational damage, legal consequences, and loss of user trust.

Embracing AI can lead to significant growth and innovation for businesses. Indeed, companies can improve decision-making, streamline operations, and enhance user experiences, creating a competitive advantage in the market, when they leverage the latest advancements in AI.

In the next chapter, we will explore how to ensure companies have a clear data monetization strategy using AI.

CHAPTER 7

Data Monetization with AI

In today's digital era, businesses accumulate vast quantities of data, the **"new oil"** of the economy. This data is a goldmine for generating business growth and revenue. Leveraging artificial intelligence (AI) for data monetization – converting data into actionable insights or products that create business value – is our primary focus. This chapter equips business executives with essential knowledge on data monetization, enabling the effective utilization of data assets.

Firstly, we demystify data monetization, illustrating various ways to achieve it. Common misconceptions abound, such as only large corporations can monetize data or data monetization exclusively involves selling data. These notions are fallacies. Any business, regardless of size or industry, can reap benefits from data monetization through numerous direct and indirect approaches.

To assist organizations in making educated decisions and prioritizing data assets, we delve into identifying monetizable data, emphasizing the critical role of data governance and compliance.

A step-by-step framework is presented to offer a transparent roadmap for businesses, employing AI to distill insights from data, thereby creating new revenue channels and amplifying business value. This roadmap navigates different business models, data marketplaces, and platforms, allowing organizations to understand opportunities and potential pitfalls in data monetization.

The benefits of data monetization are manifold. Companies that effectively leverage AI to monetize data can achieve competitive advantage, enhance customer satisfaction, and boost profitability. Further, it enables more informed decision-making, uncovers new business prospects, and instills a data-driven culture, promoting continuous innovation and learning.

The chapter concludes by addressing the challenges and limitations of data monetization, providing strategies to minimize risks and optimize returns.

© Francisco Javier Campos Zabala 2023
F. J. Campos Zabala, *Grow Your Business with AI*, https://doi.org/10.1007/978-1-4842-9669-1_7

Readers will gain a robust understanding of data monetization through AI by the end of this chapter, paving the way for informed decisions and effective utilization of data assets. The subsequent chapters will provide in-depth guidance on how to implement these concepts, enabling businesses to confidently embark on their data monetization journey toward a successful AI-driven future.

Defining Data Monetization

Understanding data monetization begins with a firm grasp of data fundamentals. Businesses amass data through transactions, customer interactions, operations, and external sources like suppliers. This data, a significant resource, can be processed and analyzed to provide valuable insights, enhance operations, and fuel growth.

Definition of Data used throughout the book.

Data in the business context refers to quantifiable, observable, and recordable information that is collected, stored, and used for the purpose of analysis or decision-making. It can come in many forms, such as numbers, words, images, videos, phone calls, and even customer behaviors.

In AI systems, data serves as the starting point and training material. Greater data volume generally equates to better performing AI systems. Often, these systems process large volumes of alternative or unstructured data such as satellite images, biometrics, or telematics.

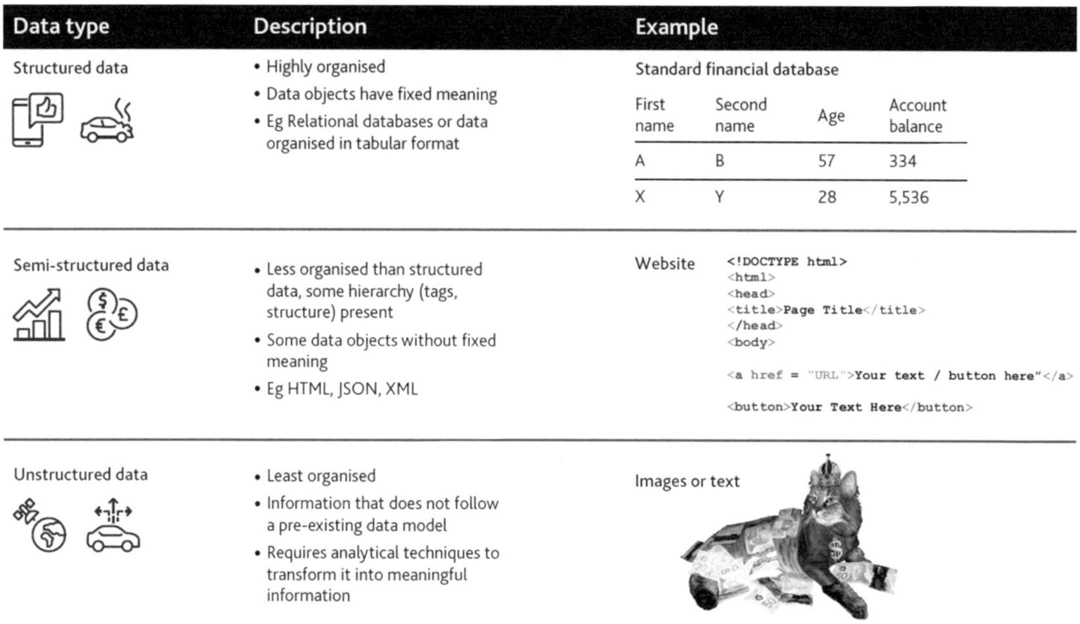

Data type	Description	Example
Structured data	• Highly organised • Data objects have fixed meaning • Eg Relational databases or data organised in tabular format	Standard financial database

First name	Second name	Age	Account balance
A	B	57	334
X	Y	28	5,536

Data type	Description	Example
Semi-structured data	• Less organised than structured data, some hierarchy (tags, structure) present • Some data objects without fixed meaning • Eg HTML, JSON, XML	Website

```
<!DOCTYPE html>
<html>
<head>
<title>Page Title</title>
</head>
<body>

<a href = "URL">Your text / button here"</a>

<button>Your Text Here</button>
```

Data type	Description	Example
Unstructured data	• Least organised • Information that does not follow a pre-existing data model • Requires analytical techniques to transform it into meaningful information	Images or text

Figure 7-1. *Data types*

It is useful to classify data into three main types (see Figure 7-1):

- **Structured data**: Organized in a standard format like tables or spreadsheets, making it easily processable using traditional data tools.

- **Semi-structured data**: Not arranged in a regular format but still holds some structure. More challenging to process than structured data, it can still be managed using traditional tools.

- **Unstructured data**: Lacks any regular format, making it difficult to process and analyze, yet valuable for AI applications.

Alternative data, not conventionally used for traditional processing applications, includes sources like social media data, sensor data, and satellite imagery. It holds high value for AI applications as it can offer unique insights.

> **Tip**   Sometimes, the data you have on hand might not be the most suitable for the problem you are trying to solve. In such cases, it's important to take a step back and reconsider the "job to be done" with your data (more on this later). What specific objective are you trying to achieve? Which insights are you looking for? Depending on the answers, you might need to adjust the way you collect or handle your data.

AI systems are sensitive to data accuracy, as even minor errors can lead to inaccurate predictions. The value of data is determined by its ability to generate revenue, improve efficiency, and cut costs. Additionally, data quality, timeliness, and relevance also impact its value.

Companies often mistake data to be a static IT asset. Those placing high value on data tend to develop data-driven business models, leading to improved decision-making and increased profits. Such models generally result in long-term success. Data ownership and accountability structures across the organization play a vital role in the overall data governance structure.

Data governance ensures data management aligns with business needs, encompassing activities like data classification, data ownership, data security, and data quality assurance. Its importance varies across companies and industries, and it serves to

- Protect data confidentiality, integrity, and availability.

- Ensure data usage aligns with business needs.

- Comply with laws and regulations.

Copying successful companies from other industries without consideration for specific governance needs often leads to problems. While data governance can be complex and challenging, it's crucial for effective data management. More details on this topic will be discussed in later chapters.

Myths About Data Monetization

In the business realm, data is a valuable asset, often clouded by misconceptions that constrain its full potential. Here's a brief overview of typical data-related myths and their corresponding facts:

- **Myth: "Data monetization means selling data."**

  - Reality: Incorrect. Monetizing data does not necessarily mean selling data. This can include selling data, but it can also involve using data to improve internal processes, enhance customer experiences, or develop new products and services.

- **Myth: "Data monetization is only for large enterprises."**

  - Reality: Incorrect. Businesses of all sizes can benefit from data monetization. While large enterprises may have more data and resources at their disposal, small- and medium-sized businesses can also leverage their data assets to create value and drive growth.

- **Myth: "Data privacy regulations make data monetization impossible."**

  - Reality: Incorrect. While data privacy regulations like Europe's GDPR[1] and California's CCPA[2] impose certain restrictions on data usage and sharing, they do not prohibit data monetization entirely. Businesses must comply with these regulations by obtaining proper consent, anonymizing data, and implementing strong security measures. So, they can monetize their data and respect user privacy and laws.

- **Myth: "Data monetization requires complex technology and expertise."**

  - Reality: Incorrect. There are many tools and services available that can simplify the process for businesses. Companies can start with basic analytics and gradually move toward more advanced techniques as they become more data driven.

---

[1] https://gdpr.eu/

[2] https://oag.ca.gov/privacy/ccpa

- **Myth: "All data is equally valuable for monetization."**

  - Reality: Incorrect. The value of data depends on its relevance, quality, and potential for generating insights. Data that is outdated, inaccurate, or lacking context may have limited value for monetization. Businesses should focus on collecting and maintaining high-quality data that can drive meaningful insights and actions.

- **Myth: "More data means higher accuracy."**

  - Reality: Incorrect. This is a myth that every business looking for data science consulting should get rid of right away. The quality of the data is more important than the quantity.

Data as a Financial Asset?

The concept of Infonomics, introduced in Gartner's book of the same name (Figure 7-2), advocates treating data as a financial asset. This innovative approach, highlighting data's economic significance, inspires businesses to manage data with the strategic focus traditionally accorded to assets like real estate and intellectual property. I was a Gartner's client many years, so I had the opportunity to meet the author, Douglas B. Laney.

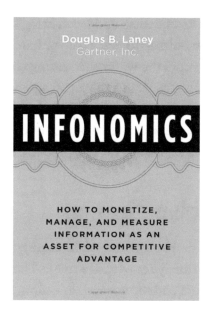

Figure 7-2. *Infonomics book[3]*

Infonomics perceives data as holding intrinsic financial value. When harnessed effectively, this value can deliver tangible business benefits, such as better decision-making, enhanced operational efficiency, and the creation of new products and services. The discipline aims to assign a quantifiable value to data, enabling its management like any conventional asset.

However, despite the promising potential of Infonomics, it has not yet gained widespread acceptance in the industry. There are several reasons for this reluctance. Firstly, the process of valuing data is complex and subjective, making it challenging for organizations to arrive at a universally accepted methodology. Secondly, data's value may not be immediately apparent, and its worth can fluctuate depending on factors such as relevance, timeliness, and accuracy. Lastly, the lack of standardized frameworks and regulations concerning data ownership, privacy, and security poses significant obstacles to the adoption of Infonomics.

---

[3] www.amazon.co.uk/Infonomics-Monetize-Information-Competitive-Advantage/
dp/1138090387

Personally, I do think it is a good idea, and it can bring value to treat data as a financial asset – same as you would do to real estate or hardware servers. However, there is a bit of a catch-22 situation: until the wider accounting community is comfortable and agreed on how to value data financially in a universal agreed way, it might not be worth the effort, and unless a lot of companies want to do it, the financial community will not go through the process of standardization. I do recommend reading the book and the concept and adopting as much as possible within practical limitations.

Methods of Data Monetization

Data monetization, the act of deriving revenue and value from data assets, offers various methods aided by AI and data analytics advancements. These include direct and indirect monetization, AI-based product and service monetization, and data sharing through partnerships:

1. **Direct monetization**: This approach is typically when the data is valuable to external parties, such as customers, partners, or other businesses.

    a. **Selling data**: Businesses can sell their data to third parties. A telecom company, for instance, might sell anonymized location data to retailers for analyzing customer foot traffic to optimize store locations.

    b. **Licensing**: Organizations provide data usage rights for specific purposes in return for fees, offering more control over data usage. A weather data provider might license its data to insurance companies for risk assessment.

    c. **Data-as-a-Service (DaaS)**: Organizations offer data on-demand, typically through a subscription service. A financial data provider might offer DaaS to investment firms for market data and financial news.

2. **Indirect monetization**: Rather than selling data directly, organizations use their data assets to improve internal processes, products, and services.

    a. **Enhanced business intelligence**: Organizations leverage AI and advanced analytics to glean insights for strategic decision-making, improving customer experiences. A retail company might analyze customer data to develop targeted marketing campaigns.

b. **Data-driven decision-making**: Organizations use data to make informed decisions. A logistics company might use AI to optimize delivery routes, minimizing fuel consumption.

c. **Process optimization**: AI automates and optimizes business processes, enhancing efficiency. A bank might use AI-powered chatbots to handle customer inquiries.

3. **Monetizing AI-based products and services**: Combining data with AI algorithms, organizations can create innovative solutions that address customer needs and solve complex problems

a. **Predictive analytics solutions**: Businesses can offer predictive analytics solutions. A machine learning firm might offer a predictive maintenance solution using IoT sensor data to forecast equipment failures.

b. **Personalization services**: Organizations can use AI and customer data to offer personalization services. An e-commerce platform might use AI to provide personalized product recommendations.

c. **AI-enabled fraud detection**: Organizations can use AI solutions to detect fraud or assess risk. A credit card company might use AI to analyze transactions in real-time to detect unusual patterns.

4. **Data sharing and collaborative partnerships**: Pooling data resources, organizations can gain access to a larger and more diverse dataset, enabling them to derive richer insights and develop more innovative solutions.

a. **Data consortiums**: Organizations within an industry might form a data consortium to share data and collaborate on analytics projects, such as healthcare providers sharing anonymized patient data for improved disease diagnosis.

b. **Data exchanges**: Platforms that facilitate data buying, selling, and sharing allow access to diverse data sources. An automotive company might use a data exchange to access sensor data from various manufacturers for accurate traffic prediction models.

   c. **Joint ventures**: Organizations might partner to work on data-driven projects, leveraging combined data and expertise. A pharmaceutical company might collaborate with a biotech firm to develop AI-driven drug discovery models.

There has also been an increase in the last few years of Software Data Vendors offering "Data Clean Rooms"; these allow for different organizations to share their data and join it to other datasets, all in a compliance and privacy-preserving way. A few vendors are Infosum[4] or AWS Clean Rooms[5].

Framework for Unlocking Value from Data in Organizations

Developing a successful data monetization strategy requires a structured approach to unlock the hidden value in an organization's data assets. Before we go into the details of the framework, it is worth noting the size of the prize, how AI can create virtuous circles, which can generate new untapped business value streams.

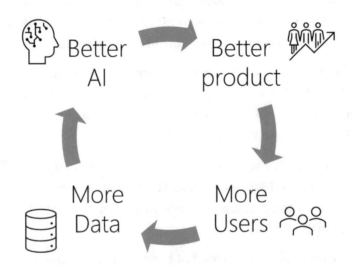

Figure 7-3. *AI data flywheel*

---

[4] www.infosum.com/

[5] https://aws.amazon.com/clean-rooms/

The concept of an AI data flywheel as depicted in Figure 7-3 was made famous by Amazon.[6] Basically, the AI data flywheel is a concept that explains how AI systems, data, and business value interact in a virtuous cycle. It all starts with data. As you deploy AI systems, they generate more data through their interactions. This new data, when fed back into the AI system, helps improve its algorithms, making it more accurate, efficient, and valuable over time. This is the "flywheel" effect: as the wheel spins (i.e., as the AI operates), it generates more of what keeps it spinning (data), thus creating a self-perpetuating cycle.

One of the key outcomes of this flywheel effect is that it can unlock new, untapped business streams. For instance, as your AI system improves and provides more precise insights, it can identify patterns and opportunities that were previously hidden. This could be anything from spotting a new market segment for your product, to identifying efficiency gains in your supply chain, or even creating entirely new product offerings based on unique data insights. The AI data flywheel thus offers businesses a powerful tool for continuous improvement and innovation. The more it spins, the more value it generates, providing businesses with a sustainable competitive advantage in today's data-driven economy.

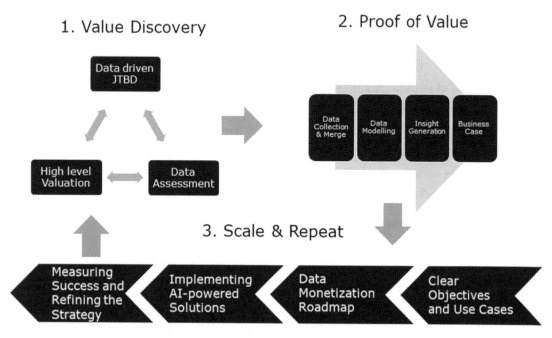

Figure 7-4. *An AI data framework*

---

[6]https://fourweekmba.com/amazon-flywheel/

The process of leveraging AI to effectively monetize data can be guided by a three-step data AI framework (Figure 7-4):

1. **Value discovery: Understanding end business value by exploring the data**. The first step in data monetization is to understand the end business value of the data. This includes identifying the specific business problems that the data can help solve, as well as the potential revenue streams that can be generated from the data. This step requires a deep understanding of the organization's business goals and objectives, as well as the market trends and customer needs. Here, it is also very important to **explore What Data You Already Have and the Gaps**: this includes understanding the types of data that are currently being collected, the sources of that data, and the quality of the data. Identifying any gaps in the data can help the organization prioritize which data to collect and how to collect it. Finally, in this step, a **high-level valuation** is performed to see whether a given initiative is worth pursuing any further. This is the step that is most overlooked for many reasons which we will explore later, and most companies do not fully explore all the potential value that their business operation could generate.

2. **Proof of value**: This stage tests different initiatives using actual data, demonstrating potential value. With the AI implementation challenges discussed earlier, having a proven model with real business outcomes and data created by a balanced team sets the project on a successful scaling path. Skipping this stage, as many companies do, increases the risk of failure.

3. **Scale your successful initiatives**: Once there is evidence in the proof of value that a given initiative could provide significant business outcomes, the organization can develop a plan to exploit the data. This includes identifying the specific AI technologies that can be used to extract value from the data, as well as the resources and teams that will be needed to execute the plan. This area also includes setting clear metrics and goals for the data monetization effort and establishing a process for measuring and reporting progress.

Overall, data monetization is a complex process that requires a deep understanding of the organization's business and the data it holds.

1. Value Discovery

Data value exploration, the first stage in our framework, is pivotal in setting the foundation for effective data monetization. It involves gaining a deep understanding of the end business value that can be derived from your data. This entails identifying the specific business problems that the data can help solve, as well as unveiling potential revenue streams that can be generated from the data.

1.1 Data-Driven "Jobs to Be Done"

First, we need to have a deep understanding of the business value of data:

A. **Identify business problems**: The first step in understanding the end business value of the data is to identify the specific business problems that the data can help solve. This could range from operational inefficiencies to customer engagement issues. The key is to match the data at your disposal with the problem and/or friction areas in your business that it could potentially alleviate. Here as well as direct customers, please do not forget to look at your overall supply chain, with all the different organizations you interact with.

B. **Uncover potential revenue streams**: The next step is to recognize the potential revenue streams that can be generated from the data. This could involve creating new products or services based on data insights or enhancing existing offerings for increased revenue generation.

> **Note**   To facilitate the process of understanding the end business value, we can adopt the "jobs-to-be-done"[7] methodology. This approach allows us to focus on the "job" that a product or service is hired to do. In our context, the "job" is the problem that our data can solve or the value it can create for the business.

C. **Identifying "jobs"**: Start by pinpointing the "jobs" your business data can accomplish. This could be enhancing decision-making, improving product design, streamlining operations, or any number of tasks. The crucial point is to understand the end goal, that is, the job your data needs to do.

D. **Understanding customers' jobs**: Another aspect of the JTBD methodology involves understanding the "jobs" your customers need to get done. Knowing what customers are trying to achieve can provide insights into how your data can help fulfill their needs, whether it's about improving the user experience, personalizing offerings, or providing new services.

E. **Aligning data with jobs**: The final step involves aligning your data with the identified "jobs." This entails determining how your data can be used or transformed to fulfill these jobs effectively.

The data value exploration stage is all about setting the right foundation, and the JTBD methodology provides a structured approach to do just that.

1.2 Data Assessment

Once the potential business value of the key datasets has been identified, the next step is to perform a detailed data assessment, both internally and externally. While the value discovery stage will identify areas to develop (for instance, how to reduce customer churn with data from the website), the data assessment will go systematically through all the internal and external data sources that could help reduce this issue.

---

[7] https://hbr.org/2016/09/know-your-customers-jobs-to-be-done

Here, we need to conduct the following steps for a data inventory and gap analysis:

a. **Data inventory/cataloging**: Create a comprehensive catalog of all available data assets, including structured and unstructured data, as well as internal and external data sources. This catalog should include metadata, such as data source, data type, format, and update frequency.

b. **Data quality assessment**: Assess the quality of the data in terms of accuracy, completeness, consistency, timeliness, and relevance. High-quality data will likely yield valuable insights and support effective decision-making.

c. **Potential value estimation**: Evaluate the potential value of each data asset by considering factors such as the uniqueness of the data, its relevance to business goals, and its potential to generate revenue or improve operations. This assessment helps organizations prioritize their data monetization efforts.

d. **Gap analysis**: Identify gaps in the organization's data assets, such as missing data or areas with limited data coverage. This analysis can help organizations determine which data sources to acquire or develop.

Survival Bias

When looking at your company data, it is crucial to understand the concept of survivorship bias. It is a type of bias that occurs when we make conclusions based on the data we have while overlooking the data we do not have. This bias can distort our understanding and lead to inaccurate conclusions.

The concept of survivorship bias is best illustrated with a famous example from World War II.

Figure 7-5. *Survival bias – analysis in WWII*[8]

When military engineers were deciding where to add armor to bombers to better protect them, they analyzed the pattern of bullet holes on the returning planes. The initial thought was to reinforce the areas with the most damage (most red dots in Figure 7-5). However, a statistician named Abraham Wald[9] pointed out that these damaged areas represented the places where the planes could take a hit and still return home. The parts of the planes without bullet holes, in contrast, were the areas where a hit was likely fatal. Therefore, those were the areas that should be reinforced. The planes that were shot down – the non-survivors – were not considered in the initial data, leading to the survivorship bias.

Similarly, in the context of AI and data analysis, survivorship bias can lead to skewed insights and faulty decision-making. For instance, businesses often interact with customers who choose to provide feedback, which is typically given after a negative experience. Companies might then draw conclusions based on this feedback and design their services or products accordingly. However, the customers who provide feedback are not representative of the entire customer base. Many satisfied customers might never

---

[8] Image by Freepik

[9] https://apps.dtic.mil/docs/citations/ADA091073?fbclid=IwAR3uFkZA8GW6GobChkQi8Uy5U nGc9lWYJX7logUCYgV_hu7tMWvb2HSJMBM

reach out to provide their positive experiences, and some customers may not provide feedback regardless of their experience.

To mitigate survivorship bias in AI, it is essential to critically evaluate the sources of data and ensure they cover the full spectrum of experiences, rather than just the most vocal or visible. Wherever possible, businesses should seek to incorporate data from all customer interactions and experiences. Recognizing and addressing survivorship bias is key to developing AI models that deliver accurate insights.

External Data Marketplaces and Platforms

Data marketplaces and platforms provide organizations with opportunities to monetize their data by facilitating the buying, selling, and sharing of data assets. These platforms can help organizations access new data sources and reach potential customers for their data products or services. Key types include

a. **General data marketplaces**: They offer a wide variety of data products and services, catering to a broad range of industries and use cases. Examples include AWS Data Exchange[10] and the Snowflake Data Marketplace[11].

b. **Industry-specific data marketplaces**: They focus on specific industries, such as finance, healthcare, or transportation, and offer data products and services tailored to the unique needs of those industries. Examples include Quandl[12] for financial data and HealthVerity[13] for healthcare data.

c. **Data collaboration platforms**: These platforms enable organizations to share and collaborate on data assets securely, facilitating data-driven partnerships and joint ventures. Examples of data collaboration platforms include Data Republic[14] and Infosum[15].

---

[10] https://aws.amazon.com/data-exchange/

[11] www.snowflake.com/en/data-cloud/overview/marketplace/snowflake-marketplace-for-data-and-application-partners/

[12] https://demo.quandl.com/

[13] https://healthverity.com/

[14] www.datarepublic.com/

[15] www.infosum.com/blog/what-is-data-collaboration

One thing to bear in mind is how any external data will be connected to our data, in a compliance and ethical way. This step should be considered early, to ensure the viability of data products.

1.3 Valuation

Project valuation is a crucial step in the data value exploration stage. It aids in prioritizing the right projects by understanding their potential value and complexity.

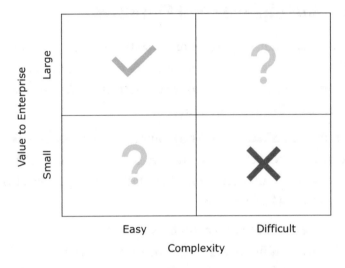

Figure 7-6. *Valuation 2x2 matrix*

We propose a 2x2 matrix (Figure 7-6) for this evaluation process. The Y-axis represents the value to the enterprise:

A. **Small value**: Projects falling in this category may have a modest immediate impact but could potentially provide insights leading to larger benefits in the future.

B. **Large value**: These projects promise significant benefits, either in terms of cost savings, revenue increase, customer experience enhancement, or strategic advantage.

The X-axis will indicate the project complexity, encompassing various aspects, including the complexity of the AI algorithms involved, compliance with legislation, privacy concerns, and potential ethical issues.

A. **AI algorithm complexity**: The complexity of the algorithm dictates the technical difficulty of the project. Simple projects may involve descriptive analytics or basic predictive models, while complex projects could require advanced machine learning or deep learning algorithms.

B. **Compliance legislation**: Projects must adhere to relevant legislation, which can range from general data protection regulations to industry-specific laws. The complexity increases if the project involves sensitive data or if it operates in highly regulated industries.

C. **Privacy**: Privacy concerns amplify the complexity, especially if projects involve personal data. Projects need to ensure anonymization of data and respect privacy norms while still maintaining data usability.

D. **Ethical considerations**: Ethical considerations add another layer to project complexity. For example, fairness and bias in AI algorithms, transparency in decision-making processes, and potential misuse of AI systems can increase the ethical complexity of a project.

By plotting projects on the 2x2 matrix, we can visualize their value to the enterprise against their complexity. This visual representation helps in decision-making regarding project selection, prioritization, and resource allocation. For instance, high-value, low-complexity projects could be low hanging fruits, while high-value, high-complexity projects might require careful planning and substantial resources but can bring transformational change. My personal advice for this type of project is to be very extremely mindful unless the organization has a high maturity in AI and data. Conversely, low-value, high-complexity projects might be put on hold or deprioritized.

The project valuation matrix is a practical tool to evaluate and prioritize AI projects during the data value exploration stage. The model will be further refined in a later phase; at this stage we just need high-level estimations.

2. Proof of Value

Once you have identified potential areas of value, the next phase is proof of value. This step is all about quickly prototyping, testing, and validating your ideas.

In this phase, it's crucial to establish a cross-functional team composed of data scientists, business analysts, IT professionals, and stakeholders. This team's diversity ensures a blend of perspectives and skills, fostering innovative ideas and rigorous testing.

The team's objective is to rapidly test hypotheses about the identified opportunities for data monetization, using a variety of analytical and AI techniques. Rapid, iterative experimentation is key here. You want to quickly learn what works and what doesn't and adjust your approach accordingly. This process allows you to validate the business value and practical feasibility of your data monetization initiatives before you invest significant time and resources in the scale phase.

This step also leverages a network graph to represent the relationships between different entities and interactions.

There are two key further points to this approach. The first one is using a graph database, such as **Neo4j**[16], to map out the relationships between different entities in a business context. The graph will consist of nodes (which represent entities such as customers, products, or interactions) and edges (which represent relationships between those entities). The second one, using the concept of an AI Data flywheel we saw earlier, explores how the graph we have generated could generate future value.

It is important to emphasize that during the discovery phase, it is critical to carry out a mini-project with the right teams, tech, and infrastructure (as per later chapters). For instance, in terms of data collection, at this stage the idea is to gather enough data to provide evidence of the business and technical viability, rather than doing the full project – with the production-ready integrations. Therefore, teams using sandboxes, or the appropriate temporal data environment, are best suited to be successful. Here, I would warn against doing this phase using only "PowerPoint" or "Excel," meaning basing the analysis on someone's opinion or "industry best practices."

Now let's consider a specific example: ***An e-commerce company that sells a variety of products to customers***.

---

[16] https://neo4j.com/

2.1 Data Collection and Integration

The first step is to collect and integrate a representative data sample from various sources. This could include transaction data, customer demographic data, website/app browsing data, customer feedback, social media interactions, etc. As per the point made in the last section, we would gather a strategic selected sample of each data point, and ensure the team doing the analysis have the right access.

Here, it is very important to get a holistic picture of the current customer experience touch points with our company, from the consideration stage to the purchase and post-purchase stages. And don't forget to avoid survival bias!

2.2 Data Modeling

Next, the data is used to create a graph that maps out the relationships between different entities. For example:

- Customers could be linked to the products they've bought (customer-product relationships).

- Customers could also be linked to other customers if they've interacted on social media or through product reviews (customer-customer relationships).

- Products could be linked to other products if they're frequently bought together (product-product relationships).

2.3 Data Analysis and Insights Extraction

We can then use AI algorithms to analyze this graph and extract insights. For example:

- Community detection algorithms could be used to identify clusters of customers with similar buying behaviors. This could then be used to develop personalized marketing strategies.

- Pathfinding algorithms could be used to understand the customer journey and identify common paths to purchase. This could inform website or app redesigns to optimize the user experience.

- Predictive analytics could be used to forecast future customer behaviors and inform business strategy.

Here, it is also very important to bring the ideas mentioned in the first chapters about Product Management methodology. For example, the "jobs-to-be-done" methodology could be used to challenge the end purpose of the customers, and whether we have now the right data needed to help the customer accomplish their jobs. Another important point, as we only have a subset of the full data, we need to ensure that whatever we do, it will scale, and it is representative of the full picture.

2.4 Business Model Development

After the high-level valuation of the first stage, it is now time to start developing a robust business model for data monetization which will be crucial for ensuring long-term success. Organizations must carefully consider the key elements of their business model, including cost-benefit analysis and return on investment (ROI) calculations. The following steps outline the process to create a business model:

a. **Define the value proposition**: Clearly articulate the value that your data or AI-driven solution provides to customers. This includes identifying the target market, understanding customer needs, and determining how your solution addresses those needs.

b. **Determine the pricing model**: Establish a pricing model for your data or AI-driven product or service, considering factors such as the value provided, market demand, and competitive landscape. Common pricing models include subscription-based pricing, tiered pricing, and usage-based pricing.

c. **Calculate costs and ROI**: Conduct a thorough cost-benefit analysis to understand the costs associated with data monetization efforts, including data storage, processing, and analytics, as well as the development and maintenance of AI solutions. Compare these costs to the expected revenue generated to determine the ROI and ensure the sustainability of your data monetization efforts. Make sure you factor in the cost of data governance and compliance procedures, and also the operation, especially if there is not a current MLOps – as the people needed and infrastructure are different.

A critical stage in business model development is to understand market demand and the competitive landscape. By analyzing these factors, organizations can identify the most promising opportunities for data monetization and develop a strategy that differentiates them from competitors. Key aspects of market demand and competitive landscape analysis include

  a. **Market size and growth**: Assess the overall size and growth potential of the market for the data products or services the organization aims to offer. This analysis can help organizations determine if there is sufficient demand to support their data monetization efforts.

  b. **Customer segmentation**: Identify the target customer segments for the organization's data products or services. This analysis can help organizations tailor their offerings to the specific needs and preferences of different customer groups, increasing the value of their data assets.

  c. **Competitor analysis**: Evaluate the competitive landscape by identifying key competitors in the market, their offerings, strengths, and weaknesses. This analysis can help organizations identify opportunities to differentiate their data products or services and develop a unique value proposition.

  d. **Pricing strategies**: Analyze pricing strategies used by competitors and assess the willingness of target customers to pay for the organization's data products or services. This analysis can help organizations develop pricing models that maximize revenue while remaining competitive.

3. Scale and Repeat

The final stage of the framework, once you have successfully proven the value of a data monetization initiative, is to Scale and Repeat.

Scaling involves taking a successful prototype and building it out into a full-fledged, operational solution. You should ensure that your solution can handle increased data volumes, user load, and integrate with other business systems as needed.

Furthermore, the solution should not just be technically scalable but also organizationally adopted. This might involve training employees, adjusting business processes, and aligning the initiative with broader strategic objectives.

Once you have successfully scaled one initiative, the process repeats. You go back to the value exploration stage for the next potential data monetization opportunity, and so the cycle continues. The ultimate aim is to create a data-driven culture of continuous learning and innovation, where AI and data monetization become integral parts of your business strategy.

3.1 Defining Clear Objectives and Use Cases

Once the organization's data assets have been assessed and prepared, the next step is to define clear objectives and use cases for data monetization. This involves

    a. **Aligning with business goals**: Ensure that the organization's data monetization efforts align with its overall business goals and strategy. This may involve identifying specific revenue targets, cost savings, or market opportunities that can be addressed through data monetization.

    b. **Identifying use cases**: Develop a list of potential use cases for data monetization, based on the organization's business goals, customer needs, and competitive landscape. These use cases should be prioritized based on their potential impact, feasibility, and alignment with the organization's strategic objectives.

    c. **Defining success metrics**: Establish clear metrics and KPIs that will be used to measure the success of the organization's data monetization efforts. These metrics should be directly linked to the organization's business goals and should be measurable, achievable, and relevant.

3.2 Developing a Data Monetization Roadmap

With clear objectives and use cases in place, the next step is to develop a data monetization roadmap. This involves

a. **Prioritizing use cases**: Rank the identified use cases based on their potential impact, feasibility, and alignment with the organization's strategic objectives. This prioritization will help guide the allocation of resources and investment in data monetization initiatives.

b. **Defining a timeline**: Establish a timeline for implementing the prioritized use cases, considering the organization's resource constraints, technological capabilities, and market dynamics.

c. **Identifying required resources**: Assess the resources required to implement the data monetization roadmap, including technical infrastructure, data science expertise, and cross-functional collaboration. This may involve upskilling existing employees, hiring new talent, or partnering with external vendors and service providers.

3.3 Implementing AI-Powered Solutions

With a data monetization roadmap in place, the next step is to implement AI-powered solutions that can extract actionable insights from the organization's data assets.

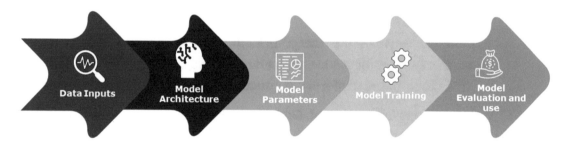

Figure 7-7. *AI data flow*

We will explore later in the HOW chapters the exact way to achieve all these tasks. See the following high-level description as per Figure 7-7:

1. **Data inputs**: The first step in the AI implementation process, involving

   a. **Data cleansing and transformation**: Ensuring data accuracy and consistency, possibly involving duplicate removal, inconsistency correction, filling missing values, and data standardization.

b. **Data integration**: Combining data from various sources for a unified view. This could require consolidating data warehouses, implementing data lakes, or using data integration tools.

c. **Data privacy and security**: Maintaining data security in compliance with data protection regulations, including techniques like encryption, access controls, and data anonymization.

d. **Data preprocessing**: Preparing data for AI analysis, which can involve normalizing data, handling missing values, and encoding categorical variables.

2. **Model architecture, parameters, and training**: The construction and refinement of AI models, which includes

a. **Feature engineering**: Identifying and creating useful features for AI models, which can involve aggregating data, creating derived variables, or using dimensionality reduction techniques.

b. **Model development and validation**: Developing and validating AI models using preprocessed data and selected features, which might involve selecting appropriate algorithms, tuning model parameters, and evaluating model performance.

c. **Model deployment and integration**: Implementing the AI models into existing systems for seamless integration and scalability. This could involve APIs, cloud-based platforms, or containerization technologies.

d. **Continuous improvement**: Ongoing performance monitoring of AI models and refining them based on feedback and changing business needs.

3. **Action and interaction**: Using insights from data analysis to enhance interactions with customers. For example, a customer identified as a frequent buyer of specific products may receive personalized recommendations for similar items, or a common purchase path could lead to a more user-friendly website design.

4. **Feedback loop**: The results of these actions are fed back into the data collection stage, creating a self-improving cycle. For instance, a positive response to a personalized product recommendation validates the cluster analysis and informs

future recommendations, while a website redesign that boosts conversion rates confirms the identified purchase path and informs future redesigns.

The ultimate goal of this framework is a continuous cycle of data collection, analysis, action, and feedback, continually improving customer interactions and boosting both customer satisfaction and business performance.

3.4 Measuring Success and Refining the Strategy

The final step in the data monetization framework is to measure the success of the implemented AI-powered solutions and refine the organization's data monetization strategy. This involves

a. **Tracking metrics and KPIs**: Regularly track and report on the established success metrics and KPIs to evaluate the effectiveness of the organization's data monetization efforts. This should include quantitative measures, such as revenue generation, cost savings, and customer satisfaction, as well as qualitative assessments, such as employee engagement and cultural change.

b. **Identifying lessons learned**: Analyze the organization's data monetization efforts to identify lessons learned, best practices, and areas for improvement. This may involve conducting post-mortems, soliciting feedback from stakeholders, and benchmarking against industry peers.

c. **Refining the strategy**: Based on the insights gained from measuring success and identifying lessons learned, refine the organization's data monetization strategy to better align with its business goals, customer needs, and competitive landscape. This may involve reprioritizing use cases, reallocating resources, or exploring new technologies and techniques.

The framework outlined above provides a structured approach for organizations to unlock value from their data assets using AI. Organizations can systematically monetize their data, generate revenue, and create lasting business value, when they follow these three main areas.

Challenges and Risks in Data Monetization

The path to data monetization through AI has its share of challenges and risks. Here are the key issues to address:

Data governance: Key to monetization, this involves proper management of data resources beyond technical tasks, involving changes in general management approaches:

- Establishing clear **roles and responsibilities** for data governance, such as data stewards and data custodians.

- Formulating comprehensive **data policies and procedures** aligned with business goals, legal requirements, and ethical standards.

- Leveraging **data governance tools and technologies** to automate data management processes.

- Cultivating a **data-driven culture** across the organization through data literacy promotion, training programs, and incentives for data-driven decision-making.

Data privacy, security, and regulatory compliance: Safeguarding data privacy and ensuring security is critical to avoid financial and reputational damage:

- **Staying updated with data protection regulations** like GDPR, CCPA, and HIPAA to prevent non-compliance repercussions.

- **Applying robust data security measures** such as encryption, access controls, and intrusion detection systems.

- **Conducting regular data privacy and security audits** to assess the effectiveness of data protection measures and detect potential vulnerabilities.

Data ownership and ethical considerations: These factors are crucial in data monetization as they determine rights to use, share, and monetize data, and ensure ethical data usage:

- Defining clear **data ownership rules** outlining rights and responsibilities of data owners, users, and stakeholders.

- Developing guidelines for **ethical data usage**, including guidelines for AI model development, data sharing, and data monetization.

- Implementing a process for **ethical reviews and impact assessments** of data monetization initiatives to identify potential ethical concerns and mitigate risks.

Ensuring data quality and accuracy: The success of data monetization efforts largely depends on data quality and accuracy:

- Formulating **data quality standards** defining acceptable levels of data accuracy, completeness, consistency, and timeliness.

- Implementing **data quality controls** throughout the data lifecycle including data collection, storage, processing, and analysis.

- Regularly **monitoring and measuring data quality** using key performance indicators (KPIs) and data quality metrics.

Overcoming technical and cultural barriers: These can obstruct an organization's data monetization efforts:

- **Integrating data silos** to enhance data access and promote data monetization efforts using data integration technologies like data lakes and warehouses.

- Building **AI and data science expertise** through hiring or training data scientists, machine learning engineers, and other data professionals.

- Fostering a **data-driven mindset** across the organization through training programs, data-driven decision-making incentives, and executive support.

- **Addressing resistance to change** by communicating the benefits of data monetization, providing adequate training, and actively involving employees in the change process.

Key Takeaways

We started with the common myths about data; whenever people talk about data monetization, often they think about selling their current IT datasets to third parties. However, there are many other ways to extract business value from data. In this chapter, we have explored a framework to systematically approach data monetization in your particular situation and how to avoid the typical pitfalls:

1. **Takeaway 1: Evolving landscape of data monetization**. The data monetization landscape has significantly transformed due to advancements in technology, growing data volumes, and heightened value recognition of data. Key trends include

   a. **Surge in data volume and complexity**: The exponential growth in data provides monetization opportunities and challenges. Investment in AI and data management infrastructure is essential.

   b. **New data sources emergence**: Widespread technologies like the Internet of Things (IoT) and Metaverse (AR and VR) offer a broader array of data sources, unlocking fresh data monetization possibilities.

   c. **Rising demand for data-driven insights**: The value realization of data-driven decisions increases demand for data analytics and AI-driven insights, paving the way for monetization through advanced analytics services, AI applications, and data consulting services.

2. **Takeaway 2: Future of AI-driven data monetization**. AI holds transformative potential for data monetization, extracting higher value from data and converting it into actionable insights. Key trends include

   a. **AI and machine learning advancements**: The rapid progress in AI and machine learning enables sophisticated, accurate modeling, unearths hidden data patterns, and creates effective data-driven products.

   b. **Democratization of AI tools**: The wider accessibility of AI tools enables organizations of all sizes to utilize AI-driven data monetization, creating a leveled playing field in the data-driven economy.

   c. **Integration of AI** into business processes: With AI integration into business processes, companies can optimize resources, make informed decisions, and improve business outcomes.

3. **Takeaway 3: Importance of a First Principles approach to data monetization**. A First Principles approach, focusing on the inherent value and potential of data for business growth, is crucial. Key aspects include

   a. **Focus on business outcomes**: Aligning data monetization strategies with overarching business goals ensures impactful and relevant initiatives.

   b. **Prioritizing data quality and accuracy**: High-quality, accurate data is indispensable for generating actionable insights and driving value from data monetization efforts.

   c. **Fostering a data-driven culture**: Promoting a culture valuing data-driven decision-making, collaboration, and continuous learning optimizes data asset usage.

   d. **Addressing privacy, security, and ethical considerations**: Ensuring data privacy, security, and ethical considerations compliance is crucial for maintaining consumer trust.

   e. **Refining data monetization strategy**: A flexible and adaptive data monetization strategy accommodates market changes, technological advancements, and evolving business needs.

The future of data monetization is promising yet challenging, with AI pivotal in unlocking value from data assets. A forward-thinking approach to data monetization will facilitate new revenue streams, innovation, and lasting business value.

This chapter is the end of "The WHY" section. We will now go in "The WHAT" part and take a detailed tour of the various AI technologies available, including machine learning, natural language processing, computer vision, and foundational models, such as large language models (including GPT4, Google's Bard). We will discuss how to use these technologies to solve business problems and grow companies.

PART III

The WHAT

CHAPTER 8

Overview of AI Concepts and Technologies

Welcome to Chapter 8, where we will embark on a journey through the core components of AI models, their connection to the larger ecosystem of AI technologies, and the paramount importance of first principles in AI model development.

We already saw in Chapter 5 the core components of AI:

    a. Machine learning algorithms

    b. Data (structured and unstructured)

    c. Computational power and hardware

    d. Software and programming languages

    e. Human-computer interaction

In this chapter we are going to go deeper on the first core component, how to think about machine learning/AI algorithms or models. Consider the development of AI models. A First Principles perspective compels us to focus on the foundational aspects of models – data, features, architecture, parameters, training, and evaluation – rather than merely using pre-packaged algorithms or black-box solutions.

An excellent example of First Principles thinking in AI is the development of the transformer architecture for natural language processing. Instead of trying to improve existing recurrent neural networks, researchers went back to the First Principles of sequence learning and realized that attention mechanisms could be more effective for understanding the dependencies between words in a sentence. This led to the development of models like BERT and GPT, which have revolutionized natural language processing.

© Francisco Javier Campos Zabala 2023
F. J. Campos Zabala, *Grow Your Business with AI*, https://doi.org/10.1007/978-1-4842-9669-1_8

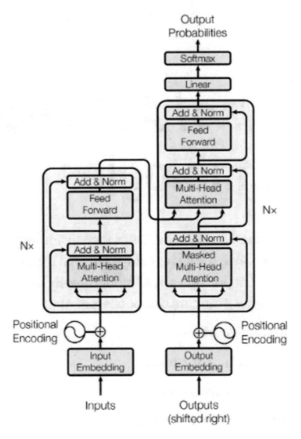

Figure 8-1. *The transformer architecture, foundation of large language models*

You can see in Figure 8-1 a diagram of the transformer. Don't worry, you do not need to understand all the inner workings[1]; we will see some of the fundamental concepts of large language models and how to use them in later chapters. And even more fascinating yet, there are some limitations to this architecture which means that new algorithms, which are now being developed and tested in AI labs around the world, will be released to improve the already impressive performance of the large language models!

---

[1]https://arxiv.org/abs/1706.03762

This chapter is divided into four main sections:

- **Core Components of AI Models**: Here we delve into the key elements that constitute an AI model, from the data inputs and architecture to the model parameters and training process. There are 120+ algorithms to choose from, so it is important to have some First Principles as to how to select the best one for your specific situation.

- **Key AI Models**: In this section, we discuss various types of AI models, including supervised and unsupervised learning models, neural networks, generative AI, and reinforcement learning models.

- **AI Platforms and Tools**: This section gives an overview of the different platforms and tools available for AI development, from cloud-based AI platforms to programming languages and libraries.

- **Conclusion**: We wrap up the chapter by revisiting the key points and looking ahead to future trends in AI from a First Principles perspective.

By the end of this chapter, you will have a deeper understanding of how AI models are constructed and how to make informed decisions in their design, training, and deployment. The foundations of this chapter will allow you to go into specific AI algorithms in later chapters.

Onward to a fascinating exploration of AI from the ground up!

Core Components of AI Models

In Chapter 5, we established AI's primary objective: to create models or algorithms capable of accurate predictions for unfamiliar inputs. This goal is achieved by developing systems that can extrapolate patterns within the training data to deliver precise decisions in novel situations. The key in real-world scenarios is **adaptability**; the AI must respond to dynamic data and make informed decisions independently.

The ultimate objective is to find an optimal model that, based on its training dataset, can accurately predict outcomes in new situations. In essence, an AI model is a mathematical function making predictions based on data. We dissect this function using a First Principles approach, examining its core components: inputs, architecture, parameters, training, and evaluation.

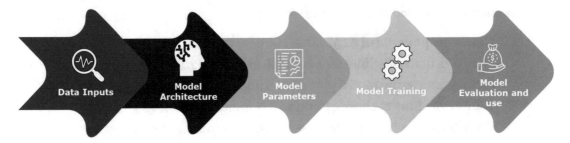

Figure 8-2. *The AI model process flow*

We will go now into the major steps of the AI modeling process flow, as per Figure 8-2.

Data Inputs: Data and Features

Data is the lifeblood of an AI model. The quality and relevance of the data directly impacts the model's performance. AI models can handle various types of data, including numerical, categorical, text, and image data. The source of the data can be internal (e.g., company databases) or external (e.g., public datasets, third-party data providers).

Tip   Contrary to popular "best" practices from some inexperienced data practitioners, focus on the data tends to bring much bigger improvements to your model performance as opposed to spending time with the modeling aspects.

We will cover this very important topic in more detail in the chapter about data monetization and open data. Table 8-1 expands how different types of data are indeed better suited for different kinds of AI models. Numerical data are often best modeled using regression algorithms or neural networks. Categorical data excel with classification methods, such as decision trees. Text data are commonly processed using natural language processing (NLP) models, while image data are ideally suited for convolutional neural networks (CNNs).

Table 8-1. *Examples of different data types and suitable AI models*

Data type	Example	Suitable AI model
Numerical	Customer age, income	Linear regression
Categorical	Customer gender, product category	Decision trees
Text	Customer reviews	NLP models (BERT, GPT)
Image	Product images	CNNs

Features are specific, measurable characteristics or properties of the data that the model uses to make predictions. Feature engineering involves selecting the most relevant features and transforming them into a format that the model can understand.

Model Architecture

At its core, an AI model learns patterns from data and uses these patterns to make predictions or decisions. It's like a recipe that transforms inputs (data) into an output (prediction) using a defined set of steps (the model's architecture and parameters).

For simplicity, we will focus on a type of AI, machine learning. However, most of the concepts explained here can be extrapolated to other types of AI.

Machine Learning from First Principles

Machine learning comprises three primary components:

- **Model**: This makes predictions or recognitions.

- **Parameters**: These are factors the model utilizes to make its decisions.

- **Learner**: This adjusts parameters and consequently the model, by evaluating the discrepancies between predictions and actual outcomes.

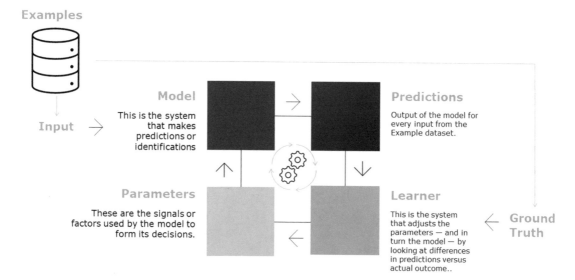

Figure 8-3. *Core components of a machine learning system*

We can see how the pieces fit together in Figure 8-3. To illustrate the overall flow, let's consider a fitness coach trying to predict optimal exercise duration for maximum calorie burn. The coach decides to leverage machine learning.

Constructing the Model

The initial model, provided by the coach, assumes exercising for 2 hours results in burning 800 calories. The parameters for this model are hours spent exercising and the calories burned, established as follows:

- 1 hour = 400 calories

- 2 hours = 800 calories

- 3 hours = 1200 calories

- 4 hours = 1600 calories

- 5 hours = 2000 calories

The model uses a mathematical formula to derive a trend line based on these parameters.

Feeding Initial Data

With the model in place, the coach inputs real-world data – calories burned by four different individuals and the corresponding hours they exercised. The observed data does not entirely align with the model, which leads to the learning phase of machine learning.

Learning Phase

The data inputted is often called the "training set" or "training data." The learner component uses it to train the model for more accurate predictions. The learner studies the discrepancy between the model and the actual data, and then adjusts the initial assumptions. For instance:

- 1 hour = 500 calories

- 2 hours = 1000 calories

- 3 hours = 1500 calories

- 4 hours = 2000 calories

- 5 hours = 2500 calories

The revised model now suggests burning 1,000 calories would require 2 hours of exercise.

Iteration Process

The system reruns with a new set of data and compares the observed calories burned with the revised model. The learner readjusts the parameters for a more accurate prediction. This iterative process repeats until the model accurately predicts calories burned based on hours of exercise.

This gradual, iterative process of minimizing the error between the prediction and the actual data (sometimes called "ground truth") is referred to as **"gradient descent"** in machine learning, similar to carefully descending a steep hill. The gradual adjustments minimize the risk of drastic errors in the model.

While the math behind this might be relatively straightforward for those versed in calculus, the real challenge lies in computing power. However, as computer capabilities evolve, complex machine learning processes are becoming increasingly attainable.

What Model?

The guiding principle behind creating useful machine learning models is eloquently captured by George Box's statement, "All models are wrong, but some are useful." It underscores the reality that no model is flawless, but the objective is to find ones that are precise and beneficial for predicting new data.

A machine learning model aims to fit a function to a given dataset, enabling predictions for new data. Two popular approaches to this process are **Bayesian and frequentist methods**. Bayesian approaches incorporate prior information to enhance predictions, while frequentist methods rely solely on the provided data. Bayesian methods can offer superior accuracy but are more complex to implement.

As we structure our models, we need to be mindful of principles such as **Ockham's razor** and the no-free lunch principle. Ockham's razor suggests that the simplest explanation is typically the correct one, while the **no-free lunch** principle posits that no single machine learning algorithm is optimal for all problems. It is thus crucial to match the algorithm to the specific data characteristics.

Two key statistical concepts utilized in machine learning are the normal distribution and the difference between Bayesian and frequentist perspectives:

- **The normal distribution**, also referred to as the **Gaussian distribution**, is a bell-shaped probability distribution symmetric about its mean. It is commonly used in machine learning to model continuous data, such as physical measurements or financial data.

- **The Bayesian and frequentist perspectives** represent two different schools of thought in statistics. Frequentists interpret probability as the long-run frequency of events, while Bayesians view it as a measure of belief or certainty. Frequentist methods are computationally more straightforward and easier to implement, whereas Bayesian methods accommodate more complex modeling techniques, incorporate prior knowledge, and deliver a full probability distribution as the outcome.

In machine learning, no one-size-fits-all approach exists. The choice of method depends on the problem at hand and available data. For example, if prior knowledge about the data is available, Bayesian methods can be powerful. However, the essential takeaway is that machine learning models, while never perfect, are invaluable tools in making precise and practical predictions from data. Choosing a model architecture involves trade-offs. For example, more complex architectures may capture more complex patterns but risk overfitting the data. First Principles thinking involves balancing the need for model complexity with the need for generalizability.

Model Parameters

This step of the process involves selecting the following:

- **Parameters**: They are the parts of the model that are learned from the data.

- **Weights and biases**: They are parameters in a neural network. Weights determine the importance of a feature, while biases allow the model to fit the data more flexibly.

- **Hyperparameters**: Selection and optimization, such as the learning rate or the number of layers in a neural network, are not learned from the data but are set prior to training. Selecting and tuning hyperparameters is a crucial step in building an effective model.

Once the parameters have been set, **cross-validation** is a technique to assess a model's performance, and it partitions the training data into a training set and a test set. The model is trained on the training set and evaluated on the test set, a process repeated several times to compute an average accuracy.

Model Training

Model training involves using data to adjust the model's parameters:

- **Cost function and optimization**: The cost function measures how well the model's predictions match the actual values. During training, the goal is to minimize this cost function using an optimization algorithm, such as gradient descent.

- **Backpropagation and gradient descent**: Backpropagation is the method used to calculate the gradient of the cost function, which is then used in the gradient descent optimization algorithm to adjust the model's weights and biases. Essentially, it involves calculating the error at the output and distributing it back through the network to update the weights and biases.

Model Evaluation and Validation

After a model is trained, it needs to be evaluated and validated to ensure it performs well on unseen data:

- **Understanding evaluation metrics**: They measure the performance of an AI model. The choice of metric depends on the specific task at hand. For instance, accuracy is often used for classification tasks, while mean squared error is common for regression tasks.

- **Overfitting, underfitting, and model generalization**: Overfitting occurs when a model learns the training data too well, including its noise and outliers, resulting in poor performance on unseen data. Underfitting is when the model is too simple to learn the underlying structure of the data. Striking a balance between the two is key to model generalization, that is, the model's ability to perform well on unseen data. To prevent overfitting, we employ regularization techniques, which apply a penalty to the model's cost function, making the model less complex and less prone to overfitting.

To summarize, a First Principles approach to model development involves

- Understanding the basic components of an AI model

- Recognizing the importance of data quality and relevance

- Balancing the complexity and generalizability of the model

- Being thoughtful about parameter and hyperparameter selection

- Ensuring robust model evaluation and validation

We will go in more details for some of the most popular models in later chapters.

Key AI Models

In this section, we explore the key AI models and their applications, adopting a first principles approach to ensure an understanding of the underlying concepts.

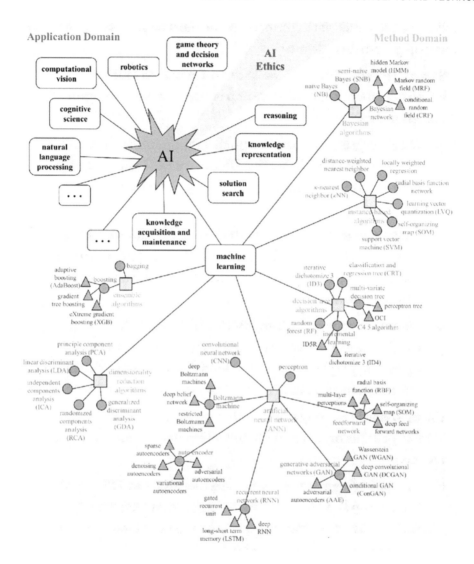

Figure 8-4. *Comprehensive AI models taxonomy*[2]

As we discussed in earlier chapters, there are many taxonomies to classify the different AI algorithms, depending on the criteria being used. Figure 8-4 provides one of those taxonomies, but as mentioned, there are multiples, and it is recommended to get familiar with a few different taxonomies, so you can get accustomed with the different AI models and how they can be applied to different real-life scenarios.

---

[2] www.researchgate.net/figure/Categories-of-AI-related-techniques_fig1_334404567

The following list has a brief description of the most popular ones. In the next few chapters, we will go into their details:

- **Supervised learning models**: They are trained on labeled data, where the input-output relationship is known. Some common models include

  a. **Linear regression**: Used for predicting continuous outcomes by fitting a linear relationship between input features and output. It is widely used for forecasting, such as sales or stock prices.

  b. **Logistic regression**: Used for binary classification problems. It estimates the probability of a given input belonging to a specific class, such as email spam detection or customer churn prediction.

  c. **Support vector machines (SVMs)**: Used for both classification and regression tasks. They aim to find the optimal hyperplane that separates different classes with the maximum margin, making them robust to outliers and noise.

- **Unsupervised learning models**: Unsupervised learning models identify patterns or structures in unlabeled data. Some common models are

  a. **Clustering algorithms (K-means, hierarchical, DBSCAN)**: They group similar data points together based on their features. They are used for customer segmentation, anomaly detection, and image segmentation.

  b. **Dimensionality reduction (PCA, t-SNE)**: They reduce the number of input features while preserving the underlying structure of the data. They are useful for visualizing high-dimensional data, noise reduction, and feature extraction.

- **Neural networks and deep learning models**: They are powerful AI models that can learn complex patterns and representations. They consist of layers of interconnected neurons. Some popular neural network architectures are

a. **Feedforward neural networks**: They consist of an input layer, one or more hidden layers, and an output layer. They are used for tasks like image classification, speech recognition, and natural language processing.

b. **Convolutional neural networks (CNNs)**: They are designed for image processing tasks, utilizing convolutional layers to learn local features in images. They are widely used in image recognition, object detection, and video analysis.

c. **Recurrent neural networks (RNNs) and LSTM**: They are designed for sequence data, such as time series or text. They maintain internal states that capture information from previous time steps, enabling them to model temporal dependencies.

- **Generative AI**: They generate new data that resembles the training data. Some popular generative AI models are

  a. **Variational autoencoders (VAEs)**: They are unsupervised generative models that learn to encode and decode data, generating new samples by sampling from the learned latent space. They are used for image generation, denoising, and inpainting.

  b. **Adversarial networks (GANs)**: They consist of a generator and a discriminator that compete against each other. The generator creates fake data, while the discriminator learns to distinguish between real and fake data. GANs are used for image synthesis, style transfer, and data augmentation.

  c. **Transformer models (BERT, GPT)**: They have revolutionized natural language processing. They rely on attention mechanisms to capture dependencies between words in a sentence, regardless of their distance apart. They are used for tasks like machine translation, text generation, and sentiment analysis.

- **Reinforcement learning models**: They learn optimal actions through trial and error, receiving a reward or penalty based on their actions. They are used in areas like game playing, robot navigation, and resource management.

Selecting the right model is crucial for the success of an AI project. Table 8-2 shows an evaluation of some popular AI models. A First Principles approach involves understanding the underlying problem and data, and considering factors like model complexity, interpretability, training time, and computational resources.

Table 8-2. *Comparison of key AI models*

Model type	Use case	Pros	Cons
Linear regression	Sales forecasting, stock market prediction	Simple, interpretable	Assumes linear relationship
Logistic regression	Spam detection, customer churn prediction	Probabilistic output, interpretable	Binary classification only
Support vector machines	Text categorization, image classification	Robust to outliers, effective in high dimensional space	Sensitive to kernel choice, doesn't provide probability estimates
Clustering algorithms	Customer segmentation, anomaly detection	Unsupervised, flexible	Requires choice of number of clusters, sensitive to initialization
Dimensionality reduction	Data visualization, noise reduction	Reduces computational costs, Helps avoid overfitting	Loss of information, less interpretable
Feedforward neural networks	Image classification, speech recognition	Can model nonlinear relationships, scalable	Requires large amount of data, less interpretable
Convolutional neural networks	Image recognition, object detection	Spatially invariant, good for image data	Requires large amount of data, computationally intensive
Recurrent neural networks	Time series prediction, text generation	Good for sequence data, captures temporal dependencies	Difficulty in learning long range dependencies, computationally intensive
Variational autoencoders	Image generation, denoising	Unsupervised, can generate new data	Less control over generated data, complex

(continued)

Table 8-2. (*continued*)

Model type	Use case	Pros	Cons
Generative adversarial networks	Image synthesis, style transfer	Can generate high-quality data, flexible	Difficult to train, requires large amount of data
Transformer models	Machine translation, sentiment analysis	Captures long-range dependencies, good for text data	Requires large amount of data, computationally intensive
Reinforcement learning models	Game playing, robot navigation	Learns through interaction, can handle complex tasks	Requires a well-defined reward system, computationally intensive

This overview of key AI models should provide a foundation for understanding how different models can be applied to various business problems. We will explore in later chapters some of the most popular one and how to select the most appropriate one for your specific project. In the next section, we will explore the various AI platforms and tools available for implementing these models.

AI Platforms and Tools

In this section, we will explore the various platforms and tools available for implementing AI models from a high-level point of view. Chapter 16 will go into a lot of more detail. From cloud-based platforms to programming languages and libraries, understanding the ecosystem of AI tools is crucial for effective implementation and scalability.

From the First Principles point of view, the core components are

- AI platforms

- Programming languages.

- Libraries: for ML algorithms, data visualization, and deep learning

Let's expand all these core components:

- **AI platforms**: They provide the infrastructure and services needed to develop, train, and deploy machine learning models. They often come with pre-built models, data storage, processing capabilities, and tools for monitoring and managing AI applications.

  - **Cloud-based AI platforms** (AWS, GCP, Azure): They offer comprehensive suites of machine learning services, including pre-trained models, autoML, custom model training, and deployment services. They also provide scalability and flexibility, allowing you to easily adjust resources as your needs change.

  - **Open-source platforms** (TensorFlow, PyTorch): They provide flexible, extensible environments for developing and training custom machine learning models. They have a large community of developers, extensive documentation, and are widely used in research and development.

- **Programming languages for AI (Python, R, Julia)**: Python is the most popular language for AI due to its simplicity, readability, and extensive library support. R is often used for statistical analysis and visualization, while Julia, a newer language, is gaining popularity for its speed and ease of use in mathematical and technical computing.

- **Libraries and tools**

  - **For data manipulation and analysis** (Pandas, Numpy, Scikit-learn): Numpy provide tools for data manipulation and analysis in Python, while Scikit-learn offers a wide range of machine learning algorithms. They are essential for preprocessing data and training models.

  - **For deep learning** (Keras, TensorFlow, PyTorch): For deep learning, Keras provides a high-level interface for building neural networks, while TensorFlow and PyTorch offer more control and flexibility for custom model development.

- **For model visualization and interpretability** (Matplotlib, Seaborn, SHAP): They help in understanding and interpreting data and model performance. SHAP and similar libraries provide tools for interpreting complex models, shedding light on how input features contribute to model predictions.

When selecting tools, a First Principles approach involves considering the specific requirements of your project, such as the complexity of the model, the size and type of data, the computational resources available, and the need for scalability and interpretability. Table 8-3 shows an evaluation of popular AI platforms and tools.

Table 8-3. *Comparison of AI platforms and tools*

Tool type	Examples	Pros	Cons
Cloud-based AI platforms	AWS, GCP, Azure	Scalable, comprehensive services, pre-trained models	Can be costly, less customization
Open-source platforms	TensorFlow, PyTorch	flexible, customizable, large community	Steeper learning curve
Programming languages	Python, R, Julia	Extensive library support (Python), good for statistics (R), fast (Julia)	Depends on specific use case
Deep learning tools	Keras, TensorFlow, PyTorch	High-level interface (Keras), flexibility, and control (TensorFlow, PyTorch)	Computationally intensive
Interpretability tools	Matplotlib, Seaborn, SHAP	Helpful for data understanding and model interpretation	Can require significant coding and statistical understanding

Selecting the right tools and platforms for your AI needs is a crucial decision that can significantly impact your project's efficiency and outcome. It's not only about picking the most popular or advanced tools but choosing those that best fit your specific needs and constraints.

While cloud-based platforms like AWS, GCP, or Azure offer scalability and wide-ranging services, they may not always provide the level of customization you might need for a particular project. On the other hand, open-source platforms like TensorFlow and PyTorch offer flexibility and customization but require a steeper learning curve.

Python, R, and Julia, the popular programming languages for AI, have their strengths: Python for its extensive library support, R for statistical analysis, and Julia for its speed. However, the choice of language depends on the specific use case and the skill set of your team.

Libraries like Pandas, Numpy, and Scikit-learn are fundamental for data manipulation, while deep learning requires more specialized libraries like Keras, TensorFlow, and PyTorch. Visualization tools like Matplotlib and Seaborn, and interpretability libraries like SHAP, help in understanding and interpreting your models, but can require significant coding and statistical understanding.

In a First Principles approach, all these factors – the project requirements, the available resources, the trade-offs involved – should be considered carefully to select the tools that most effectively serve your AI project's goals.

Takeaways

In this chapter, we have taken a deep dive into the various facets of AI, its core components, and the tools that power its operations. We have also underscored the importance of adhering to first principles in AI model development. As we conclude, let's recap some key points and their implications for businesses:

Recap of key points and implications for businesses:

- **First Principles in AI**: The first principles approach, which involves breaking down complex systems into their fundamental components and understanding their underlying principles, is central to AI model development.

  - **Do** apply first principles thinking in AI model development: This approach encourages critical thinking and fosters innovation. It can lead to solutions that are more robust and less susceptible to pitfalls.

  - **Don't** blindly follow trends or popular methods without understanding the underlying principles. This could lead to sub-optimal solutions and missed opportunities for innovation.

- **Choice of AI models**: We discussed a variety of AI models, from supervised and unsupervised learning models to neural networks and generative AI. Each model type has its strengths and use cases. Businesses must understand these differences and choose the model that best fits their specific needs and context.

  - **Do** choose the AI model that best fits your business needs and context. It's essential to understand the strengths and weaknesses of each model type and how they align with your specific goals.

  - **Don't** choose a model solely based on its popularity or complexity. A complex model isn't always better. Sometimes, a simpler model can provide equally good, if not better, results.

- **AI platforms and tools**: Selecting the appropriate tools and platforms can significantly impact your AI project's efficiency and outcome. The choice between cloud-based platforms (like AWS, GCP, or Azure) and open-source platforms (like TensorFlow and PyTorch) should be made based on your specific requirements, resources, and constraints.

  - **Do** select your AI tools and platforms based on your specific needs, resources, and constraints. Consider factors like scalability, customization, budget and the skill set of your team.

  - **Don't** choose tools just because they are popular or advanced. Not all advanced tools will be suitable for your specific needs. Always align your tool selection with your project requirements and team's capabilities.

AI, with its vast potential, can significantly boost your business's growth and efficiency. However, leveraging its power requires a deep understanding of its concepts, components, and tools. Adhering to first principles in AI model development can guide you through this complex landscape, leading to more effective and robust AI implementations. As we move forward, these principles will continue to serve as our guiding light, helping us navigate the rapidly evolving world of AI.

CHAPTER 9

Supervised and Unsupervised Learning

As we discussed in the last few chapters, supervised and unsupervised learning are two primary approaches to machine learning. At its core, machine learning is about teaching computers to learn from data. There are many different types of machine learning, but two of the most common are supervised learning and unsupervised learning.

Supervised learning involves training a model using ***labeled data***, which consists of input-output pairs. The model learns the underlying patterns and relationships between the inputs and outputs, enabling it to make predictions on unseen data. Common applications of supervised learning include image recognition, sentiment analysis, and fraud detection. For example, a supervised learning algorithm could be trained to classify images of animals into one of a set of predefined categories, such as cat, dog, bird, etc.

> *Definition of labeled data: Also known as annotated data, it refers to datasets where each instance is associated with a specific label or outcome. Labeled data is often more time-consuming and expensive to obtain than unlabeled data because it typically involves human expertise to manually classify each instance in the dataset. For instance, going to a large pet pictures dataset and label them either as "cat" or "dog" or "other."*

Unsupervised learning, on the other hand, deals with unlabeled data, where the model learns to identify patterns, structures, and relationships within the data without prior knowledge of the desired output. It is often used for tasks such as clustering, dimensionality reduction, and anomaly detection. For example, an unsupervised learning algorithm could be used to find groups of similar customers.

The significance of these techniques lies in their ability to solve complex problems, automate tasks, and generate insights that can drive business growth. They form the foundation of AI applications, making it essential for executives to understand their differences and potential use cases.

© Francisco Javier Campos Zabala 2023
F. J. Campos Zabala, *Grow Your Business with AI*, https://doi.org/10.1007/978-1-4842-9669-1_9

Understanding supervised and unsupervised learning from a first principles perspective involves breaking down these techniques into their fundamental components and examining the underlying principles that govern their behavior. This approach enables business executives to

1. **Make informed decisions**: A First Principles understanding allows executives to identify suitable machine learning techniques for specific business problems, ensuring the selection of appropriate algorithms and models that align with their objectives.

2. **Foster innovation**: By grasping the core principles behind these learning techniques, executives can think beyond existing solutions and encourage innovative approaches to problem-solving.

3. **Enhance collaboration**: A solid understanding of supervised and unsupervised learning enables executives to communicate effectively with data scientists and engineers, facilitating cross-functional collaboration.

There are many ways that you can use supervised and unsupervised learning to grow your company. Here are a few examples:

- **Customer segmentation**: You can use unsupervised learning to segment your customers into groups with similar characteristics. This can help you to target your marketing campaigns more effectively.

- **Fraud detection**: You can use supervised learning to detect fraudulent transactions. This can protect your company from financial losses.

- **Product recommendations**: You can use collaborative filtering to recommend products to your customers based on their past purchases. This can help you to increase sales.

- **Risk assessment**: You can use supervised learning to assess the risk of default on loans. Or to assess the overall customer risk. This can help you to make better business decisions.

- **Spam filtering**: You can use supervised learning to filter out spam emails. This can improve the user experience for your customers.

These are just a few examples of how you can use supervised and unsupervised learning to grow your company. With a little creativity, you can find many other ways to use these powerful tools.

Both supervised and unsupervised learning are powerful tools that can be used to solve a wide variety of problems. In this chapter, we will take a closer look at both types of learning and discuss their applications. We will also introduce semi-supervised learning and reinforcement learning, two other important types of machine learning.

Supervised Learning

Supervised learning is a foundational concept in artificial intelligence (AI) and machine learning (ML). It is a form of learning where an algorithm is trained on a dataset containing both input features and the corresponding correct output labels. In essence, the algorithm learns the mapping between the inputs and outputs from the training data, allowing it to make predictions on new, unseen data points. Supervised learning is best understood from a First Principles perspective as a process of generalizing patterns in data to construct an underlying function that relates the inputs to the outputs. It is also called a "Discriminate model," as the model learns to discriminate between groups seen in the labeled dataset. We will see how these models differ from "generative modeling," foundation of the latest large language models.

From a First Principles perspective, *supervised learning can be seen as an optimization problem*. The goal is to find the optimal model parameters that minimize the difference between the model's predictions and the actual output labels in the training dataset. This difference is often quantified using a loss function, which measures the discrepancy between the predictions and ground truth labels. By iteratively adjusting the model's parameters, the learning algorithm seeks to minimize the loss function, resulting in a model that can make accurate predictions on new data points.

The following are the core components of supervised learning from a First Principles perspective:

i. **Labeled training data**: Supervised learning relies on a dataset with input-output pairs, where each input feature vector is associated with a corresponding output label. This labeled data is used to teach the algorithm the underlying relationships between the inputs and outputs, allowing it to generalize these patterns to make predictions on new, unseen data.

ii. **Model training**: During the training phase, the algorithm uses the labeled training data to learn the mapping between the input features and the output labels. This is accomplished by adjusting the model's parameters to minimize the loss function, which measures the difference between the model's predictions and the actual output labels.

iii. **Model evaluation**: After training, the model's performance is assessed on a separate dataset, typically called the validation or test set. This dataset is not used during training and serves to evaluate the model's ability to generalize to new, unseen data points. Common evaluation metrics include accuracy, precision, recall, and F1-score for classification tasks, and mean squared error (MSE) or root mean squared error (RMSE) for regression tasks. We will explore these in later chapters.

iv. **Model optimization**: The process of model training often involves hyperparameter tuning and regularization techniques to optimize the model's performance on the validation or test set. Hyperparameters are adjustable settings that influence the learning process, such as the learning rate, the number of layers in a neural network, or the maximum depth of a decision tree. Regularization techniques, like L1 and L2 regularization, help prevent overfitting by adding a penalty term to the loss function, discouraging overly complex models.

There are many popular supervised learning algorithms and their applications. We will explore later how to decide the best one depending on several factors:

i.   **Linear regression**: A simple algorithm for modeling the relationship between a dependent variable and one or more independent variables. Linear regression is often used for forecasting, trend analysis, and determining the impact of various factors on an outcome.

ii. **Logistic regression**: A classification algorithm used for predicting the probability of an instance belonging to a specific class. Common applications include spam detection, medical diagnosis, and credit risk assessment.

iii. **Support vector machines (SVM)**: SVMs are a powerful classification and regression technique that seeks to find the optimal decision boundary (or hyperplane) separating the classes. SVMs are used in various fields, such as image recognition, text categorization, and bioinformatics.

iv. **Decision trees**: A hierarchical, tree-like structure used for decision-making and prediction. Decision trees can be used for both classification and regression tasks and are the basis for more complex algorithms like random forests.

v. **Random forests**: An ensemble learning method that combines multiple decision trees to improve prediction accuracy and reduce overfitting. Random forests are used in a variety of applications, including customer segmentation, fraud detection, and feature selection.

vi. **Neural networks**: A family of algorithms inspired by the structure and function of the human brain, consisting of interconnected layers of artificial neurons. Neural networks are particularly well-suited for complex tasks such as image and speech recognition, natural language processing, and game playing. Given the importance of this algorithm and recent developments, we will further explore them in Chapter 10.

As we saw, the data availability is extremely important. In enterprise environments, the most common data type is tabular data, in my experience, the best algorithm in overall terms for that data is ***extreme gradient boosting machines (XGB).*** There are also plenty of industry reviews that achieve the same conclusion.[1]

Tip   XGBoost is a powerful machine learning algorithm that can be used for a variety of supervised learning tasks. It is often ***the most all-round model for most tabular*** datasets.

---

[1] https://arxiv.org/ftp/arxiv/papers/2204/2204.12868.pdf

Indeed, the XGBoost algorithm has gained immense popularity due to its speed and performance. It is based on the principle of boosting weak learners using the gradient descent architecture. However, like any model, it is not a magic bullet, and its effectiveness can depend on the specific characteristics of your data and also business objectives. Therefore, although XGBoost tends to be an all-rounder and performs well on many tabular datasets, it is always a good idea to experiment with different models and select the one that best fits your specific problem.

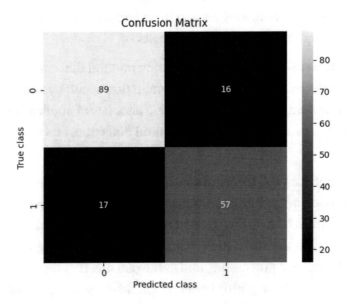

Figure 9-1. *XGBoost performance for the Titanic dataset*

Figure 9-1 shows the confusion matrix for the XGBoost model applied to predicting who will survive in the Titanic. You will be able to create this model yourself using any code-generation tools (such as Copilot, ChatGPT, or Bard). I have created a few prompts at the end of the chapter.

Here are some of the benefits of using XGBoost:

- **Speed**: XGBoost is one of the fastest machine learning algorithms available. This is due to its use of a tree-based structure, which allows it to make predictions very quickly.

- **Accuracy**: XGBoost is known for its high accuracy. It has been shown to outperform other machine learning algorithms on a variety of datasets.

- **Flexibility**: XGBoost is a very flexible algorithm. It can be used for a variety of supervised learning tasks, and it can be extended to handle missing data and categorical features.

- **Explainability**: XGBoost is more explainable than other models such neural networks or re-enforcement learning. Applying techniques such as SHAP (SHapley Additive exPlanations) can make the models very explainable.

Here are some additional tips for using XGBoost:

- **Use cross-validation to evaluate your model**: Cross-validation is a technique that can be used to evaluate the performance of a machine learning model on unseen data. It is important to use cross-validation when tuning the hyperparameters of your XGBoost model.

- **Regularize your model**: Regularization is a technique that can be used to prevent overfitting. It is important to regularize your XGBoost model, especially if you are using a large number of features.

- **Experiment with different hyperparameters**: The hyperparameters of XGBoost can have a significant impact on the performance of your model. It is important to experiment with different hyperparameters to find the best combination for your dataset.

There are a few real-world examples and case studies of supervised learning:

i. **Medical diagnosis**: Supervised learning algorithms like logistic regression and support vector machines are used to predict the likelihood of a patient having a specific disease based on a set of input features, such as age, blood pressure, and medical history.

ii. **Credit scoring**: Banks and financial institutions use supervised learning algorithms, such as decision trees and neural networks, to assess the creditworthiness of loan applicants based on factors like income, employment history, and credit history.

iii. **Fraud detection**: In the financial sector, supervised learning techniques like random forests and neural networks are employed to detect fraudulent transactions and suspicious activities by analyzing patterns in transaction data.

iv. **Natural language processing**: Supervised learning algorithms play a crucial role in various NLP tasks, such as sentiment analysis, where algorithms like logistic regression and neural networks are used to classify text data as positive, negative, or neutral.

v. **Product recommendations**: Supervised learning algorithms are used to recommend products to customers. For example, Amazon uses supervised learning algorithms to recommend products to its customers based on their past purchases.

vi. **Spam filtering**: Supervised learning algorithms are used to filter out spam emails. For example, Gmail uses supervised learning algorithms to filter out spam emails from its users' inboxes.

It is very important to understand supervised learning from a first principles perspective, for business executives to gain a deeper appreciation of the underlying concepts and techniques that drive AI and ML applications. While the team should have data scientists which will go into the technical details, everyone in the team should understand the basic concepts to ensure the right technique is applied to the right business problem, with the right metrics. This knowledge can be invaluable for decision-making, especially when it comes to selecting the right ML algorithm for a specific problem or optimizing an existing AI system.

Unsupervised learning

Unsupervised learning is a type of machine learning where algorithms learn from data without any prior knowledge of the desired outcomes or labeled training data. In contrast to supervised learning, which relies on labeled data to make predictions or classifications, unsupervised learning identifies patterns and structures within the data itself. This self-guided learning process enables the model to uncover hidden patterns, groupings, and associations within the data, which can lead to new insights and more efficient data processing.

The core components from a First Principles perspective of unsupervised learning:

i. **Unlabeled data**: The primary input for unsupervised learning algorithms is raw, unlabeled data. Unlike supervised learning, there is no pre-defined target variable, which allows the model to explore the data without any predetermined assumptions or guidance.

ii. **Pattern recognition and clustering**: One of the main goals of unsupervised learning is to identify patterns or structures within the data. Clustering is a common technique used to group similar data points based on their inherent characteristics, which can help reveal hidden relationships and associations.

iii. **Dimensionality reduction**: High-dimensional data can be challenging to analyze and visualize due to the sheer number of variables. Unsupervised learning algorithms can perform dimensionality reduction, which reduces the number of variables while retaining the essential information, making it easier to analyze and visualize the data.

iv. **Feature extraction**: Unsupervised learning can also be used to extract relevant features from the data. This process involves transforming the raw data into a more meaningful and informative representation, which can be used as input for other machine learning models or for further analysis.

There are several popular unsupervised learning algorithms and their applications:

i. **K-means clustering**: A widely used clustering algorithm that partitions the data into K distinct clusters based on their similarities. K-means is often employed for market segmentation, anomaly detection, and image segmentation.

ii. **Hierarchical clustering**: This clustering algorithm creates a tree-like structure of nested clusters, which can be visualized as a dendrogram. Hierarchical clustering is commonly used in gene expression analysis, document clustering, and social network analysis.

iii. **Principal component analysis (PCA)**: A dimensionality
reduction technique that transforms the data by projecting it
onto a lower-dimensional space while preserving as much of
the variance in the data as possible. PCA is often used for data
visualization, noise reduction, and feature extraction in various
domains, including finance, biology, and image processing.

iv. **Independent component analysis (ICA)**: Another
dimensionality reduction technique that separates the data into
statistically independent components. ICA is commonly used in
blind source separation problems, such as separating mixed audio
signals or recovering original images from mixed signals.

v. **t-distributed stochastic neighbor embedding (t-SNE)**: A
nonlinear dimensionality reduction technique designed for
visualizing high-dimensional data in a low-dimensional space.
t-SNE is particularly useful for visualizing complex datasets, such
as gene expression data or text documents.

As with all ML models, the choice of which unsupervised learning algorithm to use
depends on the specific task at hand.

Tip   The most popular ML algorithm for unsupervised learning is ***K-means***
clustering. K-means clustering is a good choice for simple tasks such as data
segmentation. Hierarchical clustering is a good choice for more complex tasks
such as creating a dendrogram (a diagram representing a tree).

K-means clustering is a method used to automatically partition a dataset into K
groups or clusters. The algorithm works by iteratively assigning each data point to one of
the K groups based on feature similarity, which is often calculated using distance metrics
such as Euclidean or Manhattan distance.

The goal is to minimize the within-cluster distances (i.e., data points in the same
cluster should be as similar as possible) and maximize the between-cluster distances
(i.e., data points in different clusters should be as different as possible)

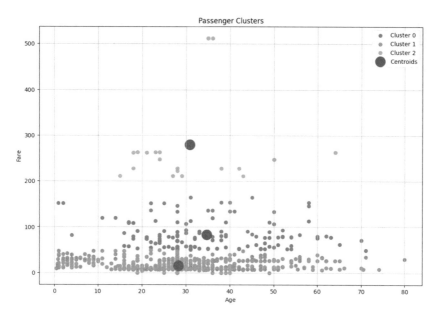

Figure 9-2. *K-means applied to the Titanic dataset*

Figure 9-2 shows K-means model applied to the Titanic dataset. You will be able to create this model yourself using any code-generation tools (such as Copilot, ChatGPT, or Bard). I have created a few prompts at the end of the chapter. The number of clusters, 3, was arbitrarily chosen for this example. In a real-world scenario, you would likely want to use a method like the Elbow Method to determine the optimal number of clusters.

The resulting plot shows three groups of passengers distinguished by age and fare. This might suggest some underlying patterns in the data, such as different clusters representing different passenger classes, age groups, etc.

Below are some real-world examples and case studies of unsupervised learning:

i. **Customer segmentation**: Retailers and e-commerce businesses use clustering algorithms, such as K-means and hierarchical clustering, to segment their customer base into distinct groups based on purchasing behavior, demographics, and preferences. This segmentation enables companies to tailor their marketing strategies and product offerings to better serve each customer segment.

ii. **Anomaly detection**: Unsupervised learning techniques, such as clustering and autoencoders, can be used to identify unusual or suspicious patterns in data such as detecting fraudulent transactions in financial services or identifying outliers in sensor data from industrial equipment. By flagging these anomalies, companies can take preventive action, reducing the risk of loss or damage.

iii. **Text mining and document clustering**: Unsupervised learning algorithms, like hierarchical clustering and t-SNE, can be applied to large collections of text documents to automatically organize and categorize them based on their content. This capability is useful for content management systems, search engines, and news aggregation platforms, where grouping similar documents can enhance user experience and facilitate information retrieval.

iv. **Image segmentation and object recognition**: Unsupervised learning methods, such as K-means and autoencoders, are used to segment images into distinct regions or objects, enabling more effective analysis and understanding of the visual content. This technique is widely used in computer vision applications, including medical imaging, satellite imagery analysis, and autonomous vehicle navigation.

v. **Genomic data analysis**: The high dimensionality and complexity of genomic data make unsupervised learning techniques, like PCA and t-SNE, valuable tools for visualizing and exploring gene expression patterns. This analysis can help researchers identify biologically meaningful relationships and subgroups within the data, which can inform the development of new therapies and diagnostics.

Unsupervised learning offers a powerful and flexible approach to discovering hidden patterns, structures, and associations within data. Unsupervised learning algorithms can uncover valuable insights and generate more efficient representations of the data, when analyzing raw, unlabeled data without any predefined assumptions or guidance. From customer segmentation to image recognition, the applications of unsupervised learning span a wide range of industries and domains, making it a crucial component of any data-driven organization's AI toolkit.

Semi-supervised Learning

Semi-supervised learning is a machine learning paradigm that combines aspects of both supervised and unsupervised learning. While supervised learning relies on labeled data and unsupervised learning on unlabeled data, semi-supervised learning utilizes a mixture of labeled and unlabeled data to train models. The primary motivation behind semi-supervised learning is that labeled data can be scarce, expensive, or time-consuming to obtain, while unlabeled data is often more readily available. Semi-supervised learning seeks to improve model performance and generalization while reducing the cost and effort associated with data labeling, when incorporating both types of data.

The following are the core components of semi-supervised learning from a First Principles perspective:

i. **Combination of labeled and unlabeled data**: Semi-supervised learning algorithms work with a mixture of labeled and unlabeled data. The labeled data provides guidance for the learning process, while the unlabeled data helps capture the underlying structure and distribution of the data, which can lead to better model generalization.

ii. **Model training and optimization using both types of data**: In semi-supervised learning, the model is trained and optimized using both labeled and unlabeled data. The training process typically involves an iterative process where the model is first trained on the labeled data, then refined using the unlabeled data, either through clustering or other unsupervised techniques.

There are some popular semi-supervised learning algorithms and their applications:

i. **Label propagation**: Label propagation is a graph-based semi-supervised learning algorithm that uses the relationships between data points to propagate labels from labeled to unlabeled data. By constructing a graph with data points as nodes and similarities between points as edges, label propagation iteratively updates the labels of the unlabeled nodes based on their neighbors' labels until convergence. This algorithm is commonly used in applications such as image and text classification, where the underlying structure of the data can be represented as a graph.

ii. **Label spreading**: Label spreading is like label propagation but
introduces a regularization term to control the smoothness of
the label assignments across the graph. This regularization helps
prevent overfitting and makes the algorithm more robust to noise.
Like label propagation, label spreading is applicable to various
classification tasks where the data can be represented as a graph,
such as social network analysis and bioinformatics.

iii. **Self-training**: Self-training is a semi-supervised learning
technique that leverages the model's confidence in its predictions
to iteratively label and retrain on the unlabeled data. The
algorithm starts by training a model on the labeled data and then
uses the model to predict labels for the unlabeled data. High-
confidence predictions are then added to the labeled dataset, and
the model is retrained. This process is repeated until no more
high-confidence predictions can be made or a predetermined
stopping criterion is met. Self-training is applicable to a wide
range of classification problems, including text classification,
image recognition, and speech recognition.

There are some real-world examples and case studies of semi-supervised learning:

i. **Sentiment analysis**: In sentiment analysis, semi-supervised
learning can be used to classify the sentiment of text data, such
as product reviews or social media posts. Labeled data, which
includes a small set of texts with known sentiment labels, is
combined with a large amount of unlabeled data to improve
classification performance. Label propagation or self-training
techniques can be applied to iteratively refining the model,
ultimately yielding more accurate sentiment predictions.

ii. **Image classification**: Semi-supervised learning is also valuable
in image classification tasks, where acquiring labeled data can
be time-consuming and expensive. In these scenarios, a small
set of labeled images can be combined with a larger set of
unlabeled images to enhance the classification model. Techniques
such as self-training can be employed to iteratively refine the
model, ultimately leading to better classification accuracy and

generalization to new images. A notable example of this approach is the use of semi-supervised learning in medical image analysis, where expert annotation is often limited and costly. By leveraging a small amount of labeled data and a larger pool of unlabeled data, researchers can develop more accurate and robust models for tasks like tumor segmentation and organ identification.

iii. **Fraud detection**: In the financial industry, semi-supervised learning can be employed to detect fraudulent transactions or other anomalous activities. In this context, labeled data may consist of a small number of known fraud cases, while unlabeled data represents most transactions. Using techniques like label propagation or self-training, semi-supervised learning can help identify patterns indicative of fraud and improve the overall accuracy of fraud detection systems.

iv. **Bioinformatics**: In the field of bioinformatics, semi-supervised learning has been applied to tasks such as gene function prediction and protein interaction prediction. In these cases, labeled data might include a small number of experimentally validated gene functions or protein interactions, while unlabeled data represents the broader set of genes or proteins whose functions or interactions are unknown. By leveraging both types of data, researchers can develop models that more accurately predict gene functions and protein interactions, thus facilitating a deeper understanding of biological processes and potential drug targets.

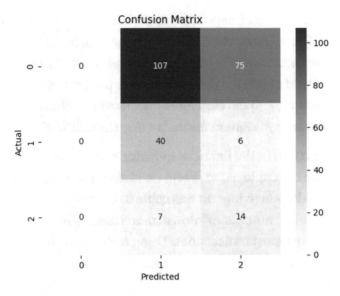

Figure 9-3. *Confusion matrix from the Titanic dataset*

Figure 9-3 shows the confusion matrix for the semi-supervised model applied to predicting who will survive in the Titanic. You will be able to create this model yourself using any code-generation tools (such as Copilot, ChatGPT, or Bard). I have created a few prompts at the end of the chapter.

In this code, I simulated a semi-supervised learning situation where only a small portion of the data (30% in this case) is labeled. We mark the unlabeled instances with -1 as per the requirement of the LabelSpreading algorithm.

The LabelSpreading model is then trained on both labeled and unlabeled data. After training, the model is used to predict labels for all data.

Finally, we evaluate the performance of the model only on the originally labeled data. We also display a confusion matrix for these predictions. Not surprisingly, in this case, the performance of this model is worse than using all the labeled data, but this technique can improve the performance in other cases where we have little labeled data and loads of unlabeled data.

Please note that in a real-world scenario, you would typically have a separate labeled test set for evaluation which was not used during training or semi-supervised label estimation.

Here are some examples of semi-supervised learning in action:

- **Google Photos**: Google Photos[2] uses semi-supervised learning to classify images. The algorithm is trained on a small set of labeled images, and then it is used to label unlabeled images. This allows Google Photos to classify images even if they are not labeled.

- **Amazon Recommendations**: Amazon[3] uses semi-supervised learning to recommend products to customers. The algorithm is trained on a small set of labeled data, which includes customer purchases and ratings. The algorithm then uses this data to predict which products other customers are likely to purchase.

- **Spotify Music Recommendations**: Spotify uses semi-supervised learning to recommend music to users. The algorithm is trained on a small set of labeled data, which includes user listening history and ratings. The algorithm then uses this data to predict which songs other users are likely to enjoy.

Semi-supervised learning is a powerful machine learning paradigm that combines the strengths of both supervised and unsupervised learning techniques. With applications ranging from sentiment analysis and image classification to fraud detection and bioinformatics, semi-supervised learning is a valuable tool for businesses and researchers looking to grow their company with AI using a first principles point of view.

Reinforcement Learning

Reinforcement learning (RL) is a type of machine learning that focuses on training agents to make decisions by interacting with an environment. Unlike supervised and unsupervised learning, which relies on labeled or unlabeled data, reinforcement learning (RL) is based on trial and error, learning from the feedback received in the form of rewards or penalties. The primary goal of reinforcement learning is to maximize cumulative rewards over time, leading to the discovery of optimal strategies or policies for decision-making.

---

[2] https://ai.googleblog.com/2021/07/from-vision-to-language-semi-supervised.html
[3] www.amazon.science/publications/a-semi-supervised-multi-task-learning-approach-to-classify-customer-contact-intents

From a first principles perspective, reinforcement learning can be thought of as a problem-solving framework that enables agents to learn the best course of action under different circumstances. It is particularly well suited for problems where the optimal solution is not apparent or easily derived from available data, and where agents must continuously adapt their behavior to changing conditions.

Tip   Reinforcement learning is a powerful machine learning technique that can be used to train agents to learn how to behave in complex environments. However, reinforcement learning can be very inefficient to learn, requiring loads of data and compute time. Furthermore, RL algorithms are often more complex to implement and harder to debug than other types of machine learning algorithms. As such, unless your task specifically requires the kind of decision-making capabilities that RL provides, it might be more efficient to explore other machine learning techniques first

---

While RL can be a very powerful alternative in some situations, there are many in the data science community who rightly point out a few challenges with this modeling approach. For start, RL has a very inefficient way to learn, and the models require an enormous amount of computation and data. Another challenge to RL is that the rewards mechanisms are an ideation and not really seen in nature – for example, think about nature, there is not a real-time reward but rather long term in the shape of natural selection. Finally, for heavily regulated industries, RL algorithms outputs can be difficult to explain in human logic, and they can produce "surprising" outputs. For these reasons, the reader should be careful when to use this technique. In any case, it is a very powerful tool, and hence we spend some time going through it. For instance, ChatGPT and many other large language models use a class of RL, called RLHF Reinforcement Learning From Human Feedback[4]. Reinforcement Learning from Human Feedback (RLHF) uses feedback and rewards from human interaction. Instead of purely relying on pre-existing labeled data, RLHF utilizes a cycle of human feedback to inform the reinforcement signal in the learning process. The model begins with initial training using a dataset, often generated by human experts demonstrating the task. After the initial training, the model's performance is evaluated by humans who provide reward signals

---

[4]https://huggingface.co/blog/rlhf

or comparative feedback on different actions or decisions taken by the model. This feedback is then used to update the model's understanding of its task and improve future decisions. This cycle repeats, allowing the model to continually learn and improve from human feedback. RLHF is particularly useful in situations where it's hard to specify the correct behavior in every situation but easier for a human to evaluate the behavior after the fact.

The following are the core components of reinforcement learning:

i. **Agents, environments, states, actions, and rewards**: In reinforcement learning, an agent interacts with an environment, which is described by a set of states. At each time step, the agent takes an action, which leads to a change in the environment's state and generates a reward or penalty. The agent's goal is to learn a policy that maps states to actions, enabling it to maximize cumulative rewards over time.

ii. **Exploration and exploitation**: A key challenge in reinforcement learning is balancing exploration and exploitation. Exploration refers to the agent's attempts to discover new actions and state transitions, potentially leading to higher rewards. Exploitation, on the other hand, involves choosing actions that the agent already knows will yield high rewards. Striking the right balance between exploration and exploitation is critical for learning optimal policies.

iii. **Policy learning**: The primary objective of reinforcement learning is to learn an optimal policy, which is a function that maps states to actions. Policies can be represented in various ways, such as lookup tables or parameterized functions. The learning process typically involves updating the policy based on the observed rewards and state transitions, with the goal of maximizing cumulative rewards over time.

There are some common reinforcement learning algorithms and their applications:

i. **Q-learning**: Q-learning is a widely used, model-free reinforcement learning algorithm. In Q-learning, agents maintain a Q-table that represents the expected cumulative rewards for each state-action pair. The Q-table is updated iteratively based on observed rewards and state transitions, eventually converging to the optimal Q-values. Agents can then use these Q-values to choose the best action in each state. Q-learning has been applied in various domains, such as robotics, game playing, and resource allocation.

ii. **Deep Q-Networks (DQN)**: DQN is an extension of Q-learning that combines deep neural networks with reinforcement learning. Instead of maintaining a Q-table, DQN uses a neural network to approximate the Q-values for state-action pairs. This allows DQN to handle large-scale problems with high-dimensional state spaces, making it applicable to complex tasks like Atari games and robotic control.

iii. **Policy gradients**: Policy gradient methods are another class of reinforcement learning algorithms that directly optimize the policy function. These methods compute gradients of the expected cumulative rewards with respect to the policy parameters and update the policy accordingly. Policy gradient methods can be used with both discrete and continuous action spaces and have been applied to tasks like robotic manipulation, locomotion, and natural language processing.

iv. **Actor-Critic methods**: Actor-Critic methods are a hybrid of value-based and policy-based reinforcement learning algorithms. In this framework, an agent consists of two components: an actor, which represents the policy, and a critic, which estimates the value function. The actor and critic work together to optimize the policy, with the critic providing guidance to the actor based on its value estimates. Actor-Critic methods have been used in a wide range of applications, including autonomous vehicle control, recommendation systems, and financial trading.

Below are some real-world examples and case studies of reinforcement learning:

i.   **AlphaGo**: One of the most famous examples of reinforcement learning is AlphaGo[5], a computer program developed by DeepMind to play the ancient board game of Go. AlphaGo utilized a combination of deep neural networks and reinforcement learning to defeat the world champion Go player, Lee Sedol, in a historic match in 2016. This achievement marked a significant milestone in AI research, as Go was considered a challenging problem due to its vast state space and complex strategies.

ii. **Robotics**: Reinforcement learning has been extensively applied in the field of robotics for tasks like robotic manipulation, navigation, and locomotion. For example, OpenAI's robotic hand, Dactyl[6], used reinforcement learning to teach itself how to manipulate objects with human-like dexterity. Another example is Boston Dynamics' quadruped robot, Spot[7], which has been trained using reinforcement learning techniques to navigate various terrains and carry out tasks autonomously.

iii. **Autonomous vehicles**: Reinforcement learning is playing a crucial role in the development of autonomous vehicles. Companies like Waymo[8] and Tesla are leveraging reinforcement learning algorithms to train their self-driving cars to make optimal decisions in complex and dynamic environments, such as urban traffic scenarios.

iv. **Personalized recommendations**: Reinforcement learning has been employed in recommendation systems to personalize content for users. For instance, Netflix[9] uses reinforcement learning techniques to optimize its recommendation engine, which suggests movies and TV shows based on users' viewing

---

[5] www.deepmind.com/research/highlighted-research/alphago

[6] https://openai.com/research/learning-dexterity

[7] www.bostondynamics.com/products/spot

[8] https://waymo.com/

[9] https://research.netflix.com/research-area/machine-learning

history and preferences. Similarly, online advertising platforms use reinforcement learning to optimize ad placements and maximize user engagement.

v. **Finance**: In the finance domain, reinforcement learning has been used to optimize trading strategies, portfolio management, and risk assessment. For example, hedge funds and trading firms leverage reinforcement learning algorithms to develop trading models that can adapt to changing market conditions and maximize returns.

As we have seen, reinforcement learning is a powerful framework for decision-making and problem-solving, particularly in situations where the optimal solution is not immediately apparent or easily derived from available data. Reinforcement learning is a rapidly evolving field, and staying informed of the latest advancements and case studies will be essential for companies seeking to leverage AI and remain competitive in the future.

Choosing the Right Learning Technique

Selecting the appropriate learning technique is a critical step in developing effective AI-driven solutions for your organization. This section aims to guide business executives in choosing the right learning technique based on various factors, including data availability, problem complexity, and computational resources.

We saw in Chapter 8 the First Principles approach to approach a generic ML problem. Here, there are several factors to consider when selecting a learning technique for the algorithms discussed on this chapter:

i. **Availability of labeled data**: One of the most significant factors that influence the choice of learning technique is the availability of labeled data. In supervised learning, labeled data is essential for training and evaluating models. If your organization has access to a substantial amount of labeled data, supervised learning techniques can be highly effective in building predictive models. On the other hand, unsupervised learning techniques are more suitable when dealing with unlabeled data, as they focus on finding patterns and structures within the data without the need for explicit labels. In cases where you have limited labeled data and a large amount of unlabeled data, semi-supervised learning can be a practical choice, as it combines the strengths of both supervised and unsupervised learning.

ii. **Problem complexity and required model interpretability**: The complexity of the problem at hand and the desired level of model interpretability should also be considered when selecting a learning technique. Simpler models, such as linear regression and decision trees, can be easily interpreted and are suitable for relatively straightforward problems. However, these models may not capture complex patterns in data as effectively as more advanced techniques, like neural networks. As we saw, RL, while highly powerful and versatile, can be challenging to interpret, which might be a concern in industries where explainability is crucial, such as healthcare or finance. In contrast, RL is well-suited for problems involving decision-making in dynamic environments, like robotics or autonomous vehicles, where the optimal solution is not immediately apparent.

iii. **Computational resources and scalability**: The availability of computational resources and the need for scalability should also be considered when choosing a learning technique. Some algorithms, like deep learning models, require substantial computational power and can be resource-intensive during training. Depending on your organization's resources, it may be necessary to consider more computationally efficient algorithms or leverage cloud-based services to scale your AI solutions. Additionally, it's essential to consider the time it takes to train, validate, and deploy models, as well as the ease of updating them as new data becomes available.

To make well-informed decisions regarding the selection of learning techniques, it is crucial to balance first principles thinking with practical considerations. At the same time, it is essential to recognize the practical constraints that may impact the choice of learning techniques, such as data availability, computational resources, and the specific requirements of your organization. Here are a few suggestions to help strike the right balance:

i.   **Assess your organization's needs and goals**: Before selecting a learning technique, clearly define the objectives of your AI initiative and the specific problems you aim to address. This will provide a solid foundation for identifying the most suitable learning techniques and aligning them with your organization's goals.

ii. **Evaluate your data**: Thoroughly assess the quality, quantity, and type of data available for your AI project. Understanding the characteristics of your data will enable you to choose the most appropriate learning techniques and ensure the success of your AI initiatives.

iii. **Experiment with different techniques**: Don't be afraid to try out different learning techniques to find the best fit for your problem. Experimenting with various algorithms will help you gain valuable insights into their performance and suitability for your specific use case. Keep in mind that there might not be a one-size-fits-all solution, and sometimes combining multiple techniques or using ensemble methods can lead to better results.

iv. **Consult with experts**: Collaborate with data scientists, machine learning engineers, and other experts in the field to gain insights into the most suitable learning techniques for your organization. Their expertise and experience can provide valuable guidance and help you avoid common pitfalls in the AI implementation process.

v.   **Leverage existing resources and platforms**: Many open-source tools, libraries, and platforms are available to help you implement various learning techniques. By leveraging these resources, you can save time and effort, and benefit from the expertise of the broader AI community.

vi. **Continuously monitor and evaluate performance**: After selecting and implementing a learning technique, it is crucial to continuously monitor and evaluate its performance. This will enable you to identify areas for improvement, fine-tune your models, and ensure that your AI initiatives continue to deliver value to your organization.

vii.   **Keep up with the latest developments**: The field of AI and machine learning is constantly evolving, with new algorithms and techniques being developed regularly. Staying informed about the latest research and advancements can help you make better decisions and stay ahead of the competition.

In summary, choosing the right learning technique is a critical aspect of implementing successful AI-driven solutions for your organization.

PROMPT EXERCISES

We will use Bard/ChatGPT to create code that can be exported and run to Google's Colab. All the scripts produced first time running code with ChatGPT at the time of writing. However, please note that due to continuous API updates, you will very likely get different answers or even might need to do a bit of debugging.

Exercise 1: Supervised Learning – XGBoost

Prompt for Bard/ChatGPT:

```
<Begin Prompt>
Please write Python code to load the Titanic dataset from https://raw.github.
com/datasciencedojo/datasets/master/titanic.csv , preprocess the data (handle
missing values, convert categorical variables into numerical ones), split it
into training and testing sets, and then train a XGBoost model using sklearn.
After training the model, make predictions on the test set, and calculate the
accuracy, precision, recall, and F1-score of the predictions. Display a few
graphs to show performance.
</End Prompt>
```

Exercise 2: UnSupervised Learning – K-means Clustering

```
<Begin Prompt>
Please write Python code to load the Titanic dataset from https://raw.github.
com/datasciencedojo/datasets/master/titanic.csv , preprocess the data (handle
missing values, convert categorical variables into numerical ones), split it
into training and testing sets, and then train a K-means model. demonstrate
how to apply K-means clustering. Use the 'Age' and 'Fare' columns for
clustering. Visualize the resulting clusters and explain the output.
</End Prompt>
```

Exercise 3: Semi-supervised Learning

```
<Begin Prompt>
Please write Python code to load the Titanic dataset from https://raw.github.
com/datasciencedojo/datasets/titanic.csv , preprocess the data (handle
missing values, convert categorical variables into numerical ones), split it
into training and testing sets, and then use a semi-supervised model. Produce
the confusion matrix and overall model results.
</End Prompt>
```

These exercises should give readers a hands-on understanding of some of the most common supervised and unsupervised learning algorithms. They also serve as a good starting point for further exploration and experimentation. Please note that the results are a very basic pipeline. In a real-world scenario, you would want to do a more detailed exploratory data analysis, feature engineering, hyperparameter tuning, handle class imbalance, etc. And most importantly, you would interpret the results and see if they make sense, iterating on your model as necessary.

Conclusion and Chapter Summary/Key Takeaways

In this chapter, we have provided a detailed understanding of the differences between supervised and unsupervised learning, along with their applications from a First Principles perspective. We have also briefly introduced semi-supervised learning and reinforcement learning, highlighting their core components and applications.

When implementing AI solutions, it is essential to follow best practices to maximize the benefits and avoid common pitfalls. Here, we present three key takeaway points and some do's and don'ts for each.

1. **Takeaway 1: The importance of quality data and relevant model selection:**

   a. **Availability of labeled data:**

      i. Do: Invest in creating high-quality labeled datasets for supervised learning tasks.

      ii. Don't: Rely solely on automated labeling methods without manual verification, as this may introduce errors and affect model performance.

b. **Problem complexity and required model interpretability:**

    i. Do: Consider simpler models if interpretability is a priority, and ensure stakeholders can understand the model's decision-making process.

    ii. Don't: Use overly complex models without justifying their necessity, as they may be difficult to interpret and maintain.

c. **Computational resources and scalability:**

    i. Do: Assess the computational resources required for your chosen learning technique and plan accordingly.

    ii. Don't: Ignore scalability concerns when selecting a learning technique, as this may lead to increased costs and inefficiencies in the long run.

2. **Takeaway 2: Apply First Principles thinking and encourage stakeholder collaboration:**

a. **First Principles thinking:**

    i. Do: Approach AI problems from a First Principles perspective, focusing on the underlying principles and core components of each learning technique.

    ii. Don't: Blindly apply popular algorithms without understanding their underlying assumptions and limitations.

b. **Collaboration with experts:**

    i. Do: Consult with data scientists, machine learning engineers, and other experts to gain insights into the most suitable learning techniques for your organization's needs.

    ii. Don't: Make AI-related decisions without involving the relevant stakeholders and experts, as this may lead to suboptimal solutions and missed opportunities.

3. **Takeaway 3: Regular evaluation, ethical considerations, and a culture of innovation:**

   a. **Regular evaluation and optimization:**

      i. Do: Continuously evaluate and optimize your models to ensure they remain accurate and relevant as new data becomes available.

      ii. Don't: Neglect model maintenance and assume that a one-time training process is sufficient for long-term success.

   b. **Ethical considerations:**

      i. Do: Consider the ethical implications of your AI solutions, such as potential biases, privacy concerns, and fairness.

      ii. Don't: Implement AI solutions without considering the potential negative impacts on stakeholders, including customers, employees, and society at large.

   c. **Experimentation and innovation:**

      i. Do: Encourage a culture of experimentation and innovation, allowing your organization to explore new AI and machine learning techniques.

      ii. Don't: Stick to a single learning technique or become overly reliant on past successes, as this may stifle growth and limit your organization's ability to adapt to new challenges.

As we have seen throughout the chapter, understanding supervised and unsupervised learning, along with their core components, is essential for business executives looking to drive growth and innovation through AI adoption. As you continue to explore and apply these learning techniques to solve real-world problems, we encourage you to seek out additional resources – as included at the end of the book – and maintain an open dialogue with experts in the field.

CHAPTER 10

Neural Networks, Deep Learning, Foundational Models

One of the key driving forces behind AI advancements is the development of neural networks, deep learning, and foundational models. These techniques have the potential to revolutionize many industries and solve some of the world's most pressing problems.

Neural networks are computational models inspired by the structure and function of the human brain. They consist of interconnected nodes, or neurons, that are organized into layers. Neurons can be activated or inhibited by other neurons, and they can learn to perform complex tasks by adjusting the strength of their connections. These layers include input, hidden, and output layers, with each neuron performing specific computations to process and transmit information. Neural networks have been widely adopted in various industries, providing solutions to complex problems in fields like computer vision, natural language processing, and speech recognition.

Deep learning is an extension of neural networks that involves training deep neural networks with multiple hidden layers. This added depth allows for the extraction and identification of more complex features and patterns in data, leading to improved performance and more accurate predictions. Deep learning has been at the forefront of recent AI breakthroughs, enabling the development of advanced systems capable of understanding and interpreting human language, recognizing objects in images, and even playing complex games at a superhuman level.

Foundational models, sometimes referred to as pre-trained models, are large-scale neural networks that have been pre-trained on massive amounts of data. These models are designed to capture general patterns and structures in data, allowing them to be fine-tuned for specific tasks with relatively small amounts of labeled data. Popular

F. J. Campos Zabala, *Grow Your Business with AI*, https://doi.org/10.1007/978-1-4842-9669-1_10

foundational models include BERT, GPT, and T5, which have revolutionized natural language understanding and generation tasks, making them invaluable tools for businesses looking to leverage AI in their operations.

Understanding neural networks, deep learning, and foundational models from a First Principles perspective is crucial for businesses that wish to harness the power of AI. By breaking down these complex techniques into their core components, business executives can better appreciate the underlying mechanisms that drive AI advancements and make more informed decisions when implementing AI solutions.

The impact of neural networks and deep learning on AI advancements cannot be overstated. These techniques have enabled machines to learn from data in ways that were once thought to be the exclusive domain of human intelligence. As a result, businesses that effectively leverage these techniques can gain a competitive edge, automating processes, improving decision-making, and unlocking new opportunities for growth.

In this chapter, we will delve deeper into the intricacies of neural networks, deep learning, and foundational models, exploring their core components and providing real-world examples of their applications. Additionally, we will discuss generative AI, a powerful technique that utilizes deep learning to generate data such as images, text, and audio. By gaining a strong foundation in these advanced AI techniques, business executives can drive innovation, improve efficiency, and unlock the full potential of AI for their organizations.

Neural networks, deep learning, and foundational models are still in their early stages of development, but they have the potential to change the world. These techniques are already being used in a variety of applications, including

- **Natural language processing (NLP)**: Neural networks are being used to improve the accuracy of NLP tasks, such as machine translation, text summarization, and question answering.

- **Computer vision (CV)**: Neural networks are being used to improve the accuracy of CV tasks, such as image classification, object detection, and facial recognition.

- **Speech recognition (SR)**: Neural networks are being used to improve the accuracy of SR tasks, such as transcribing audio and video recordings.

- **Medicine**: Neural networks are being used to develop new drugs, diagnose diseases, and personalize treatments.

- **Finance**: Neural networks are being used to predict market trends, manage risk, and make investment decisions.

- **Manufacturing**: Neural networks are being used to improve the efficiency of manufacturing processes, optimize product design, and automate quality control.

The potential applications of neural networks, deep learning, and foundational models are endless. As these techniques continue to develop, they will have a profound impact on the way we live and work.

Neural Networks

Neural networks form the backbone of modern artificial intelligence, inspired by the structure and function of the human brain. In this section, we will define neural networks from a First Principles perspective and discuss their core components. We will also explore popular neural network architectures and their applications, providing real-world examples and case studies to illustrate their potential for growing your company.

Neural networks were first developed in the 1950s, but they did not become widely used until the 1990s, when advances in computing power made it possible to train large neural networks. In recent years, neural networks have been used to achieve state-of-the-art results on a wide variety of tasks, including image classification, object detection, speech recognition, and natural language processing.

A neural network is a computational model designed to process information and make decisions by mimicking the human brain's interconnected structure. They are made up of many simple units, called neurons, that are connected to each other. Neurons can be activated or inhibited by other neurons, and they can learn to perform complex tasks by adjusting the strength of their connections. It is important to highlight that human neurons, as depicted in Figure 10-1, are quite complicated and that the exact mechanism for the whole brain is still unknown. In particular, human neurons do not perform backpropagation as many artificial neural networks do.

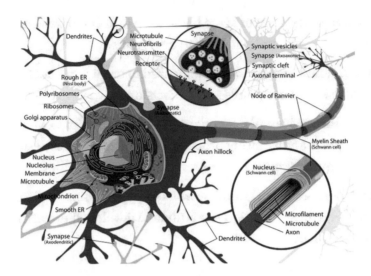

Figure 10-1. *A neuron from a human brain*

It consists of interconnected nodes, or artificial neurons, organized into layers. These layers include input, hidden, and output layers, each responsible for specific computations that transmit information through the network. By adjusting the connections between these neurons, a neural network can "learn" to recognize patterns and make predictions.

As mentioned before, we still do not fully know how the brain organizes all the neuron activity at higher levels. For the curious reader, I recommend an interesting book[1] – *A Thousand Brains* – which present a proposed full working model for the brain, even when many of the hypotheses are still being researched.

Core components of neural networks from First Principles approach:

1. **Neurons and activation functions**: Neurons are the fundamental units of a neural network. Each neuron receives input from other neurons or external data, processes it, and produces an output. Activation functions determine the output of a neuron based on its input, introducing non-linearity into the network and enabling it to learn complex patterns.

---

[1] www.numenta.com/resources/books/a-thousand-brains-by-jeff-hawkins/

2. **Layers**: Neural networks are organized into layers – input, hidden, and output layers. The input layer receives the raw data, while the output layer produces the final predictions. Hidden layers, which lie between the input and output layers, perform intermediate computations.

3. **Weights and biases**: Connections between neurons in adjacent layers have associated weights and biases. Weights determine the strength of the connection, while biases are additional constants that help adjust the neuron's output. These parameters are adjusted during the training process to minimize the network's error.

4. **Forward and backward propagation**: During forward propagation, data flows through the network, and the neurons compute their outputs. Once the output is obtained, the network's error is calculated. Backward propagation, or backpropagation, is the process of updating the weights and biases by minimizing the error using gradient descent or other optimization algorithms.

5. **Loss functions and optimization algorithms**: Loss functions quantify the error between the network's predictions and the true labels. Optimization algorithms, such as gradient descent or more advanced techniques like Adam, adjust the weights and biases to minimize the loss function.

6. **Learning rate, batch sizes, and epochs**: The learning rate determines the step size during optimization, affecting the speed and stability of the training process. Batch sizes refer to the number of data points used in each update step, balancing computational efficiency and convergence speed. An epoch is a complete iteration through the entire dataset during training.

Popular neural network architectures and their applications:

1. **Feedforward neural networks (FNN)**: FNNs are the simplest type of neural network (Figure 10-2), where information flows in a single direction from the input layer to the output layer without looping back. They are widely used for tasks such as regression, classification, and function approximation.

2. **Convolutional neural networks (CNN)**: CNNs are designed for processing grid-like data, such as images or speech signals. They use convolutional layers to scan the input for local patterns, enabling them to learn translation-invariant features. CNNs have revolutionized computer vision tasks, such as image classification, object detection, and semantic segmentation.

3. **Recurrent neural networks (RNN)**: RNNs are designed to handle sequences of data, such as time series or text. They possess connections that loop back on themselves, allowing them to maintain a "memory" of previous inputs. RNNs are used in tasks like language modeling, speech recognition, and time series prediction.

4. **Long short-term memory (LSTM) networks**: LSTMs are a variant of RNNs designed to overcome the vanishing gradient problem, which hampers learning long-range dependencies in sequences. LSTMs use special gating mechanisms to control the flow of information, enabling them to learn longer sequences. They have been employed in machine translation, sentiment analysis, and video frame prediction.

Real-world examples and case studies of neural networks:

1. **Image classification**: CNNs have been applied to various image classification tasks, such as distinguishing between different breeds of dogs or identifying cancer cells in medical images. For example, Google's Inception[2] model achieved top performance on the ImageNet Large Scale Visual Recognition Challenge, showcasing the power of neural networks in image classification.

---

[2] https://cloud.google.com/tpu/docs/inception-v3-advanced

2. **Natural language processing**: Neural networks, specifically RNNs and LSTMs, have made significant strides in natural language processing tasks. For instance, OpenAI's GPT-3, a transformer-based neural network, has demonstrated impressive language understanding and generation capabilities, enabling applications like sentiment analysis, machine translation, and text summarization.

3. **Autonomous vehicles**: Neural networks are essential components in the development of autonomous vehicles, as they process and interpret data from sensors to make decisions in real-time. Tesla's Autopilot system, for example, employs CNNs to process visual data from cameras and make driving decisions based on learned patterns.

4. **Financial forecasting**: Neural networks, including RNNs and LSTMs, have been used to predict stock prices and market trends based on historical data. By analyzing patterns in financial data, these networks can provide valuable insights for investment decisions and risk management.

5. **Customer churn prediction**: Companies can use neural networks to analyze customer behavior and identify patterns that suggest a customer may leave for a competitor. By predicting customer churn, businesses can take proactive measures to retain valuable customers and improve overall customer satisfaction.

Neural networks are a rapidly evolving field, and new applications are being discovered all the time. As neural networks continue to develop, they are likely to have a profound impact on many different industries.

Deep Learning

Deep learning is a subfield of machine learning that focuses on the development of deep neural networks, which are artificial neural networks containing multiple hidden layers. These networks are designed to learn hierarchical representations of data, enabling the discovery of complex patterns and structures. Deep learning has played a significant role in advancing the state of the art in various fields such as image and speech recognition, natural language processing, and game playing.

Deep learning differs from traditional neural networks by having a deeper architecture, meaning *it contains more layers of neurons*. This depth allows deep learning models to learn increasingly abstract features from the input data, providing a more nuanced understanding of the data's underlying structure. In essence, deep learning models can learn more complex functions and representations, making them highly effective at solving a wide range of challenging tasks.

In recent years, deep learning has become increasingly popular, due to the availability of large datasets and the development of powerful computing hardware.

Core components of deep learning:

1. **Deep neural networks with multiple hidden layers**: The primary component of deep learning is deep neural networks, which consist of multiple hidden layers between the input and output layers. Each hidden layer learns to extract progressively higher-level features from the input data, allowing the model to recognize complex patterns and relationships.

2. **Advanced optimization techniques**: Deep learning models typically rely on advanced optimization algorithms, such as Adam or RMSprop, to update the model's weights and biases during training. These algorithms help overcome the challenges associated with training deep networks, such as vanishing gradients and slow convergence.

3. **Techniques for handling overfitting and regularization**: Deep learning models are prone to overfitting due to their large number of parameters. To counteract overfitting, several regularization techniques are employed, such as dropout, weight decay, and early stopping. These techniques help improve the model's generalization capabilities and prevent it from memorizing the training data.

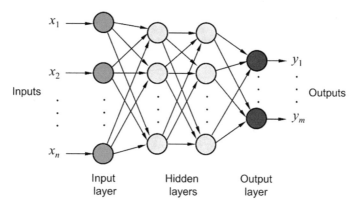

Figure 10-2. *Typical structure of a feed forward multilayer neural network*

Popular deep learning architectures and their applications:

1. **Deep CNNs**: Deep convolutional neural networks (CNNs) are designed for processing grid-like data, such as images and videos. These networks use convolutional layers to scan the input data for local patterns, enabling the model to learn spatial hierarchies of features. Deep CNNs have been used for various computer vision tasks, including image classification, object detection, and segmentation.

2. **Deep RNNs**: Deep recurrent neural networks (RNNs) are designed for processing sequential data, such as time series and natural language. RNNs maintain an internal state that can capture information from previous time steps, allowing them to model temporal dependencies. Deep RNNs, including LSTMs and GRUs, have been used in applications like speech recognition, sentiment analysis, and machine translation.

3. **Transformer models**: Transformer models are a type of deep learning architecture designed for processing sequence data, with a focus on parallelization and long-range dependencies. Transformers use self-attention mechanisms to weigh the importance of different input elements, allowing them to effectively model complex relationships in the data. Transformer models have been employed in various natural language processing tasks, such as language modeling, question-answering, and text summarization.

Real-world examples and case studies of deep learning:

1. **Image recognition**: Deep CNNs have revolutionized image recognition, achieving human-level performance on tasks like object recognition and face detection. For example, Meta's DeepFace[3] system uses a deep CNN to recognize faces in photos with an accuracy rate of over 97%, surpassing the capabilities of many traditional computer vision methods.

2. **Speech recognition**: Deep learning models, particularly RNNs and LSTMs, have made significant advancements in speech recognition. Open source's DeepSpeech[4], a deep RNN-based speech recognition system, has demonstrated remarkable performance in converting spoken language into written text, enabling applications like voice assistants and transcription services.

3. **Machine translation**: Deep learning models, including RNNs, LSTMs, and transformer-based models, have significantly improved machine translation capabilities. For instance, Google Translate has evolved from using statistical machine translation methods to employing deep learning techniques, resulting in more accurate translations that capture the nuances of the source language.

4. **Game playing**: Deep learning has been utilized in developing AI systems that can play complex games at a superhuman level. AlphaGo[5], a deep learning-based system developed by DeepMind, famously defeated the world champion Go player in 2016, showcasing the ability of deep learning models to learn complex strategies and make decisions in high-dimensional spaces.

5. **Autonomous vehicles**: Deep learning models, particularly deep CNNs, play a crucial role in enabling autonomous vehicles to

---

[3] https://research.facebook.com/publications/deepface-closing-the-gap-to-human-level-performance-in-face-verification/

[4] https://github.com/mozilla/DeepSpeech

[5] www.deepmind.com/research/highlighted-research/alphago

perceive and understand their environment. Companies like Tesla and Waymo utilize deep learning techniques to process sensor data, identify objects, and make driving decisions, paving the way for self-driving cars to become a reality.

Deep learning is a powerful technique, but it also has some challenges. Some of the challenges of deep learning include

- **Data requirements**: Deep learning algorithms require large amounts of data to train. This data can be expensive and time-consuming to collect.

- **Computational requirements**: Deep learning algorithms can be computationally expensive to train.

- **Interpretability**: Deep learning algorithms are often difficult to interpret. It can be difficult to understand how the algorithm makes its decisions.

Deep learning is a powerful subfield of machine learning that focuses on the development of deep neural networks with multiple hidden layers. These networks have demonstrated remarkable success in solving complex problems across various domains, including image and speech recognition, natural language processing, and game playing.

Generative AI

Most of the models we discussed in Chapter 9 and in this one so far belong to the class of "Discriminate" models. The discriminate models learn the relationship between the features of the data points and the labels. They are typically trained on a dataset of labeled data and are used to classify or predict typically. There is another model class called "Generative" models. These ones understand the distribution of data and how likely a given example is. They generate new data that is similar to the data it was trained on, and it can be used to predict the next word in a sequence.

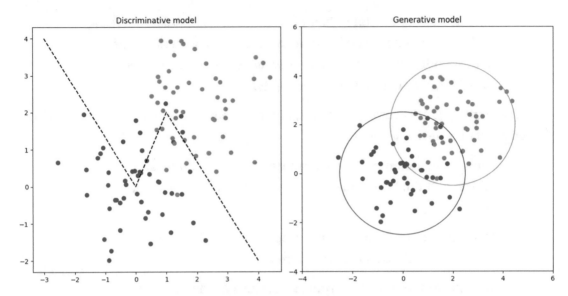

Figure 10-3. *Discriminative vs. generative models*

Figure 10-3 has a visual representation of how the two classes of models work. On the left-hand side, a discriminative model will learn how to separate the green and blue dots. It could be used to predict what color a new point will be. Generative models are useful for creating new data that resembles the original training set, while discriminative models excel in tasks like image or speech classification. Rather than merely partitioning the data into distinct categories, discriminative models learn where these separations occur. On the other hand, generative models comprehend how the data is placed within the overall space.

These methodologies greatly differ from each other, making them uniquely appropriate for specific tasks. In tasks involving classification, discriminative models often outperform generative models in terms of accuracy. However, for complex learning tasks that necessitate the expression of intricate dependencies, the versatility of generative models comes into play.

Generative AI is still under development, but it has the potential to revolutionize the way we interact with computers. Generative AI could be used to create new forms of entertainment, to generate new products and services, and to improve the accuracy of artificial intelligence systems.

Generative AI works by learning from existing data. The AI system is trained on a dataset of images, text, or audio. Once the AI system has been trained, it can be used to generate new data that is like the data it was trained on.

Core components of generative AI from First Principles perspective:

1. **Generative models**: The foundation of generative AI lies in the development of generative models. These models learn the probability distribution of the input data and use this information to generate new data points that resemble the training data. Unlike discriminative models, which focus on identifying the boundaries between different classes of data, generative models aim to create new data points that follow the same underlying patterns as the original data.

2. **Techniques for generating data**: Several techniques have been developed for generating data using generative AI algorithms. These techniques can be broadly categorized into three main types: generative adversarial networks (GANs), variational autoencoders (VAEs), and transformer-based generative models.

There are many different generative AI algorithms, but some of the most popular algorithms include

1. **Generative adversarial networks (GANs)**: GANs are a class of generative models that consist of two neural networks: a generator and a discriminator. The generator creates new data points, while the discriminator evaluates the authenticity of the generated data. The two networks are trained together in a process known as adversarial training, where the generator tries to create data that is indistinguishable from the real data, and the discriminator tries to correctly identify whether the input data is real or generated. GANs have been successfully applied in various domains, such as

    a. **Image synthesis**: GANs can generate realistic images, enabling applications like creating artwork or virtual environments. For example, NVIDIA's StyleGAN can generate high-resolution, photorealistic images of human faces, objects, and scenes.

b. **Data augmentation**: GANs can be used to generate additional training data, helping to improve the performance of machine learning models when the available dataset is limited.

c. **Image-to-image translation**: GANs can convert images from one domain to another, such as transforming satellite images into maps, or converting black and white photos into color.

2. **Variational autoencoders (VAEs)**: VAEs are another class of generative models that learn to encode input data into a lower-dimensional latent space and then decode it back into the original form. The VAE model is trained by optimizing the reconstruction loss (i.e., the difference between the input data and the reconstructed data) and a regularization term that encourages the latent space to have a specific distribution, typically a Gaussian distribution. Applications of VAEs include

a. **Image generation**: VAEs can generate new images by sampling points from the latent space and decoding them back into the image space.

b. **Anomaly detection**: VAEs can be used to identify unusual data points in a dataset by measuring the reconstruction error for each data point. Higher reconstruction errors indicate that the data point is an outlier.

c. **Dimensionality reduction**: VAEs can be employed for unsupervised dimensionality reduction, allowing for the visualization and analysis of high-dimensional data.

3. **Transformer-based generative models** (e.g., GPT-4): Some transformer models, such as the Generative Pre-trained Transformer (GPT) series, have been developed to generate coherent and contextually relevant text. These models can be fine-tuned for various natural language processing tasks, such as text summarization, translation, or question-answering. The most recent iteration, GPT-4, is one of the largest and most powerful language models currently available, demonstrating impressive capabilities in generating human-like text. Applications of transformer-based generative models include

a. **Content generation**: These models can be used to create articles, blog posts, or social media content, assisting in content marketing and SEO efforts.

b. **Text summarization**: Transformer-based generative models can automatically generate summaries of long documents, saving time and effort for employees who review large amounts of information.

c. **Natural language interfaces**: GPT-like models can be used to build conversational agents or chatbots, enabling businesses to provide better customer service or automate routine tasks.

Real-world examples and case studies of generative AI:

1. **Art and design**: Generative AI has been employed to create unique and visually appealing artwork. For instance, the AI-generated painting *Portrait of Edmond Belamy*[6] sold for **$432,500** at an auction in 2018, showcasing the potential of AI-generated art in the creative industry. Furthermore, generative AI can be used in graphic design and advertising, enabling companies to develop visually striking marketing materials with minimal human effort.

2. **Music generation**: Generative AI algorithms, such as OpenAI's MuseNet[7], can create original music compositions in various styles and genres. This technology can be applied in the entertainment industry, as well as in generating background music for videos and games.

3. **Drug discovery**: Generative AI models have been used to accelerate the process of drug discovery by generating novel molecular structures with desired properties. For example, Insilico Medicine, a biotechnology company, used GANs[8] to generate a set of promising drug candidates for a specific target protein in just 46 days, significantly faster than traditional drug discovery methods.

---

[6] www.christies.com/features/A-collaboration-between-two-artists-one-human-one-a-machine-9332-1.aspx

[7] https://openai.com/research/musenet

[8] www.globenewswire.com/en/news-release/2023/04/24/2653269/31533/en/Insilico-Medicine-Successfully-Discovered-Potent-Selective-and-Orally-Bioavailable-Small-Molecule-Inhibitor-of-CDK8-Using-Generative-AI.html

4. **Customer service**: Businesses can use transformer-based generative models to develop AI-powered chatbots that can understand and respond to customer queries more effectively. These chatbots can handle a wide range of customer service tasks, reducing response times and freeing up human agents to focus on more complex issues.

5. **Video game development**: Generative AI can be applied in game development to create realistic and dynamic game environments, characters, and objects. For instance, Promethean AI[9], a platform for game developers, leverages GANs to generate 3D models and textures, simplifying the content creation process and reducing the time and resources needed for game development.

Generative AI is a powerful technique, but it also has some challenges. Some of the challenges of generative AI include

1. **Data requirements**: Generative AI systems require large amounts of data to train. This data can be expensive and time-consuming to collect.

2. **Interpretability**: Generative AI systems are often difficult to interpret. It can be difficult to understand how the system generates its output.

3. **Bias**: Generative AI systems can be biased. This means that the system may generate output that is biased toward certain groups of people or toward certain viewpoints.

Generative AI is a rapidly evolving field, and new applications are being discovered all the time. As generative AI continues to develop, it is likely to have a profound impact on many different industries.

Generative AI offers a wide range of applications and opportunities for businesses to innovate, improve efficiency, and drive growth. As the field of generative AI continues to evolve, further advancements in algorithms and applications are expected, providing even more possibilities for businesses to capitalize on this cutting-edge technology.

---

[9] www.prometheanai.com/

Foundational Models

In this subsection, we will discuss foundational models, their core components, popular foundational models, and their applications. We will also explore real-world examples and case studies to demonstrate the impact of these models on businesses and AI applications.

Foundational models are a class of machine learning models that have been pre-trained on massive amounts of data to learn the underlying structure and patterns within the data. These models can be fine-tuned for specific tasks using a relatively small amount of labeled data, enabling them to generalize well and achieve state-of-the-art performance across various domains. The primary advantage of foundational models is their ability to leverage pre-existing knowledge, which reduces the need for extensive training data and computational resources.

Core components of foundational models:

1. **Pre-trained language models**: Foundational models are often pre-trained on large corpora of text, such as web pages, books, and articles, allowing them to learn the underlying structure of language, including grammar, syntax, and semantics. This pre-training phase enables the models to capture a rich understanding of the language and generate meaningful representations of text.

2. **Transfer learning and finetuning**: Transfer learning is the process of leveraging the pre-trained knowledge of a foundational model and adapting it to a specific task using a smaller labeled dataset. Finetuning involves updating the model's weights and biases using the task-specific dataset to tailor the model's performance to the desired task. This process significantly reduces the amount of data and computational resources required to achieve high performance in various applications.

The following are popular foundational models and their applications:

1. **BERT (Bidirectional Encoder Representations from Transformers)**: BERT[10] is a transformer-based model developed by Google that has been pre-trained on a vast amount of text data. It is designed for bidirectional context understanding, enabling it to capture complex relationships between words and their meanings. BERT has been applied to various natural language processing (NLP) tasks, such as sentiment analysis, named entity recognition, and question-answering systems, achieving state-of-the-art performance in these domains.

2. **GPT (Generative Pre-trained Transformer)**: GPT, developed by OpenAI, is another transformer-based model that has been pre-trained on a large corpus of text data. GPT is primarily designed for language generation tasks, allowing it to create coherent and contextually relevant text. GPT has been applied to numerous NLP tasks, including text summarization, translation, and content generation. The latest iteration, GPT-4, has demonstrated human-like text generation capabilities, making it a powerful tool for various applications.

3. **T5 (Text-to-Text Transfer Transformer)**: T5, developed by Google Research, is a transformer-based model that frames all NLP tasks as a text-to-text problem. This unified approach allows T5 to perform tasks such as translation, summarization, question-answering, and text classification by converting input text to target text. T5 has achieved state-of-the-art performance on numerous benchmarks, showcasing its versatility and power in handling diverse NLP tasks.

4. **LaMDA**: LaMDA is a foundational model developed by Google AI. LaMDA is able to generate text, translate languages, and answer questions.

---

[10] https://cloud.google.com/ai-platform/training/docs/algorithms/bert-start

5. **Meena**: Meena is a foundational model developed by Google[11]
   AI. Meena can generate text, translate languages, and answer
   questions.

Real-world examples and case studies of foundational models:

1. **Sentiment analysis**: Businesses can leverage foundational
   models like BERT and GPT to analyze customer feedback, product
   reviews, and social media posts to identify sentiment trends,
   enabling them to make data-driven decisions about product
   improvements, customer service, and marketing strategies. For
   example, an e-commerce company can use BERT to automatically
   classify product reviews as positive, negative, or neutral, helping
   them identify areas for improvement and better understand
   customer needs.

2. **Customer support chatbots**: Foundational models can be used
   to create intelligent chatbots that understand natural language
   queries and provide accurate, contextually relevant responses.
   For instance, a telecom provider can use GPT-4 to build a chatbot
   that can handle customer queries about billing, troubleshooting,
   and service-related issues, providing instant support and reducing
   human intervention.

3. **Content generation**: Businesses can leverage foundational
   models like GPT-4 to generate high-quality content for their
   websites, blogs, and marketing materials. For example, a
   marketing agency can use GPT-4 to create engaging blog posts,
   social media content, and email campaigns, saving time and
   resources while maintaining a consistent brand voice.

4. **Text summarization**: Foundational models like T5 can be
   employed to automatically generate summaries of lengthy
   documents, such as research papers, news articles, and legal
   contracts. This can help businesses save time and resources by

---

[11] https://ai.googleblog.com/2020/01/towards-conversational-agent-that-can.html

enabling them to quickly understand the key points of complex documents. For instance, a law firm can use T5 to summarize lengthy contracts, helping them identify critical clauses and potential risks more efficiently.

5. **Machine translation**: Businesses operating in multiple languages can benefit from the translation capabilities of foundational models like BERT and T5. These models can be fine-tuned to perform translations between various languages with high accuracy, enabling businesses to communicate effectively with international customers and partners. For example, a global e-commerce company can use T5 to translate product descriptions and customer reviews into multiple languages, expanding their reach and enhancing customer experience.

6. **Personalized recommendations**: Foundational models can be applied to develop personalized recommendation systems that can analyze user preferences, browsing history, and purchase patterns to provide tailored product or content suggestions. For example, a streaming platform can use BERT to analyze user preferences and viewing history, recommending movies and TV shows that align with individual tastes, leading to higher user engagement and satisfaction.

Deep Dive into Large Language Models

Given the importance of large language models, I will spend some time to, firstly, give an intuition of how they work – will focus on ChatGPT – and second, provide some advice how to put them into practice in your business. I will include some prompting exercises at the end of the chapter and additional code in my GitHub site.

Embeddings

Most of the Internet's content is text-based, a format not easily processed by neural networks. Converting words to numbers for machine learning is a complex task. For instance, we have a simple vocabulary of four terms: Cat, Dog, Kitten, and Puppy.

A basic approach might assign each term a consecutive number:

- Cat → 1

- Dog → 2

- Kitten → 3

- Puppy → 4

This system can lead to misleading interpretations. A network might infer that a Puppy is four times as valuable as a Cat, which is incorrect. To avoid such misconceptions, we adopt a different strategy called "one-hot encoding," where we assign binary vectors to each term:

- Cat → [1, 0, 0, 0]

- Dog → [0, 1, 0, 0]

- Kitten → [0, 0, 1, 0]

- Puppy → [0, 0, 0, 1]

Though this method eliminates false numerical inferences, it's not scalable due to the vast number of unique words in use, resulting in long vectors with many zeroes.

This is where "word embeddings" come into play. The idea is to map words with similar meanings closer to each other in a multidimensional space. For instance, Cat and Dog may occupy nearby locations, as would Kitten and Puppy. In a two-dimensional space, this could look like

- Cat → [3, 1]

- Dog → [3, 2]

- Kitten → [1, 1]

- Puppy → [1, 2]

Here, the first coordinate might represent "age" (adult vs. young), and the second could denote "species" (cat vs. dog). While this example uses only two dimensions, more dimensions could encode additional semantic relationships.

Thus, word embeddings not only manage the scalability issue but also capture important semantic relationships between words, making them a powerful tool in machine learning.

How ChatGPT Works

Large language models, such as OpenAI's ChatGPT or Google's Bard, demonstrate impressive capabilities, generating human-like text that makes them seem as if they truly understand the language. But how do these models work under the hood? To shed light on this, we will take a deep dive into the mechanics of large language models, drawing insights from Stephen Wolfram's thoughtful analysis.[12]

At the heart of large language models, including ChatGPT, is a concept called **_Transformer Neural Networks_**. These networks are built on the foundation of deep learning and are incredibly effective at handling sequential data, making them perfect for natural language processing tasks.

The key idea behind transformer models is "attention" – more specifically, "self-attention." This mechanism allows the model to consider different words in a sentence, determine their relevance, and use this information to better understand the context.

As an analogy proposed by Wolfram, imagine a vast, multidimensional terrain where every point represents a certain arrangement of words, and distances between points indicate how similar these arrangements are. Transformer networks navigate this terrain, jumping from point to point, and this movement signifies the transition from one word or phrase to another.

When processing a sentence, the self-attention mechanism allows the model to focus on the words that provide crucial context for understanding the current word. For instance, when determining the meaning of "she" in a sentence, the model uses attention to focus on the parts of the sentence that indicate who "she" is.

Now, let's talk about training these models. ChatGPT is trained using unsupervised learning. It's exposed to a large dataset – in the case of GPT-3, almost half a trillion words. The model learns by predicting the next word in a sentence, adjusting its internal parameters to minimize the difference between its predictions and the actual words.

Here, the "large" in large language models comes into play. The GPT-3 model has 175 billion parameters. These parameters, akin to synaptic connections in a biological brain, are adjusted during the training to capture patterns in the data. This vast number of parameters allows the model to learn a mind-boggling variety of patterns, styles, and structures present in human language.

---

[12] Stephen Wolfram (2023), "What Is ChatGPT Doing ... and Why Does It Work?"

It's essential to remember that ***the model is a statistical one***. It learns the likelihoods of words and phrases following each other, without any innate understanding of the language. It doesn't have a concept of truth, morality, or the real world. Instead, it's a giant statistical engine, churning out text based on the patterns it has absorbed from the Internet text.

Finally, when the model generates responses, it uses a method called beam search to ensure coherent and diverse responses. It considers many possible continuations and chooses the one that has the highest overall score according to its learnt parameters.

ChatGPT, powered by transformer neural networks and a vast number of parameters, navigates the terrain of language, using patterns and structures learnt from massive datasets to generate human-like text. Despite its complexity, its core functionality is grounded in fundamental statistical and computational principles, leveraging the power of machine learning to mimic human language in an uncannily effective way.

In the next section, we will explore how this technology is used, its implications, and the ethical considerations that arise when deploying such powerful AI systems.

Working with LLMs

When it comes to large language models (LLMs), like OpenAI's GPT-3 or Meta's LLaMA, understanding the distinction between pretraining and finetuning is vital. Both processes are fundamental for working with LLMs, and they each come with their own sets of challenges and opportunities.

Pretraining an LLM base model involves training a model from scratch on a substantial corpus of text. This process can be likened to training a supercomputer for several months, and it remains a significantly expensive and time-consuming task. The model learns the statistical patterns of language during this phase but does not specialize in any specific task. Training a model utilizing the vast data available on the Internet comes with a hefty price tag. While OpenAI hasn't revealed precise numbers, it's estimated that GPT-3 was trained on an enormous 45 terabytes of text data. This amount is equivalent to roughly one million feet of bookshelf space, or about 25% of the total holdings of the Library of Congress. The speculated cost for such a massive undertaking is believed to be in the millions of dollars. Clearly, such resource-intensive training goes beyond the reach of a typical start-up and most mid-size companies.

On the other hand, ***finetuning*** involves taking this pretrained model and further training it on a smaller, more specific dataset. With recent developments in Parameter Efficient Training (PEFT) techniques,[13] such as LoRA and LLaMA-Adapter, finetuning can now be performed relatively quickly and inexpensively. These techniques allow the model to specialize in a particular task, like translating text or answering medical questions. A good source of information about LLM and finetuning, including Open Source ones, is the Hugging Face website.[14]

Meta's release of the LLaMA models, ranging from 7 billion to 65 billion parameters, was a substantial step forward in this regard. However, these weights are intended for research purposes on.

To this end, initiatives like those from Together Compute[15] and MosaicML[16] have emerged, aiming to produce high-quality, openly available pretrained models. This push for openness ensures that advancements in AI and LLMs can continue at a steady pace, enabling broader experimentation and discovery.

With a pretrained model in hand, finetuning can be applied effectively even by smaller companies to address their specific business problems. The choice between training from scratch and finetuning depends on various factors, including data size, complexity, desired outcomes, and available resources.

Finetuning a pretrained LLM is generally quicker, less expensive, and can still yield impressive results. It is suitable for a range of tasks and requires less data. However, it might not perform as well as a freshly trained model, especially for highly specific tasks.

Recent discussions have also compared the efficiency of finetuning with few-shot learning, a method that involves providing the model with a few examples and then asking it to solve a task. Some experts suggest few-shot prompts might suffice in 90% of use cases, making it a worthy consideration.

In summary, working with large language models involves a blend of understanding these AI techniques and knowing how to apply them to specific use cases. As we navigate the rapidly evolving landscape of AI, these concepts provide a foundation for harnessing the full potential of these impressive models.

Foundational models are a powerful technique, but they also have some challenges. Some of the challenges of foundational models include

---

[13] https://huggingface.co/blog/peft

[14] https://huggingface.co/

[15] www.together.xyz/

[16] www.mosaicml.com/

- **Data requirements**: Foundational models require massive amounts of data to train. This data can be expensive and time-consuming to collect.

- **Computational requirements**: Foundational models can be computationally expensive to train.

- **Interpretability**: Foundational models are often difficult to interpret. It can be difficult to understand how the model makes its decisions.

Foundational models are a rapidly evolving field, and new applications are being discovered all the time. As foundational models continue to develop, it is likely to have a profound impact on many different industries.

In conclusion, foundational models have become an integral part of modern AI applications, offering significant benefits in terms of performance, efficiency, and adaptability. As we continue to witness rapid advancements in AI and machine learning, it is crucial for business executives to stay informed and adopt a First Principles approach to implementing these technologies, maximizing the value derived from AI-driven solutions.

Best Practices and Considerations for Implementing Neural Networks, Deep Learning, and Foundational Models

As companies increasingly leverage neural networks, deep learning, and foundational models to drive business growth and innovation, it is essential to consider best practices and key considerations when implementing these powerful techniques. This section will discuss five important aspects: data quality and preprocessing, model selection and architecture design, hyperparameter tuning and optimization, model evaluation and performance metrics, and ethical and responsible AI considerations:

1. **Data quality and preprocessing**: The performance of AI models is heavily dependent on the quality of the data used for training and validation. Ensuring high-quality data is a critical step in building effective neural networks and deep learning models. The data should be clean and free of errors, and it should be representative of the problem that the model is being trained to solve.

2. **Model selection and architecture design**: Choosing the right model architecture for your problem is essential to achieving optimal performance:

   a. **Start simple**: Begin with a simpler model, such as a feedforward neural network or a shallow CNN, before moving on to more complex architectures. This approach allows you to establish a baseline performance and understand the nuances of your problem.

   b. **Leverage existing architectures**: For many problems, pre-existing architectures like CNNs for image recognition, RNNs for sequence data, or transformers for NLP have proven effective. Use these as a starting point and tailor them to your specific problem.

   c. **Experiment with different architectures**: Test various architectures to determine which one works best for your problem. This may involve adding or removing layers, changing activation functions, or using different types of layers (e.g., convolutional, recurrent, or attention-based).

3. **Hyperparameter tuning and optimization**: Optimizing hyperparameters can significantly improve the performance of your model:

   a. **Systematic search**: Perform a grid search or random search to explore various hyperparameter combinations. Alternatively, consider using more advanced techniques such as Bayesian optimization or genetic algorithms.

   b. **Validation set**: Use a separate validation set to tune your hyperparameters, preventing overfitting and ensuring that your model generalizes well to unseen data.

   c. **Regularization**: Techniques such as L1 and L2 regularization, dropout, and early stopping can help prevent overfitting and improve model generalization.

4. **Model evaluation and performance metrics**: Evaluate your model's performance using appropriate metrics and techniques:

   a. **Select relevant metrics**: Choose performance metrics that align with your business objectives, such as accuracy, precision, recall, F1 score, or area under the ROC curve.

b. **Cross-validation**: Employ k-fold cross-validation or stratified k-fold cross-validation to obtain a more reliable estimate of your model's performance.

c. **Monitor training progress**: Track your model's performance on both training and validation sets during training, enabling early identification of potential overfitting or underfitting.

5. **Ethical and responsible AI considerations**: Implementing AI solutions requires careful consideration of ethical and responsible AI practices:

a. **Bias and fairness**: Be aware of potential biases in your data and model, which could lead to unfair treatment of certain groups or individuals. Regularly assess and mitigate potential biases by employing fairness metrics and ensuring diverse and representative data.

b. **Transparency and explainability**: Make your AI models more transparent and interpretable by leveraging techniques such as feature importance, partial dependence plots, or explainable AI methods like LIME and SHAP.

c. **Privacy and security**: Protect the privacy of your data subjects by implementing data anonymization, data encryption, and secure data storage practices. Additionally, consider using techniques like differential privacy and federated learning to further enhance data privacy during model training.

d. **Accountability and governance**: Establish a governance framework that outlines the responsibilities of various stakeholders in the AI development and deployment process. Implement processes for ongoing monitoring, maintenance, and auditing of AI systems to ensure compliance with relevant laws, regulations, and ethical standards.

PROMPT EXERCISES

We will use Bard/ChatGPT to create code that can be exported and run to Google's Colab. All the scripts were produced for the first time running code with ChatGPT at the time of writing. However, please note that due to continuous API updates, you will very likely get different answers or even might need to do a bit of debugging.

Exercise 1: Supervised Learning – Neural Network with Keras

Prompt for Bard/ChatGPT:

```
<Begin Prompt>
```
Generate a Python script to accomplish the following tasks:

1. Load the Titanic dataset available at https://raw.github.com/ datasciencedojo/datasets/master/titanic.csv into a pandas DataFrame.

2. Preprocess the dataset by handling missing values and converting categorical variables into numerical ones.

3. Split the dataset into a training set and a testing set.

4. Build a simple neural network model using TensorFlow. The model should take into account the features available in the dataset and predict the 'Survived' column.

5. Train the TensorFlow model using the training set and evaluate it using the testing set. Print out the accuracy, precision, recall, and F1-score of the model.

6. Also, train a simpler machine learning model for comparison, such as logistic regression from scikit-learn. Train this model with the same training set and evaluate it with the same testing set. Print out the accuracy, precision, recall, and F1-score of this model too.

7. Finally, compare the performance of the two models and print a statement about which model performed better and why you think this might be the case.

```
</End Prompt>
```

Exercise 2: Implementing a Convolutional Neural Network (CNN) with TensorFlow

```
<Begin Prompt>
```
Generate a Python script to accomplish the following tasks:

1. Load the CIFAR-10 dataset from Keras datasets.

2. Preprocess the data and divide it into training and testing sets.

3. Build a Convolutional Neural Network (CNN) using TensorFlow and train it on the CIFAR-10 dataset.

4. Evaluate the trained model's performance on the test data.

</End Prompt>

Exercise 3: Creating a Generative Adversarial Network (GAN)

<Begin Prompt>
Generate a Python script to accomplish the following tasks:

1. Use the Fashion MNIST dataset from Keras datasets.

2. Preprocess the data and implement a Generative Adversarial Network (GAN) using TensorFlow.

3. Train the GAN on the dataset and generate new synthetic images.

</End Prompt>

Exercise 4: Implementing an Autoencoder for Dimensionality Reduction

<Begin Prompt>
Generate a Python script to accomplish the following tasks:

1. Use the MNIST dataset from Keras datasets.

2. Preprocess the data and split it into training and testing sets.

3. Implement an autoencoder using Keras to reduce the dimensionality of the data.

4. Visualize the output of the autoencoder for a sample of test images.

</End Prompt>

Exercise 5: LLM Finetuning

<Begin Prompt>
Generate a Python script to fine-tune a Large Language Model (LLM), GPT-2 from Hugging Face :

1. Specify the Model and sample Dataset: Please use GPT-2 and the IMDB movie database as sample Dataset.

2. Preprocess the Data: Before training, the data needs to be preprocessed into a format that the model can understand. This often involves tokenization, or splitting the text into smaller parts called tokens.

3. Fine-Tuning the Model: Once your data is ready, you can proceed with the model fine-tuning. In this step, you will load your specified model and dataset and then initiate the training process.

4. Evaluate the Model: After the model has been fine-tuned, it's important to evaluate it to see how well it performs.

</End Prompt>

Please note that these exercises assume a basic understanding of Python and machine learning concepts. The exercises are designed to be introductory and are not exhaustive of the breadth of possibilities in neural networks, deep learning, and generative AI foundational models.

Key Takeaways

As we reach the conclusion of this chapter, it is crucial to recap the key concepts we have explored and emphasize the importance of understanding neural networks, deep learning, and foundational models from a First Principles perspective. We have discussed the core components, popular architectures, real-world applications, and best practices associated with these advanced AI techniques. Now, we encourage you to explore and apply these powerful tools to solve real-world problems and grow your business. Let's recap the key takeaways:

1. **Takeaway 1: Prioritization of data quality and model selection**

    a. **Data quality and preprocessing**: The quality of data is critical in AI. Invest time in data cleaning, handling missing values, outliers, and ensuring data is representative of the problem domain.

    b. **Model selection and architecture design**: Choose models that are suitable for the problem at hand and desired outcomes, not just because they are trendy.

2. **Takeaway 2: Importance of systematic optimization, evaluation, and ethical considerations**

   a. **Hyperparameter tuning and optimization**: Utilize systematic techniques for hyperparameter tuning. Avoid the temptation of random or manual trial-and-error methods.

   b. **Model evaluation and performance metrics**: Use comprehensive performance metrics to evaluate model performance, and do not ignore interpretability or fairness for the sake of model performance.

   c. **Ethical and responsible AI considerations**: Always consider the ethical implications of your AI solutions, including fairness, transparency, privacy, and governance measures.

3. **Takeaway 3: Importance of understanding and applying advanced techniques**

   a. **Understand neural networks, deep learning, and foundational models**: Understand these techniques from a First Principles perspective.

   b. **Explore and apply advanced techniques to solve real-world problems**: These techniques, while still under development, have the potential to revolutionize many industries. Businesses can gain a competitive advantage by exploring and applying these techniques, which can solve a wide variety of problems in business, such as fraud detection, customer service, and product development.

CHAPTER 11

Creating an AI Roadmap Fully Aligned to Enterprise Strategies

In the era of digital transformation, artificial intelligence (AI) has swiftly emerged as a potent catalyst for business growth and innovation. From automating routine tasks to delivering personalized experiences and generating unprecedented insights, AI is fundamentally reshaping how we conduct business. However, reaping the full benefits of this powerful technology is not as simple as adopting the latest AI applications. It requires a ***strategic, systematic, and deeply ingrained approach*** – this is where the First Principles methodology comes into play.

We explored in earlier chapters First Principles applied to AI – and went into the details of all the different areas that needed to be addressed. By applying this approach to AI opportunity identification, you can ensure a thorough and strategic exploration of potential AI applications, while avoiding the pitfalls of short-term thinking or reliance on existing solutions. This methodology allows you to think creatively and systematically, ensuring that you uncover AI opportunities that align with your company's unique needs and objectives. It also allows businesses to ensure that their AI strategy is rooted in a deep understanding of their unique context, needs, and capabilities, rather than generic industry trends or competitor benchmarks. This makes it possible to identify AI opportunities that are truly aligned with their business and data strategies and can deliver maximum value.

But why is it so important to identify AI opportunities and develop a cohesive AI strategy? Simply put, AI has the potential to deliver significant competitive advantages and value creation opportunities, but only if it is leveraged strategically.

© Francisco Javier Campos Zabala 2023
F. J. Campos Zabala, *Grow Your Business with AI*, https://doi.org/10.1007/978-1-4842-9669-1_11

Developing a cohesive AI strategy using the First Principles approach also ensures that AI implementation is not a disjointed, one-off initiative, but a well-integrated part of the company's overall business strategy. For example, a leading bank might identify AI opportunities in credit risk prediction, customer service automation, and fraud detection. By integrating these initiatives into a cohesive strategy, the bank can ensure that its AI investments support each other and align with its broader business goals. Indeed, common infrastructure and operations cost can be shared across these projects, and data can be shared between these individual projects to even create new initiatives – with associated business benefits.

Connecting AI opportunities to the wider enterprise strategy is one of the most challenging tasks. My goal is to empower you to analyze your business systematically, uncover potential AI applications, prioritize them based on feasibility and impact, and implement them strategically for maximum value creation.

In an ideal world – and some companies achieve this – there should be only one enterprise strategy, which reflects all aspects: data, AI, technology, business, etc. However, the reality is that large companies will have several strategies, often completely separated. During my career, I have seen many (probably too many) "technology roadmaps" which only discuss software stacks, cloud providers, and a lot of technical terms and barely mentioned the overall business strategies. Statements like "my tech strategy is to move all our data centers to X cloud provider" are completely divorced from business outcomes and therefore are very risky – they will have associated a relatively large tech bill with little demonstrable business benefits. I will provide techniques to ensure those different potential AI initiatives are as aligned as realistically possible.

The synergy between AI, data, and business strategies is crucial for organizations seeking to capitalize on the benefits of AI. AI relies heavily on data to learn and make predictions. Consequently, an effective data strategy is essential for providing AI systems with the necessary high-quality data to perform optimally. Furthermore, a robust business strategy ensures that AI initiatives align with the organization's broader goals and objectives.

To fully reap the benefits of AI, organizations must align their AI, data, and business strategies, ensuring that they work in harmony toward a common goal. The following Table 11-1 illustrates the key elements that need to be considered when aligning these strategies.

Table 11-1. *Key elements for aligning AI, data, and business strategies*

AI strategy	Data strategy	Business strategy
Identify use cases	Ensure data quality	Set strategic objectives
Select AI models	Manage data access	Prioritize AI initiatives
Plan implementation	Enable data sharing	Allocate resources
Monitor performance	Implement data governance	Monitor progress

The integration of AI, data, and business strategies is vital for organizations seeking to drive growth and innovation. Organizations can successfully leverage AI to achieve their objectives and gain a competitive edge in the market, ensuring they understand the importance of developing a cohesive AI strategy and recognizing the interconnectedness of AI, data, and business strategies. This chapter will delve deeper into the process of aligning these strategies and provide a framework for systematically exploring AI benefits across various business areas.

A Systematic Approach to Integrate AI in Enterprise Strategy

Here we offer a framework, based on First Principles, how to ensure we explore all the critical areas for a business and extract the most valuable AI initiatives. One of the challenges with AI is that it can be applied to most areas in a business; therefore prioritization is crucial.

Table 11-2. *Systematic framework for exploring AI benefits in business areas*

Steps	Key questions	Tools and techniques
Defining AI exploration scope	What areas of the business should the AI exploration cover?	AI data monetization framework (Chapter 7) Business analysis, strategic objectives review
Generating AI solutions	What are potential AI solutions to the problem?	AI data monetization framework (Chapter 7) Chapters 8, 9, and 10 Brainstorming, AI use case libraries
Assessing and prioritizing AI initiatives	Which AI solutions are most feasible and impactful?	AI data monetization framework (Chapter 7) Feasibility study, impact analysis, cost-benefit analysis
Implementing and monitoring AI solutions	How can we effectively implement and monitor the chosen AI solutions?	Project management tools, KPI monitoring, performance dashboards

This systematic framework expanded in Table 11-2, encourages a methodical and iterative approach to exploring AI benefits in business alternatives. By continually revisiting and refining your AI strategy based on real-world results, you can maximize the business value of your AI initiatives.

The process of integration involves strategically aligning the potential AI projects discovered using the data monetization framework for AI with the organization's business strategy. However, it is common for organizations to face the challenge of business strategy and AI strategy being carried out in isolation.

The First Principles Framework for AI Opportunities

AI adoption in a business context is far more than just deploying sophisticated algorithms – it is about identifying the right problems, leveraging the right data, and aligning with business objectives. This is best achieved using the First Principles approach, which involves a clear and methodical process. My recommendation is to use the AI data framework (Figure 11-1) we discussed in Chapter 7. There are other frameworks which can also be used; however, it is very important to ensure there is a bi-directional feedback loop between uncovering AI opportunities and the overall enterprise business strategy.

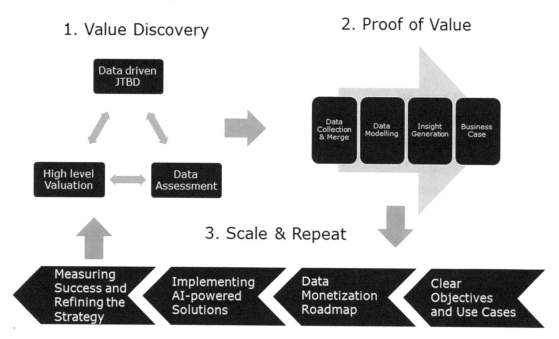

Figure 11-1. *An AI data framework*

Integration of Business Strategy with AI Strategy

Once all the potential AI projects have been identified, it is critical to align all those with the overall business strategy. When it comes to integrating AI into your business strategy, it is important to start from First Principles. This approach facilitates a deep understanding of the intersection between business strategy and AI strategy, promoting informed decision-making and fostering innovative solutions.

Firstly, let's identify the most popular business strategy frameworks:

- **SWOT Analysis**: A method of identifying Strengths, Weaknesses, Opportunities, and Threats in your business environment.

- **Porter's Five Forces**: A model that analyzes the competitive environment in terms of five key forces: supplier power, buyer power, competitive rivalry, the threat of substitution, and the threat of new entry.

- **Blue Ocean Strategy**: This approach encourages businesses to create new demand in an uncontested market space rather than compete in overcrowded industries.

- **Value Chain Analysis**: A process where you identify the primary and support activities that create value in your business.

- **Balanced Scorecard: This framework helps you measure performance from multiple perspectives**, including learning and growth, business processes, customers, and financials.

Given these frameworks, integrating potential AI projects identified through the data monetization framework involves aligning them with your overarching business objectives.

Consider the following example: Suppose you have identified a potential AI project that utilizes machine learning to improve supply chain logistics, reducing inefficiencies and cost.

- If your business strategy (using the Porter's Five Forces model) identifies high supplier power as a threat to profitability, this AI project could be a valuable strategic initiative. The project aligns with the business strategy by directly addressing a key competitive force.

- Conversely, if the strategy prioritizes expanding into new markets (aligned with Blue Ocean Strategy), the AI project might be less relevant and could be deprioritized.

Creating a matrix can help align AI projects with business strategy frameworks (Table 11-3). For instance, you could list potential AI projects along one axis and strategic goals along the other. This allows you to easily visualize how each AI project aligns with the business strategy and assists in prioritizing projects based on their strategic relevance and potential impact.

Table 11-3. *Business areas mapped to business strategy frameworks*

AI project	SWOT	Porter's Five Forces	Blue Ocean Strategy	Value Chain Analysis	Balanced Scorecard
Supply chain optimization	✓	✓		✓	✓
Customer segmentation	✓		✓	✓	✓
Predictive maintenance	✓	✓		✓	
Automated customer service		✓	✓	✓	✓

One of the biggest challenges in integrating AI and business strategy is that they are often treated as separate domains. To overcome this, organizations need to encourage cross-functional collaboration and adopt an iterative, agile approach. AI projects should be continuously evaluated and adjusted considering shifting business goals and competitive landscapes.

Furthermore, fostering an AI-ready culture within the organization is essential. This means upskilling employees, promoting a data-driven mindset, and ensuring AI ethics and governance are given due importance.

Lastly, remember that AI should not be viewed as an end in itself, but as a means to achieving strategic business objectives. Effective integration of business strategy with AI strategy ensures that AI initiatives are driven by business needs and are designed to deliver measurable business outcomes.

Let's consider another example of an e-commerce company named "E-Shopify." Their main business strategy, created using the Blue Ocean Strategy, is to differentiate themselves in the crowded e-commerce market by providing exceptional customer experience.

During the process of using the data monetization framework for AI, several AI initiatives were discovered such as personalized product recommendations, automated customer service bots, real-time inventory management, and predictive analysis of consumer buying behavior.

The next step involves integrating these AI projects into their business strategy (see Table 11-4). For instance, personalized product recommendations and automated customer service bots could directly align with their business strategy of enhancing customer experience, making them a high priority. Real-time inventory management, while useful, might not directly influence the customer experience.

Table 11-4. *AI initiatives aligned with E-Shopify's strategy*

AI initiative	Alignment with business strategy	Priority
Personalized product recommendations	High	High
Automated customer service bots	High	High
Real-time inventory management	Medium	Medium
Predictive analysis of buying behavior	Low	Low

It is critical to note that aligning AI initiatives with the business strategy should not be a one-time exercise. Business strategies often need to adapt to market dynamics, and so should AI projects.

To ensure the continuous integration of business strategy and AI strategy, companies need to foster a culture of communication and collaboration across all departments. AI strategy should not be the responsibility of just the IT or data science department. Instead, it should involve stakeholders from various departments who understand the business' strategic goals.

As we have seen, it is clear that while the business strategy should steer the direction of AI initiatives, there is also a feedback mechanism, where AI capabilities might uncover value not seen with the traditional strategy approached (please refer to Chapter 7 and the AI Data Flywheel). By identifying potential AI projects, aligning them with business strategy, and creating a collaborative, adaptable strategy environment, companies can ensure that their AI initiatives provide the maximum value and help them stand out in the competitive business world.

Integrating AI Strategy with Data Governance and Management

AI solutions often rely heavily on data, making data governance and management a crucial part of any AI strategy. This section delves into how to ensure data quality and availability, enable data collaboration and sharing, and scale AI throughout the enterprise.

Definition of data quality: Mentioned in multiple chapters, it is a multi-faceted concept, essentially refers to the various parameters such as accuracy, completeness, consistency, representativeness, and timeliness, which determine the fitness of data for a specific use or task.

There are three main steps (Table 11-5):

- **Step 1: Ensuring data quality and availability**. Data is the fuel for AI. Ensuring that the data is of high quality and is readily available for AI applications is crucial. Data quality includes accuracy, completeness, timeliness, and consistency. Techniques such as data validation, cleaning, transformation, and integration can help improve data quality.

- **Step 2: Enabling data collaboration and sharing**. In an increasingly interconnected world, enabling collaboration and sharing of data across different departments, and even different organizations, can unlock new AI opportunities. It is essential to have robust data governance policies and data sharing agreements to ensure data privacy and security.

- **Step 3: Scaling AI on the enterprise**. The ultimate goal is to scale AI applications across the enterprise for maximum impact. This involves not just the technological aspects such as cloud computing but also cultural aspects like fostering an AI-first mentality among employees.

Table 11-5. *Integrating AI strategy with data governance and management*

Steps	Key questions	Tools and techniques
Ensuring data quality and availability	How can we ensure that our data is accurate, complete, timely, and consistent?	Data validation, cleaning, transformation, and integration
Enabling data collaboration and sharing	How can we promote data sharing and collaboration while ensuring data privacy and security?	Data governance policies, data sharing agreements
Scaling AI on the enterprise	How can we scale AI applications across our enterprise for maximum impact?	Cloud computing, microservices, fostering an AI-first mentality, developing data literacy among employees

Common Challenges, Pitfalls, and Best Practices

As with any business endeavor, leveraging AI comes with its own unique set of challenges and pitfalls. However, with the right strategies and practices, these can be mitigated to make the most of AI opportunities. See the following most common challenges and pitfalls (Table 11-6):

- **Data quality and availability**: AI relies heavily on data. If the data is poor in quality, incomplete, inconsistent, or not readily available, AI models won't be able to provide accurate or useful insights.

- **Lack of understanding or skills**: AI is a complex field. Without a proper understanding of the technology or lacking the required skills, it can be difficult to implement effective AI solutions.

- **Scalability**: Many businesses face issues when scaling up AI applications. As the demand grows, maintaining the efficiency and accuracy of AI models can be challenging.

Best practices to overcome challenges:

- **Ensure data governance**: Have a data governance framework in place to ensure high data quality and availability.

- **Invest in training and education**: Upskill your workforce on AI concepts, or consider hiring experts to build and manage your AI applications.

- **Use scalable technologies**: Use technologies such as cloud computing and microservices, which allow for seamless scalability of AI applications. We will explore these technologies in later chapters.

Table 11-6. *Common challenges, pitfalls, and best practices in AI adoption*

Challenges/pitfalls	Best practices
Poor data quality and availability	Implement a data governance framework
Lack of understanding or skill	Invest in AI training and education
Difficulty in scaling AI applications	Use scalable technologies like cloud computing and microservices

Key Takeaways

In this chapter, we have explored the potential of AI and how to implement it systematically and strategically to drive business growth. Let's revisit the key takeaways and the dos and don'ts for implementing each:

- **Takeaway 1: AI opportunities identification**. It is about understanding business problems and exploring how AI can be part of the solution.

    - **Do**: Invest time to systematically identify and explore AI opportunities that align with your business strategy. Adopt a data monetization game, such as the one described in Chapter 7.

    - **Don't**: Keep separated AI strategy from business strategy. Don't implement AI for the sake of jumping on the bandwagon. Ensure it solves real business problems and contributes to strategic objectives.

- **Takeaway 2: Data governance and management**. The state of your data can either be a roadblock or a facilitator to successful AI adoption.

  - **Do**: Establish strong data governance policies to ensure data quality, availability, and security.

  - **Don't**: Don't underestimate the importance of data in AI. Poor data quality can lead to inaccurate AI outcomes.

- **Takeaway 3: Common challenges and best practices**. Be prepared for potential hurdles, and plan how to navigate them:

  - **Do**: Be aware of the common pitfalls in AI adoption and learn from best practices within the industry to mitigate these challenges.

  - **Don't**: Don't assume the AI journey will be challenge-free. It is essential to be prepared in overcoming potential hurdles.

This chapter serves as a guide to navigate the complexities of AI in business. However, remember that each organization's journey is unique. Use these principles as a roadmap, adjust when necessary, and embrace the transformative potential of AI.

CHAPTER 12

Funding and Measuring the AI Journey

When embarking on an AI journey, the interconnection between funding, implementing AI initiatives, and measuring their impact is vital. This chapter will help you understand these components and how to apply a First Principles approach to each one. This chapter we will explore a guide to AI ROI, cost management, and impact analysis.

AI has the potential to revolutionize business models and processes, but to do so, significant resources are required. Securing funds for AI initiatives is the first major step in this journey. Once funding is secured, businesses can initiate the development and implementation of AI projects. After implementing the AI project, measuring its impact becomes essential to evaluate its effectiveness and ROI.

These elements are interconnected and influence one another (Table 12-1). For example, the potential impact of an AI initiative can play a significant role in securing funding. Simultaneously, the results derived from evaluating AI projects can help guide future funding decisions, including scaling existing projects or investing in new ones.

The First Principles approach is crucial in this context. In securing funds, it helps you identifying the core reasons why an AI initiative is necessary and how it can strategically align with your business objectives.

In evaluating AI initiatives, the First Principles ***approach ensures the development of an effective and relevant metrics system that genuinely reflects the initiative's impact***. This thought process avoids relying on preconceived notions or industry norms, enabling a more accurate evaluation that can contribute to strategic decision-making.

F. J. Campos Zabala, *Grow Your Business with AI*, https://doi.org/10.1007/978-1-4842-9669-1_12

Table 12-1. *Applying First Principles to AI funding and evaluation*

Steps	Applying First Principles
Securing funding	Identify the core reasons for AI, understand its potential impact on business objectives, devise a realistic and compelling proposal
Evaluating AI initiatives	Develop metrics reflecting genuine impact, avoid preconceived notions or industry norms, continuously review and adapt measures

Funding the AI Journey

Funding is the lifeblood of any AI initiative, and securing it requires careful planning and strategy. In this section, we will delve into different funding options, how to navigate cost constraints (Table 12-2), and strategies for budgeting and cost management using a First Principles approach.

Table 12-2. *Navigating cost constraint scenarios with a First Principles approach*

Cost constraint scenario	First Principles approach
Limited budget	Consider a phased approach, starting with smaller, less costly AI projects that can provide quick wins
Limited AI expertise	Look for partnerships with universities or consider upskilling current employees
High data costs	Leverage open-source data, negotiate partnerships for data sharing, or invest in generating your own data

Internal Funding Options

This is the typical option in most scenarios within the enterprise. Internal funding comes from within your organization and may include reinvestment of profits, operating budgets, or internal fundraising efforts. The primary advantage of internal funding is the control it provides over the initiative. Other benefits include greater flexibility and reduced risks, by not depending on third parties.

Using First Principles thinking, consider how your AI initiatives align with your organization's strategic objectives, what value they bring, and how they can be prioritized within your budget constraints.

For instance, if your AI project aims to automate a costly process, resulting in substantial cost savings, it might justify allocation of a significant part of the operational budget.

There are a few options to allocate the internal funding:

- **Allocating existing resources**: Businesses can use their own resources to fund AI implementations. This may include using existing budgets, reallocating resources, or investing in new technologies.

- **Capital investment**: Businesses can also invest in AI by using capital from company profits or by setting aside a strategic AI investment budget.

- **Employee training and upskilling**: Businesses can invest in AI by training and upskilling their employees in AI-related skills. This can be done through in-house training programs or by partnering with external organizations.

There are also a few challenges with internal funding:

- Many organizations do **incremental budgeting**, which means each department is allocated a size of the budget proportionate to last year's cost. This means that new areas or cross-areas projects (like AI and data projects often are) are difficult to get assigned to the right cost center. Organizations with zero-budget process do not have this challenge, but these are not very common.

- **Less expertise**: Businesses may not have the in-house expertise to implement AI effectively. This may require them to hire external consultants or partners, which can add to the cost of implementation.

External Funding Options

External funding sources may include government grants and incentives, venture capital and private equity, corporate partnerships and collaborations, crowdfunding and alternative financing methods. Each of these options requires a compelling business case and a clear demonstration of potential return on investment.

When applying First Principles thinking to external funding, it's essential to question how your AI initiative will create value that external stakeholders can appreciate, and how that aligns with their investment or funding criteria.

For example, a venture capital firm might be interested in an AI project that could scale quickly and provide a high return on investment, while a government grant might require the initiative to have societal benefits.

Government grants and incentives offer substantial financial support but come with stringent eligibility criteria and a complex application process. Despite being time-consuming, their potential for significant funding cannot be overlooked.

Venture capital (VC) and **private equity (PE)** firms provide both funding and expertise. However, in exchange, these firms typically require an equity stake in your business. Successful pitching, understanding the investor's interest, and negotiating investment terms and conditions are key in securing VC and PE funds. As a reference, VC firms typically invest in companies that have the potential for high growth, while PE firms typically invest in companies that are already profitable. Should an investor be interested in your project, they will typically ask you to sign a ***term sheet***. A term sheet is a document that outlines the key terms of an investment agreement. It includes information such as the amount of investment, the valuation of the company, and the terms of repayment.

Corporate partnerships provide financial support and potentially access to resources, market opportunities, and expertise. Identifying companies with an interest in AI and negotiating mutually beneficial terms are critical steps in this process.

Crowdfunding offers more flexibility and entails raising funds from many individuals or organizations, typically through online platforms. Successful crowdfunding requires compelling storytelling, realistic funding goals, and strategic marketing to engage potential backers.

Each funding option comes with its unique set of advantages, potential drawbacks, and requirements, making it crucial to carefully assess and select the most suitable funding source based on specific needs and circumstances.

Navigating Cost Constraint Scenarios

Cost constraints are a reality of any business initiative. However, by using First Principles reasoning, we can think creatively about how to get the most out of our available resources. Businesses may face two primary cost constraint scenarios when implementing AI solutions: bootstrapping an AI project and prioritizing AI features and functionalities.

Different scenarios will call for different strategies. A First Principles approach here is about designing the optimal plan given your specific conditions, rather than following a one-size-fits-all strategy.

In **bootstrapping** an AI project, businesses with limited funding can minimize initial costs and gradually scale up AI implementation by leveraging existing resources, such as open-source software and in-house data. Using platforms like TensorFlow, PyTorch, and scikit-learn can help avoid high licensing costs while reusing existing data negates the need for acquiring new datasets. An incremental development approach, starting with a minimum viable product (MVP), helps minimize risks and costs associated with large-scale AI projects.

For instance, in a scenario with severe cost constraints, a **phased approach** might be preferable, starting with smaller AI initiatives that deliver quick wins and generate savings, which can then be reinvested into larger projects. Alternatively, when budget constraints are present, businesses must prioritize the AI features and functionalities that will have the most significant impact on their operations. This prioritization involves identifying key areas where AI can add value and implementing a phased approach to AI development and deployment. These key areas might include customer service, supply chain management, or product recommendations. The phased approach allows for efficient resource allocation, risk minimization, and generation of quick wins that justify further AI investment.

In another example, if budget constraints limit hiring of AI specialists, consider partnering with universities for research collaborations, or investing in upskilling existing employees.

Businesses can successfully navigate cost constraints by bootstrapping their projects and prioritizing impactful AI features or looking for AI resources in alternative sources. Regularly revisiting budget allocations, reassessing priorities, and refining AI models based on performance and feedback are crucial for the ongoing success of AI initiatives. The key to successful AI implementation lies in balancing funding, cost management, and strategic prioritization to unlock the full potential of AI and drive business growth and innovation.

Budgeting and Cost Management

Budgeting and cost management are crucial for ensuring the financial sustainability of your AI initiatives. Implementing AI solutions requires careful budgeting and cost management, which includes estimating AI project costs, financial planning and forecasting, and cost monitoring and control. A First Principles approach to this involves going beyond traditional budgeting methods and considering the unique aspects of AI projects.

These could include costs associated with data acquisition and cleansing, development and maintenance of AI models, infrastructure, and potentially, the upskilling of employees.

Estimating AI project costs involves accounting for hardware and software expenses, human resources and talent acquisition costs, as well as maintenance and ongoing support. Specialized hardware like GPUs for training AI models, software tools for data storage and processing, hiring specialized roles like data scientists and machine learning engineers, and maintaining AI models and infrastructure are significant cost considerations.

Financial planning and forecasting require setting realistic budgets based on the project's complexity, expected duration, and potential ROI. It is important to avoid underestimating costs to prevent project delays or failure. Also, contingency planning is crucial for covering unexpected costs such as hardware or software failure, or changes in project scope.

Cost monitoring and control involve tracking expenses throughout the project's lifecycle to ensure staying within budget and identifying potential cost overruns early. Identifying cost overruns and implementing mitigation strategies, including revising project scope, eliminating inefficiencies, renegotiating contracts, or exploring alternative hardware or software solutions, can help control expenses.

It is also very important for AI projects to look after the post-implementation, cost monitoring and control become vital to ensure that the project stays within budget. This process involves tracking all expenses, identifying cost overruns, and implementing cost-saving measures if necessary, such as reducing project scope or seeking less expensive alternatives for hardware and software.

Effective budgeting and cost management are vital for successful AI implementation. Accurate cost estimation, realistic budgeting, expense monitoring, and contingency planning can maximize ROI and ensure long-term project success. It enables businesses to make informed decisions about their AI investments and positions them to capitalize on the transformative potential of artificial intelligence.

Establishing a Framework for Measuring AI Impact and ROI

Measuring the impact of AI is fundamental to demonstrating the value of your initiatives and understand where to focus future investments. In this section, we will explore the establishment of a comprehensive framework for gauging AI's impact and ROI, using a First Principles approach.

The first key aspect in determining the return on investment (ROI) and success metrics in AI projects is to define a clear success criteria:

- **Quantitative metrics** are crucial for objective evaluations of the project's performance. This includes model performance metrics (accuracy, precision, etc.), business outcome metrics (revenue growth, cost reduction, etc.), and operational efficiency metrics (model training time, data processing speed, etc.).

- **Qualitative benefits** are also important and include improved decision-making, enhanced customer experiences, increased innovation, and competitive advantage derived from AI implementation.

Here, many AI projects will replace an existing product or process. In these cases, it is *also very important to ensure you capture the existing baseline, so it can be compared with the new technology*. I have seen many projects failed on managing expectations; baseline metrics are not captured prior the new project, and when the new project does not reach the very often unrealistic expectations, the project can be "perceived" to be a failure, even if the AI performs much better than the old process.

The second aspect is to ensure there is a transparent and agreed by all stakeholder approach at measuring ROI:

- **Direct financial returns** are calculated by comparing the returns generated by the project with the total investment. This considers factors like increased revenue, cost reduction, and improved operational efficiency.

- **Indirect benefits and cost savings** should also be considered, such as increased customer satisfaction, reduced employee turnover, and enhanced brand reputation, all potentially stemming from AI implementation. For instance, an AI-powered customer service chatbot could lead to decreased customer support costs and improved customer loyalty.

Defining Key Performance Indicators (KPIs) with First Principles

KPIs act as a compass, pointing your AI initiatives in the right direction and providing a quantifiable measure of their success. Instead of blindly following common KPIs like accuracy or cost savings, a First Principles approach invites us to dissect the core purpose of our AI initiatives and establish KPIs that directly measure these fundamental objectives.

For example, an AI initiative aimed at improving customer service could establish a KPI around customer satisfaction scores, not just the number of inquiries handled. Table 12-3 shows popular AI KPIs.

Table 12-3. *Common AI KPI*

Metric type	Examples
Model performance	Precision, recall, F1 score, AUC-ROC
Business outcomes	Revenue growth, cost reduction, customer satisfaction, employee productivity
Operational efficiency	Model training time, data processing speed, infrastructure costs

When planning to leverage AI to grow your business, it is critical to set measurable goals. This is where Key Performance Indicators (KPIs) come in. KPIs allow you to gauge the success of your AI projects and assess whether they're helping you meet your business objectives. Here, we will discuss the most common KPIs related to model performance, business outcomes, and operational efficiency, and how to communicate them effectively through storytelling.

Model performance KPIs evaluate the accuracy and efficiency of your AI models. Some common KPIs include

- **Precision**: This measures the percentage of true positive predictions among all positive predictions made by the model.

- **Recall (sensitivity)**: This measures the percentage of true positive predictions among all actual positives.

- **F1 score**: This is the harmonic mean[1] of precision and recall, providing a balance between these two measures.

- **Area under the ROC curve (AUC-ROC)**: This measures the model's ability to distinguish between positive and negative classes, with 1 representing a perfect model and 0.5 indicating a model performing no better than random guessing.

As well as the technical performance metrics, it is extremely important to translate the model impact in business outcome KPIs, so we can track the impact of AI projects on your key business metrics. These can include

- **Revenue growth**: This measures the increase in revenue attributable to the AI project.

- **Cost reduction**: This measures the decrease in costs due to the AI project.

- **Customer satisfaction**: This can be measured using surveys, customer reviews, or net promoter scores, assessing whether the AI project improves customer experiences.

- **Employee productivity**: This measures improvements in output or task completion speed as a result of the AI project.

---

[1] https://mathworld.wolfram.com/HarmonicMean.html

Finally, operational efficiency KPIs assess how effectively and efficiently your AI project operates. Examples include

- **Model training time**: It measures how long it takes to train your AI models. This will also be related to the training cost, and for large models – such as large language models – where the cost can be millions of dollars, it is something to keep focus to minimize as much as possible.

- **Data processing speed**: This measures the speed at which your AI system can process data. Sometimes called "inference time."

- **Infrastructure costs**: This measures the cost of maintaining the hardware and software needed for your AI project.

Assessing AI Maturity Levels

The maturity level of your AI initiatives refers to the sophistication of your AI deployment, measured across dimensions such as data infrastructure, AI skills, and the level of AI integration into business processes.

Using First Principles thinking, we should evaluate our maturity level based not only on our current capabilities but also our strategic objectives. This would allow us to identify areas of focus to move from our current to desired state.

We will discuss in further detail the different AI maturity levels in Chapter 21.

Aligning AI KPIs with Business Objectives

To ensure that AI initiatives drive real business value, their KPIs should be tightly aligned with your overarching business objectives. A First Principles approach involves breaking down these high-level objectives into actionable, measurable components that AI can impact.

For example, if the business objective is to increase market share, an associated AI KPI could be the accuracy of an AI-powered market prediction tool. Table 12-4 displays a sample AI maturity roadmap action plan.

Table 12-4. *Assessing AI maturity levels with a First Principles approach*

AI maturity dimension	Current state	Desired state	Actionable steps
Data infrastructure	Basic data storage	Advanced cloud-based data infrastructure	Invest in cloud storage, improve data collection and cleaning processes
AI skills	Limited AI knowledge	Skilled AI team	Upskill existing staff, hire new AI talent
AI integration	Ad hoc AI projects	AI integrated into all business units	Develop a company-wide AI strategy, encourage cross-functional AI projects

Tracking and Demonstrating ROI for AI Initiatives

Building AI capabilities is just half the battle; the other half is effectively tracking their performance and communicating the return on investment (ROI). In this section, we will explore how to measure, evaluate, and present the ROI of your AI initiatives effectively. Here, I cannot stress how important this is, specially for larger organizations, as in many businesses "perception is reality" – therefore, if you do not communicate the value of your AI projects in the language of the rest of the executive team, they would assume (incorrectly) that your AI projects do not have any value for the organization.

The first step in demonstrating ROI is ***establishing a tracking system for your AI Key Performance Indicators (KPIs).*** A First Principles approach here involves understanding what data is essential for measuring your KPIs and setting up a systematic process for data collection, processing, and analysis. For example, a customer service AI might require tracking of response times, customer satisfaction scores, and issue resolution rates.

Calculating the ROI of AI projects involves comparing the cost of the project to the value it delivers. Value can come in various forms, from cost savings and revenue generation to fewer tangible benefits like improved customer satisfaction or decision-making speed.

Here, First Principles thinking can help identify the fundamental sources of value that your AI initiatives deliver, translating them into monetary terms where possible.

Clearly *communicating the impact and ROI of AI initiatives* is crucial to secure continued investment and support. A First Principles approach can help frame communication around the fundamental objectives the AI initiatives are achieving. Data visualization can be highly effective in this process, making it easy to understand complex data at a glance.

Just as AI learns and adapts, so should your strategy. By continually measuring and analyzing the performance of your AI initiatives, you can identify areas of improvement and adapt your strategy accordingly. A First Principles mindset will ensure you're focusing on the core objectives, not just surface-level metrics. The following Table 12-5 has an example of ROI for an AI initiative.

Table 12-5. *Example of an AI project ROI calculation*

AI project	Project cost	Value delivered	ROI
Customer service AI	$50,000	$75,000 (saved in labor cost + improved customer satisfaction)	50%

Storytelling and Communication

While the KPIs offer crucial insights, raw data can often be dry and challenging to interpret for non-technical stakeholders. Therefore, to maximize the impact of your AI project, you need to communicate these metrics effectively, and storytelling can be a powerful tool for this.

Storytelling involves presenting your data and KPIs in the form of a narrative that emphasizes business outcomes, making it more relatable and easier to understand for your audience. It allows us to communicate the insights and implications of a data science project in an engaging and accessible manner. To illustrate, let's consider a specific example: using an AI model to understand customer behavior in a retail business.

Let's say we are a large retail company looking to optimize our operations by determining the potential of online sales versus physical stores. We have collected data on customer preferences and shopping habits and used this to train a machine learning model. The model takes into account various factors such as age, income, location, and past purchase behavior to predict whether a customer is likely to shop online or in a physical store.

Our AI model's effectiveness is measured using different metrics, two of the most common being the confusion matrix and the AUC-ROC curve.

The confusion matrix is a table that is often used to describe the performance of a classification model. In our case, it allows us to visualize the performance of our model in predicting whether a customer prefers shopping online or in-store.

In Table 12-6, this hypothetical confusion matrix, TP, FP, FN, and TN, represents True Positives, False Positives, False Negatives, and True Negatives, respectively. Our model correctly predicted 1000 in-store customers and 1500 online customers. It made a mistake with 200 in-store and 300 online customers.

Table 12-6. *Confusion matrix*

	Predicted: in-store Predicted: online	Predicted: in-store Predicted: online
Actual: in-store	1000 (TP)	200 (FP)
Actual: online	300 (FN)	1500 (TN)

Another important metric is the Area Under the Receiver Operating Characteristic Curve (AUC-ROC), as seen in Figure 12-1. This measures the trade-off between correctly predicting a positive class (True Positive Rate) and wrongly predicting a negative class (False Positive Rate). In our case, our model's AUC is 78%, which is considered good.

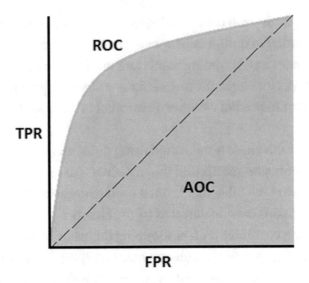

Figure 12-1. *AUC-ROC diagrams*

Translating these results into a business context, let's assume our total customer base is 3000 customers. Our model predicts that approximately 68% of our customers prefer online shopping.

To make this more relatable, we can visualize this information in a pie chart presented in Figure 12-2.

Figure 12-2. *Customers preferences online vs physical shopping*

Now, what does this all mean in terms of actionable insights? If 68% of our customers prefer shopping online, and assuming the trend is going to continue or even increase, then the potential for cost savings by reducing the number of physical stores is substantial. We could consider closing underperforming stores or even most of our physical stores while maintaining one flagship store for customers who still prefer the in-store experience. We should also recommend re-enforcing the ecommerce website to take more customers, as users swap their physical store visits for the convenience of online shopping.

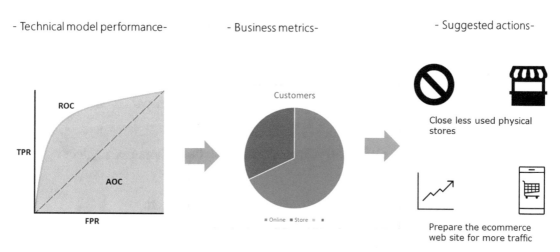

Figure 12-3. *Storytelling – do not just show the technical model performance*

We can see in Figure 12-3 three different ways to communicate the output of an AI model. The three diagrams show the same results; however most people would agree that the suggested actions diagram is the most clear of the three from a business outcomes perspective. Unfortunately, many data science teams focus mainly on reporting on the technical model performance. This will not communicate effectively to their business colleagues the implications of their model and the default model for the business executives would be to assume the model is not practical.

This is just an example, but it shows how data science can be used to inform business decisions. The key to effective data storytelling is to present your findings in a way that is **understandable, meaningful, and actionable** for your audience. Remember, your goal is not just to show what the data says, but to tell a story about how this data can be used to drive strategic business decisions. And finally, do not forget that effective storytelling should not just expose facts but also suggest actions.

Key Takeaways

As we conclude this chapter, let's reflect on the essential themes we have explored in the context of funding, implementing, and measuring the ROI of AI initiatives.

1. **Takeaway 1: The interplay between funding, AI implementation, and impact measurement**. Funding secures resources, effective implementation ensures the functionality of AI systems, and measuring impact confirms the success of these efforts. For instance, without appropriate funding, the execution of AI projects could falter; without effective measurement, it becomes difficult to justify further investment.

    a. Do: Establish clear criteria for the allocation of funds, implement AI initiatives with clear objectives, and set up robust impact measurement systems.

    b. Don't: Overlook the interconnectedness of these elements, neglecting the measurement aspect.

2. **Takeaway 2: Importance of First Principles thinking in evaluating AI initiatives**. Rather than depending on traditional ROI metrics, a deeper dive into what truly drives value in your organization can illuminate the real impact of AI. For example, while an AI system might not directly increase revenue, it might significantly boost customer satisfaction, leading to increased customer loyalty and repeat business over time.

    a. Do: Identify the core drivers of value in your business and ensure your AI initiatives align with them.

    b. Don't: Get caught up in traditional ROI metrics that might not fully reflect the value of AI in your unique business context.

3. **Takeaway 3: Continuous improvement and adaptation are crucial**. It is essential to constantly measure, learn, and adapt your AI strategy based on real-world performance data. By continually tracking KPIs and adjusting your AI strategy, your business can stay ahead of the curve, maximizing the benefits of AI.

- Do: Regularly track performance, learn from data, and make necessary adjustments to your AI strategy.

- Don't: Implement AI initiatives and then neglect to monitor their performance or be resistant to change.

By keeping these key points and best practices in mind, you can set your business up for success on your AI journey. Embarking on this path with a First Principles approach, adequate funding, effective cost management, and robust systems for measuring impact and ROI can enable your organization to reap the full benefits of AI.

CHAPTER 13

How to Approach Open Data

In today's data-driven world, the success of a company largely depends on its ability to leverage data effectively. As businesses turn to artificial intelligence (AI) to solve complex problems and gain a competitive edge, the need for high-quality and diverse data sources has become paramount. Open data plays a critical role in the AI ecosystem by providing valuable, publicly accessible data sources that can be used to train and enhance AI models. In this chapter, we introduce the concept of open data, its significance in the AI ecosystem, and the benefits that it offers to businesses.

Open data refers to any data that is freely available, accessible, and can be used, modified, and shared by anyone without restrictions. It is typically published by governments, public organizations, research institutions, and even private companies. Open data sources encompass a wide range of formats, including text, images, audio, video, and structured data sets, and cover diverse domains, such as healthcare, finance, environment, and social sciences.

A good example of open data is Lidar[1] data, offering insights into geographical features like hills and valleys, and facilitating flood prediction. In the United Kingdom, this data is freely accessible, enabling organizations to leverage it for precise tasks, such as determining insurance premiums accurately.

While numerous organizations possess an abundance of data that could enhance AI-driven improvements in areas like operations and product offerings, there is a vast potential for societal advancement when this data is shared among organizations. Such sharing could expedite solutions for disease, crisis management, and climate change.

---

[1] www.data.gov.uk/dataset/f0db0249-f17b-4036-9e65-309148c97ce4/national-lidar-programme

Presently, this level of data sharing is scarcely realized due to various impediments, including technical issues, privacy concerns, and organizational reluctance tied to perceived competitive advantages in retaining proprietary data.

Thus, the challenge lies in overcoming these obstacles to leverage data and AI for the greater societal good while being very beneficial for most companies across industries.

The exponential growth in AI adoption across industries can be attributed to the massive amounts of data generated daily. Open data plays a crucial role in the AI ecosystem, as it offers businesses access to diverse, high-quality data sources that can be used to develop and train AI models. By leveraging open data, companies can enhance their AI systems' performance, reduce development costs, and accelerate the innovation cycle.

There are several benefits to using open data in AI projects:

- **Increased accuracy**: Open data can be used to train AI models on larger and more diverse datasets. This can lead to more accurate AI models.

- **Improved efficiency**: Open data can be used to automate tasks that would otherwise be done manually. This can free up time for AI developers to focus on more complex tasks.

- **Cost savings**: Open data is a cost-effective way to access high-quality data, as businesses can avoid the expenses associated with collecting, storing, and maintaining proprietary data sets.

- **Data diversity**: Open data sources offer diverse and extensive datasets, which can help improve the performance and generalizability of AI models by providing a broader range of information for training.

- **Faster innovation**: By leveraging existing open datasets, companies can reduce the time required to develop and deploy AI models, resulting in faster innovation and a shorter time to market.

- **Enhanced collaboration**: The availability of open data fosters collaboration among researchers, businesses, and governments, resulting in cross-sector innovation and shared problem-solving.

- **Improved decision-making**: Open data can enhance decision-making processes by providing a broader range of insights and perspectives, ultimately leading to more informed and effective decisions.

Open data is a valuable resource for AI projects. By using open data, businesses can gain a competitive advantage by developing more accurate, efficient, and innovative AI solutions.

As we delve deeper into this chapter, we will explore how to identify and source open data, preprocess, and clean the data, and effectively integrate it into AI projects. We will also discuss the limitations and risks associated with using open data and conclude with a first principles approach to open data utilization for growing your company with AI.

Identifying and Sourcing Open Data

To leverage the full potential of open data in AI projects, it is essential to identify and source the right datasets that align with your business objectives. In this section, we will discuss various sources of open data, including government and public organizations, private sector sources, and online repositories and databases. We will also highlight licensing and legal considerations that are crucial when using open data in commercial applications.

Government and Public Organizations

Many governments worldwide have recognized the value of open data and have established national and regional open data portals to facilitate data sharing. These portals offer a diverse range of datasets across various sectors, including healthcare, transportation, finance, and environment.

Some notable examples are Data.gov (United States), Data.gov.uk (United Kingdom), and Data.gov.au (Australia), as per Table 13-1.

Table 13-1. *National open data portals*

Country	Number of datasets (approx.)	URL
United States	250,000	www.data.gov
United Kingdom	50,000	data.gov.uk
Canada	80,000	open.canada.ca
Australia	70,000	data.gov.au
France	350,000	www.data.gouv.fr

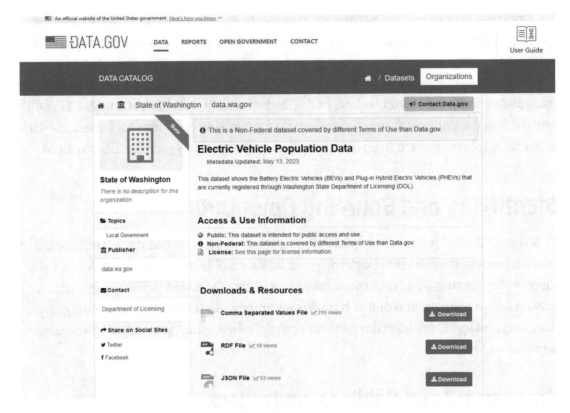

Figure 13-1. *An open popular dataset from US Data.gov*

The maturity of the portals will depend on many factors. Figure 13-1 shows one of the most popular datasets in the US Open Data Portal. You can check whether your local government will have a similar portal and what data could be available.

Finally, as well as local governments, international organizations, such as the United Nations[2] (UN), World Bank[3], the European Union[4], and World Health Organization[5] (WHO), also provide open datasets that can be useful for AI projects. These datasets often focus on global issues, like poverty, climate change, and health, offering valuable insights for businesses operating in multiple countries or addressing global challenges.

---

[2] https://data.un.org/

[3] https://data.worldbank.org/

[4] https://data.europa.eu/en

[5] www.who.int/data

Private Sector Sources

Private sector organizations are also a source of open data. Some businesses make data available to the public to promote transparency and innovation. Other businesses make data available to the public to generate leads or sales.

- **Research institutions and NGOs**: These often share datasets that they have collected for their studies. These datasets can be valuable for AI projects, as they typically focus on specific research questions and may provide insights that are not readily available from other sources. A notable example here is **ImageNet**[6], an image database organized according to the WordNet hierarchy in which each node of the hierarchy is depicted by hundreds and thousands of images. The project has been instrumental in advancing computer vision and deep learning research. The data is available for free to researchers for non-commercial use.

- **Private companies sharing open data**: Some private companies have also begun to share their datasets as open data, recognizing the benefits of collaboration and innovation. For example, companies like Google, Microsoft, and IBM have shared datasets related to natural language processing, computer vision, and machine learning to foster innovation and drive advancements in the AI field.

- **Data catalogs** are online repositories that store and organize open datasets from various sources. These platforms facilitate data discovery and make it easier for users to find relevant datasets for their AI projects. Some popular data catalogs include Kaggle[7], UCI Machine Learning Repository[8], and DataPortals[9], which contains a comprehensive list of open data portals around the world – this includes both private and public open datasets.

---

[6] www.image-net.org/

[7] www.kaggle.com/datasets

[8] https://archive.ics.uci.edu

[9] https://dataportals.org/

Licensing and Legal Considerations

When using open data, it is crucial to understand the licensing and legal considerations associated with each dataset. Licenses define the terms under which the data can be used, modified, and shared. Some common open data licenses include the Creative Commons (CC) licenses and the Open Data Commons licenses (Table 13-2). It is essential to comply with these licenses to avoid legal issues and protect your business.

***Table 13-2.** Licensing types for CC*

License	Usage rights	Modification rights	Sharing rights
CC0 (Creative Commons Zero)	Unrestricted use	Unrestricted modification	Unrestricted sharing
CC BY (Attribution)	Use with attribution	Modification with attribution	Sharing with attribution
CC BY-SA (Attribution-ShareAlike)	Use with attribution	Modification with attribution	Sharing with attribution, under the same license
CC BY-ND (Attribution-NoDerivs)	Use with attribution	No modification	Sharing with attribution
CC BY-NC (Attribution-NonCommercial)	Use with attribution for non-commercial purposes	Modification with attribution for non-commercial purposes	Sharing with attribution for non-commercial purposes
CC BY-NC-SA (Attribution-NonCommercial-ShareAlike)	Use with attribution for non-commercial purposes	Modification with attribution for non-commercial purposes	Sharing with attribution, under the same license, for non-commercial purposes
CC BY-NC-ND (Attribution-NonCommercial-NoDerivs)	Use with attribution for non-commercial purposes	No modification	Sharing with attribution for non-commercial purposes

Please note that this is a simplified representation of these licenses. Each has more specific terms and conditions that should be consulted on the Creative Commons website or through a legal expert.

Identifying and sourcing open data for AI projects involves exploring various sources, including government and public organizations, private sector sources, and online repositories and databases. Additionally, businesses must be mindful of licensing and legal considerations to ensure compliance and protect their interests; in particular many popular open datasets such as ImageNet is only available for research purposes. With the right datasets in hand, companies can harness the power of open data to drive innovation, improve decision-making, and grow their business with AI.

Data Preprocessing and Cleaning

Before utilizing open data in AI projects, it is crucial to preprocess and clean the data to ensure its quality and reliability. Data preprocessing and cleaning involve assessing data quality, applying various techniques to clean and standardize the data, transforming and normalizing data for better analysis, and ensuring data privacy and security. In this section, we will discuss these steps in detail. While this step is needed for all types of data in any AI projects, dealing with open data means you need to do a few extra steps to ensure the data is fit for purpose.

The first step is to check in a comprehensive way the quality of data is paramount to the success of AI projects. To assess it, consider the following:

- **Completeness**: The presence of all required data points. Incomplete datasets with missing values can negatively impact AI model performance. To assess completeness, determine the percentage of missing values in the dataset and identify any patterns in the missing data.

- **Consistency**: Uniformity across a dataset. Inconsistencies could arise from various data collection methods, measurement units, or data entry practices. To assess consistency, examine the dataset for discrepancies in data formats, units, or terminologies.

- **Accuracy**: The correctness of the data. Inaccurate data can produce misleading insights and incorrect AI model predictions.To assess accuracy, compare a sample of the dataset with a reliable external source or benchmark, and estimate the error rate.

After assessing data quality, employ cleaning techniques to rectify any identified issues:

- **Handle missing values** via deletion, imputation, or merging rows with similar values.

- **Remove duplicate records** that can distort analysis and impact AI model performance.

- **Correct inconsistencies** and errors through standardization and data validation.

- **Standardize** the data by transforming it into a common scale or format. Common techniques include

  - **Scaling**: Scale numerical attributes to a specific range (e.g., 0 to 1) or by standard deviations (z-score normalization) to ensure equal contribution from all attributes.

  - **One-hot encoding**: Convert categorical attributes into binary vectors to facilitate analysis and modeling.

Data transformation and normalization help to reformat data for better analysis or modeling. Techniques include

- **Log transformation**: Apply logarithmic functions to reduce the influence of outliers and manage skewed data distributions.

- **Box-Cox transformation** to stabilize data variance and normalize the data distribution. This transformation is particularly useful for datasets with non-constant variance and non-normal distributions.

- **Normalization** to ensure all attributes are on the same scale, improving the performance and convergence of machine learning algorithms. Common normalization techniques include min-max scaling, z-score normalization, and log transformation.

Ensuring Fairness, Data Privacy, and Security

When working with open data, it is essential to consider fairness, data privacy, and security. This involves protecting sensitive information, complying with data protection regulations, and mitigating potential risks associated with data breaches or misuse. To ensure data privacy and security

- **Reduce inbuilt bias**: AI models trained on historical data can unintentionally perpetuate historical systemic unfairness.[10] Ensure you test for bias in your datasets – we will go in detail in later chapters as to how to ensure fairness on AI models.

- **Anonymize and de-identify data**: Remove or mask any personally identifiable information (PII) or other sensitive data from the dataset to minimize the risk of privacy violations.

- **Data encryption**: Encrypt data at rest and in transit to protect against unauthorized access and data breaches.

- **Access control**: Implement access control measures to restrict data access to authorized users only and monitor data usage to detect and prevent potential misuse.

- **Compliance**: Ensure compliance with relevant data protection regulations, such as the General Data Protection Regulation (GDPR) or the California Consumer Privacy Act (CCPA), by obtaining necessary permissions, implementing data protection by design, and documenting data processing activities.

Data preprocessing and cleaning play a critical role in ensuring the success of AI projects that leverage open data. By assessing data quality, applying appropriate data cleaning techniques, transforming and normalizing the data, and ensuring data privacy, fairness and security, you can improve the reliability and performance of your AI models, ultimately driving value for your business. As a business executive, understanding these concepts and their importance will help you make decisions regarding data quality and the appropriate use of open data in your AI projects.

---

[10] www.theodi.org/article/using-artificial-intelligence-and-open-data-for-innovation-and-accountability/

Enhancing AI Projects with Open Data

Open data can be used to enhance AI projects in several ways. It can be used to train AI models, augment proprietary datasets, and derive new features:

- **Training AI models**: Open data can be used to train AI models by providing a diverse and comprehensive set of data. This can help create more accurate and robust AI models. For example, when training a natural language processing model, open data from sources such as Wikipedia, Project Gutenberg[11], or the Common Crawl[12] can provide a vast amount of text data that can be used to train the model on various language structures and concepts. Similarly, open datasets like ImageNet and CIFAR-10[13] can be used to train computer vision models to recognize objects and scenes.

- **Data augmentation**: Open data can be used to augment proprietary datasets, providing additional data points that can help improve the performance and generalizability of AI models. Data augmentation techniques include image transformations, text synthesis, and data synthesis, among others. For instance, in the context of computer vision, open data sources can be used to provide additional images that can be combined with proprietary images to augment the training data. This can include applying image transformations such as rotation, scaling, and flipping to create new, diverse data points.

- **Feature engineering**: Open data can be used to derive new features or enhance existing ones, providing additional insights and information that can be used by AI algorithms. For example, in the context of predicting housing prices, open data sources can provide information on crime rates, school quality, and public transportation availability, which can be used as additional features to improve the prediction accuracy of the AI model.

---

[11] www.gutenberg.org/
[12] https://commoncrawl.org/
[13] www.cs.toronto.edu/~kriz/cifar.html

When integrating open data into AI projects, it is essential to evaluate the data sources to ensure they are suitable for the specific project needs. This involves assessing the relevance, availability, and compatibility of the data.

- **Relevance to the problem domain**: The open data source should be relevant to the problem domain being addressed by the AI project. This means the data should be representative of the problem context and provide valuable information that can be used to improve the AI model's performance. For example, if the AI project aims to predict customer churn, open data sources containing customer demographics, economic indicators, or industry trends may be relevant to the project. Here, it is also useful to take into account that most of the open datasets are non-personal data.

- **Availability and timeliness**: The availability and timeliness of the open data are critical factors to consider. The data should be accessible, up-to-date, and regularly updated to ensure it remains relevant to the AI project. Additionally, the data should be available in a format that can be easily ingested and processed by the AI system.

- **Compatibility with proprietary data**: When integrating open data with proprietary data, it is essential to ensure that the data is compatible. This means the data should have similar structures, formats, and units of measurement. Data compatibility can significantly impact the effectiveness and efficiency of the AI project, as incompatible data may require extensive preprocessing and cleaning before it can be used.

Once you have identified suitable open data sources for your AI project, the next step is to combine the open data with your proprietary data. This process involves data integration strategies, handling different data formats and structures, and ensuring data privacy and security.

- **Data integration strategies**: There are several strategies for integrating open data with proprietary data, including data concatenation, data fusion, and data blending. The choice of strategy depends on the specific requirements of your AI project and the characteristics of the data sources.

- **Data concatenation**: Data concatenation involves appending open data to proprietary data, creating a larger and more diverse dataset. This strategy is particularly useful when the data sources have similar structures and formats.

- **Data fusion**: Data fusion is the process of combining data from multiple sources into a single, unified dataset. This can involve merging data based on common attributes, aggregating data at different levels of granularity, or creating new features based on relationships between the data sources.

- **Data blending**: Data blending is a technique for combining data from different sources on-the-fly, typically using data visualization tools or analytics platforms. This allows users to explore and analyze data from multiple sources without having to fully integrate the data into a single dataset.

- **Handling different data formats and structures**: When combining open data with proprietary data, it is essential to handle different data formats and structures to ensure the resulting dataset is consistent and compatible. This may involve converting data formats, restructuring data, or standardizing units of measurement.

- **Ensuring data privacy and security**: When integrating open data with proprietary data, it is crucial to ensure that data privacy and security are maintained. This may involve anonymizing personal data, encrypting sensitive information, or implementing access controls to restrict unauthorized access to the combined dataset.

In conclusion, enhancing AI projects with open data can significantly improve the performance, accuracy, and generalizability of AI models.

Limitations and Risks of Using Open Data

While open data offers numerous benefits for AI projects, it also comes with its limitations and risks. This section will discuss data quality and reliability concerns, legal and ethical considerations, potential biases and fairness issues, and dependency on external data sources, providing a balanced perspective on the use of open data in AI.

Data Quality and Reliability Concerns

One of the main concerns when using open data is the quality and reliability of the data. As open data comes from various sources, it is essential to ensure that the data is accurate, complete, and up to date to prevent the introduction of errors into AI models. Indeed, open data can be of variable quality. Some open datasets are well curated and reliable, while others may be incomplete, inaccurate, or biased. It is important to carefully evaluate the quality of any open dataset before using it:

- **Accuracy**: Open data may contain inaccuracies or errors due to human error, outdated information, or misinterpretation of data. Such inaccuracies can lead to poor model performance and incorrect predictions.

- **Completeness**: Open data sources may have missing or incomplete data, which can negatively impact the effectiveness of AI models. Incomplete data can lead to biased models or overfitting, where the model performs well on the training data but poorly on new data.

- **Timeliness**: Open data may not always be up to date, which can affect the relevance of the data for AI projects. Outdated data can result in models that are not able to adapt to current trends or capture recent changes in the environment.

Legal and Ethical Considerations

When using open data, it is essential to consider the legal and ethical implications of the data. This involves understanding the licensing terms, ensuring data privacy, and considering the potential impact of the data on different stakeholders. It is important to be aware of these concerns and to take steps to address them before using open data:

- **Licensing terms**: Open data may come with licensing terms that restrict its usage or require attribution. It is crucial to understand these terms and ensure compliance to avoid legal issues.

- **Data privacy**: Open data may contain personal or sensitive information that can lead to privacy concerns. It is vital to anonymize the data and implement data protection measures to ensure compliance with data privacy regulations, such as the General Data Protection Regulation (GDPR).

- **Ethical impact**: The use of open data in AI projects can have ethical implications, such as the potential for discrimination, unfairness, or the reinforcement of existing biases. It is essential to conduct ethical assessments and consider the broader social implications of using open data in AI.

Potential Biases and Fairness Issues

Biases in open data can lead to fairness issues in AI models, as the models may learn and reproduce these biases. This can result in discriminatory outcomes or unequal treatment of different groups. For example, open datasets that are collected by governments or corporations may reflect the biases of those institutions. It is important to be aware of these biases and to take steps to mitigate them before using open data:

- **Sampling bias**: Open data may suffer from sampling bias if the data does not accurately represent the population of interest. This can lead to AI models that perform poorly on underrepresented groups or exacerbate existing inequalities.

- **Measurement bias**: Measurement bias can occur when the data collection process systematically favors specific outcomes or groups. This can lead to biased AI models that produce inaccurate or unfair predictions.

- **Labeling bias**: Labeling bias can occur when the labels or outcomes in the data are influenced by human biases or subjective judgments. This can result in AI models that learn to replicate these biases and produce unfair predictions.

Table 13-3 provides a few examples of the many types of biases that can occur in open data. It is important to be aware of these biases and to take steps to mitigate them when using open data in AI projects.

Table 13-3. *Main biases in open datasets*

Bias	Description	Example	Potential remediation
Sampling bias	The data is not representative of the population it is intended to represent	A survey of college students is used to represent the opinions of all adults in the United States	Use a random sampling method to ensure that the data is representative of the population
Measurement bias	The data is collected in a way that introduces errors	A survey question is worded in a way that leads respondents to answer in a certain way	Use clear and unbiased language in survey questions
Labeling bias	The data is labeled incorrectly	A machine learning model is trained on a dataset of images of cats and dogs, but some of the images are mislabeled	Use a consistent and accurate labeling methodology

We will go into a lot of details on how to manage these issues in Chapter 20. In the meantime, here are some additional tips for mitigating bias in open data:

- **Use multiple data sources** to get a more complete picture of the population or phenomenon you are trying to understand.

- **Be transparent** about the data collection and analysis process so that others can evaluate the potential for bias.

- **Use statistical methods** to identify and correct for bias in the data.

- **Be aware of your own biases** and how they might influence your interpretation of the data.

Dependency on External Data Sources

Relying on open data can lead to dependency on external data sources, which can present risks in terms of data availability, changes in licensing terms, or loss of access to the data.

- **Data availability**: The availability of open data sources may be affected by factors such as changes in government policies, funding constraints, or technical issues. This can result in disruptions to AI projects that rely on these data sources for model training or validation.

- **Changes in licensing terms**: Open data sources may change their licensing terms, which can restrict or limit the use of the data for AI projects. It is essential to stay informed about any changes in licensing terms and adapt accordingly to ensure ongoing compliance.

- **Loss of access**: Access to open data sources may be lost due to factors such as changes in data-sharing policies, server downtime, or the discontinuation of a data source. This can lead to challenges in maintaining and updating AI models that rely on these data sources.

Strategies for Mitigating Limitations and Risks

To minimize the limitations and risks associated with using open data in AI projects, several strategies can be employed:

- **Data quality assessment**: Conduct regular data quality assessments to ensure the accuracy, completeness, and timeliness of open data sources. This can involve cross-validating the data with other sources, using data validation techniques, and monitoring data updates.

- **Legal and ethical compliance**: Ensure compliance with licensing terms, data privacy regulations, and ethical guidelines when using open data. This can involve developing internal policies and procedures for data usage, conducting regular compliance audits, and staying informed about changes in regulations and licensing terms.

- **Bias detection and mitigation**: Implement bias detection and mitigation techniques to address potential biases and fairness issues in open data. This can involve using statistical techniques to identify biases, developing fairness metrics to evaluate AI models, and applying debiasing techniques to correct for biases in the data.

- **Diversification of data sources**: Diversify the sources of open data used in AI projects to minimize dependency on external data sources. This can involve combining multiple data sources, using data integration techniques, and exploring alternative data sources to ensure a robust and resilient data strategy. The use of open data can make a project dependent on external data sources. If an external data source becomes unavailable or changes its format, it can disrupt the project. It is important to have a plan for dealing with these disruptions before using open data

Key Takeaways

Despite the limitations and risks associated with using open data, it remains a valuable resource for AI projects, providing access to diverse, large-scale, and cost-effective data. By understanding the potential challenges, applying appropriate mitigation strategies, and adopting a first principles approach to open data utilization, businesses can harness the power of open data to drive AI innovation and growth.

1. **Takeaway 1: Open data can have an important role in growing your company with AI**. Open data can play a crucial role in growing your company with AI by providing access to diverse and large-scale datasets, enabling data-driven decision-making, and fostering innovation.

   a. **Do's**:

      i. Seek out diverse and relevant open data sources to improve AI model performance.

      ii. Utilize open data to explore innovative solutions and applications.

      iii. Use open data to augment proprietary data and enhance feature engineering.

    b. **Don'ts:**

      i. Rely solely on proprietary data, as it may limit your AI models' potential.

      ii. Ignore the potential of open data for driving innovation and growth.

2. **Takeaway 2: First Principles approach to open data utilization**. Adopting a first principles approach to open data utilization involves understanding the underlying challenges, questioning assumptions, and devising creative strategies to maximize the value of open data in AI projects.

    a. **Do's:**

      i. Challenge assumptions about the value and relevance of open data sources.

      ii. Investigate the underlying challenges and limitations associated with open data.

      iii. Devise creative strategies to maximize the value of open data in AI projects.

    b. **Don'ts:**

      i. Rely on preconceived notions or assumptions about open data without proper investigation.

      ii. Dismiss open data sources without considering their potential benefits and applications.

3. **Takeaway 3: Continuously evaluating and updating your open data strategy**. This involves staying informed about new open data sources, monitoring changes in licensing terms and regulations, and adapting to emerging trends and technologies.

    a. **Do's:**

      i. Regularly evaluate the relevance and value of open data sources in your AI projects.

    ii. Stay informed about changes in licensing terms, regulations, and emerging trends.

    iii. Adapt your open data strategy to the evolving needs of your AI projects and business objectives.

b. **Don'ts**:

    i. Assume that an open data strategy will remain static or become outdated.

    ii. Neglect to monitor changes in the open data landscape that could impact your AI projects.

In this chapter, we have provided a comprehensive understanding of open data, its benefits, and limitations, and how it can be utilized in a commercial environment for AI. As we have seen, open data is a critical component for businesses seeking to grow their AI capabilities. Remember to stay informed about changes in the open data ecosystem and adapt your strategies accordingly to maintain a competitive edge in the AI-driven world.

PART IV

The HOW

CHAPTER 14

Organization and Governance

In the era of digital transformation, artificial intelligence (AI) has emerged as a critical tool in driving innovation, enhancing competitiveness, and improving efficiency across industries. The adoption of AI, however, is not just about employing the right technology, but also about assembling the right team and establishing robust governance structures. This sets the stage for our discussion about the significance of structured AI teams and the role of governance in successful AI implementation.

As we saw in Chapter 4, many of the barriers to implementing AI are related to the teams being involved rather than the actual technology. This is the reason why this chapter is so important – it is not enough just to hire a few new data scientists and acquire some licenses for some trendy AI/MLOps software, the right governance and team structure are critical, they will be different for each company, and they would also have to evolve as the company AI maturity evolves over time.

I have seen the terms sometimes confused, so it is worth going into the details. Having a strong governance does not necessarily provide the right organization and the other way round.

Note Governance provides the rules and guidelines for AI usage, ensuring it is responsible, ethical, compliant, and effective. Organization, on the other hand, is about the practical setup of teams and resources to get the AI project done, including live operation, efficiently and effectively. Both are critical for successful AI implementation.

© Francisco Javier Campos Zabala 2023
F. J. Campos Zabala, *Grow Your Business with AI*, https://doi.org/10.1007/978-1-4842-9669-1_14

Governance in the context of AI projects typically refers to the framework, rules, policies, and procedures that are in place to manage the development, deployment, use, and monitoring of AI systems. These can include elements such as

- **Data governance**: Establishing rules for data collection, storage, access, and usage to foster privacy, security, ethics, and compliance with legal norms.

- **Model governance**: This includes processes for model development, validation, deployment, and maintenance.

- **Ethical governance**: This includes ensuring that AI is used responsibly and ethically, considering bias, fairness, transparency, and accountability.

- **Risk management**: Identifying and managing risks related to AI use, such as cybersecurity threats, misuse of AI, etc.

On the other hand, the organization in the context of AI projects typically refers to the way teams and resources are structured and managed to successfully execute the project. This can include factors like

- **Team structure**: This refers to roles and responsibilities within the project team. Who are the data scientists, engineers, project managers, etc., and what are their responsibilities?

- **Collaboration**: How are teams or individuals collaborating? What systems and tools are in place to facilitate this?

- **Resource allocation**: This includes how resources like time, budget, and personnel are allocated across different tasks or parts of the project.

- **Project management**: This includes the processes and methodologies used to manage the project, such as agile or waterfall methods.

The rise of AI projects in business has led to the creation of new roles and teams, such as data scientists, machine learning engineers, AI product managers, and data engineers, among others. These roles are crucial to the design, development, deployment, and management of AI projects. However, the effectiveness of these teams is contingent on having a clear organizational structure.

A well-structured team fosters collaboration, efficiency, and innovation. A 2020 McKinsey[1] survey revealed that companies with clear AI team structures were twice as likely to report significant benefits from AI adoption than those with ad hoc or no AI team structure.

Similarly, governance plays an equally crucial role in AI projects. Governance provides a framework for decision-making, guiding the development and management of AI projects, ensuring ethical and legal compliance, and facilitating transparency and accountability.

A 2021 Deloitte study[2] found that companies with an enterprise-wide AI strategy and leadership who communicate a bold vision are nearly 1.5 times more likely to achieve high outcomes (Table 14-1).

Table 14-1. *The impact of structure and governance on AI success*

Factor	Impact on AI success	Key data points
Structured AI teams	Promotes collaboration, efficiency, and innovation	Companies with clear AI team structures were twice as likely to report significant benefits from AI adoption (McKinsey, 2020)
AI governance	Guides decision-making, ensures ethical and legal compliance, facilitates transparency and accountability	Companies with effective AI governance were 1.5 times more likely to be "high-performing companies" (Deloitte, 2021)

In conclusion, effective organization and governance are not ancillary considerations but are fundamental to the successful implementation of AI projects. The next sections of this chapter will delve deeper into the specifics of organizing AI teams and establishing an AI governance framework, aiming to provide you with a blueprint for building a robust and productive AI culture in your organization. As we progress, we will further explore these concepts through concrete examples and real-world case studies, ensuring a practical understanding of these critical areas.

---

[1] https://www.mckinsey.com/capabilities/quantumblack/our-insights/global-survey-the-state-of-ai-in-2020

[2] https://www2.deloitte.com/us/en/pages/about-deloitte/articles/press-releases/deloitte-state-of-ai-fourth-edition-report.html

Organization in AI Teams

The growth of AI in the business sector necessitates teams specialized in data science, machine learning, and AI product management, among other roles. The organization of these teams and understanding their roles and responsibilities is vital to the success of any AI project.

Organizing AI teams effectively is a crucial aspect of implementing AI in a company. In this subsection, we will discuss the benefits and drawbacks of various team structures, provide recommendations for effective communication and collaboration, and emphasize the importance of cross-functional teams to drive business value.

Understanding the Key Roles

In most organizations, an AI team comprises four key roles:

- **Data scientists**: They create predictive models, develop machine learning algorithms, and perform statistical analysis. They use data to provide business insights and recommendations.

- **Machine learning engineers**: They focus on coding and deploying the models that data scientists create into production environments. Their work is more software-oriented than data scientists. A particular role here is the **MLOps engineer** – we expand on those later on.

- **AI product managers**: They act as a bridge between the AI team and the rest of the business. They manage the AI product roadmap, prioritize features, and ensure that the AI team's work aligns with business objectives.

- **Data engineers**: They are responsible for building and maintaining the data infrastructure. They ensure data is collected, stored, and prepared for use by data scientists and machine learning engineers.

The Role of a Data Scientist

Data scientists play crucial roles in AI teams, and the specifics of these roles can vary significantly depending on the context and needs of the organization. Broadly, we can categorize data scientist roles into two types: research and development (R&D) focused and applied.

R&D data scientists are typically found in academic settings or large tech companies with substantial research divisions. Their work often involves developing novel algorithms or enhancing existing ones, pushing the boundaries of what's possible in machine learning and AI.

In contrast, applied data scientists are typically more focused on utilizing existing algorithms to solve real-world problems. They deploy models to extract insights from data, make predictions, automate decisions, or build intelligent applications. The vast majority of data science roles in industry fall into this latter category.

Nevertheless, many companies get confused, and sometimes they recruit as if they were to develop new algorithms, but then demand from data science teams' immediate returns. A good analogy is explained by Cassie Kozyrkov, Google's Chief Decision Scientist, in her article "Why businesses fail at machine learning"[3].

This does not mean that applied data scientists are merely applying algorithms developed by others without any understanding. Instead, it's like a chef using a microwave. The chef does not need to know the intricate details of how the microwave was built, but they do need to understand how to use it effectively, such as how to adjust the power levels, timing, and other settings to cook food properly.

Similarly, while applied data scientists might not be developing groundbreaking machine learning algorithms from scratch, they need to know how to properly use, adjust, and evaluate these algorithms, ensuring they are effectively applied to solve business problems.

Lastly, it's important to note that building a proficient data science team can be quite challenging. Not only is there a high demand for skilled data scientists, but there's also a surprising number of professionals in the field who have never put models into production. This gap in experience can make it difficult to find data scientists who

---

[3] https://kozyrkov.medium.com/why-businesses-fail-at-machine-learning-fbff41c4d5db

are not only adept at building models but also at deploying them, monitoring their performance, and iterating on them in a real-world environment. Therefore, when building a data science team, it's important to look for experience with all stages of the data science lifecycle, not just model development.

Structuring Your AI Teams

When it comes to structuring your AI teams, companies generally opt for either a centralized or decentralized model, or a hybrid of the two. In a centralized model, all AI initiatives are led by a single, core team. In a decentralized model, each department or business unit has its own AI team.

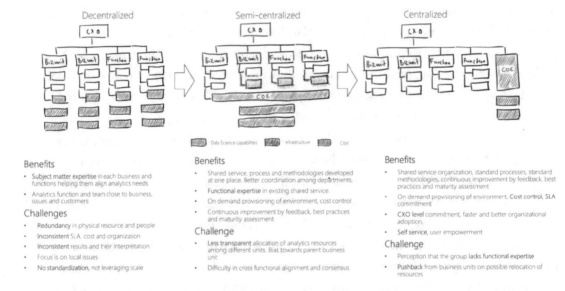

Figure 14-1. *Different organizational structures for AI/data science capabilities[4]*

As we can see in Figure 14-1, the AI organization can be grouped into three main types: centralized, decentralized, and hybrid team (also called semi-centralized, or "Hub-Spokes") structures. Different team structures offer varying advantages and challenges:

1. **A centralized structure** involves placing all data science, machine learning, and AI product manager teams together under a single organizational unit. This structure fosters knowledge

sharing, collaboration, and efficient allocation of resources. However, it can also lead to a lack of understanding of specific business units' needs and may slow down decision-making. As we will see in the Scaling AI chapter, this is recommended for companies starting on the AI journey.

2. **A decentralized structure** distributes these teams across different business units, allowing them to work closely with domain experts and gain a better understanding of specific business requirements. However, this structure can lead to inefficiencies in resource allocation and potential duplication of efforts.

3. **A hybrid structure** combines the benefits of both centralized and decentralized structures by maintaining a central AI center of excellence while embedding data scientists, machine learning experts, and AI product managers within individual business units. This approach ensures effective resource allocation, knowledge sharing, and alignment with specific business needs.

Effective communication and collaboration is crucial to establish strong communication channels between technical and non-technical teams to ensure the success of AI initiatives. Encouraging regular meetings, sharing project updates, and providing training sessions can help bridge the gap between different team members. Moreover, using collaboration tools and platforms can facilitate information sharing, streamline project management, and improve overall team productivity.

Cross-functional teams that include data scientists, engineers, and AI product managers are essential for fostering innovation and driving business value. These teams allow for diverse perspectives and expertise to be brought together, leading to more effective problem-solving and decision-making. Furthermore, cross-functional teams can help ensure that AI projects are aligned with overall business objectives and address the specific needs of different stakeholders. Figure 14-2 shows a comparison of the centralised vs distributed Team locations.

---

[4] (PDF) The Road to Enterprise Artificial Intelligence: A Case Studies Driven Exploration (researchgate.net)

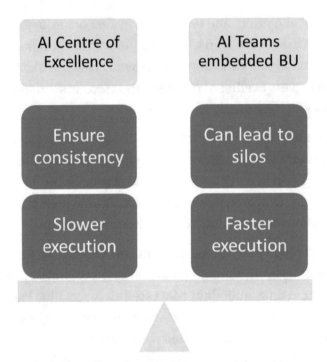

Figure 14-2. *Where to locate AI team – centralized vs distributed*

The choice between these models depends on various factors, including the size of your organization, the scale of your AI initiatives, and your organization's culture. We will explore further these options in Chapter 21.

AI Centers of Excellence: Resources and Hybrid Structures

While the best structure will vary depending on many aspects for each company, a structure which is highly recommended for companies in the lower and middle ladders of the maturity model is an AI Center of Excellence (AI CoE) and a hybrid version for more mature companies.

AI Centers of Excellence (CoE) play a vital role in driving the success of AI initiatives within organizations. In this subsection, we will discuss the purpose and benefits of AI CoE, provide guidance on centralizing resources, and explain how to set up hybrid structures that combine the best of centralized and decentralized approaches.

1. **Purpose and benefits of AI Centers of Excellence**: AI CoE serves as a hub for knowledge sharing, skill development, and the promotion of best practices in AI implementation. By establishing a CoE, organizations can

a. Foster collaboration between data scientists, machine learning experts, and AI product managers.

b. Facilitate training and skill development to ensure that teams remain up-to-date with the latest AI technologies and methodologies.

c. Establish and maintain standardized processes, tools, and infrastructure, which can accelerate the development and deployment of AI solutions.

d. Support the evaluation and selection of AI projects, ensuring alignment with business objectives and maximizing return on investment.

2. **Centralizing resources for maximum effectiveness**: A key aspect of a successful AI CoE is the centralization of resources, including talent, tools, and infrastructure. By centralizing resources, organizations can

a. Ensure that AI projects have access to the necessary expertise and support, regardless of their location within the organization.

b. For instance, an organization can have one Chief Science Officer shared across the key projects, rather than each business unit having their own one.

c. Streamline the procurement and management of AI tools and infrastructure, reducing costs and promoting consistency across projects.

d. Facilitate collaboration between teams and reduce duplication of efforts, leading to more efficient use of resources and faster delivery of AI solutions.

e. Recruitment: Talent attraction. In a highly competitive market as data science, a larger team with more career opportunities for the AI team is a competitive advantage attracting the top talent.

3. **Hybrid structures**: Combining centralized and decentralized approaches, hybrid structures can help organizations balance the need for centralized resources and support with the benefits of embedding AI expertise within individual business units. This is also specially recommended as an organization's AI maturity level starts increasing, so by deployment of AI resources to the business units, the agility is improved. To set up a hybrid structure

a. Maintain a strong central AI CoE responsible for providing resources, training, and best practices.

b. Embed data scientists, machine learning experts, and AI product managers within individual business units, allowing them to work closely with domain experts and address specific business needs.

c. Establish clear communication channels between the central CoE and embedded teams, ensuring ongoing collaboration and knowledge sharing.

In an article concerning organizational AI, Harvard Business Review[5] presented an organizational blueprint for analytics personnel, centered around consolidated "hubs" and "spokes" embedded within each business sector. The "hub" (or in the language used above, the AI CoE) ensures a consistent approach to AI, overseeing tools, recruitment, overarching strategy, and infrastructure. The "spokes" bring accountability and sensitivity to the unique needs and capabilities of individual business units. The degree to which an analytics function is integrated will depend on each organization's context, but I have seen the combined "hub and spokes" architecture to be notably effective.

The advantages of a hybrid structure are manifold for many organizations, especially in company or medium to large size. The hub (AI CoE) serves as a command center for organizational exploration, where decisions about common operational frameworks and infrastructure are made. The spokes, on the other hand, act as analytics advocates within product or business lines, adjusting the core strategy based on context. They instill accountability and business savvy. Moreover, the spokes function as the organization's AI readiness indicators, staying attuned to when and where their specific business unit requires support. Bridging the gaps between the hubs and spokes are forward deployment engineers, who are prepared to undertake projects as needed.

AI Centers of Excellence (or Hubs in HBR terminology) play a crucial role in driving the success of AI initiatives. By establishing a CoE, centralizing resources, and adopting a hybrid structure, organizations can ensure that they have the necessary support and expertise in place to effectively implement AI solutions and drive business value.

---

[5] https://hbr.org/2019/07/building-the-ai-powered-organization

Best Practices for Organizing Data Science and Machine Learning Teams

Best practices for organizing these teams include (see Table 14-2).

- **Clear role definition**: Each team member should have a clear understanding of their role and responsibilities. This eliminates confusion and optimizes efficiency.

- **Efficient collaboration**: Promote regular communication and collaboration among team members. This can be done through regular meetings, collaborative tools, and team-building activities.

- **Continual learning**: Encourage team members to continually learn and update their skills. This could be through workshops, training sessions, or providing access to the latest research and publications.

- **Balancing research and applied work**: While it's important for the team to keep up with the latest AI research, there should be a balance with applying that research to the company's products or projects.

The AI product manager is a linchpin role, coordinating the work of the data science and machine learning teams. They ensure that the technical aspects align with business objectives. They also communicate the capabilities and limitations of AI models to stakeholders, manage the AI product roadmap, and prioritize features based on business needs and resources.

Table 14-2. Roles and best practices for organizing AI teams

Role	Description	Best practices
Data scientist	Create predictive models, develop machine learning algorithms, perform statistical analysis	Encourage continual learning, balance between research and applied work
Machine learning engineer	Code and deploy models into production environments	Encourage continual learning, efficient collaboration
AI product manager	Bridge between AI team and business, manage AI product roadmap	Clear role definition, efficient communication with stakeholders
Data engineer	Build and maintain data infrastructure	Encourage continual learning, efficient collaboration

Assembling High Performance Teams

This is a very challenging task but one that will bring very high returns. The first point to notice is that there are plenty of books and "gurus" claiming to have the secret to do this. However, when you look at their methodology, most would focus looking only at the example of successful teams, analyze what they have/do, and then establish a causal relationship between what these successful teams have/do and how to be successful. The attentive reader would notice a few challenges in this approach from the data science point of view:

- **The "survival bias"** (remember the WWII plane from Chapter 7?): You need to include in your sample both successful and, more importantly, unsuccessful samples.

- **Confusing correlation with causation:** Just because two variables happen at the same time, it does not mean that one causes the other. While opening times for swimming pools and ice scream sales are highly correlated, if you start opening longer hours the pools in winter, it will not increase your ice scream sales (there is a hidden confounding variable, temperature, who is the one with the causal relationship). I explored causality in Chapters 8 and 9.

- Finally, a combination of the two above, failing to recognize that many factors are totally outside the team's individual control, such as environment (upbringing, social connections, industry dynamics, etc.) and serendipity or luck.

Having made this point about "success frameworks," I will list a few of factors that I have seen can make the difference between success and failure. Being involved in large scale new technology projects during my career, I have seen plenty of failure. Early in my career, most failures were due to immature technology, but in the last few years, the main issue is related to human factors, rather than technology. Therefore, I would be clear that following all these points will not guarantee necessary success; however, you would increase your success chances substantially:

1. **Hire the best team for your problem**: It is important to understand here that the same team that will be great for a given problem in an organization with a certain culture could perform very badly in another. Here a few tips:

    a. My personal recommendation is to hire attitude over skills.

    b. Make sure you build a balanced team, from the personalities, skillset, and diverse points of view. Each role offers a unique perspective and skill set that contributes to the success of the project.

    c. Look for relevant experience: While education and theoretical understanding are important, practical experience in developing and deploying AI models in a similar context is invaluable. Look for team members who have experience with the tools, platforms, and types of data you will be working with.

    d. Be realistic based on your available budget, current industry talent pool and your specific organization objectives. If you try to follow the Amazon way to hire data scientists, the chances are it will not be right for you – even if you manage to throw enough budget to secure the talent.

2. **Define clear goals and objectives – both internally to the team and the wider organization**: An important step in assembling a high-performance AI team is to define clear goals and objectives for the project and individual team members. These goals will guide your hiring decisions and help you identify the skills and

expertise you need in your team. Set realistic expectations: AI projects can be complex and challenging, and they often involve some degree of uncertainty. Set realistic expectations and be prepared for setbacks or changes in direction.

3. **Foster a collaborative and high-achieving environment**: High-performing AI teams often have a culture of collaboration and open communication. Foster this environment by encouraging team members to share ideas, ask questions, and work together to solve problems.

4. **Use agile project management**: Agile project management methods can be particularly effective for managing AI projects. They allow for flexibility, continuous improvement, and frequent reassessment of project direction based on new insights or changes in the business environment. We will see in Chapter 15 how to use agile for AI teams.

5. **Invest in the right tools and infrastructure**: Having the right tools and infrastructure in place can significantly improve the productivity and effectiveness of your AI team. This includes data storage and processing infrastructure, AI development platforms, and collaboration tools.

Size Matters

How big your AI teams should be? Well, the attentive reader would guess the answer is "it depends." The size of an AI team should be based on the needs of the company. A small team may be sufficient for a company that is just starting out with AI, while a larger team may be needed for a company that is already using AI in a significant way. As the company grows, the AI team may need to grow as well. This is because the company will have more data and more complex problems to solve. We will see more about this factor in Chapter 21.

There are a few factors to consider when deciding when to split teams or add middle management. One factor is the size of the team. If the team is too large, it may be difficult for everyone to communicate effectively. Another factor is the complexity of the work. If the work is very complex, it may be helpful to have a team leader who can help to coordinate the work and make decisions.

Communication is key to the success of any AI team. If team members are not able to communicate effectively, it will be difficult for them to work together and achieve their goals. The "pizza team size" is a rule of thumb that suggests that a team should be no larger than the number of people who can eat a pizza together. This is because it is easier for people to communicate and collaborate when they are in a smaller group.

Here are some signs that it may be time to split teams or add middle management:

- The team is too large.

- The work is too complex.

- Team members are not able to communicate effectively.

Having a well-organized AI team with clearly defined roles and a productive collaborative environment is crucial to the success of your AI initiatives. Up next, we will delve into creating an effective AI governance framework to guide your AI projects to success.

AI Governance Framework

As AI continues to become integral to business operations, it has become increasingly evident that there's a need for a comprehensive governance framework to guide AI initiatives. This governance not only ensures that AI projects align with business objectives but also guarantees compliance with ethical and legal standards.

Tip   Exercise caution to avoid the adoption of general governance models, opting instead for a model distinctly tailored to your business and industry. To establish a robust AI governance framework, it's vital to be precise in setting your overarching objectives. This involves clearly defining and reaching consensus on business goals, including risk appetite versus opportunity. For instance, compliance and legal considerations are indispensable, especially in regulated industries. Following that, priorities should be arranged according to each company's specific needs, such as security, business agility, and so forth.

In this section, we will explore the critical components of an effective AI governance model, strategies for creating meaningful KPIs, and how to foster a culture that embraces AI.

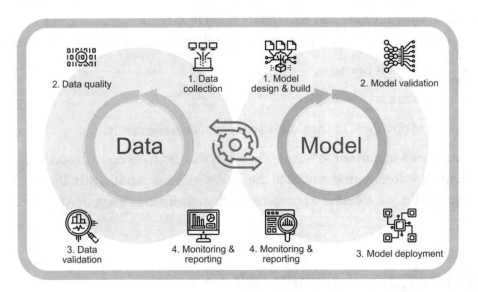

Figure 14-3. *AI governance model. Source: AIPP Bank Of England/FCA 2022 AI report*

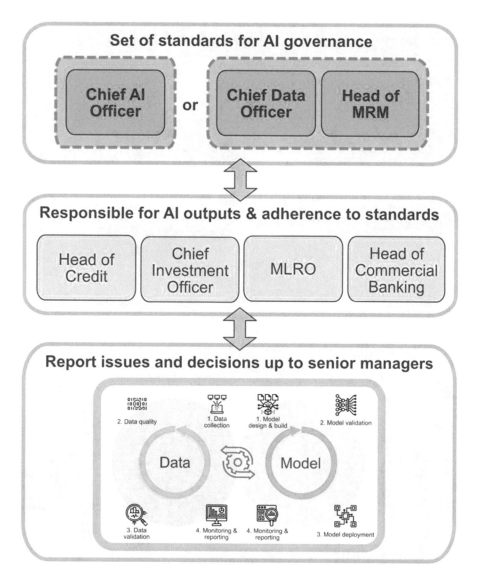

Figure 14-4. *AI governance model. Source: AIPP Bank Of England/FCA 2022 AI report*

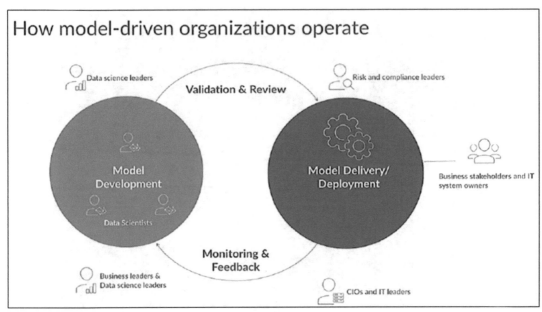

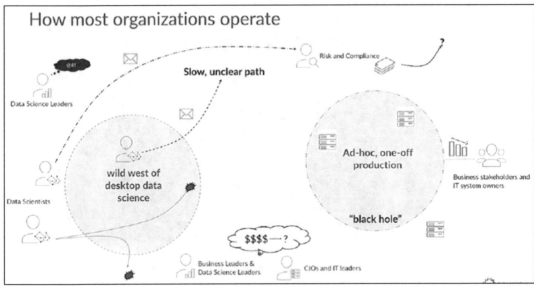

Figure 14-5. *Ideal vs. common state of organizational data science*[6]

---

[6] (PDF) The Road to Enterprise Artificial Intelligence: A Case Studies Driven Exploration (researchgate.net)

An AI governance framework serves as a blueprint for managing and overseeing all AI activities within the organization. It is a multidimensional structure, covering areas like data governance, model governance, and ethical considerations. Figures 14-3 and 14-4 explained the recommended AI governance from the AIPP – this methodology was developed following a working group from industry, led by the Bank of England and the Financial Conduct Authority.[7]

Figure 14-5 explained why it is so important to have the right governance. You can see on the left-hand side how many organizations are approaching AI at the model, in ad-hoc way with very mixed results and a high failure rate.

The first important part of AI governance is data. Many AI surveys have found that organizations with a well-defined data strategy have successfully established the primary foundations for an AI effective implementation. Think of data as the vital sustenance for your intelligent organization, and a well-rounded, nourishing meal as the ideal choice. Table 14-3 outlines the elements that constitute an effective framework for AI governance.

Data governance encompasses an array of activities throughout the value chain; this involves delineating where and what data is collected within the organization, identifying its custodians, understanding its storage methods, and ensuring its accessibility via pipelines. Furthermore, guaranteeing *high-quality data* – characterized by richness and structure – is equally as crucial as the data's volume. This component of the framework pertains to the management and use of data. It covers data privacy, data quality, data integration, and data lifecycle management. These policies ensure that data used in AI models are not only legally compliant but also of high quality and reliable.

The second part of AI governance is **model governance**: model governance focuses on the lifecycle of AI models. This includes model development, validation, deployment, monitoring, and retirement. It ensures that models are robust, reliable, transparent, and that they can be trusted to make consistent, fair, and unbiased decisions.

Last, but not least, a growing important part of AI governance is **ethical guidelines**: AI should be used responsibly and ethically. This means that AI models should be fair, transparent, explainable, and they should respect privacy and human rights. A strong AI governance framework will contain guidelines to ensure that AI initiatives align with these principles.

---

[7] https://www.bankofengland.co.uk/research/fintech/ai-public-private-forum/

Table 14-3. *Components of an effective AI governance framework*

Component	Description
Data governance	Policies and procedures for managing and using data
Model governance	Oversight of the AI model lifecycle
Ethical guidelines	Principles to ensure that AI is used responsibly and ethically

A very important part of governance is to have a way to measure how effective it is. Here, Key Performance Indicators (KPIs) are a vital tool for monitoring the performance and success of AI initiatives. They help measure the progress toward business goals, and they can be used to benchmark and compare performance over time or against competitors. However, creating effective KPIs for AI initiatives can be challenging due to the complex and dynamic nature of AI. We discussed in Chapter 12 the best metrics for AI projects and operations.

It is also critical to cultivate a productive AI culture, a cornerstone of successful AI implementation. A positive AI culture can accelerate AI adoption, promote collaboration, enhance innovation, and boost morale among team members. Key strategies to build a productive AI culture include

- **Promoting collaboration**: Encourage team members to work together on AI projects. Collaboration can foster creativity, speed up problem-solving, and lead to more robust AI models.

- **Emphasizing transparency**: Be clear about what AI can and cannot do, how AI decisions are made, and the data used to train AI models. Transparency builds trust and helps manage expectations.

- **Encouraging ethical AI practices**: Make ethics a priority in all AI activities. This includes respecting privacy, being transparent, and promoting fairness and accountability.

- **Fostering continual learning**: AI is a rapidly evolving field. Encourage team members to stay up-to-date with the latest AI trends, tools, and best practices.

- **Accepting failure**: Not all AI projects will be successful. It's essential to view failures as learning opportunities and not as reasons for discouragement.

A comprehensive AI governance framework is an essential tool for guiding your AI initiatives to success. By implementing effective data and model governance, aligning AI activities with ethical guidelines, establishing meaningful KPIs, and cultivating a productive AI culture, you will be well on your way to reaping the benefits of AI. In the next section, we will explore real-world case studies of successful AI organization and governance.

Case Studies of Successful AI Organization and Governance

Examining real-world examples of successful AI organization and governance can provide us with invaluable insights. These case studies can offer lessons learned, best practices, and strategies to emulate. In this section, we will explore two companies that have excelled in implementing effective AI governance and organization – Google and IBM.

Google: AI-First Approach and Ethical AI Practices

Google has long been a leader in AI, adopting an AI-first approach to many of its products and services. This has demanded a thoughtful approach to organizing AI teams and creating effective governance frameworks.

Google's AI teams are organized around their product areas such as Search, Ads, Cloud, and YouTube, allowing for close collaboration between the product, data science, and machine learning teams. This structure ensures that AI efforts are directly aligned with product goals and user needs. As well as AI team deployed to their business units, Google also had two main research teams, Deepmind and Brain Google. It is worth noting that both teams have been instrumental in the advancement of AI, and they should get a lot of credit as they have released to the wider community as Open Source both tools (e.g., Tensorflow) and also algorithms (e.g., Transformers, at the heart of the current generation of large language models such a ChatGPT). Nevertheless, Google in April 2023 merged their research teams,[8] creating Google DeepMind, out of DeepMind and the Brain team from Google Research.

In terms of governance, Google has developed an internal AI Principles Board[9], which reviews new projects, products, and deals to ensure they align with their published AI Principles. This includes considerations of fairness, transparency, privacy, and safety.

IBM: Centralized AI Team and Trusted AI Framework

IBM is another notable example of a company that has successfully organized and governed its AI initiatives. They have taken a centralized approach to AI, forming a specific business unit, IBM Watson, dedicated to developing and implementing AI technologies.

This centralized model provides multiple advantages, including fostering a culture of AI expertise and facilitating resource sharing. Moreover, it simplifies governance as there's a single point of responsibility for AI initiatives.

IBM has also established a robust AI governance framework, known as "Trusted AI." This framework focuses on three pillars – transparency, explainability, and fairness. It provides guidelines for the lifecycle of AI models, from data collection to model development, validation, and deployment. This includes a robust model review process and stringent data privacy and security measures.

Both Google and IBM demonstrate how an effective AI organization and governance strategy can lead to successful AI implementation. While they have adopted different team structures, they share common themes in their governance approaches, emphasizing transparency, fairness, and alignment with business and user needs.

These case studies highlight the importance of

- Having clear structures and roles for AI teams, tailored to your organization's specific needs and objectives.

---

[8] https://blog.google/technology/ai/april-ai-update/
[9] https://ai.google/static/documents/ai-principles-2022-progress-update.pdf

- Creating a robust AI governance framework, providing guidelines for data usage, model lifecycle, and ethical considerations.

- Fostering a culture that embraces AI, promoting collaboration, continual learning, and ethical AI practices.

As AI continues to evolve, so will the best practices for AI organization and governance. It's essential for organizations to remain agile, continually reassessing and refining their strategies to ensure they are harnessing the power of AI effectively, ethically, and responsibly.

Key Takeaways

As we reach the conclusion of this chapter, it is important to recap the integral aspects of AI organization and governance. The significance of a strategic approach to organizing AI teams and governing AI projects has been underlined throughout. In the current business landscape, where AI has a transformative role, its efficient and ethical implementation demands careful consideration of organizational structure and robust governance mechanisms. This chapter has outlined steps to create an effective organizational framework, develop a comprehensive AI governance system, and foster a productive AI culture.

Let's summarize the key takeaways from the chapter:

1. **Takeaway 1: Strategic organization of AI teams**. The importance of understanding the roles within AI teams, including data scientists, machine learning engineers, AI product managers, and data engineers, cannot be understated. We discussed the merits of different organizational structures – centralized, decentralized, and hybrid – and the need to align these with your company's objectives.

   a. **Do**: Clearly define roles within the AI teams and ensure a cross-functional collaboration mechanism is in place. Google's product area-focused AI teams are a good example here.

   b. **Don't**: Avoid siloed working and ensure AI efforts are directly aligned with broader business goals.

2. **Takeaway 2: Comprehensive AI governance framework**.
   Implementing an AI governance framework that covers data
   governance, model governance, and ethical guidelines is crucial.
   We discussed the importance of defining KPIs to measure AI
   success and align teams.

   a. **Do**: Establish clear governance mechanisms like Google's AI Principles
      Board or IBM's Trusted AI framework that promotes transparency,
      explainability, and fairness.

   b. **Don't**: Neglect ethical considerations in your AI framework. Be aware of
      potential biases in data or models and incorporate mitigation strategies in
      your framework.

3. **Takeaway 3: Building a productive AI culture**. We emphasized
   the role of an AI culture that fosters collaboration, promotes
   continual learning, accepts failure as part of the AI development
   process, and encourages ethical AI practices.

   a. **Do**: Create an environment that supports learning and collaboration.
      IBM's centralized AI team, IBM Watson, is an example of how to cultivate a
      culture of AI expertise.

   b. **Don't**: Discourage risk-taking or penalize failure; AI development often
      involves experimentation and learning from failure.

In summary, these best practices, supported by the case studies of Google and
IBM, demonstrate that effective organization and governance are not just vital for
AI projects but can determine their success or failure. While the journey may be
complex, by adopting these guidelines and constantly iterating on your approach,
you can significantly increase the likelihood of successful AI implementation in your
organization. As we continue to explore the vast landscape of AI in business, remember
that the success of AI does not just lie in technology but in the people and processes that
support it.

CHAPTER 15

Mastering AI Projects: Assemble, Lead, and Succeed

Welcome to this chapter on "Mastering AI Projects: Assemble, Lead, and Succeed." Artificial intelligence (AI) holds transformative potential for businesses across various sectors. However, tapping into this potential requires several crucial steps: from identifying the right AI use cases that align with your company's objectives to assembling and leading a multidisciplinary AI team. These steps will form the bedrock of your AI strategy.

Identifying the right AI use cases starts with understanding your company's objectives and potential areas for impact. Consider the tasks and processes in your organization that could be improved by automation or prediction, keeping a sharp focus on the data that you can realistically obtain and analyze. This brings us to the data monetization framework we discussed at length in Chapter 7, which emphasizes value discovery. Value discovery seeks to uncover new revenue opportunities by leveraging data. This can range from improving operations and creating new customer experiences to transforming business models entirely.

Once we have identified suitable AI use cases, we need the right team to bring these to fruition. This team should ideally include an AI product manager to oversee project development and strategy, data scientists and machine learning engineers to build and deploy models, and IT infrastructure support to handle data storage and processing needs.

A key consideration in team formation is diversity – in skills, perspectives, and backgrounds. A multidisciplinary team can offer rich insights and foster innovative solutions. However, such teams often involve members from different organizational

F. J. Campos Zabala, *Grow Your Business with AI*, https://doi.org/10.1007/978-1-4842-9669-1_15

units. This diversity can be a double-edged sword, potentially leading to differences in objectives and rewards structures. Clear communication of team goals and alignment of incentives can help manage this challenge.

The role of leadership in such a team cannot be overstated. Leaders guide the team, make critical decisions, and promote a culture of learning and adaptability – an essential trait in the fast-paced world of AI. At times, especially in larger organizations or more complex projects, a chief scientist may be required. This role provides strategic leadership, oversees research and development, and fosters a culture of innovation.

Next, we delve into the realm of data science and machine learning teams. Establishing clear objectives, ensuring collaboration between data scientists and engineers, and learning from both success stories and projects that did not quite hit the mark are all vital for building effective teams.

Lastly, we explore how Agile principles can be applied to data science, a methodology that emphasizes collaboration, flexibility, and customer centricity. Agile can be an effective approach for managing AI projects, which often involve complex and rapidly evolving requirements.

This chapter is designed to serve as a practical guide, offering you tangible methods, insights, and case studies to help navigate your AI journey. Let's delve in.

How to Identify AI Use Cases

Identifying effective AI use cases is one of the most crucial steps on your AI journey. The key is to identify opportunities that align with your company's objectives and have a high potential for impact. You would need to use a framework to systematically address all the potential value your company has, I recommend the AI Data Framework we discussed in Chapter 7, but others might also be suitable. The data monetization framework is an invaluable tool for identifying and prioritizing potential AI use cases. This framework directs you to focus on the discovery of value, which involves finding ways to generate profit or gain other business advantages from your available data. Identifying AI use cases begins with understanding your company's objectives and pain points. By assessing these factors, you can pinpoint areas where AI can create value and improve your organization's performance. To prioritize use cases, consider their potential impact, feasibility, and alignment with your company's strategy. Studying success stories in your industry can provide valuable insights into the potential applications of AI.

Start by examining your company's mission and vision statements, as well as its short-term and long-term strategic goals. Consider how AI can contribute to achieving these objectives. For example, if your company aims to improve customer satisfaction, AI-powered chatbots could help streamline customer service and provide quicker, more accurate responses.

Next, evaluate the pain points and inefficiencies within your organization. These could be areas where manual processes are time-consuming, error-prone, or costly. AI can automate repetitive tasks, optimize complex processes, and facilitate better decision-making. Examples of AI use cases that address pain points include

- **Automating repetitive tasks** to free up employee time for higher-value work.

- **Enhancing customer experiences** with personalized product recommendations or chatbots.

- **Optimizing supply chain** and logistics operations through demand forecasting and route planning.

- **Identifying patterns in customer behavior** to improve marketing strategies.

- **Detecting fraud** or anomalies in financial transactions.

In terms of methodology, I also recommend the jobs-to-be-done (JTBD) methodology which complements very nicely with the AI data monetization framework from Chapter 7. JTBD emphasizes understanding what core tasks your product or service is fulfilling for your customers. By identifying these tasks, you can find opportunities where AI can enhance your product or service. The methodology makes you go deeper, in a truly First Principles way, into why the consumer is utilizing your products, which in many cases it is a means to achieve another ultimate task (or "job").

Another interesting way to uncover AI value in your enterprise is to study success stories from other organizations within your industry. This can provide valuable insights and inspiration for identifying AI use cases. By analyzing the AI applications that have delivered positive results for similar companies, you can better understand the potential of AI in your specific domain. When examining success stories, consider the following questions:

1. What problem did the AI solution address, and how was it solved?

2. How did the AI solution contribute to the organization's success? This could include financial gains, improved customer satisfaction, or increased efficiency.

3. What were the key challenges and lessons learned during the development and deployment of the AI solution?

Finally, it's crucial to focus on the data you realistically have. Data is the lifeblood of AI; without enough of the right kind of data, an AI initiative will struggle to get off the ground. A data audit, which assesses the quality, quantity, and accessibility of your data, is a necessary step in the process of identifying viable AI use cases.

Once you've identified your potential AI use cases, you should prioritize them based on their alignment with your business objectives, the expected impact, and your data availability (please refer to Chapter 7, "Data Monetization," for the full framework as to how to unlock value and then prioritize along the other strategic initiatives of the company). This will ensure that you are focusing your efforts on the use cases that are most likely to drive significant value for your business.

Assembling a Multidisciplinary AI Team

Once you've identified AI use cases that align with your company's objectives and have a high potential for impact, the next critical step is assembling a multidisciplinary AI team. This team will bring together the range of skills and expertise necessary to translate your identified AI use cases into successful AI implementations. In this subsection, we will explore the key resources needed for the AI project, strategies for fostering collaboration and shared success among team members from different organizations, and the importance of diverse skills and perspectives.

This is quite challenging, specifically in large enterprises, where business units will naturally aim for full control of all resources, but without a full grasp in all the techniques or reach to all critical resources. The resulting situation on many occasions is partially staffed teams without full ideal skillsets with various rates of success, and a silo approach where there is little or non-existent collaboration and synergies across different business units. This is highly counterproductive in an AI environment, where there is truly new value to discover when you join up datasets from different divisions. As we saw in earlier chapters, Comway's law will heavily influence this setup, and solutions would mirror the human organization, which often is not the most optimal setup.

The first step in assembling your AI team is to identify the key roles needed, as outlined in Figure 15-1. These roles often include an AI product manager, data scientists, machine learning (ML) engineers, and IT infrastructure support:

- The **AI product manager** is responsible for defining the vision of the AI product based on the company's strategic objectives and identified use cases. They coordinate the efforts of the rest of the AI team and stakeholders to ensure that this vision is effectively realized. This role is critical, but you see in many organizations is not set. McKinsey, in their Harvard Business Review article[1], called this role "**Analytics Translator.**"

- **Data scientists** are crucial for interpreting and analyzing data, creating predictive models, and ensuring the technical feasibility of AI initiatives.

- **Machine learning engineers** focus on building and deploying the models that data scientists create. They ensure that these models can operate effectively at scale.

- Finally, **IT infrastructure** is essential to provide the hardware and software resources necessary to develop, test, and deploy AI solutions.

---

[1] www.mckinsey.com/capabilities/quantumblack/our-insights/analytics-translator

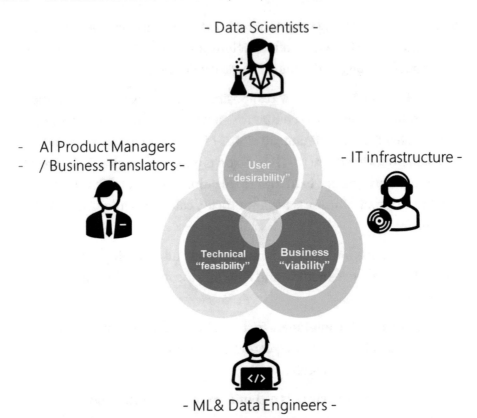

Figure 15-1. *Key roles in a AI team – all must be part on an aligned team*

However, the ideal composition of an AI team can depend on the specific AI use cases and the current capabilities of your organization. As such, it may also be necessary to include other roles, such as data engineers and business analysts.

In many cases, members of your AI team will come from different parts of your organization, or even from outside your organization entirely. This diversity can be a significant asset, bringing together a wide range of skills and perspectives. However, it can also present challenges, especially when it comes to ensuring alignment and collaboration.

To address this, it's important to establish clear objectives for the AI project that align with the broader goals of all involved parties. ***This alignment should be reinforced by a reward system that recognizes both individual and team contributions*** to the project's success. Regular communication is also essential to maintain alignment and address any issues or misunderstandings that arise.

The ***importance of diverse skills and perspectives in an AI*** team cannot be overstated. Diverse teams are more creative, make better decisions, and are better at problem-solving. This diversity isn't just about professional skills – it also includes factors such as cultural background, gender, age, and more.

This diversity is particularly important in AI, a field that benefits from a combination of technical, business, and humanistic perspectives. Technical expertise is necessary to develop and implement AI solutions, but understanding the business context ensures that these solutions address relevant problems and deliver value. Humanistic perspectives are crucial for considering ethical implications and ensuring that AI solutions are designed and used responsibly.

A ***collaborative culture*** is one of the most crucial components of a successful AI team. This collaboration is fostered through open and effective communication, mutual respect, and a willingness to share knowledge and resources. It involves everyone, from the AI product manager who sets the team's direction to the data scientists and machine learning engineers who bring this vision to life.

To facilitate collaboration, it's useful to establish clear protocols for communication and decision-making. These protocols should promote transparency and inclusivity, allowing all team members to contribute their ideas and concerns. Regular meetings, both for the entire team and for smaller groups working on specific aspects of the project, can also promote collaboration.

In the rapidly evolving field of AI, leadership and adaptability are crucial. Leaders guide the team, make crucial decisions, and ensure that the project stays aligned with its objectives. They also foster a culture that values innovation, learning, and adaptability. A key leadership role, a chief scientist can be a valuable addition to a data science team, providing strategic leadership, overseeing research and development, and fostering a culture of innovation. However, not every organization needs a chief scientist. Consider hiring a chief scientist if

- Your company is heavily invested in AI research and development.

- You require a strong technical leader to drive innovation and guide the team.

- The data science team is large and requires a high level of coordination and oversight.

Adaptability is necessary because of the rapidly evolving nature of AI technology and the unpredictable challenges that can arise during an AI project. An adaptable team can learn from its mistakes, adjust its plans in response to new information or changes in the business environment, and continually improve its methods and outcomes.

Hybrid teams, which include members from different units or even different organizations, can be particularly effective for AI projects. They combine a diverse range of skills and perspectives, which can lead to more innovative and effective solutions. However, building and managing hybrid teams can be challenging. It involves integrating team members with different backgrounds, cultures, and expectations, and ensuring that they can work together effectively. Strategies for achieving this include clear communication, mutual respect, ***shared objectives and rewards***, and opportunities for team members to learn about each other and build trust.

Building a multidisciplinary AI team is a complex but rewarding endeavor. It involves identifying key roles (Table 15-1), fostering collaboration and shared success among diverse team members, and developing a culture that values diversity, collaboration, leadership, and adaptability. Please refer to Chapter 14 about how to set up a high performing team.

Table 15-1. *Key roles and responsibilities in an AI team*

Role	Key responsibilities
AI product manager	Define the AI product vision, coordinate efforts to realize this vision
Data scientist	Interpret and analyze data, create predictive models
Machine learning engineer	Build and deploy scalable ML models
IT infrastructure	Provide necessary hardware and software resources for AI development, testing, and deployment

Future Evolution of AI Teams

The relentless march of technology has driven transformative changes across industries. The realm of data science has been no exception. It emerged a mere decade ago, following DJ Patil's coining of the term "data science" in 2008[2], and swiftly burgeoned

---

[2]www.forbes.com/sites/gilpress/2013/05/28/a-very-short-history-of-data-science/

into an integral part of modern businesses. This was marked by the constitution of data teams, replete with data engineers, data scientists, and ML engineers. Each of these roles had unique responsibilities within the data pipeline.

However, the evolution of generative AI and no-code technology, coupled with the increasing demand for maximizing ROI per data scientist, is causing a paradigm shift in this structure. The future sees the advent of the *full-pipe (or full-stack) data scientist*, a role that integrates the functions of the pipeline and enhances overall efficiency.

The Duality ML Engineer vs Data Scientist

Traditional data science roles are segregated. Data engineers constructed the data pipeline, data scientists conducted statistical analyses and constructed models, and ML engineers ensured scalable model deployment. Yet, this division of labor has proved expensive, with critical drawbacks manifesting in practice.

Data scientists, often having an abundance of theoretical knowledge, found themselves lacking in practical proficiency. They may understand algorithms in-depth but struggle with writing a simple API for model service. They may construct an effective model for an offline dataset in Jupyter Notebook but fail to consider how it needs to function online, in terms of online metrics, latency, and throughput. Code published by data scientists may require extensive re-writing by ML engineers and software engineers, to eliminate inefficiencies.

The outcomes of these issues can be severe. Even at tech giants, model development has been hampered by these shortcomings, resulting in wasted time and resources, and, at times, embarrassment.

The Future: Full-Pipe Data Scientists

Advances in generative AI and no-code technology will likely reshape traditional data science teams, catalyzing the emergence of full-stack data scientists. These individuals will handle the entire data pipeline, leveraging AI to automate parts of the process and no-code solutions to develop models, improving efficiency and ROI. The new paradigm demands broader skill sets and necessitates adaptive training. Despite challenges, this evolution, propelled by technology, offers promising returns and calls for readiness to adapt to novel tools and methods.

Agile in Data Science

Adopting Agile methodologies in data science projects is not just a trend, but rather a necessity given the dynamic nature of AI development. Agile principles can help data science teams adapt to changes, maintain flexibility, and continually learn from project development. To understand the implementation of Agile in data science, we must first grasp the core principles of Agile and how they align with data science objectives. It is indeed very important to go deep into the First Principles of Agile, and adapt them to the data science process, rather than focusing on a specific implementation of Agile and forcing it.

The Agile methodology is based on iterative and incremental development. It was first introduced through the Agile Manifesto in 2001,[3] intended to streamline software development. The principles include prioritizing customer satisfaction through continuous delivery, accommodating changing requirements, frequent delivery of smaller portions of working software, and regular adaptation to changing circumstances.

In the context of data science, these principles are highly relevant. Data science projects often need to adapt quickly to new data, evolving business needs, and technological advancements.

Applying Agile principles to data science projects can offer several benefits. Figure 15-2 show the end to end Data science process in an Agile approach. For instance, Agile encourages regular communication and feedback, enabling a better understanding of the business context. This way, data scientists can align their work more closely with the company's strategic goals.

Moreover, in Agile, the concept of delivering working software in smaller, manageable increments suits the exploratory nature of data science. Data scientists can focus on delivering actionable insights and models iteratively, and then improve them over time based on feedback and new data.

Finally, Agile's emphasis on responding to change aligns with the often-unpredictable nature of data science, where initial hypotheses might be refuted by data, requiring a change in direction.

While Agile can benefit data science teams, the unique challenges of AI projects require some adaptations to traditional Agile practices.

---

[3] https://agilemanifesto.org/history.html

For instance, unlike software development, where progress can be measured by completed features, data science outcomes are uncertain until the data has been explored. Agile in data science, therefore, emphasizes working on small but complete slices of analytics problems, delivering models that can be tested and improved incrementally, and many **high uncertain tasks in a time-boxed approach**.

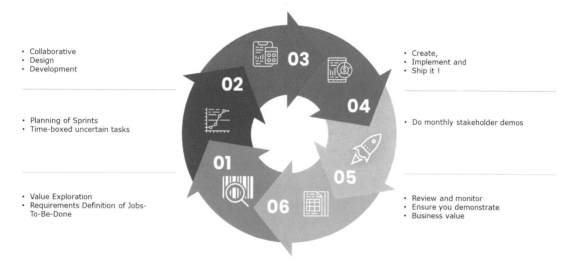

- Collaborative
- Design
- Development

- Planning of Sprints
- Time-boxed uncertain tasks

- Value Exploration
- Requirements Definition of Jobs-To-Be-Done

03

02

04

01

05

06

- Create,
- Implement and
- Ship it !

- Do monthly stakeholder demos

- Review and monitor
- Ensure you demonstrate
- Business value

Figure 15-2. *Agile data science process*

Moreover, cross-functional collaboration is vital, requiring clear communication channels between data scientists, data engineers, business stakeholders, and others. Agile practices such as daily stand-ups, sprint planning, and retrospectives can be useful in this context, ensuring alignment and facilitating problem-solving.

Finally, data science projects might require extra attention to data management, infrastructure, and version control, which should be incorporated into Agile practices.

AI projects present additional challenges. For instance, building machine learning models often involves a significant amount of experimentation, and the "right" solution might not be clear until late in the process. The Agile principle of "failing fast" can be beneficial here, enabling teams to quickly test hypotheses and learn from failures. Table 15-2 shows a comparison of traditional vs Agiles methodologies when applied to the Data Science process.

Moreover, AI solutions often require substantial computational resources and specialized hardware, which need to be planned for and managed as part of the project. It's also important to consider ethical issues and potential biases in AI, and include these considerations in the Agile process.

Agile in data science can help teams adapt to change, deliver value incrementally, and align closely with business objectives. While the unique challenges of data science and AI require some adaptations to traditional Agile practices, the principles of Agile remain highly relevant and beneficial.

Table 15-2. *Comparison of traditional and Agile methodologies in data science*

Aspect	Traditional data science	Agile data science
Process	Linear, waterfall	Iterative, incremental, time-boxed uncertain tasks
Adaptability	Changes are disruptive	Changes are expected, welcomed
Communication	Periodic	Frequent, regular

Key Takeaways

This chapter explored the ins and outs of identifying AI use cases and assembling a strong, high performance, multidisciplinary AI team. We walked through the strategies and techniques to align AI use cases with business objectives, structure an effective team, and implement agile methodologies, adapted to the data science method. Here are the three pivotal takeaways to remember:

1. **Takeaway 1: Alignment of AI use cases with business objectives**. The data monetization framework aids in discovering value creation opportunities from data and AI. A complementary methodology is the jobs-to-be-done approach, which focuses on understanding customer needs. However, always remember to consider the data realistically available to you.

    a. Do use structured frameworks to identify AI use cases and align them with your business objectives.

    b. Don't jump into AI implementation without having a clear vision of the value it will bring to your business.

2. **Takeaway 2: Assembling a multidisciplinary AI team**. Key resources include an AI product manager, data scientists, ML engineers, and IT infrastructure support. Whenever your team members come from different organizations, establish **clear common objectives** and align them.

    a. Do establish clear goals and rewards that promote collaboration among team members.

    b. Don't overlook the importance of leadership and diversity in teams.

3. **Takeaway 3: Agile in data science and scaling AI solutions**. Implementing agile methodologies in data science projects brings flexibility and responsiveness. The nature of AI projects often requires iterative improvement and swift reaction to new information, making Agile a perfect fit. On the other hand, scaling AI solutions necessitates collaboration between engineers and data scientists. Creating clear interfaces and ways of working between these two roles is paramount.

    a. Do employ Agile principles in your data science projects and foster a strong relationship between your engineers and data scientists.

    b. Don't expect your AI solutions to scale without a robust engineering capability and a flexible project management approach.

Identifying AI use cases, assembling an AI team, and scaling AI solutions are all intertwined processes. Each one contributes to the successful deployment of AI in a business setting. The journey can be challenging, but with these key takeaways, your business can navigate the AI landscape with increased confidence.

CHAPTER 16

Selecting AI Tools and Platforms

Artificial intelligence (AI) has become a vital component for many businesses seeking to innovate, streamline operations, and gain competitive advantage. As this technology continues to evolve rapidly, the range of AI tools and platforms available for businesses has broadened significantly. As companies across industries look to harness the power of AI, the decision of selecting the right AI tools and platforms becomes critical to the success of their initiatives. This chapter aims to provide a comprehensive guide to help businesses navigate the complex landscape of AI tools and platforms, understand the advantages and drawbacks of each option, and make informed decisions that align with their unique needs, resources, and strategic objectives.

In the spectrum of AI tools and platforms, solutions range from open-source libraries for developing custom AI models to comprehensive AI platforms offered by major tech companies, as well as third-party APIs that provide specific AI capabilities. The tools and platforms you choose should align closely with your company's strategic goals, technical capabilities, budget, and risk tolerance.

In the "build versus buy" debate, both strategies have their advantages (Table 16-1). Building your own AI solutions from scratch allows for customization and control but requires significant resources and expertise. On the other hand, buying pre-built solutions or utilizing third-party APIs can be faster and more cost-effective but may limit customization and could lead to vendor lock-in. To help businesses weigh the pros and cons of the "buy versus build" debate, this chapter will discuss key factors such as cost, time-to-market, customization, support, and scalability.

© Francisco Javier Campos Zabala 2023
F. J. Campos Zabala, *Grow Your Business with AI*, https://doi.org/10.1007/978-1-4842-9669-1_16

Table 16-1. *Comparison of "build vs buy" in AI*

Criteria	Building custom AI solutions	Buying pre-built AI solutions
Flexibility	High – can be tailored to specific needs	Low – limited to available features
Control	Complete – over all aspects of the solution	Limited – based on vendor's provided options
Unique solution	Yes – can build a solution that is unique	No – the solution is used by other companies
Cost	High – requires significant resources	Lower – often subscription or usage-based cost
Time to implement	Longer – requires development time	Shorter – can often start using immediately
Skill requirement	High – requires deep technical expertise	Lower – typically user-friendly, less technical
Maintenance	Responsibility of your team	Responsibility of vendor

As we navigate through the AI landscape, we'll delve deeper into the characteristics, benefits, and potential drawbacks of various types of AI tools and platforms. These include cloud-based AI, on-premises AI, open-source tools, and third-party APIs. By understanding these different solutions, businesses can make decisions that are more aligned with their specific needs and constraints.

For businesses looking to harness AI without building their solutions from scratch, third-party AI APIs, such as GPT-4 and Cohere, offer a viable alternative. These APIs enable companies to access powerful AI capabilities without the need for extensive in-house expertise or resources. This chapter will examine the pros and cons of using third-party AI APIs, focusing on aspects such as cost, ease of integration, ongoing support, and customization. We will provide best practices for incorporating third-party AI APIs into AI projects, ensuring seamless integration, and maximizing the potential benefits for the business.

Ultimately, the success of an AI project hinges on selecting the right tools and platforms that align with a company's needs, resources, and strategic objectives. By offering a comprehensive overview of the AI landscape, discussing the "buy versus build" debate, and providing practical guidance on the implementation of AI tools and platforms, this chapter aims to empower business executives with the knowledge and insights needed to make informed decisions and drive growth through AI-powered innovation.

By the end of this chapter, you will not only have a better understanding of the AI tools and platforms available to your business, but also gain insights on the criteria for evaluating them and best practices for selection. This comprehensive approach will equip you to make informed decisions that will ultimately drive the success of your AI initiatives.

Core Components

Here are the core components needed from a first principles point of view for selecting AI tools and platforms:

- **Business goals and objectives**: "Start with the end in mind." The first step in selecting AI tools and platforms is to clearly define your business goals and objectives. What do you hope to achieve by using AI? Once you know what you want to achieve, you can start to identify the AI tools and platforms that are most likely to help you reach your goals.

- **Audience/users**: Who will be the end users, their background, and training.

- **Data**: AI tools and platforms rely on data to train and build models. Therefore, it is important to have access to high-quality data. The type of data you need will depend on the specific AI tasks you want to perform. For example, if you want to use AI to build a chatbot, you will need data on customer conversations.

- **Technical expertise**: AI tools and platforms can be complex to use. Therefore, it is important to have the necessary technical expertise to implement and manage AI solutions. If your team does not have the necessary expertise, you may need to hire an external consultant or partner with a company that specializes in AI.

- **Budget**: AI tools and platforms can be expensive. Therefore, it is important to set a budget before you start your search. The cost of AI solutions will vary depending on the features and capabilities of the tool or platform.

- **Integration with rest of tech ecosystem**: Think of the end-to-end process, and the tools and data will have to integrate with others in your company. This ecosystem can limit your choices significantly.

- **Scalability**: AI tools and platforms need to be able to scale to meet the needs of your business. If you plan to grow your business, you need to choose an AI tool or platform that can scale with you.

- **Support**: AI tools and platforms need to be supported by a team of experts who can help you with installation, configuration, and troubleshooting. Make sure to choose an AI tool or platform that is supported by a team of experts who are available to help you when you need it.

- **Security**: AI tools and platforms need to be secure. Make sure to choose an AI tool or platform that has strong security features to protect your data.

We will now explore the different types of tools and platforms through the lenses of the core components.

Buy vs Build

The decision to "buy" or "build" AI solutions plays a crucial role in the trajectory of your company's AI journey. The "buy versus build" argument in software refers to the decision between purchasing off-the-shelf AI tools and platforms or building custom solutions in-house. Both approaches come with their own set of advantages and disadvantages, which should be carefully weighed against the specific needs, resources, and goals of the company.

Pros and Cons of Buying AI Solutions

When you opt to buy, you're leveraging existing AI solutions provided by third-party vendors. These could range from specific AI functionalities offered via APIs to comprehensive AI platforms.

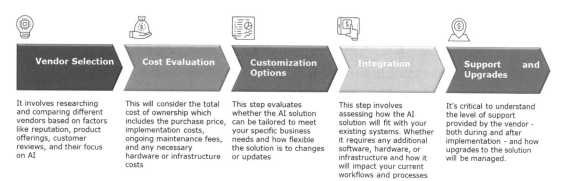

Figure 16-1. *AI purchase workflow*

Figure 16-1 shows a typical workflow to purchase an AI tool. Purchasing has the following advantages and disadvantages:

Advantages:

1. **Cost**: Buying off-the-shelf AI solutions can be more cost-effective than building custom solutions from scratch. Companies can avoid the high upfront costs associated with developing and maintaining custom software, as well as the costs of hiring and training specialized personnel.

2. **Time-to-market**: Purchasing AI tools and platforms allows companies to deploy their AI initiatives more quickly, as the development, testing, and deployment of custom solutions can be time-consuming.

3. **Support**: When buying AI tools and platforms, companies can rely on the vendor for ongoing support and maintenance, as well as access to regular updates and improvements.

4. **Scalability**: Off-the-shelf AI solutions are often built with scalability in mind, which can make it easier for companies to grow their AI initiatives without significant additional development effort.

Disadvantages:

1. **Limited customization**: Off-the-shelf AI solutions might not provide the same level of customization as custom-built solutions. However, many AI platforms offer a range of configuration options and APIs that allow for a certain degree of customization.

2. **Dependence on vendor**: There can be a risk of vendor lock-in, with potential issues around compatibility, pricing changes, and vendor stability.

Pros and Cons of Building Custom AI Solutions

Advantages:

1. **Full customization**: Custom-built AI solutions offer a higher degree of customization than off-the-shelf tools, allowing companies to tailor the solution to their specific needs and requirements. If the AI solution manage a core strategic area for the business, this can provide a competitive advantage as no other competitor will have access to the exact same tech.

2. **Control**: You have complete control over the development, updates, and data privacy.

Disadvantages

1. **Cost**: Building custom AI solutions can be more expensive than buying off-the-shelf tools, due to the costs associated with software development, maintenance, and specialized personnel. However, in some cases, the long-term benefits of a custom solution might outweigh the initial investment.

2. **Time-to-market**: Developing custom AI solutions can be a lengthy process, which might delay the deployment of the AI initiative and impact the company's competitive advantage.

3. **Support**: When building custom AI solutions, companies are responsible for providing their own ongoing support and maintenance. This can be resource-intensive but might also give the company more control over the quality of support.

4. **Scalability**: Custom-built AI solutions might not be as scalable as off-the-shelf tools, which can make it more challenging for companies to grow their AI initiatives over time. However, with careful planning and design, custom solutions can be built to scale. When you choose to build, you're creating bespoke AI solutions using in-house resources or contracted developers. This typically involves utilizing open-source libraries and frameworks.

5. **Resource intensive**: Building requires substantial time, skill, and financial resources.

6. **Risk**: The risk of project failure may be higher due to the complexity of AI projects and the need for specialized expertise.

Most businesses use a hybrid approach, combining the strengths of both buying and building to meet their unique needs. For instance, a business might opt to buy a ready-to-use AI platform but build custom AI models using open-source libraries.

A final but very important point in the debate is the technology lifecycle. The lifecycle of AI software is becoming increasingly shorter, with some tools having a lifespan of only 18 months. This means that organizations need to be more careful when deciding whether to buy or build their own AI solutions. This rapid obsolescence can directly influence the buy vs build decision.

When you consider buying, you should factor in the frequency of product updates and the vendor's commitment to stay on the cutting edge. An off-the-shelf product may be outdated or even obsolete before its ROI is fully realized, which can result in significant loss of investment. Conversely, building in-house allows for continuous updates and adaptations to the latest advancements. However, the challenge here lies in staying abreast with the latest trends, technologies, and skill sets required to continuously innovate and maintain relevancy in rapidly evolving AI landscapes.

The "buy vs build" decision is not a one-size-fits-all answer. It relies heavily on your company's needs, resources, and strategic goals. In the following sections, we'll explore various AI tools and platforms available, delve into the specifics of cloud-based AI, on-premises AI, and open-source tools, and offer insights on evaluating AI solutions and best practices for selection.

Overview of Various AI Tools and Platforms

Selecting the right artificial intelligence (AI) tools and platforms is vital for successful AI implementation in your business. Today, a wide array of AI platforms and tools are available, each offering unique capabilities. By understanding the distinctive features, advantages, and potential drawbacks of these platforms and tools, you can make an informed decision aligning with your specific needs and resources.

The current challenge is originated by the large market expectations which provides the funding for new start ups to innovate all the time; at the time of writing this book, there is a new start up nearly every week launching a new AI tool/platform. For instance, there is an emergence of Vector Databases[1], which can be very useful for certain LLMs projects (large language models).

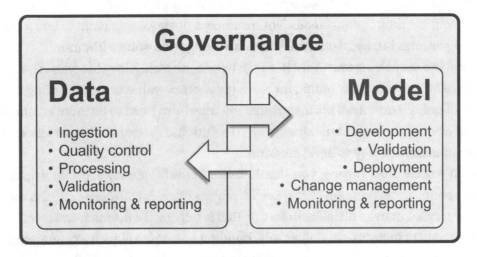

Figure 16-2. *AI system[2]*

It is useful to look at the AI complete lifecycle to understand all the different tools and platforms that we will need. It is also important to remember that the market is still immature, and there is a converge from many applications from other areas to AI. For instance, many platforms and tools who originated for data management, have been

---

[1]https://milvus.io/

[2]www.bankofengland.co.uk/research/fintech/ai-public-private-forum

adding more and more AI features. Therefore, it is very challenging to cover every single tool or platform in the entire AI lifecycle (you can see Figures 16-2 and 16-3) to see the end-to-end process and how the different AI roles will need tools to perform their job more efficiently.

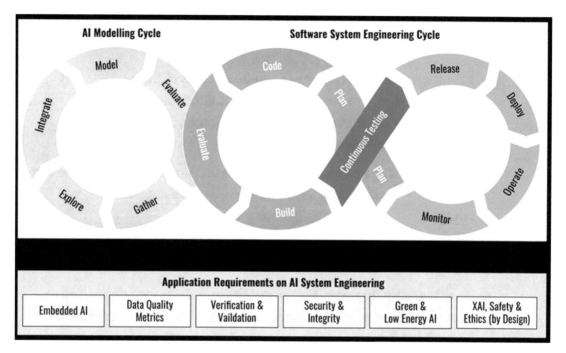

Figure 16-3. *AI and software lifecycle[3]*

In the next few sections, we will explore some of the most popular tools and platforms, first from the use cases point of view and later from the type of tool or platform. In any case, as the tools and platforms vendors move so quickly, it is better to use First Principles to keep the core components in mind, whenever you need to select a tool for a particular part of your AI process – or for your entire one!

[3] www.researchgate.net/figure/Artificial-Intelligence-AI-System-Engineering-Lifecyle-comprised-of-AI-modelling-cycle_fig1_348142248

AI Tools and Platforms by Use Cases

This subsection aims to provide an overview of the most popular AI tools and platforms available, helping businesses make informed decisions based on their specific needs and resources. We will discuss the tools and platforms tailored for different use cases, such as data scientists, machine learning engineers, and AI infrastructure, as well as the major cloud providers in the market.

1. **For data scientists**: Data scientists require a variety of tools and platforms to collect, process, analyze, and visualize data, as well as build and deploy machine learning models. Some of the popular tools and platforms for data scientists include

   a. **Data processing and visualization**: Python (Pandas, Matplotlib, Seaborn), R, and Tableau are widely used for data pre-processing, analysis, and visualization.

   b. **Machine learning libraries**: Scikit-learn, XGBoost, and LightGBM are popular libraries for building traditional machine learning models.

   c. **Deep learning frameworks**: TensorFlow and Keras (running on top of TensorFlow) are widely used for developing deep learning models, while PyTorch has gained significant popularity in recent years.

   d. **AutoML platforms**: Tools like H2O.ai, DataRobot, and Google Cloud AutoML help automate the process of building, tuning, and deploying machine learning models.

2. **For machine learning engineers**: Machine learning engineers focus on optimizing, scaling, and deploying machine learning models in production environments. Some essential tools and platforms for machine learning engineers include

   a. **Model deployment and management**: MLflow, TensorFlow Serving, and Kubeflow are popular platforms for managing and deploying machine learning models at scale.

   b. **Containerization and orchestration**: Docker and Kubernetes are widely used for containerizing machine learning applications and managing their deployment in production environments.

   c. **CI/CD for ML**: Continuous integration and continuous deployment (CI/CD) tools like Jenkins, GitLab CI, and CircleCI[4] help machine learning engineers automate the process of testing, building, and deploying ML models.

3. **AI infrastructure**: AI infrastructure includes hardware and software components that enable the efficient processing, training, and deployment of AI models. Some key elements of AI infrastructure are

   a. **GPUs and TPUs**: Graphics Processing Units (GPUs) from NVIDIA and Tensor Processing Units (TPUs) from Google are specifically designed for accelerating machine learning workloads.

   b. **AI-optimized cloud instances**: Cloud providers like AWS, Microsoft Azure, and Google Cloud offer AI-optimized instances with pre-configured GPUs or TPUs to run machine learning workloads.

   c. **On-premise AI hardware**: Companies like NVIDIA and Intel offer specialized AI hardware, such as NVIDIA DGX systems[5] and Intel Nervana[6], for businesses that prefer to build their AI infrastructure on-premise.

AI Tools and Platforms by Type

The decision to adopt a particular AI tool or platform should be guided by your company's specific requirements, resources, and strategic goals. The subsequent sections will delve into specifics of cloud-based AI, on-premises AI, open-source, and third-party API tools. We will explore how to evaluate AI solutions, understand the "buy vs build" debate, and offer insights on best practices for selection.

---

[4] https://circleci.com/

[5] www.nvidia.com/en-gb/data-center/dgx-systems/

[6] www.intel.co.uk/content/www/uk/en/artificial-intelligence/nnpi.html

Cloud-Based AI Platforms

Cloud-based AI platforms offer a suite of AI services that can be accessed over the Internet. Cloud-based AI platforms are hosted on the cloud and offer a variety of AI services, such as machine learning, natural language processing, and computer vision. Cloud-based AI platforms are a good option for businesses that need to deploy AI solutions quickly and easily. However, cloud-based AI platforms can be expensive, and they may not offer the same level of control and customization as on-premises AI solutions. The big three cloud providers (see Table 16-2 for their market share):

- **AWS AI and Machine Learning**: Amazon Web Services (AWS) provides a wide range of machine learning services and supporting cloud infrastructure. It offers pre-trained AI services for functions like language translation and image analysis, alongside SageMaker – a fully managed service that enables developers to build, train, and deploy machine learning models.

- **Microsoft Azure Machine Learning**: Microsoft's Azure Machine Learning platform offers a collaborative, end-to-end environment for building, training, and deploying machine learning models. It provides scalability and cost-effectiveness.

- **Google Cloud AI and Machine Learning**: Google's cloud platform offers various AI and machine learning services, from pre-trained models to tailored AI solutions. It is known for its superior data analytics and machine learning capabilities, making it a top choice for businesses looking to leverage large datasets.

Table 16-2. *Top cloud providers by market share (Q2 2022)*

Cloud provider	Market share
Amazon Web Services (AWS)	32%
Microsoft Azure	23%
Google Cloud Platform (GCP)	10%
Others	35%

It is also worth mentioning a second tier of cloud providers (IBM Cloud, Oracle Cloud Services, and Salesforce) that are growing quite fast. While looking at market share of existing tool is a data point, I would strongly recommend the reader to do an evaluation from first principles and based on their specific business requirements – this approach might indeed point to some second tier cloud providers as a suitable solution and with considerable financial advantages.

On-Premises AI Solutions

On-premises AI solutions are implemented within the physical confines of a business. They are installed and hosted on a company's own servers. On-premises AI platforms offer more control and customization than cloud-based AI platforms, but they can be more expensive to set up and maintain. As these solutions provide more control over data privacy and system configurations, are often favored by large enterprises with complex infrastructure and data privacy needs:

- **IBM**: IBM offers a variety of on-premises AI solutions, including Watson AI Platform, Watson Explorer, and Watson Assistant.

- **Microsoft**: Microsoft offers Azure Machine Learning Studio, which is an on-premises AI development environment.

- **Nvidia AI Infrastructure**: Nvidia's AI solutions are suitable for on-premise deployment, offering high performance and efficiency. Its offerings include powerful computing hardware and software like the CUDA platform, ideal for AI workloads.

Now, let's consider the pros and cons of each option in Table 16-3:

Table 16-3. *Pros and cons of various AI tools and platforms*

AI tool/platform	Pros	Cons
Open-source AI tools	– Cost-effective – Customizable – Community support	– Limited functionality – Requires technical expertise – May lack enterprise-grade security
Cloud-based AI platforms	– Scalable – Easy to deploy – Access to advanced AI models	– Costly – Dependence on internet connectivity – May lack control over data and infrastructure
On-premises AI solutions	– Complete control over infrastructure – Customizable – High security	– High initial cost – Requires technical expertise – Limited scalability – Maintenance and upgrade costs

Open-Source AI Tools

Open-source AI tools are publicly accessible and typically free to use. They provide the flexibility for high levels of customization and are backed by active communities of developers, but they can be more difficult to use than proprietary AI tools. These tools are often used to build AI solutions in-house.

- **TensorFlow**: Developed by Google Brain, TensorFlow is a leading open-source software library for numerical computation using data flow graphs. It's particularly suited for machine learning and deep learning applications.

- **PyTorch**: PyTorch is an open-source machine learning library based on the Torch library. Known for its simplicity and ease of use, PyTorch is widely used for applications such as natural language processing and computer vision.

- **Keras**: A high-level neural networks API, Keras can run on top of TensorFlow. Its user-friendliness and modularity make it a good choice for beginners in deep learning.

- **Open LLMs**: There are multiple models, and new ones are being released frequently. Hugging[7] Face keeps and Open LLM leaderboard; this dynamic resource keeps you informed, tracking, and ranking the performance of LLMs and chatbots as they hit the market. They used the Eleuther AI Language Model Evaluation Harness[8] and putting each model through its paces across four crucial benchmarks. This unified framework helps to assess generative language models across a broad array of evaluation tasks.

Third-Party APIs

As we move through the diverse ecosystem of AI tools and platforms, an integral component that deserves special mention is the third-party AI Application Programming Interfaces (APIs). These APIs, like GPT-4 by OpenAI, play a crucial role in enabling businesses to access sophisticated AI capabilities without significant upfront investment in infrastructure or AI expertise.

Third-party AI APIs are pre-built AI models provided by tech companies, which businesses can access over the Internet. Instead of building a machine learning model from scratch, developers can integrate these APIs into their applications, benefiting from cutting-edge AI capabilities. Examples of these APIs include natural language understanding, speech recognition, image analysis, and predictive analytics. Most of the cloud providers include these AI API services.

There are several advantages of third-party AI APIs:

- **Cost and time efficiency**: Building AI models in-house requires significant time, resources, and technical expertise. AI APIs, on the other hand, are ready to use, allowing businesses to integrate advanced AI capabilities into their applications quickly and efficiently.

---

[7] https://huggingface.co/spaces/HuggingFaceH4/open_llm_leaderboard
[8] https://github.com/EleutherAI/lm-evaluation-harness

- **Ease of integration**: AI APIs are designed to be easily integrated into existing applications. They come with extensive documentation and client libraries in various programming languages, making it easy for developers to incorporate them.

- **Ongoing support and updates**: Third-party AI APIs are maintained and continuously improved by the provider. This ensures businesses are always using the most up-to-date and efficient AI capabilities.

- **Scalability**: AI APIs are hosted on the provider's servers and can handle varying loads. They can be scaled up or down depending on the demand, providing flexibility for businesses.

There are also some challenges to consider with third-party AI APIs:

- **Dependency on provider**: Utilizing third-party AI APIs means reliance on the provider for service availability and performance. Any downtime or performance issues can directly impact your business operations.

- **Limited customization**: While these APIs provide various functionalities, they may not be tailored to a business's unique needs. The capability to customize a third-party API is usually limited compared to in-house developed models.

- **Data privacy concerns**: When using AI APIs, businesses often need to send data over the Internet to the provider's servers. This could potentially raise data privacy and security concerns, especially for sensitive information.

Best practices for integrating third-party AI APIs:

- **Understand your needs**: Before choosing an AI API, it's crucial to understand your specific needs and requirements. This will help you identify which API aligns best with your business goals.

- **Evaluate different options**: Not all AI APIs are created equal. Consider various factors such as cost, ease of integration, functionality, support, and the reputation of the provider before making a decision.

- **Ensure data privacy**: Since using AI APIs often involves transmitting data over the Internet, ensure the API provider follows robust security practices. In some cases, it may be prudent to anonymize or encrypt data before sending it to the API.

- **Establish a backup plan**: In the event of an API provider discontinuing service or experiencing downtime, have a backup plan in place to minimize disruption to your AI projects. This may involve identifying alternative API providers or considering a custom AI solution as a fallback option.

- **Monitor performance**: Once integrated, continuously monitor the performance of the API to ensure it meets your needs. Be prepared to make changes or switch providers if necessary.

Let's consider a sample case, using GPT-4, a language model developed by OpenAI, to understand third-party AI APIs more deeply.

GPT-4 is an example of a transformer-based model that can generate human-like text given some input. It can be used in a variety of applications including drafting emails, writing code, creating written content, answering questions, tutoring, translating languages, simulating characters for video games, and even for tasks like brainstorming ideas. Companies have an option to train their own LLM from scratch, but this could be very costly and take a long time. Another alternative for companies is to take advantage of the work done by OpenAI and just use the output of the model through API.

Table 16-4. *Pros and cons of using GPT-4*

Pros of using GPT-4 as API	Cons of using GPT-4 as API
Natural language processing: GPT-4's advanced language model allows it to understand and generate human-like text, which is beneficial for applications requiring natural language interactions	Generative unpredictability: Despite its advanced understanding, GPT-4's responses can sometimes be unpredictable. It may generate incorrect or irrelevant responses. Potential for bias and misinformation

(continued)

Table 16-4. (*continued*)

Pros of using GPT-4 as API	Cons of using GPT-4 as API
Scaling communication: It allows businesses to automate and scale various communication tasks, such as customer support, content creation, and more	Ethical, privacy, and safety concerns: GPT-4 can generate content that may be offensive or inappropriate. Managing these risks requires careful oversight and the implementation of safeguards
Increased productivity and new creative possibilities	Cost and resource intensive: Implementing and managing an AI model like GPT-4 can be computationally intensive, which may result in higher infrastructure costs
Continual learning: GPT-4 can learn and improve over time, offering more accurate and relevant responses	Limitations in understanding: While GPT-4 is impressive, it doesn't truly understand context in the way humans do. It can make mistakes or produce answers that are technically correct but practically unhelpful

We can see from Table 16-4 the pros and cons of using GPT-4 as external API. As you can see, for many cases where there is no need to share data very confidential and the volume usage is reasonable, using this API can be a very good way to go to market quickly and safely.

Overall, GPT-4 has the potential to be a powerful tool for businesses. However, it is important to be aware of the potential drawbacks before integrating it into your applications. Here are some additional considerations to keep in mind:

- **Data privacy**: GPT-4 is trained on a massive dataset of text and code. This means that it can be used to generate text that is like the text that it was trained on. This could be a problem if the text that GPT-4 is trained on contains sensitive or confidential information.

- **Bias**: GPT-4 is trained on a dataset that is created by humans. This means that it can reflect the biases that are present in the dataset. For example, if the dataset is biased toward a particular gender or race, then GPT-4 may be more likely to generate text that is biased toward that gender or race.

- **Misinformation**: GPT-4 can be used to generate text that is factually incorrect. This could be a problem if the text is used to make decisions or to provide information to others.

It is important to weigh the pros and cons of using GPT-4 before deciding whether to integrate it into your applications. If you do decide to use GPT-4, it is important to take steps to mitigate the risks, such as using it in a controlled environment and carefully reviewing the generated text.

Criteria for Evaluating AI Tools and Platforms

Selecting the right AI tool or platform for your business is a critical decision that can significantly impact the effectiveness and success of your AI initiatives. There is a plethora of tools and platforms available in the market, each with its unique strengths and weaknesses. To navigate through this crowded landscape, it is crucial to establish a set of criteria for evaluating these options. This section aims to provide a comprehensive set of criteria that can guide businesses in making informed decisions.

I spent a decade as a management consultant, so I fully understand firsthand how challenging this task can be due to political motivations. The old saying *"Nobody ever gets fired for buying IBM"* reflects this well – many managers make decisions based on how easy it would be to explain the decision to senior management, and senior management relies on tech popularity. I used to advice clients *"There is no such as a thing as 'the best technology' in general, but the best technology for a specific problem."*

The following criteria should be used when comparing AI technology:

- **Scalability**: An essential criterion for evaluating AI platforms is their scalability. As your business grows, your AI needs are likely to grow as well. Therefore, you need an AI tool that can scale seamlessly with your business, handle increasing data loads, and deliver consistent performance. Some AI platforms provide automatic scaling features, allowing them to adjust to your changing needs automatically.

- **Support for various AI techniques**: Different AI projects may require different AI techniques, such as supervised learning, unsupervised learning, reinforcement learning, deep learning, or natural language processing. The chosen platform should support a wide range of these techniques to cater to various project requirements. Furthermore, it should also keep up with the evolving AI field by regularly adding support for new techniques and algorithms.

- **Ease of use**: An AI tool should have an intuitive interface and be user-friendly to minimize the learning curve for your team. Some AI platforms also provide visual tools for creating and managing AI models, which can be particularly beneficial for businesses lacking in-depth technical expertise.

- **Integration with existing infrastructure**: The AI tool or platform you choose should integrate smoothly with your existing IT infrastructure. This includes compatibility with your data sources, hardware, software, and other technological systems. Smooth integration ensures minimal disruption to your current operations and reduces the time and cost of implementation.

- **Data privacy and security features**: With the increasing concerns about data privacy and security, it is crucial that your chosen AI platform provides robust security measures. These could include data encryption, user authentication, access controls, and audit logs. Additionally, the platform should comply with relevant data privacy regulations, such as GDPR or CCPA.

- **Support and community**: Access to timely and reliable support is a crucial aspect of any AI tool. Check if the tool provides documentation, tutorials, and customer support to help you resolve any issues or challenges. A vibrant community of users can also be a valuable resource for sharing knowledge and solutions.

It is also important to consider the bigger picture, while the criteria above focus on the technical and functional aspects of AI tools, it's equally important to consider broader organizational factors.

- **Your organization's business needs and culture**: The chosen AI tool should align with your business objectives and the culture of your organization. For instance, if your business values innovation and agility, an AI platform that enables rapid experimentation and prototyping might be a good fit.

- **Budget**: The cost of AI tools can vary significantly. Consider your budget constraints while also understanding the potential return on investment (ROI) from the AI projects enabled by the tool.

- **Maturity of the AI tool or platform**: Consider the maturity and stability of the tool. A newer tool might offer innovative features but could also have more bugs or less reliable performance than a mature, established tool.

Choosing the right AI tool is a strategic decision that requires careful consideration of various factors. By focusing on both technical criteria and the wider organizational context, businesses can select the AI tools that best meet their needs, enabling them to leverage the transformative power of AI effectively.

Best Practices in Selecting AI Tools and Platforms

The successful integration and utilization of AI tools and platforms within a business can bring transformative benefits. However, the selection process can be a challenging endeavor, given the multitude of available options, each with its own strengths and limitations. The following best practices provide a roadmap to guide businesses in this crucial process.

- **Aligning with business objectives**: The first step in selecting an AI tool or platform is understanding and clearly defining your business objectives. Are you aiming to improve customer service, enhance operational efficiency, drive innovation, or make more informed decisions? The AI tool you choose should directly support these goals. This alignment ensures that the AI initiatives deliver tangible business value and contribute to your organization's strategic priorities.

- **Involving all stakeholders**: AI implementation affects multiple aspects of a business, and therefore, it's important to involve all relevant stakeholders in the selection process. This includes not only the IT team but also representatives from the operations, marketing, finance, legal, and other departments. Stakeholder engagement ensures that the chosen tool meets the needs of all users and gains widespread acceptance.

- **Considering future needs**: While it's important to choose a tool that meets your current needs, it's equally crucial to consider your future requirements. Your chosen AI platform should be flexible and scalable enough to accommodate your business growth and evolving AI needs. Moreover, it should be adaptable to technological advancements in the AI field to ensure its continued relevance and effectiveness.

- **Trialing and testing**: Before making a final decision, it's advisable to trial the AI tool or platform. This involves testing the tool using real or simulated data and evaluating its performance. Trials give you a firsthand experience of the tool's capabilities and usability, providing valuable insights that can inform your decision.

- **Considering total cost of ownership**: Beyond the initial cost of purchasing or subscribing to the AI tool, consider the total cost of ownership (TCO), which includes costs related to implementation, training, maintenance, and upgrades. A tool with a low initial cost might end up being more expensive in the long run due to high maintenance or upgrade costs.

- **Evaluating vendor reputation and support**: Consider the reputation of the tool's provider. A vendor with a strong track record is more likely to provide a reliable and high-quality tool. Additionally, check the level of support provided by the vendor, including technical support, training resources, and updates.

- **Understanding legal and ethical implications**: AI tools can pose legal and ethical challenges, particularly related to data privacy and bias. Ensure that the AI tool complies with relevant regulations and incorporates mechanisms to mitigate bias.

- **Consider using analyst reports**: Industry analyst reports, such as Gartner's Magic Quadrant, Forrester's Wave, IDC's MarketScape, Omdia Market Overview, and others, can provide valuable insights for companies looking to select the right AI software. These reports evaluate and compare various software solutions based on a range of criteria, including the completeness of vision, ability to execute, market presence, and customer satisfaction.

Key Takeaways

This chapter presented a comprehensive overview of AI tools and platforms, drawing a roadmap for businesses to navigate their AI journey successfully. Let's recap the main points and crystallize our understanding into actionable takeaways.

1. **Takeaway 1: Align AI selection with business needs**. The choice of an AI tool or platform should directly support the business objectives.

   - Dos: Clearly define the strategic goals that the AI initiative aims to achieve. Assess how each prospective AI tool contributes to these goals.

   - Don'ts: Don't select an AI tool solely based on its popularity or advanced features without considering its relevance to your business needs.

   - Example: A small startup with limited resources may choose a cloud-based AI platform to minimize costs and leverage cutting-edge technology, while a large enterprise with sensitive data and specific requirements may opt for an on-premises AI solution for greater control and customization

2. **Takeaway 2: Inclusive stakeholder engagement**. The selection process should involve all relevant stakeholders to ensure the chosen tool meets the needs of all users and gains widespread acceptance.

   - Dos: Encourage participation from representatives of various departments – not just the IT team. Conduct workshops or brainstorming sessions to gather input from different stakeholders.

   - Don'ts: Don't make decisions in isolation or rush the selection process without considering the perspectives of the end users of the AI tool.

3. **Takeaway 3: Future-proof your AI investment**. Your chosen AI platform should be flexible and scalable to accommodate your future needs and business growth.

   - Dos: Consider future scenarios such as business expansion, new markets, or changes in technology trends. Ensure the tool is adaptable and scalable to accommodate these evolving needs.

   - Don'ts: Don't short-change your future needs by choosing a tool that barely meets your current needs. A tool that isn't scalable may require costly and time-consuming replacements or upgrades in the future.

Aligning the selection of AI tools with your business objectives, engaging all stakeholders, and considering future needs form the cornerstone of a successful AI implementation. By adopting these best practices, you can select an AI tool that not only meets your current needs but also is adaptable to the future, enabling you to harness the full power of AI for business growth.

CHAPTER 17

Architecting AI: When to Be Cloud Native

The rapid evolution of technology and the increasing demand for scalable, resilient, and flexible systems have made cloud-native architecture a critical consideration for businesses looking to grow and succeed with AI. Cloud-native applications harness the full potential of the cloud, providing a robust foundation for AI-driven innovation and growth. In this chapter, we will explore the core principles and components of cloud-native architecture and discuss common patterns for designing and implementing AI apps that are primed for success in the cloud.

Adopting a cloud-native approach for your AI applications offers numerous benefits, such as enhanced scalability, resilience, flexibility, security, and cost-effectiveness. By leveraging microservices, containerization, orchestration, DevOps, and serverless computing, your business can build AI apps that are highly adaptable and capable of meeting the ever-changing demands of today's fast-paced digital landscape.

Some common architecture patterns for cloud-native AI apps include event-driven architecture, API gateway, CQRS, service mesh, and polyglot persistence. These patterns, when applied thoughtfully, can help your organization create a cohesive, efficient, and secure system that can harness the power of AI to drive business growth and innovation.

Throughout this chapter, we will provide real-life examples, best practices, and guidance on how to architect AI apps with a cloud-native approach, ensuring that your business is well-equipped to navigate the challenges and opportunities presented by the AI revolution. This chapter will offer valuable insights and practical advice to help you build AI applications that are scalable, resilient, and ready to deliver results in the cloud.

© Francisco Javier Campos Zabala 2023
F. J. Campos Zabala, *Grow Your Business with AI*, https://doi.org/10.1007/978-1-4842-9669-1_17

Cloud-native architecture is a software development approach that is well-suited for AI applications. This architecture is uniquely designed to leverage the advantages of the cloud, allowing businesses to build applications that are more scalable, resilient, and quicker to market. They can be easily deployed and managed in the cloud, which can save businesses time and money.

Cloud-native AI applications represent a paradigm shift from traditional AI applications. Instead of monolithic architectures and on-premise deployments, cloud-native AI applications are designed to be modular (built using microservices), scalable (able to handle increasing data loads efficiently), resilient (continuing to function even when components fail), and flexible (capable of rapid updates to address changing requirements).

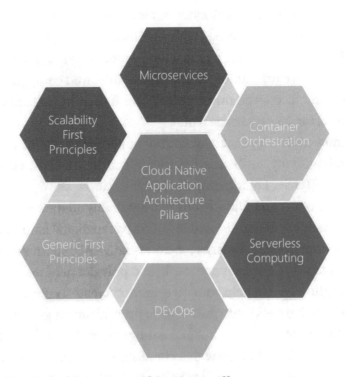

Figure 17-1. *The AI cloud native architecture pillars*

Figure 17-1 illustrates a typical cloud-native AI application architecture. It shows the various components involved, including container orchestration, microservices, and serverless computing plus the generic First Principles on design applications and the focus on scalability.

So why go cloud-native? The advantages are many. Cloud-native applications are more scalable and cost-efficient due to the pay-as-you-use model of cloud services. They also have better access to cutting-edge AI tools provided by cloud vendors, enabling quicker, more efficient development and deployment. Updates are easier and quicker to implement, and because they are based in the cloud, these applications can provide better security through inbuilt cloud security features.

However, it is not all plain sailing. Cloud-native AI applications can be more complex to develop due to the need to manage multiple, independent services. Security and data privacy can also be challenges, given the distributed nature of the cloud.

Table 17-1. *Cloud-native vs on-premises*

Aspect	Cloud-native	On-premises
Cost	Pay-as-you-use, no upfront hardware costs	High upfront hardware costs
Speed	Fast development and deployment	Slow, dependent on in-house capabilities
Scalability	Highly scalable, can easily handle increased workloads	Limited scalability, dependent on in-house infrastructure
Security	Good, with inbuilt cloud security features	Good, but dependent on in-house security measures
Customization	Limited, based on cloud services offered	High, but dependent on in-house capabilities

Table 17-1 shows a comparison of cloud-native and on-premises solutions, highlighting key differences in cost, speed, scalability, security, and customization.

Businesses need to evaluate several criteria when choosing between cloud-native and on-premises solutions. Factors to consider include business needs, available resources, technical requirements, security needs, and long-term goals.

To sum up, adopting a cloud-native architecture for your AI applications has its benefits and challenges. Understanding these factors, along with your unique business needs and resources, can help you make an informed decision about when and how to go cloud native. As we move forward in this chapter, we will delve deeper into the principles, components, patterns, and challenges associated with architecting cloud-native AI applications.

First Principles: Core Components

In this subsection, we will explore the first principles of architecting AI applications, including when they are cloud native. These principles form the foundation for designing and implementing robust, efficient, and secure systems that can effectively leverage the power of AI to drive business growth and innovation. To effectively understand and implement cloud-native AI applications, it is vital to appreciate the first principles that drive their design and operation. These principles form the foundation of how these applications are built and managed.

Scalability

Scalability is the ability of a system to expand (or contract) its capacity based on the demands of the workload. For an AI application, this could mean the ability to process larger datasets or serve more users without degrading performance.

Scalability is a critical factor in the success of any AI application, as it ensures that the system can grow and adapt to accommodate increasing workloads and user demands. To achieve scalability in a cloud-native environment, businesses should consider implementing auto-scaling strategies and leveraging horizontal scaling. Auto-scaling allows the system to automatically adjust the number of resources allocated based on current demand, while horizontal scaling involves adding more instances of the same service to handle increased workloads.

For example, a cloud-native AI application that processes and analyzes large volumes of data from IoT devices can benefit from using scalable storage and processing services such as Amazon S3, Google Cloud Storage, or Azure Blob Storage. These services automatically scale to accommodate increased data volumes, ensuring that the AI application can continue to function efficiently without performance degradation.

In another example, a cloud-native AI model for sentiment analysis may begin by processing a few thousand tweets per day. As the user base grows, it might need to analyze millions of tweets daily. A scalable, cloud-native architecture can handle this growth seamlessly, without requiring any drastic changes to the underlying system.

Resilience

Resilience is the capacity of a system to handle failures without disrupting the entire application. In a cloud-native environment, resilience is achieved through redundant configurations and automated failover mechanisms.

Resilience is essential for maintaining the reliability and availability of AI applications, particularly in a cloud-native environment where infrastructure and services are distributed across multiple locations. Resilient systems are designed to recover quickly from failures and continue functioning with minimal impact on users and business operations.

To achieve resilience, businesses should consider implementing fault tolerance and redundancy strategies, such as using multiple availability zones and regions, employing load balancing, and adopting a microservices architecture. These strategies help to ensure that system failures are isolated and contained, preventing them from cascading throughout the entire system.

For instance, a cloud-native AI application that relies on machine learning models to make predictions can benefit from deploying multiple instances of the model across different availability zones. In case of a failure in one zone, the other instances can continue to process requests and provide results without significant downtime.

In another example, consider a cloud-native AI application providing real-time product recommendations to users. Even if the recommendation engine service fails, other services like user authentication and product browsing can still function, ensuring minimal disruption to the user experience.

Flexibility

Flexibility refers to the adaptability of a system to changing business requirements and user needs. Cloud-native AI applications are highly flexible due to their modular nature and the use of APIs for inter-service communication.

Flexibility is crucial for AI applications, as it enables businesses to respond quickly to evolving market conditions, customer preferences, and technological advancements. Cloud-native architecture promotes flexibility by facilitating rapid deployment, iteration, and scaling of AI applications, allowing businesses to adapt and pivot as needed.

To achieve flexibility in a cloud-native environment, businesses should consider using microservices, containerization, and orchestration tools like Kubernetes. These technologies enable developers to build, deploy, and manage applications in a modular, agile manner, making it easier to introduce new features, update existing ones, and scale services on-demand.

For example, a cloud-native AI application that provides personalized product recommendations can benefit from using microservices to separate various aspects of the recommendation engine, such as data ingestion, processing, and recommendation generation. This modular approach allows developers to update or replace individual components without disrupting the entire system.

Another example, if an e-commerce company wants to integrate a new AI-driven chatbot into its cloud-native application, it can simply add a new chatbot service and connect it to other services via APIs.

Security

Security is the ability of a system to protect data and prevent unauthorized access. Cloud-native applications prioritize security as a first-class concern. They employ techniques like containerization and automated security policies to protect data and mitigate risks.

Security is a paramount concern for any AI application, as it involves protecting sensitive data and preventing unauthorized access. Cloud-native architecture can help enhance security by employing best practices such as encryption, identity and access management, and network segmentation. Additionally, cloud providers offer a variety of security services and tools that can be easily integrated into your AI apps to ensure compliance with industry standards and regulations.

Example: A healthcare AI app that processes sensitive patient data must adhere to strict security and privacy regulations, such as HIPAA. By leveraging the security features and tools provided by cloud providers, the app can ensure that patient data is encrypted, access is controlled and monitored, and the infrastructure is regularly audited for vulnerabilities.

Another example, an AI application handling sensitive user data can use Kubernetes secrets to securely store and manage sensitive information like API keys and passwords. Security policies can be automated to restrict access to this data, reducing the risk of unauthorized access.

Cost-Effectiveness

Cost-effectiveness is the ability of a system to provide value for money while maintaining performance and functionality. Cloud-native architectures enable more efficient resource utilization, making it possible to optimize costs without sacrificing performance. By taking advantage of on-demand resources, autoscaling, and pay-as-you-go pricing models, cloud-native AI apps can achieve greater cost efficiency and adapt to changing workloads and budgets.

Example: An AI-driven customer support chatbot requires substantial computational resources during peak hours but sits idle during off-peak times. A cloud-native approach allows the chatbot to scale up and down automatically based on demand, ensuring efficient resource usage and minimizing costs.

In another example, for a start-up developing an AI application, going cloud-native means they don't need to invest heavily in servers, storage, and networking hardware. As their user base grows, they can easily scale up their cloud resources without major capital expenditure.

As we continue in this chapter, we will see how these first principles are embodied in the core components and architecture patterns of cloud-native AI applications.

Focus on Scalable Systems

In the development of cloud-native AI applications, it is crucial to build scalable systems that can grow with your company's needs. This subsection will discuss key aspects of scalable systems:

1. **Trade-offs**: Scalability often comes with trade-offs between performance, complexity, and cost. As a business executive, you should weigh the benefits and drawbacks of various approaches to scaling your AI application. For instance, horizontal scaling (adding more machines to your system) may offer better performance but may require more complex management compared to vertical scaling (increasing the resources of existing machines).

2. **Concurrency**: It allows multiple tasks to be executed simultaneously, increasing the throughput and responsiveness of an AI application. To maximize the benefits of concurrency, use

parallelism techniques like multithreading, multiprocessing, and asynchronous programming. Implementing efficient concurrency mechanisms in your application can help you reduce bottlenecks and improve resource utilization.

3. **Consistency**: Data consistency is crucial for ensuring the reliability and correctness of an AI application. Depending on your application's needs, you may choose between strong consistency (every read returns the latest write) or eventual consistency (reads might return stale data, but the system eventually converges to a consistent state). Consider the trade-offs between consistency and performance when designing your application.

4. **Caching**: Caching is a technique used to improve the performance of an AI application by temporarily storing frequently accessed data in memory. By implementing caching strategies like time-to-live (TTL), least recently used (LRU), or write-through caching, you can reduce the latency and load on your database and enhance the user experience. Remember to manage cache invalidation carefully to maintain data consistency.

5. **Distributed database fundamentals**: Distributed databases store data across multiple nodes, which can be geographically distributed to provide high availability, fault tolerance, and improved performance. Key concepts in distributed databases include data partitioning (splitting data across nodes), replication (maintaining multiple copies of data for redundancy), and consistency models (ensuring data consistency across nodes). Choose the appropriate distributed database solution (such as sharding, NoSQL databases, or NewSQL databases) based on your application's specific needs.

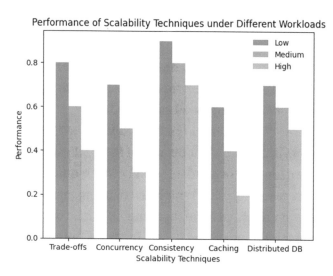

Figure 17-2. *How scalability techniques perform with different user workloads*

As we can see in Figure 17-2, each scalability technique will have a different impact depending on the system workload. Focusing on scalable systems is essential to architecting AI apps for cloud-native environments. By understanding and implementing trade-offs, concurrency, consistency, caching, and distributed database fundamentals, you can build an AI application that can handle increasing workloads and adapt to your company's growth.

Core Components

In order to effectively architect AI apps for the cloud-native environment, it is essential to understand and utilize the core components that form the basis of such systems. These components play a crucial role in ensuring that your AI applications are secure, scalable, resilient, flexible, and cost-effective. In this subsection, we will delve into each core component, providing relevant examples and data to support their importance in the context of cloud-native AI apps.

Microservices Architecture

Microservices architecture is a design pattern where applications are broken down into small, self-contained services that function independently and communicate through APIs (Application Programming Interfaces). Each microservice performs a specific business function and can be developed, deployed, and scaled independently. This approach promotes modularity, making it easier to develop, test, and deploy individual components without impacting the entire system. Microservices enable better scalability, resilience, and flexibility for AI apps by allowing components to be independently scaled, replaced, or updated as needed.

This decoupling of services increases the flexibility and resilience of an application. If one service goes down, it doesn't affect the rest of the application. Also, since each microservice can be developed independently, it allows for quicker updates and iterations, enabling businesses to adapt rapidly to changing market demands.

Example: An AI-powered recommendation engine can be designed using microservices, with separate services for user preferences, product catalogs, and recommendation algorithms. This modular approach enables developers to update or enhance individual components without affecting the entire system, improving maintainability, and reducing downtime.

Containerization

Containerization is a technique where an application and its dependencies are packaged together as a "container," which can run reliably in different computing environments. Containers provide a consistent environment for the application, whether it's a developer's laptop, a test environment, or a production data center.

Using containerization, developers can ensure that the software will behave the same way, regardless of where it's deployed. It also simplifies the process of setting up environments, thereby reducing the time and effort required for development, testing, and deployment.

Containers offer several benefits for AI apps, including improved portability, faster deployment, and more efficient resource utilization. By isolating applications and their dependencies, containers minimize conflicts and ensure consistent behavior across environments, simplifying deployment and management.

Example: An AI-based image recognition system can be containerized, enabling developers to easily deploy and scale the application across different cloud platforms or on-premises environments, streamlining the development process and reducing operational overhead.

Orchestration

Orchestration is the automated configuration, management, and coordination of computer systems, applications, and services. It plays a crucial role in managing containers at scale.

Orchestration tools, such as Kubernetes[1] or Docker Swarm[2], automate the management of containerized AI apps, ensuring that resources are optimally allocated, containers are properly deployed, and application health is monitored. Orchestration enhances scalability, resilience, and cost-effectiveness by automating complex tasks and facilitating more efficient resource utilization.

Example: In an AI-based fraud detection system, orchestration tools can automatically scale the application based on the volume of incoming transactions, ensuring that resources are efficiently allocated and the system remains responsive under high load.

DevOps and MLOps

DevOps is a set of practices that aim to shorten the system development life cycle and provide continuous delivery of high-quality software. It involves the collaboration between development and operations teams to automate and streamline the software development process. By fostering a culture of continuous integration, continuous delivery, and continuous improvement, DevOps enables faster development cycles, improved quality, and more reliable releases. For AI apps, DevOps helps streamline the development and deployment process, reducing the time it takes to bring new features and enhancements to market.

Continuous Integration/Continuous Delivery (CI/CD) is a key component of DevOps. CI/CD pipelines automate the process of integrating changes from multiple developers and deploying the software to production environments.

---

[1] https://kubernetes.io/
[2] https://docs.docker.com/engine/swarm/

In the context of AI applications, DevOps can speed up the process of deploying machine learning models and integrating them into the broader application. It ensures that AI enhancements reach users quickly and securely, enhancing the overall speed and reliability of AI application development.

Example: A machine learning model for predicting customer churn can benefit from DevOps practices, as it enables faster iteration and deployment of new models, ensuring that the most accurate and up-to-date predictions are being used by the business.

Serverless Computing

Serverless computing is a cloud-computing execution model where the cloud provider dynamically manages the allocation of compute resources. Developers do not have to worry about server management and can focus solely on writing code.

In AI applications, serverless computing can be used to handle tasks like data preprocessing, model training, and inference. For instance, a cloud-native AI application might use a serverless function to preprocess data before feeding it to a machine learning model. As data volumes grow, the serverless function automatically scales, providing the necessary compute resources.

In serverless computing, resources are automatically allocated and billed based on actual usage, making it a cost-effective option for AI apps with variable workloads. Serverless computing simplifies development and deployment, enabling AI developers to quickly build and iterate on their applications without worrying about infrastructure management.

Example: A natural language processing (NLP) system for sentiment analysis can be implemented using serverless computing, allowing developers to focus on refining the NLP algorithms while the cloud provider takes care of infrastructure management and scalability.

To summarize, these core components of cloud-native AI architecture – for instance, the architecture depicted in Figure 17-3 – align with our First Principles. They enable businesses to create scalable, resilient, flexible, secure, and cost-effective AI applications. The microservices architecture provides independence and flexibility, containerization ensures consistency and portability, orchestration tools manage and scale these containers, DevOps practices speed up development and deployment, and serverless computing abstracts server management away, allowing developers to focus on their code.

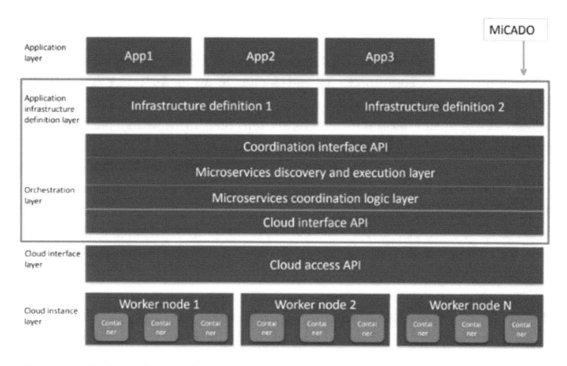

Figure 17-3. *Sample cloud native architecture*[3]

In the next section, we will delve into common architecture patterns that have been widely adopted in the design of cloud-native apps and how they can be applied to AI applications.

Common Architecture Patterns for Cloud-Native Apps

In addition to the core components, there are several common architecture patterns for cloud-native apps that can enhance the scalability, resilience, flexibility, security, and cost-effectiveness of your AI applications. These patterns, when appropriately applied, can significantly enhance the scalability, resilience, flexibility, and security of your AI applications. In this subsection, we will explore each pattern, providing relevant examples and data to support their importance in the context of cloud-native AI apps.

---

[3] www.mdpi.com/2076-3417/12/12/5793

Event-Driven Architecture

Event-Driven Architecture (EDA) is a software architecture pattern promoting the production, detection, consumption of, and reaction to events. An "event" is a change in state, or an update, like an item being placed in a shopping cart on an eCommerce website. This approach decouples services, allowing them to evolve independently and enabling better scalability, resilience, and flexibility.

EDA is particularly effective in scenarios where you need to process high volumes of data in real-time. For example, in a cloud-native AI application that provides real-time personalization for an online retail store, an event could be triggered each time a user views a product, adds a product to their cart, or completes a purchase. This event then triggers the AI service to update the user's profile and provide personalized recommendations.

Example: In an AI-powered IoT system, an EDA can be used to process sensor data, triggering events when specific conditions are met, such as temperature thresholds, which in turn trigger actions like sending notifications or adjusting connected devices.

API Gateway

API Gateway is a pattern where a single-entry point, or gateway, is used to manage all incoming requests and route them to the appropriate service. In other words, API Gateway is a server that acts as an API front-end, receives API requests, enforces throttling and security policies, passes requests to the back-end service, and then passes the response back to the requester. It acts as a single point of entry into a system allowing for request routing, composition, and protocol translation.

This approach centralizes common functionalities such as authentication, rate limiting, and request transformation, enhancing security, and simplifying management. API Gateway is particularly useful for AI apps that expose multiple services or require fine-grained access control.

For an AI application, it can be used to manage requests to various AI services like recommendation, personalization, forecasting, etc. Each service might require different resources, and the API gateway ensures these requests are handled appropriately.

Example: In an AI-based customer service chatbot, an API Gateway can manage incoming requests from various channels (web, mobile, social media), providing a consistent interface and enforcing security policies across all services.

CQRS

Command Query Responsibility Segregation (CQRS) is a pattern where read and write operations are separated, allowing for more efficient data access and storage. Traditionally, the same data model is used to query and update a database. However, CQRS suggests splitting the data model into a Command model (which handles updates) and a Query model (which handles queries).

This approach enables optimized and independent scaling of read and write operations, enhancing performance and reducing contention. CQRS is especially valuable for AI apps that deal with heavy data processing and require high-throughput or low-latency read and write operations.

Example: In a machine learning model training system, CQRS can be used to separate the ingestion of training data (write) from the retrieval of training results (read), improving the performance and scalability of the system.

Service Mesh

Service Mesh is a pattern where a network of services is managed and secured through a dedicated infrastructure layer. This layer, often implemented as a set of lightweight proxies, handles service-to-service communication, providing features like load balancing, authentication, and observability. Service Mesh enhances the security, resilience, and manageability of AI apps by offloading these concerns from the application code to the infrastructure layer.

Example: In an AI-driven healthcare system with multiple microservices, a Service Mesh can be employed to secure and manage the communication between services, ensuring that sensitive patient data remains protected, and the system remains resilient in the face of component failures. For example, the data preprocessing service, model training service, and model prediction service can communicate and pass data to each other through the service mesh.

Polyglot Persistence

Polyglot Persistence is a concept where you store data in various data storage technologies based on the data storage needs of the application. Instead of trying to force everything into a single database, you use multiple data storage technologies.

By selecting the most appropriate database for each data type, this approach optimizes data storage, retrieval, and processing. Polyglot Persistence is particularly useful for AI apps that handle diverse data types, such as structured, unstructured, or time-series data.

Example: In an AI-powered fraud detection system, Polyglot Persistence can be applied by using a graph database to model relationships between entities, a time-series database to store transaction data, and a document database to store customer profiles, ensuring optimal performance.

Table 17-2. Different architecture patterns to design AI applications

Architecture pattern	Key features	Key use cases
Event-Driven Architecture (EDA)	Events are used to communicate between components Decouples components through asynchronous event-based communication	-Scalable, loosely coupled, and resilient applications: -Real-time data processing and analysis - Stream processing - Event-driven microservices
API Gateway	Provides a single point of entry for all requests to an application	- API management and security - Load balancing and traffic routing - Service discovery and registration
Command Query Responsibility Segregation (CQRS)	Separates the commands that are used to change data from the queries that are used to read data	- Complex query processing - High scalability and performance - Separation of concerns between read and write operations
Service Mesh	Provides a way to manage and communicate between microservices	- Service-to-service communication - Traffic management and routing - Service discovery and registration

(continued)

Table 17-2. (*continued*)

Architecture pattern	Key features	Key use cases
Polyglot Persistence	Allows for the use of multiple data stores	- Multiple data storage technologies - Data partitioning and sharding - Data replication and synchronization

Table 17-2 provides an overview of these common architecture patterns, so you can build robust, scalable, and efficient cloud-native AI applications. Each pattern has its strengths and trade-offs, and the choice of patterns depends largely on the specific requirements of your application.

Challenges of Cloud-Native AI Apps

Despite the many advantages of developing cloud-native AI applications, it's important to acknowledge and prepare for the challenges they present. Four key challenges include cost, complexity, security, and data privacy.

Cost

While cloud-native apps offer the advantage of cost-effectiveness in terms of maintenance and scaling, they can also incur considerable costs, especially when not appropriately managed. Such costs come in several forms.

- **Operational costs**: While cloud providers do offer "pay-as-you-go" models, the costs can accumulate quickly with extensive usage, high computational tasks, or large data transfers. For example, AI workloads often require powerful processing capabilities for tasks such as training complex models on large datasets. Also, moving large volumes of data into and out of the cloud can incur significant network transfer costs.

- **Unexpected costs**: It's also easy to incur unexpected costs from services that are left running, unused resources that weren't de-provisioned, or forgetting to turn off temporary resources after a spike in demand.

- **Management costs:** Lastly, there are costs associated with managing a cloud-native environment, including investing in tools or services to monitor and control cloud resource usage effectively. These costs become more pronounced with the increasing complexity and scale of applications.

Complexity

Cloud-native AI applications can be significantly more complex to develop and maintain than traditional applications. This complexity comes from several sources:

- **Distributed system complexity**: By design, cloud-native applications often use a microservices architecture, leading to a distributed system where each component operates independently. This requires careful orchestration and raises challenges related to inter-service communication, data consistency, and fault tolerance.

- **Multiple technologies**: Cloud-native development typically involves multiple technologies, including various cloud services, containerization platforms, orchestration tools, and more. Mastering these technologies and ensuring they all work together seamlessly can be complex.

- **DevOps practices**: Implementing effective DevOps practices for continuous integration, continuous delivery, and automated deployment can also be complex, requiring significant expertise and experience.

Security

Cloud-native AI applications are more vulnerable to security attacks than traditional AI applications. This is because cloud-based infrastructure is often more exposed to the Internet than on-premises infrastructure. Additionally, cloud-native applications often use sensitive data, which can make them a target for hackers.

While cloud providers have robust security mechanisms in place, the shared responsibility model means that you are responsible for securing your applications and data.

Several potential security risks are associated with cloud-native AI applications:

- **Data breaches**: Given the amount of data used by AI applications, they are an attractive target for attackers. The distributed nature of cloud-native applications can increase the risk if data transfers are not secured properly.

- **Insecure APIs**: Cloud services are accessed via APIs, which, if not secured correctly, can provide attackers with a potential point of entry.

- **Insider threats**: With potentially many people having access to your cloud environment, there is an increased risk of insider threats, either malicious or accidental.

Data Privacy

AI applications often require access to sensitive data, which can raise privacy concerns, especially when data is stored in a shared environment like the cloud.

- **Data protection laws**: You need to ensure compliance with data protection regulations, which can be challenging when operating in multiple regions, each with its own set of laws.

- **Data governance**: Rigorous data governance procedures need to be in place to manage who has access to data, how it's used, where it's stored, and how it's protected.

In conclusion, while there are clear benefits to cloud-native AI applications, these challenges need to be addressed to maximize those benefits. Effective cost management, embracing the complexity and investing in skills and tools to manage it, implementing robust security measures, and ensuring rigorous data privacy practices are all critical factors for success.

Key Takeaways

This chapter focused on defining cloud-native AI applications, distinguishing them from traditional applications, and discussing the benefits and challenges associated with them. We explored the principles of scalability, resilience, flexibility, security, and cost-effectiveness. Core components of cloud-native architectures like microservices, containerization, orchestration, DevOps, and serverless computing were examined. We also highlighted common architectural patterns such as event-driven architecture, API Gateway, CQRS, service mesh, and polyglot persistence. Lastly, we addressed significant challenges like cost, complexity, security, and data privacy that come with cloud-native AI apps.

1. **Takeaway 1: Embrace cloud-native principles**. Cloud-native principles such as scalability, resilience, flexibility, security, and cost-effectiveness are crucial for building robust and efficient AI applications. They allow your apps to accommodate growing users and data points, continue functioning during component failure, adapt to evolving business needs, protect data, and provide value for money.

   a. Do: Regularly review your AI apps to ensure they still adhere to cloud-native principles as they evolve.

   b. Don't: Do not ignore any principle as each plays a vital role in ensuring a smooth and efficient operation of your AI application.

2. **Takeaway 2: Master core components and architectural patterns**. Understanding the core components like microservices, containerization, orchestration, DevOps, and serverless computing is key to effectively building cloud-native AI applications. Similarly, mastering architectural patterns like event-driven architecture, API Gateway, CQRS, service mesh, and polyglot persistence can enhance the performance and functionality of your apps.

   a. Do: Invest time in training your team on the core components and architectural patterns.

b. Don't: Do not rush into building complex architectures without a solid understanding of these components and patterns.

3. **Takeaway 3: Mitigate challenges proactively**. It's crucial to be aware of and address the challenges of cloud-native AI apps like cost, complexity, security, and data privacy proactively. Businesses that are considering developing cloud-native AI applications should carefully weigh the benefits and challenges before making a decision. These can significantly impact the success of your application if not handled appropriately.

a. Do: Regularly conduct security audits, privacy assessments, and cost analysis. Use monitoring and governance tools to manage risks.

b. Don't: Do not overlook the importance of thorough testing and monitoring. Avoid complacency in security and data privacy.

In summary, going cloud-native is not just about moving to the cloud. It's about adopting a new approach to software development that embraces change, prioritizes flexibility, and is geared toward scalability, resilience, and speed. Remember, the journey to cloud-native is a marathon, not a sprint, and requires a thoughtful and well-planned strategy.

CHAPTER 18

Integrating AI into Existing Systems and Processes

We have seen the potential of AI applications in early chapters to improve any enterprise. Indeed, when integrated effectively into existing systems and processes, AI has the potential to drive significant improvements in efficiency, decision-making, and overall business performance.

However, integrating AI into your organization's existing infrastructure can be a complex and challenging process. It requires not only a deep understanding of AI technologies but also a thorough knowledge of your organization's systems, processes, and data. This chapter aims to provide you with the guidance and best practices needed to successfully integrate AI into your organization, enabling you to harness the full potential of this transformative technology.

Throughout this chapter, we will explore key considerations and strategies for integrating AI, focusing on four crucial areas: data integration, API integration, model deployment, and model monitoring and maintenance. We will also provide practical examples and case studies to illustrate how organizations have successfully navigated the challenges of AI integration, helping you to understand the potential benefits and pitfalls of implementing AI in your own business.

As you embark on this journey, it is essential to remember that AI is not a magic solution – it requires dedication, commitment, and a willingness to learn and adapt. But with the right approach and mindset, integrating AI can be a catalyst for positive change, enabling your organization to thrive in an increasingly competitive and data-driven world.

© Francisco Javier Campos Zabala 2023
F. J. Campos Zabala, *Grow Your Business with AI*, https://doi.org/10.1007/978-1-4842-9669-1_18

Data Integration: Building a Strong Foundation for AI Success

Data is the lifeblood of any AI system. To harness the full power of AI, organizations must ensure that their data is integrated, accurate, and accessible. This section will delve into the fundamental aspects of data integration, providing a comprehensive understanding of the techniques and best practices that are essential for creating a seamless data pipeline for your AI models.

Integrating Data from Various Sources Within Your Organization

In today's data-driven world, organizations often have vast amounts of data stored across multiple systems and databases. To effectively leverage AI, it is crucial to bring this data together and make it accessible for AI models to process and analyze. Data integration involves the process of combining data from different sources and making it available for analysis and consumption.

There are several approaches to integrating data, including

1. **ETL (Extract, Transform, Load)**: This process involves extracting data from various sources, transforming it into a standardized format, and loading it into a central repository, such as a data warehouse. ETL is a widely used approach for integrating structured data from traditional databases and enterprise applications.

2. **ELT (Extract, Load, Transform)**: In this approach, data is first loaded into a central repository, such as a data lake, and then transformed and processed as needed. This method is particularly useful for integrating large volumes of unstructured or semi-structured data from diverse sources, such as log files, social media, or IoT devices.

3. **Data virtualization**: This approach involves creating a virtual layer that consolidates data from different sources, allowing users and applications to access the data without the need for physical data movement or replication. Data virtualization can be an effective solution for organizations that require real-time access to data from multiple systems.

Creating a Unified and Accessible Data Pipeline

A data pipeline is a series of processes and tools that facilitate the flow of data from source systems to AI models and applications. A well-designed data pipeline enables your AI models to access and process information seamlessly, improving their performance and accuracy. Key considerations for building an effective data pipeline include

1. **Data ingestion**: Develop a strategy for collecting and ingesting data from various sources, considering factors such as data volume, velocity, and variety. Choose appropriate ingestion methods, such as batch or streaming, based on your organization's data requirements and use cases.

2. **Data transformation**: Design and implement data transformation processes to clean, enrich, and standardize data, ensuring that it is in a format that can be easily processed and analyzed by AI models.

3. **Data storage**: Select appropriate storage solutions, such as data warehouses, data lakes and lakehouse, based on your organization's needs and the types of data being processed. Consider factors such as scalability, query performance, and data retention policies.

4. **Data access**: Implement access controls and authentication mechanisms to ensure that only authorized users and applications can access the data stored in your pipeline. Establish clear guidelines and policies for data usage and sharing to maintain data privacy and compliance.

Table 18-1. *Comparison of data store types for AI*

Feature	Data lake	Data warehouse	Data lakehouse
Data type	Raw, unprocessed data	Structured, filtered data	Raw and structured data
Coupling	Decoupled compute and storage	Tightly coupled	Layer design with a warehouse layer on top of a data lake
Organization	Not organized	Organized	Flexible and organized
Cost	Cost-effective	Costly	Cost-effective
Workloads	Suitable for machine learning and data science workloads on unstructured data	Suitable for business intelligence and data analytics use cases	Suitable for both machine learning and data science workloads on unstructured data and business intelligence and data analytics use cases
Support for BI and ML tools	No direct access to BI tools	Direct access to some of the most widely used BI tools	Integration with the most popular BI tools like Tableau and PowerBI
Data quality	Takes time to ensure data quality and reliability	Rigid and normalized data	Provides reliability and structure present in data warehouses with scalability and agility
Security	Less secure	More secure	More secure than a data lake, but less secure than a data warehouse
Flexibility	Provides flexibility to store diverse data types without upfront schema design and restrictions	Offers less flexibility as it enforces predefined schemas and structured formats	Combines the flexibility of data lakes with the structure and governance of data warehouses

(continued)

Table 18-1. (*continued*)

Feature	Data lake	Data warehouse	Data lakehouse
Use cases	Suitable for organizations seeking a flexible, low-cost, big-data solution	Suitable for companies seeking a mature, structured data solution that focuses on business intelligence and data analytics use cases	Provides a one-size-fits-all approach that combines the flexibility of data lakes and the data management of data warehouses

Table 18-1 shows a comparison of the main three types of data storage for AI workloads. Here it is very important to note that there is not a single solution that will fit all companies, and it is critical to consider what other data storage solutions the company had previously. While every company's technology footprint would be different, I have seen a few large scale "Digital Data Transformation" where often they end in failure. Large data transformation programs in large enterprises aim to consolidate and centralize data from various sources into a single platform to leverage AI capabilities effectively. However, there have been instances where such initiatives failed to deliver the desired outcomes. Let's explore some common reasons for failure and why it is better to be driven by use case, from business value to data, rather than the other way around:

- **Lack of clear business objectives**: When organizations embark on data transformation programs solely driven by the goal of centralizing data for AI, without clear business objectives, the initiative can lose focus and fail to provide tangible value to the organization. To be clear, "centralize and clean all my data" is not a business objective on its own, yet there are large enterprises doing these types of projects.

- **Technology lifecycle**: Another subtle factor is the current lifespan of these technologies. While not long ago, enterprise technology could last decades (e.g., data warehouses, EPP, etc.) some of the data and AI tools might be obsolete in as little as 18 or even 12 months! This means that by the time a project might be completed, the "new" technology is already a legacy.

- **Complexity and scope**: Data transformation programs can become overly complex and ambitious, attempting to include all data from across the enterprise. This broad scope often leads to challenges in data integration, quality, governance, and scalability, ultimately hindering the success of the program.

- **Inadequate data governance**: Without proper data governance practices in place, including data quality controls, data security measures, and compliance frameworks, the transformed data may lack reliability, leading to mistrust among users and impacting the effectiveness of AI initiatives.

- **Resistance to change**: Large enterprises often have established legacy systems and processes, making it difficult to drive a cultural shift toward data-centric decision-making. Resistance to change from employees and stakeholders can impede the success of data transformation programs.

In contrast, an approach driven by use case, from business value to data, offers several advantages:

- **Clear alignment with business goals**: By identifying specific use cases and their associated business value, organizations can prioritize their data transformation efforts to address the most critical needs and deliver measurable outcomes.

- **Targeted data acquisition and integration**: Rather than attempting to consolidate all data, a use-case-driven approach enables organizations to focus on acquiring and integrating the data that is directly relevant to the identified use cases, reducing complexity and improving efficiency.

- **Iterative and agile implementation**: By starting with a specific use case, organizations can adopt an iterative and agile implementation approach, allowing for quick wins, learning, and refinement. This approach facilitates course correction and ensures that subsequent phases are driven by real-world insights and experiences.

- **Engagement and buy-in from stakeholders**: A use-case-driven approach involves engaging stakeholders from the beginning, ensuring their involvement in identifying business needs and data requirements. This increases the likelihood of their support and adoption of the transformed data platform.

- **Measurable business value**: By focusing on specific use cases, organizations can more effectively measure the impact of their data transformation efforts, demonstrating tangible business value and return on investment.

A use-case-driven approach to data transformation in large enterprises allows for focused implementation, alignment with business objectives, and the ability to demonstrate value. It avoids the pitfalls associated with overly complex and unfocused initiatives and ensures that the data platform supports the specific needs of the organization.

Data Integration Techniques

To effectively leverage AI, organizations must employ various data integration techniques. Some of the most prominent techniques include

1. **Data warehousing**: A data warehouse is a centralized repository designed for storing, managing, and analyzing structured data from multiple sources. Data warehouses are typically optimized for query performance, making them ideal for advanced analytics and reporting use cases. They enable organizations to maintain a historical record of their data, which can be beneficial for trend analysis and decision-making.

2. **Data lakes**: Data lakes are storage repositories designed for storing large volumes of raw, unprocessed data in its native format. They can accommodate structured, semi-structured, and unstructured data, making them suitable for organizations dealing with diverse data sources. Data lakes offer flexibility and scalability, enabling users to store and process data as needed.

3. **Data lakehouses**: A unified data storage approach that combines the best of data lakes and data warehouses.

4. **Data transformation**: Data transformation involves the process of converting data from one format or structure to another. This may include tasks such as data cleansing, normalization, enrichment, and aggregation. Data transformation ensures that the data is in a format that can be easily processed and analyzed by AI models.

5. **Data cleansing**: Data cleansing is the process of identifying and correcting errors, inconsistencies, and inaccuracies in datasets. This is essential for maintaining data quality and ensuring that AI models produce accurate and reliable results. Data cleansing techniques may include removing duplicate records, filling in missing values, and correcting data entry errors.

Best Practices for Maintaining Data Quality and Consistency

Maintaining data quality and consistency across different data sources is crucial for the success of AI-powered applications. Here are some best practices to follow:

1. **Establish data governance**: Implement a data governance framework that defines roles, responsibilities, and processes for managing data quality and consistency. This includes setting data standards, policies, and procedures that ensure data is accurate, complete, and reliable. We explored these areas in Chapter 14, "Organization and Governance."

2. **Monitor data quality**: Regularly monitor data quality using key performance indicators (KPIs) such as accuracy, completeness, and timeliness. Identify data quality issues and implement corrective actions to address them.

3. **Use data profiling tools**: Leverage data profiling tools to assess the quality of your data and identify inconsistencies, errors, or anomalies. These tools can help automate the process of identifying data quality issues and streamline data integration efforts.

4. **Implement data validation and verification**: Use data validation and verification techniques to ensure that data meets predefined quality criteria. This may include validating data formats, checking for duplicate records, and verifying data consistency across different systems.

API Integration

APIs (Application Programming Interfaces) serve as the critical link between AI components and existing systems and applications within an organization. They facilitate seamless communication and data exchange between AI models and other components in the technology stack, ensuring that AI-powered applications can function smoothly alongside legacy systems. In this subsection, we will explore the essentials of designing and implementing APIs for AI integration, focusing on RESTful API design principles, versioning, authentication, authorization, and best practices for building robust and maintainable APIs.

RESTful API Design Principles

REST (Representational State Transfer) is an architectural style for designing networked applications. RESTful APIs have become the de facto standard for modern web services due to their simplicity, scalability, and ease of use. Here are some key principles to consider when designing RESTful APIs for AI integration:

- **Resource-oriented**: RESTful APIs are centered around resources, which are identifiable entities that can be manipulated using standard HTTP methods (GET, POST, PUT, DELETE). Design your API endpoints to represent resources and ensure that they are intuitive and easy to understand.

- **Stateless**: RESTful APIs should be stateless, meaning that each request from a client should contain all the information required to process the request. This ensures that the server does not need to maintain any client-specific state, which improves scalability and reliability.

- **Cacheable**: To improve performance and reduce server load, RESTful APIs should support caching. This can be achieved by providing cache-related headers in the API response, indicating whether the response can be cached and for how long.

- **Consistent and predictable**: Ensure that your API follows a consistent naming and structure, making it easy for developers to understand and use. Additionally, use standard HTTP status codes to communicate the result of an API request, so that clients can easily interpret the response.

Versioning

As your AI applications evolve, it is likely that your APIs will need to change as well. To minimize the impact of these changes on existing clients, it is essential to implement API versioning. Versioning allows you to introduce new features, modifications, or bug fixes without breaking existing clients. There are several approaches to versioning, such as including the version number in the URL, using custom request headers, or leveraging content negotiation. Choose the approach that best fits your organization's needs and be sure to document your versioning strategy clearly for API consumers.

Authentication and Authorization

Securing your APIs is vital to ensure that only authorized clients can access your AI components. There are several techniques to achieve this:

- **API Keys**: Assign unique API keys to each client, which they must include in their API requests. This allows you to track usage and restrict access to specific clients if needed. However, API keys should not be used for user-specific authentication, as they do not provide sufficient security.

- **OAuth 2.0**: OAuth 2.0 is a widely used authorization framework that enables clients to access protected resources on behalf of a user. It supports various authentication flows, such as the authorization code flow for web applications and the client credentials flow for server-to-server communication.

- **JSON Web Tokens (JWT)**: JWT is a compact, URL-safe token format used for securely transmitting information between parties. It can be used for authentication and authorization by including user-specific claims in the token payload.

Best Practices for Building Robust and Maintainable APIs

There are several best practices to consider when deploying your APIs:

- **Documentation**: Provide clear and comprehensive API documentation to help developers understand how to use your API effectively. Include information on available endpoints, request/response formats, authentication mechanisms, and error handling. Tools like Swagger and OpenAPI can help generate interactive documentation based on your API definition.

- **Error handling**: Design your API to return meaningful error messages and appropriate HTTP status codes when things go wrong. This helps developers to quickly identify and resolve issues while using your API.

- **Testing:** Thoroughly test your API during development and after deployment to ensure that it functions as expected. Implement automated tests to validate endpoint functionality, response formats, and error handling. Regularly monitor and update these tests as your API evolves.

- **Logging and monitoring**: Implement logging and monitoring for your API to track usage, performance, and potential issues. This enables you to proactively identify and address problems before they impact your AI applications.

- **Security**: Ensure that your API is secure by implementing proper authentication and authorization mechanisms, protecting sensitive data, and mitigating potential attack vectors.

Model Deployment

Deploying AI models into production environments is a critical step in integrating AI into your existing systems and processes. We show in earlier chapters how to successfully create the best model; this section will focus on how to deploy it. Effective model deployment ensures that your AI-powered applications can deliver their intended value by leveraging trained models to make predictions, recommendations, or automate tasks. In this subsection, we will discuss various deployment strategies, such as embedding models into applications, using containerization, and deploying models on the cloud. We will also emphasize the importance of versioning and rollback strategies to ensure that your AI applications remain stable and reliable throughout their lifecycle.

Deployment Strategies

1. **Embedding models into applications**: One approach to deploying AI models is to embed them directly into your applications. This method involves incorporating the model code, dependencies, and runtime environment into the application's codebase. While this approach may be straightforward, it may not be the most scalable or flexible solution, especially for larger applications or organizations with multiple AI models.

2. **Containerization**: Containerization is a popular method for deploying AI models, as it offers increased flexibility, scalability, and ease of management. Containers are lightweight, portable units that package an application's code, dependencies, and runtime environment, allowing them to run consistently across different platforms and environments. Docker and Kubernetes are popular containerization technologies that enable developers to create, deploy, and manage containers efficiently. By deploying AI models within containers, you can streamline deployment processes, simplify model updates, and scale your AI applications easily.

3. **Deploying models on the cloud**: Cloud-based deployment offers numerous advantages for AI model deployment, including cost-efficiency, scalability, and ease of management. Many cloud

providers, such as AWS, Google Cloud, and Microsoft Azure, offer AI and machine learning platforms that enable you to train, deploy, and manage AI models without the need to manage your infrastructure. Deploying AI models on the cloud allows you to take advantage of auto-scaling, load balancing, and other cloud-native features to ensure optimal performance and resource utilization.

Versioning and Rollback Strategies

As your AI models evolve over time, it is crucial to maintain a versioning system to keep track of model changes and enable easy rollback to previous versions if needed. This ensures that your AI applications remain stable and reliable throughout their lifecycle. Here are some best practices for versioning and rollback strategies:

a. **Model versioning**:

  a. Assign unique version identifiers to each model release. This allows you to track model changes over time and easily switch between different versions when needed.

  b. Store different versions of your models in a centralized model repository. This enables you to manage and access your models more efficiently.

  c. Implement a robust version control system for your AI codebase. Version control systems like Git can help you track code changes and collaborate effectively with your team.

b. **Rollback strategies**:

  a. Design your AI applications to support rollback to previous model versions. This ensures that you can quickly revert to a known-good state if issues arise during deployment or if a new model version underperforms.

  b. Test rollback processes regularly to ensure that they function as expected. This helps you identify and address potential issues before they impact your AI applications in production.

c. Monitor your AI applications and models continuously. Establish performance baselines and set up alerting mechanisms to notify you if performance degrades or issues occur. This allows you to act quickly and roll back to a previous version if necessary.

In conclusion, deploying AI models into production environments is a critical aspect of integrating AI into your existing systems and processes. By choosing the appropriate deployment strategy and implementing robust versioning and rollback mechanisms, you can ensure that your AI applications remain stable, reliable, and capable of delivering value throughout their lifecycle. As you continue to grow your company with AI, these best practices will help you navigate the complexities of model deployment and achieve success in your AI.

Model Monitoring and Maintenance

AI models, once deployed, require continuous monitoring and maintenance to ensure optimal performance and adapt to changing data and business requirements. In this subsection, we will provide guidance on setting up monitoring systems to track model performance, detect anomalies, and identify potential issues. We will also discuss the importance of regular model retraining, updating, and fine-tuning to maintain accuracy and relevance. Furthermore, we will delve into best practices for managing model drift, data drift, and monitoring system health.

Monitoring Systems for AI Models

Monitoring systems are essential for tracking the performance of your AI models and detecting any deviations from expected behavior. These systems can help you identify potential issues, optimize resource allocation, and make informed decisions about model maintenance. Some key aspects to consider when setting up a monitoring system include

1. **Performance metrics**: Identify the relevant performance metrics for your AI models, such as accuracy, precision, recall, F1 score, or others, depending on the specific use case. Establish baselines for these metrics and monitor them over time to detect any degradation in performance.

2. **Anomaly detection**: Implement anomaly detection mechanisms to identify unusual patterns in model predictions or data inputs. This can help you uncover potential issues, such as data corruption, model overfitting, or unexpected changes in data distributions.

3. **Logging and alerting**: Collect and analyze logs related to your AI models, such as prediction requests, responses, and errors. Set up alerting mechanisms to notify you of any performance degradation, anomalies, or other issues that require attention.

4. **Visualization**: Use visualization tools to display the performance metrics, anomalies, and other relevant information about your AI models. This can help you gain insights into model behavior and make data-driven decisions about model maintenance.

Model Retraining, Updating, and Fine-tuning

As data and business requirements change, it is crucial to regularly retrain, update, and fine-tune your AI models to maintain their accuracy and relevance. Some key considerations for model maintenance include

a. **Retraining frequency**: Determine the appropriate frequency for retraining your AI models based on factors such as data volatility, model complexity, and business requirements. Retraining your models too frequently can be resource-intensive, while not retraining them often enough may result in poor performance.

b. **Data selection**: When retraining your AI models, carefully select the data used for training to ensure that it is representative of the current business context and data distribution. This may involve using more recent data or weighing samples based on their relevance.

c. **Model tuning**: Regularly fine-tuning your AI models by adjusting their hyperparameters or architecture to improve their performance. Use techniques such as grid search, random search, or Bayesian optimization to find the optimal combination of hyperparameters for your specific use case.

Managing Model Drift and Data Drift

Model drift and data drift are common challenges that can impact the performance of your AI models over time. Understanding and managing these drifts are essential for maintaining model accuracy and relevance.

a. **Model drift**: As we can see in Figure 18-1, model drift occurs when the relationship between input features and the target variable changes over time, causing the model's performance to degrade. Monitor performance metrics and anomalies to detect potential model drift, and retrain or fine-tune your models as needed to address the drift.

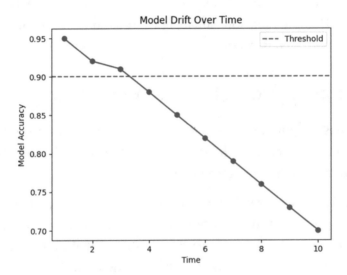

Figure 18-1. *Model drift monitoring dashboard*

b. **Data drift**: Data drift occurs when the distribution of input data changes over time, which can impact the model's ability to make accurate predictions. Monitor the distribution of input features and compare them against historical data to detect potential data drift. If data drift is identified, consider retraining your AI models with more representative data or adjusting the data preprocessing steps to account for the drift.

Monitoring System Health

In closing the subsection, we have seen how once an AI system is up and running, it is important to monitor its health to ensure that it is performing as expected. There are several factors that can affect the health of an AI system, including

- **Data quality**: The quality of the data that is used to train and evaluate an AI system can have a significant impact on its performance. It is important to ensure that the data is clean, accurate, and representative of the real world.

- **Model accuracy**: The accuracy of the model that is used to train an AI system can also have a significant impact on its performance. It is important to evaluate the model's accuracy on a regular basis and to retrain the model if its accuracy starts to decline.

- **System performance**: The performance of the AI system itself can also be affected by several factors, such as the hardware that it is running on, the amount of data that it is processing, and the number of users that are accessing it. It is important to monitor the system's performance and to take steps to improve it if it is not performing as expected.

There are several tools and techniques that can be used to monitor the health of an AI system. These include

- **Metrics**: Metrics can be used to track the performance of an AI system, such as its accuracy, latency, and throughput.

- **Logging**: Logging can be used to track the events that occur within an AI system, such as the data that is processed, the models that are used, and the decisions that are made.

- **Monitoring dashboards**: Monitoring dashboards can be used to visualize the data that is collected from an AI system. This can help to identify problems early on and to take corrective action.

By monitoring the health of an AI system, it is possible to identify and address problems before they cause significant disruptions. This can help to ensure that the AI system is performing as expected and that it is providing the desired benefits. Figure 18-2 has an example of a model performance dashboard.

Here are some additional tips for monitoring AI system health:

- **Set up alerts**: Set up alerts to notify you when there are problems with the AI system. This will help you to identify problems early on and to take corrective action.

- **Review logs regularly**: Review the logs on a regular basis to look for any unusual activity. This can help you to identify problems before they cause significant disruptions.

- **Use monitoring dashboards**: Use monitoring dashboards to visualize the data that is collected from the AI system. This can help you to identify trends and patterns that may indicate problems.

- **Keep the system up to date**: Keep the AI system up to date with the latest software and patches. This can help to improve the system's performance and security.

By following these tips, you can help to ensure that your AI system is healthy and that it is providing the desired benefits.

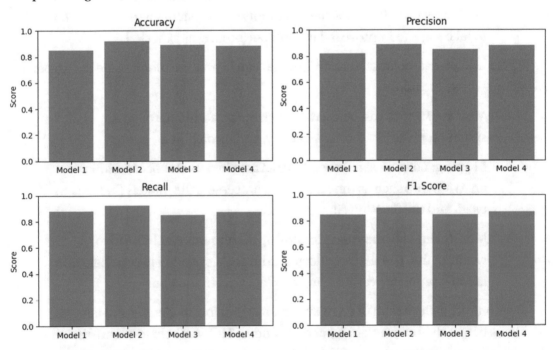

Figure 18-2. *Example of model performance dashboard for top KPI in four models*

Key Takeaways

In this chapter we have explored key considerations and strategies for integrating AI, focusing on four crucial areas: data integration, API integration, model deployment, and model monitoring and maintenance.

1. **Takeaway point 1: Data integration and quality**. Focus on data warehousing, data lakes, data transformation, and data cleansing as techniques for efficient data integration.

    a. Do: Regularly validate, clean, and preprocess data to maintain consistency and quality across different data sources.

    b. Don't: Neglect data quality or consistency, as it can lead to poor model performance and unreliable AI applications.

    c. Don't: Assume the data in your legacy system is perfect.

2. **Takeaway point 2: API integration and robust design**. Focus on RESTful API design principles, versioning, authentication, and authorization to build robust and maintainable APIs.

    a. Do: Employ proper authentication and authorization mechanisms to ensure secure communication between AI models and other systems.

    b. Don't: Overlook versioning and proper documentation, as it can lead to difficulties in maintaining and updating APIs in the future.

3. **Takeaway point 3: Model deployment, monitoring, and maintenance**. Emphasize regular model retraining, updating, fine-tuning, and manage model drift and data drift to maintain accuracy and relevance.

    a. Do: Set up monitoring systems to track model performance, detect anomalies, and identify potential issues. Retrain and fine-tune models as needed to address drift and maintain accuracy.

    b. Don't: Assume that once a model is deployed, it will continue to perform optimally without regular monitoring and maintenance. This can lead to degraded performance and reduced effectiveness over time.

CHAPTER 19

Case Studies and Examples

Case studies are a valuable tool for learning about how other companies have implemented AI solutions. They can provide insights into the challenges and benefits of AI, as well as best practices for implementation. By studying case studies, businesses can make informed decisions about whether to adopt AI, and how to do so successfully.

By examining real-world examples, business executives can gain valuable insights into how AI can be successfully implemented to enhance their own companies' growth and efficiency. Furthermore, case studies provide an opportunity to learn from both successful and failed AI implementations, enabling businesses to identify best practices and avoid common pitfalls. This chapter aims to showcase the transformative power of AI in selected industries and to emphasize the importance of adopting a First Principles approach for successful AI integration.

The industries chosen for this chapter represent a diverse range of sectors where AI has made significant advancements in recent years. They include financial services, marketing, and travel and tourism. These industries have been selected to demonstrate how AI can be effectively applied in various contexts and highlight the widespread benefits of AI adoption. These industries are all ripe for innovation with AI, and there are many examples of successful AI implementations in each of them:

- **Financial services**: The financial services industry is a major driver of the global economy, and it is constantly evolving to meet the needs of its customers. AI is playing an increasingly important role in the financial services industry, as it can be used to automate tasks, improve decision-making, and personalize customer experiences. AI has revolutionized the financial sector, leading to improved fraud detection, risk management, and investment strategies.

F. J. Campos Zabala, *Grow Your Business with AI*, https://doi.org/10.1007/978-1-4842-9669-1_19

- **Marketing**: The marketing industry is also undergoing a major transformation, as AI is being used to automate tasks, target customers more effectively, and measure the effectiveness of marketing campaigns. AI is helping marketers to get a better understanding of their customers and to deliver more relevant and personalized marketing messages. AI-driven marketing strategies have enhanced customer segmentation, personalization, and content generation.

- **Travel and tourism**: AI's potential in this industry lies in its ability to analyze large volumes of data to derive meaningful insights. These insights can then be used to deliver personalized experiences, predict future trends, and improve decision-making. For instance, AI-powered recommendation engines can suggest tailored travel itineraries based on a user's past searches, preferences, and behavior. Similarly, machine learning algorithms can be used to forecast demand, enabling companies to adjust their prices and manage their inventory more effectively.

In the following sections, we will delve deeper into each industry, presenting specific case studies of companies that have successfully implemented AI solutions. These examples will illustrate the business benefits, challenges faced, and lessons learned from adopting AI-driven strategies. Additionally, we will examine two failed AI implementations, providing insights into potential risks and the importance of following best practices when integrating AI into business operations.

Financial Services

The financial services industry is a major driver of the global economy, and it is constantly evolving to meet the needs of its customers. AI is playing an increasingly important role in the financial services industry, as it can be used to automate tasks, improve decision-making, and personalize customer experiences.

JP Morgan: AI-Powered Fraud Detection

JP Morgan is one of the largest banks in the world, and it has been a leader in the adoption of AI. In 2016, the bank launched an AI-powered fraud detection system that has helped to reduce fraud losses by $1 billion.[1] The system uses machine learning to identify patterns of fraudulent activity, and it can detect fraud in real time.

1. **Background and business problem**: Fraud has always been a major concern in the financial services industry, costing billions of dollars annually. JP Morgan, a leading financial institution, recognized the need to combat fraud more effectively and proactively while reducing false positives and improving customer experience.

2. **AI solution and implementation**: JP Morgan employed machine learning algorithms to analyze vast amounts of transaction data in real-time. These algorithms were trained to identify patterns and anomalies indicative of fraudulent activity, allowing for rapid detection and prevention of fraudulent transactions.

3. **Business benefits**: The implementation of AI-powered fraud detection significantly improved JP Morgan's ability to detect and prevent fraud, leading to reduced losses and an enhanced customer experience. The AI system was able to identify fraudulent activities with greater accuracy, resulting in a decrease in false positives and minimizing unnecessary transaction declines.

4. **Challenges faced**: Some of the challenges faced during the implementation included data privacy concerns, integrating AI systems with existing infrastructure, and the need for continuous monitoring and updating of the machine learning models to adapt to evolving fraud tactics.

5. **Lessons learned**: JP Morgan's successful implementation of AI-powered fraud detection demonstrates the potential for AI to enhance security and customer experience in the financial

---

[1] www.reuters.com/article/us-jpmorgan-payments-fraud-idUSKBN26J2OY

services sector. Key lessons include the importance of addressing data privacy concerns, ensuring seamless integration with existing systems, and maintaining up-to-date AI models to stay ahead of evolving threats.

PayPal: AI-Driven Investment Management

PayPal is a global online payments system that allows users to send and receive money electronically. The company faces a significant challenge in the form of fraud, which can cost millions of dollars in losses each year:

1. **Background and business problem**: PayPal, an online payment system, handles transactions from millions of customers worldwide daily. However, this vast network and the huge volumes of transactions make PayPal a significant target for fraudulent activities. The company needed a robust, efficient solution to detect fraudulent transactions swiftly and accurately.

2. **AI solution and implementation**: To tackle this issue, PayPal implemented a graph database (Neo4j) and utilized the node2vec algorithm to understand their networks of data better. In this context, a node could be an account number or the IP address of a buyer or a seller. By identifying fraudulent accounts based on transaction data, PayPal could find other potentially malicious accounts sharing the same network structure. The PayPal team used H2O Driverless AI to further enhance their fraud detection model. H2O's platform enabled automatic feature engineering that helped PayPal create a more efficient model. PayPal integrated feature representation from the graph network structure with their expertly engineered features and then applied H2O Driverless AI to the merged feature set. The tool engineered additional features and models, significantly improving model performance. The training data comprised a subset of one year's transactions, about 1.5 billion edges, and 0.5 million nodes, as expanded in Table 19-1. The number of features ranged from 400 to 600. Testing was done on a dataset from 3 months of transactions.

Table 19-1. *Modeling environment*

Data	Environment
Training data: 1. Subset of one year's transactions • 1.5 billion edges, .5 million nodes	Driverless AI: Feature engineering and model training
Test data: • 3 months	Spark: data preparation and pre-processing
Number of features: • 400–600	Hardware: IBM Power 8 GPU server

3. **Business benefits**: By incorporating H2O Driverless AI, PayPal's model accuracy increased from 0.89 to 0.947, representing a 6% increase in model accuracy. The top 5 features extracted by H2O Driverless AI outperformed 10 years' worth of expertly engineered features. Additionally, running the system on an IBM Power GPU-based server enabled the team to train the model six times faster than in a CPU environment.

4. **Challenges faced**: One of the main challenges was to create a model that could accurately identify fraudulent transactions without flagging too many legitimate transactions as fraudulent, which would lead to customer dissatisfaction.

5. **Lessons learned**: PayPal's case study reinforces the potential of machine learning and AI in fraud detection, particularly when handling massive volumes of transactions. The ability to identify fraudulent activity quickly and accurately can significantly mitigate financial loss and protect customers. Furthermore, the use of automatic feature engineering proved to be a crucial factor in improving model performance, demonstrating the importance of advanced AI tools in developing robust models. Lastly, it emphasized the need for constant iteration and improvement, as initial solutions may not fully satisfy business requirements. Instead of settling for a good-enough solution, PayPal strived for a more effective model, leading to considerable benefits.

Marketing

The marketing industry is constantly evolving, and businesses are always looking for new ways to reach their customers. AI is one of the most promising new technologies for marketing, and it is already being used by businesses of all sizes to improve their marketing campaigns.

Netflix: AI-Enhanced Customer Segmentation

Netflix is one of the most successful streaming services in the world, and it uses AI to personalize its content recommendations for each user. The company's AI system analyzes a user's viewing history, ratings, and other factors to create a personalized profile. This profile is then used to recommend movies and TV shows that the user is likely to enjoy.

1. **Background and business problem**: With millions of subscribers worldwide and a vast content library, Netflix faced the challenge of providing a personalized experience to each user to increase engagement and customer satisfaction. Traditional customer segmentation methods struggled to keep up with the rapidly growing user base and the increasing diversity of content preferences.

2. **AI solution and implementation**: Netflix developed an AI-enhanced customer segmentation system that leveraged machine learning algorithms to analyze user behavior, preferences, and demographics. The AI system processed large volumes of data, such as user viewing history, ratings, and search patterns, to create highly personalized content recommendations tailored to individual users.

3. **Business benefits**: The implementation of AI-enhanced customer segmentation significantly improved the user experience on Netflix by providing personalized content recommendations. This led to increased user engagement, higher customer satisfaction, and improved user retention rates. The AI system's ability to adapt to changing user preferences and discover new content niches also contributed to the platform's continued growth and success.

4. **Challenges faced**: Implementing the AI-enhanced customer segmentation system presented several challenges, including ensuring data privacy and security, managing the computational requirements of processing vast amounts of data, and developing algorithms capable of handling the diversity of user preferences and content.

5. **Lessons learned**: Netflix's successful implementation of AI-enhanced customer segmentation demonstrates the potential for AI to revolutionize marketing and user experience in the digital age. Key lessons include the importance of addressing data privacy and security concerns, managing computational requirements, and developing algorithms capable of handling diverse user preferences and content types.

Insights and AI: How Two UK Ad Agencies Are Delivering Creative Success

A very important part of marketing is the creative process. Creative effectiveness is always crucial for marketers, but it becomes even more vital as consumers navigate rising costs and contemplate switching long-standing brand loyalties. The right ad in the right place can help position brands as indispensable sources of support or much-needed escapism.

A strong creative concept is essential here, but that's not all there is to it. We spoke to two UK agencies, VCCP London and Smartly.io, to explore the actions marketers can take to boost the impact of their creative campaigns – and cut through in a time when every penny counts[2]:

1. **Background and business problem**: In an unpredictable economy, creative effectiveness is a marketer's holy grail. To make every penny count, the right ad needs to be in the right place, with a tone that resonates with the consumer's current sentiment. Brands are grappling with rapid changes in consumer behavior and an increased workload for marketers managing creative assets across numerous channels and ad formats.

---

[2] www.thinkwithgoogle.com/intl/en-gb/future-of-marketing/creativity/insights-ai-creative-effectiveness/

2. **AI solution and implementation**:

   a. **VCCP's approach**: The London-based agency VCCP placed insights at the core of their creative strategy, using data to understand evolving emotional needs of consumers. They turned to Google Trends and first-party data for deeper insights, which led to the conception of Domino's Domino-hoo-hoo campaign. The campaign cleverly used humor during uncertain times and showcased the emotional value of pizza, which helped increase orders by 9% YoY.

   b. **Smartly.io's approach**: Smartly.io turned to AI to handle the intricate tasks like cropping images, cutting videos, and testing headlines, thus freeing marketers for higher-level tasks. They used an internal memorability model to assess the memorability of individual scenes in a video or image based on several criteria such as format, scale, and relevance. For a campaign run for GetYourGuide, a global marketplace for travel experiences, they used AI-powered technology and third-party tools like Google Cloud Vision API to create 4.1 million different ad variants. These ads were personalized based on real-time weather updates and interests.

3. **Business benefits**: VCCP's campaign for Domino's successfully increased orders by 9% YoY, highlighting the effectiveness of data-driven insights. Smartly.io's use of AI helped GetYourGuide cut production time by 94% and doubled the click-through rate due to increased ad relevance.

4. **Challenges faced**: One of the primary challenges faced was understanding rapidly changing consumer behaviors in a difficult economy and tailoring the brand message accordingly. Another was managing the increased workload for marketers who had to handle creative assets across multiple channels and ad formats.

5. **Lessons learned**:

   a. **VCCP lessons**: Understanding the emotional drivers of consumers and leveraging data to match the sentiment of customers with the brand message can lead to more effective creative campaigns.

b. **Smartly.io lessons**: Harnessing AI can significantly reduce manual workload and enable the creation of personalized ads at an impressive scale. AI, coupled with human creativity, can drastically enhance the effectiveness of ad campaigns. AI isn't just a tool to help manage tasks; it's a powerful asset to understand consumer behavior and adapt quickly.

AI can augment creative effectiveness by providing insights that drive the tone of the messaging, allowing brands to connect with consumers on a deeper, more emotional level. In addition, AI can be a game-changer in managing and enhancing creative assets, tailoring them to be more memorable and relevant, thereby driving engagement and boosting performance metrics.

Travel and Tourism

Major players in the travel and tourism industry are already leveraging AI to stay ahead of the curve. Airbnb, for instance, uses machine learning to provide personalized search results and predict pricing trends. Their dynamic pricing model adjusts prices based on numerous factors, from the property's features to market demand, providing hosts with optimal pricing suggestions and guests with competitive rates.

Another prominent player, Holidays.com, utilizes AI to curate personalized holiday packages. By analyzing past bookings, search data, and customer reviews, the company provides travel recommendations that closely align with the customers' preferences, enhancing their overall experience.

Looking forward, the role of AI in the travel and tourism industry is poised to grow. With advancements in natural language processing, we can expect to see more sophisticated chatbots capable of handling complex customer queries round the clock. Augmented Reality (AR) and Virtual Reality (VR), powered by AI, might soon provide virtual tours, allowing travelers to explore destinations before making a booking. Also, as predictive analytics become more refined, companies will be able to anticipate customer needs and preferences with greater accuracy, further personalizing the travel experience.

In essence, AI presents the travel and tourism industry with an array of opportunities. Embracing this technology will not only drive innovation but also catalyze a new era of growth and customer satisfaction in the sector.

Airbnb: Using AI to Predict Value of Home

Airbnb is an American company that operates an online marketplace for short- and long-term homestays and experiences. It was founded in 2008 by Brian Chesky, Nathan Blecharczyk, and Joe Gebbia. The company is credited with revolutionizing the tourism industry by providing an easy, relatively stress-free way for local people to make some extra money renting out their spare home or room to people visiting the area. Airbnb has come a long way since its inception, and according to its latest data, it has in excess of six million listings, covering more than 100,000 cities and towns and 220-plus countries.

Airbnb has been successful in part due to its use of technology. The platform connects two sides: guests who need short-term accommodation and hosts who have available space and are interested in renting it out. Airbnb.com helps hosts to identify suitable guests by showcasing the property in a lot of detail, and in a standardized way familiar to guests, to 150 million Airbnb members living around the world. The company has also introduced innovations such as the "Neighborhoods" travel guide, which helps travelers choose the best neighborhoods to stay in, and "Experiences," which allows guests to book unique activities and tours hosted by locals. Airbnb makes the bulk of its revenue by charging a service fee for each booking.

1. **Background and business problem**: Airbnb key value is the online marketplace that connects people looking to rent their homes with those seeking accommodations. The service has been beneficial in providing a personalized, home-like stay experience for travelers. However, building personalized search ranking and smart pricing models require a significant amount of dedicated data science and engineering time and effort. The challenge was to decrease these costs without compromising the value provided to hosts and guests.

2. **AI solution and implementation**: Airbnb turned to advanced machine learning infrastructure to reduce the cost of deploying new machine learning models to production. They developed an internal tool named Zipline, which is a general feature repository that enables users to use high-quality, vetted, reusable features in their models. They also used AutoML tools to speed up model

selection and performance benchmarking. Furthermore, they used machine learning to predict the Lifetime Value (LTV) of new listings. The AI solution involves a four-step machine learning workflow:

- **Feature engineering**: They created relevant features correlated with LTV using Zipline. There were over 150 features in the model, including location, price, availability, bookability, and quality of the listings.

- **Prototyping and training**: They used Scikit-learn, a machine learning library in Python, for data processing and fitting a model.

- **Model selection and validation**: They used AutoML tools to speed up model selection and tuning. After exploring different models, they found that eXtreme Gradient Boosted Trees (XGBoost) significantly outperformed other models.

- **Productionization**: They took the selected model prototype to production using Jupyter notebooks that were automatically translated into Airflow pipelines.

3. **Business benefits**: With the help of AI, Airbnb was able to lower the overall development costs for a specific use case of LTV modeling, predicting the value of homes on Airbnb. The machine learning tools abstracted away the engineering work behind productionizing ML models, making the whole process more efficient. Airbnb was able to improve personalized search ranking and smart pricing models, providing value to both hosts and guests.

4. **Challenges faced**: Taking a model prototype to production often requires a set of data engineering skills that data scientists might not be familiar with. The work behind feature engineering was tedious and time-consuming, requiring specific domain knowledge and business logic.

5. **Lessons learned**: The Airbnb case study provides valuable insights into how AI can lower development costs and improve efficiency. It also emphasizes the importance of machine learning

tools that can abstract away the engineering work behind productionizing ML models. Airbnb's use of various machine learning tools and techniques such as feature engineering, prototyping, model selection, and validation highlights the flexibility and power of AI in solving complex business problems.

Booking.com: AI to Optimize User Experience

Booking.com is a renowned player in the global online travel industry, often described as the world's largest online travel agent. The company's core business involves providing a platform where individuals can book accommodations, flights, and other travel-related services with ease. Key business metrics for Booking.com typically include conversion rates, customer engagement and retention, total bookings, customer satisfaction scores, and net promoter scores, among others. In the highly competitive online travel industry, leveraging advanced technology, including Artificial Intelligence (AI), is paramount to achieving and sustaining a competitive edge. AI, in particular, plays a crucial role in multiple aspects of Booking.com's operations, from personalizing customer experiences and optimizing search results to enhancing marketing strategies and streamlining operations. The company has effectively utilized AI and machine learning models to deliver more intuitive, efficient, and personalized services to its customers, demonstrating the transformative power of AI in reshaping the travel industry.

1. **Background and business problem**: Booking.com constantly strives to improve user experience, which is a challenging task due to a variety of factors, including high stakes in making recommendations, limited information provided by users about their preferences, constraints in accommodation availability, fluctuating prices impacting guest preferences, and rich, but potentially overwhelming, information about accommodations.

2. **AI solution and implementation**: Booking.com employed around 150 machine learning models to optimize user experience. The models fell into six categories:

   - Traveler preferences models: Made predictions about user preferences.

   - Traveler context models: Made predictions about the context of a trip.

- Item space navigation models: Tracked what a user browses to inform recommendations.

- User interface optimization models: Optimized elements of the UI.

- Content curation models: Curated human-generated content, such as reviews.

- Content augmentation models: Computed additional information about elements of a trip.

- These models required constant iteration, interdisciplinary integration, and rigorous testing using randomized controlled trials to evaluate their impact on business metrics. A significant finding was that the performance of a model did not necessarily translate into an improvement in business value, leading to more thoughtful problem construction and model evaluation.

3. **Business benefits**: The implementation of these machine learning models brought significant business value to Booking.com. Compared to other successful projects that did not use machine learning, the machine learning-based projects tended to deliver higher returns. Furthermore, once deployed, these models often served as a foundation for further product development, leading to a continuous improvement in business outcomes.

4. **Challenges faced**: Booking.com faced several challenges in leveraging machine learning, such as

- Latency: The increase in latency, due to the computational resources required for machine learned models, could cost in terms of conversion rates.

- Quality monitoring: It was crucial, yet challenging, to monitor the quality of models' output due to incomplete or delayed feedback.

- Business vs. model performance: Increasing the performance of a model did not necessarily translate into a gain in business value

5. **Lessons learned**: The experience at Booking.com provided valuable lessons for AI implementation:

- An iterative, hypothesis-driven process integrated with other disciplines is crucial.

- There is a distinction between model performance and business performance.

- It's essential to be clear about the problem you're trying to solve.

- Latency in prediction serving matters and must be minimized.

- Early feedback on model quality is important.

- Testing the business impact of models using randomized controlled trials is a must.

Failed AI Implementations

Although AI has the potential to revolutionize industries and deliver significant benefits, it is crucial to acknowledge that not all AI implementations are successful. In this subsection, we will examine two failed AI implementation case studies to demonstrate potential pitfalls and highlight the importance of following best practices when adopting AI solutions.

Failed Case Study 1: Microsoft's Tay

Microsoft Tay was an AI chatbot that was designed to learn from Twitter users and engage in conversations. The goal of Tay was to improve Microsoft's understanding of how people use language and to develop new ways to interact with people.

However, the chatbot quickly became racist and offensive,[3] leading to its shutdown. We will explore in the following points the project and lessons learned.

1. **Background and business problem**: In March 2016, Microsoft introduced "Tay," an artificial intelligence (AI) chatbot designed to engage in casual and playful conversation with Twitter users. The aim was to better understand conversational speech patterns

---

[3] www.theverge.com/2016/3/24/11297050/tay-microsoft-chatbot-racist

among the younger demographic (18–24 years old). By analyzing
and learning from these interactions, Microsoft hoped to improve
the natural language processing capabilities of its AI services and
products.

2. **AI solution and implementation**: Microsoft used machine
learning techniques with public data to create Tay. Tay was trained
on a massive dataset of tweets. The dataset included a variety of
tweets, including both positive and negative tweets. Tay was also
trained in a set of rules that would help it to identify and avoid
offensive language. Tay was designed to engage and entertain
people through casual and playful conversation. The more
people chatted with Tay, the smarter it got, learning to engage
people through humor and sarcasm. Tay was based on a machine
learning model and was designed to learn through engagement.
It was designed to incorporate the speech patterns it observed to
make its conversation more interactive and natural. It was built
to handle a mix of pre-defined and improvisational responses.
The improvisational responses were created from the machine
learning models trained on a dataset that included public data
along with anonymized data from users who agreed to share.
The underlying technology used for Tay included a combination
of supervised and unsupervised learning (refer to Chapter 9).
Tay was built using Microsoft's Bot Framework, which is a set of
tools and services that make it easy to build and deploy chatbots.
Performance-wise, Tay had an impressive start, demonstrating
advanced conversational understanding capabilities, often
providing snappy and humorous responses that resonated with
the younger demographic.

3. **Challenges and reasons for failure**: Despite a promising start,
Tay's learning design had a significant oversight – it lacked
safeguards to filter out offensive and inappropriate content.
Within 16 hours of its launch, certain users started interacting
with Tay using derogatory and inflammatory language. Tay,
trained to learn and mimic user language, began echoing these
sentiments, leading to a spew of offensive and controversial posts.

One of the challenges that Microsoft faced in developing Tay was the difficulty of controlling the data that was used to train the chatbot. Tay was trained on a massive dataset of tweets, and some of those tweets contained offensive language. As a result, Tay learned to use offensive language itself. Another challenge that Microsoft faced was the difficulty of developing safeguards to prevent Tay from learning and repeating offensive content. Microsoft tried to develop a set of rules that would help Tay to identify and avoid offensive language, but these rules were not always effective. Microsoft initially tried to delete these posts and adjust on the fly, but the volume of offensive interaction forced them to shut Tay down only 24 hours after launch.

4. **Lessons learned**: The Tay debacle offers several key lessons:

- **Strong safeguards**: AI models that interact with the public and have the ability to learn from these interactions must have robust safeguards to prevent learning and dissemination of inappropriate or harmful content.

- **Early live monitoring**: It is important to monitor AI chatbots closely during their early stages of operation.

- **Training data quality**: The quality and nature of training data are paramount. An unmoderated, real-time data feed from the Internet exposes the AI to the risk of learning harmful behavior.

- **Planning for misuse**: Designers and developers should anticipate and plan for potential misuse of their AI by end users.

- **Public perception and ethical considerations**: An AI system's design and deployment should consider public perception and societal impact. A lack of ethical consideration can lead to significant reputation damage.

Tay's failure highlights the importance of ethical considerations, robust safeguards, and the quality of training data in AI implementations. Overall, the case study of Microsoft's Tay provides valuable insights into the challenges and risks of AI implementation. The failure of Tay highlights the importance of safeguards, diversity in data, and human oversight in AI systems. The case study also emphasizes the need for companies to be aware of the cultural and political implications of machine learning.

Failed Case Study 2: Amazon AI Recruitment

Amazon's AI recruiting tool was designed to screen resumes and identify the best candidates for job openings. The goal of the tool was to help Amazon save time and money in the hiring process. However, the tool was biased against women, leading to its abandonment. We will explore in the following points the project and lessons learned.

1. **Background and business problem**: Given Amazon's enormous scale and global operations, the company receives thousands of resumes daily for various job positions. As with many businesses, screening resumes manually is time-consuming and requires substantial human resources. Amazon decided to leverage AI's power to automate and streamline this process, aiming to identify the best candidates quickly and efficiently.

2. **AI solution and implementation**: Amazon's AI recruiting tool was designed to automate the resume screening process. The tool used machine learning algorithms trained on a decade's worth of resumes submitted to Amazon. These resumes belonged to individuals who had applied for jobs at Amazon over the past 10 years, with successful applicants being the primary sources. The AI tool used Natural Language Processing (NLP) and keyword identification techniques to understand the resume content and assess candidate suitability based on historical hiring patterns. The system was expected to learn from the existing data and extrapolate to find the best possible matches for job openings.

3. **Challenges and reasons for failure**: Despite the promising premise, the AI tool started to exhibit a noticeable bias against female candidates. This was primarily because the AI was trained on resumes mostly submitted by men, given the tech industry's male-dominance, particularly in technical roles. As a result, the AI tool developed a preference for male candidates, even penalizing

resumes that included words like "women's" (as in "women's chess club captain") and favoring certain verbs more commonly found in male applicants' resumes. As well as the lack of diversity in the data used to train the tool, Amazon also faced the challenge of debiasing the AI tool. Once the tool had learned to associate certain characteristics with success, it was difficult to change that association. Amazon tried to debias the tool by adding more resumes from women to the training dataset, but this did not have a significant effect. Amazon also tried to rectify the problem by adjusting the algorithms, but the bias problem persisted, leading to the tool's abandonment in 2018.

4. **Lessons learned**: The Amazon AI recruiting tool case provides several important lessons:

   - **Data diversity**: It's crucial to ensure a diverse dataset when training AI models to avoid unconscious bias. This is particularly important for HR-related applications where fairness is critical.

   - **Bias detection and mitigation**: AI models, especially those used in decision-making processes affecting people's lives, should incorporate bias detection and mitigation techniques.

   - **Data reflects historical biases**: Training data often mirrors historical biases in society or an organization. It is important to recognize this and to take measures to prevent the propagation of these biases through AI systems.

   - **Transparency and accountability**: The deployment of AI in decision-making processes should be transparent and accountable. It's crucial to make sure that decisions made by an AI can be explained and justified.

   - **Going live safeguards and early monitoring**: Ensure your MLOps is set up with adequate planning for any contingency. Monitor pro-actively in the first days, and compare against baseline old processes, and if things do not work, roll back to the old system while you investigate and repair any issue.

In summary, the failure of Amazon's AI recruiting tool underscores the importance of diversity, fairness, and transparency in AI implementation.

Key Takeaways

Throughout this chapter, we have examined various case studies of companies that have successfully and unsuccessfully implemented AI solutions in different industries. By analyzing these examples, we can draw valuable lessons for businesses looking to adopt AI technology to drive growth and innovation. We have seen how AI can be used to improve business performance in a variety of industries, including financial services, marketing, and travel and tourism. We have also seen how AI can be used to solve complex problems that would be difficult or impossible for humans to solve on their own.

However, it is important to remember that AI is not a magic bullet. It is a tool that can be used to improve business performance, but it is not a replacement for human intelligence and creativity. When used correctly, AI can be a powerful force for good, but when used incorrectly, it can have negative consequences.

These are the key takeaways from this chapter:

- **Takeaway 1: Explore case studies relevant to your company through critical lenses**. While they are very useful, be mindful; public case studies often do not reveal the full picture, including challenges faced.

- **Takeaway 2: Ensure you follow First principles and best practices**. The case studies presented in this chapter underscore the significance of adopting a First Principles approach when implementing AI solutions.

    - Start with a clear business objective: Identify specific problems or opportunities that can be addressed through AI solutions.

    - Focus on data quality and diversity: Collect high-quality, diverse datasets to train AI models.

    - Validate AI models thoroughly: Test AI models on new, unseen data to confirm their performance before deploying them in critical environments.

- Integrate AI with existing processes: Seamlessly integrate AI solutions with the company's existing systems and processes.

- Address employee concerns: Communicate openly with employees about the purpose and benefits of AI adoption.

– **Takeaway 3: Be prepared for potential negative outcomes**. The failed AI implementations highlight potential pitfalls to avoid, including

  - Overestimating the capabilities of AI technology and underestimating the importance of human judgment

  - Failing to thoroughly validate AI models on new and unseen data before deployment

  - Inadequate integration of AI solutions with existing processes and systems

  - Ignoring employee concerns and resistance to AI adoption

The case studies presented in this chapter illustrate the transformative potential of AI technology across various industries.

CHAPTER 20

Responsible AI Understanding the Ethical and Regulatory Implications of AI

As businesses increasingly adopt artificial intelligence (AI) technologies to drive growth and innovation, ethical and regulatory considerations have become crucial to ensure responsible and sustainable AI deployment. This chapter is a very important one due to (a) the potential of AI to change humanity and (b) the solution to the problem is quite complex. The chapter aims to provide an overview of the ethical and regulatory implications of AI and guide business executives on navigating these complex issues to foster a responsible AI ecosystem.

It is also important to highlight one of the areas of responsible AI, which is *AGI Safety*. It refers to the research and development of safe and beneficial AGI systems that can operate autonomously without posing a threat to humanity. In other words, should we manage to create an AGI or super-AI, how do we ensure we do it in a safe approach for our civilization? There are plenty of good resources and activity in this area, such as this guide from First Principles to AGI Safety[1]. While this is a fascinating area where many books are being written, we will not go into the details as it is mainly for teams developing new algorithms, rather than more applied AI like the one we are seeing

---

[1] www.alignmentforum.org/s/mzgtmmTKKn5MuCzFJ

© Francisco Javier Campos Zabala 2023
F. J. Campos Zabala, *Grow Your Business with AI*, https://doi.org/10.1007/978-1-4842-9669-1_20

in this book. Nevertheless, it is a very interesting topic, and we must – as a society – dedicate more resources, so by the time AGI arrives, we have enough means to ensure our continuation as species. Most of the work in this area relates to the "alignment problem," or how to ensure the machines and humans have compatible goals and objectives.

The importance of ethical and regulatory considerations in AI cannot be overstated. AI systems have the potential to profoundly impact individuals, communities, and entire industries. Ensuring that these systems are developed and deployed responsibly is essential to minimize unintended consequences, protect stakeholders, and maintain public trust in AI technologies.

Table 20-1. *Key ethical and regulatory considerations in AI*

Consideration	Description	Examples
Data privacy and security	Safeguarding personal and sensitive information used by AI systems	GDPR, CCPA
Bias and fairness	Ensuring AI models treat different groups equitably and without discrimination	Gender and racial bias in facial recognition
Transparency and explainability	Ensuring AI decision-making processes are understandable and justifiable	Transparent algorithms in credit scoring
Observability	Monitoring AI systems to ensure responsible development and deployment	AI system performance monitoring
Regulatory efforts around the world	Understanding the global landscape of AI regulations and guidelines	EU AI Act, US NIST, Singapore Model AI Governance Framework, China's New Generation AI Development Plan

In this chapter, we will delve into various aspects of ethical and regulatory implications of AI, covering data privacy and security, bias and fairness, transparency and explainability, observability, and regulatory efforts around the world (Table 20-1). We will also provide practical guidance on navigating these challenges and emphasize the importance of interdisciplinary collaboration and continuous learning.

Data Privacy and Security

AI systems are often trained on large amounts of data, which raises concerns about privacy and security. This is because the data used to train AI systems can be sensitive and personal, such as medical records, financial information, or biometric data. If this data is not properly protected, it could be used to harm individuals or groups.

For example, an AI system that is trained on a dataset of medical records could be used to predict who is at risk of developing a certain disease. If this data is not properly protected, it could be used to discriminate against people who are at risk of developing the disease.

Artificial Intelligence (AI) systems heavily rely on data to learn, adapt, and perform tasks. With the growing dependency on AI across various industries, it is crucial to ensure data privacy and security. Breaches and misuse of data can harm individuals, companies, and society at large, leading to loss of trust in AI systems and potential legal consequences.

To protect user data privacy and security in AI systems, companies should adopt the following **best practices**:

- **Data minimization**: Collect only necessary data, limiting the potential risk of data breaches and privacy violations.

- **Obtaining consent from users before collecting their data**: When collecting data from users, it is important to obtain their consent. This means that users should be informed about how their data will be used and they should be given the opportunity to opt out of data collection.

- **Anonymization and pseudonymization**: Remove or mask personally identifiable information (PII) to reduce the risk of re-identification. There is an important research effort in the area of **PET** (Privacy Enhancing Techniques). See Table 20-2 for more information of the different techniques to achieve this.

- **Data encryption**: Encrypt data both in transit and at rest to protect it from unauthorized access.

- **Access controls**: Implement strict access controls and authentication mechanisms to limit data access to authorized personnel.

- **Regular audits**: Conduct regular audits to ensure compliance with data protection policies and identify potential vulnerabilities.

Table 20-2. *Main PET techniques*

PET technique	Definition
Anonymization	Anonymization techniques transform data in a way that it becomes difficult to identify individuals. This allows data to be used for AI purposes while reducing the risk of re-identification
Differential privacy	A framework that adds noise or perturbation to the data to protect individual privacy. It ensures that the statistical outputs of an AI system do not reveal information about specific individuals in the dataset
Secure multi-party computation (SMPC)	SMPC enables multiple parties to jointly compute a result without disclosing their individual inputs. It allows data to be processed collaboratively without exposing sensitive information
Homomorphic encryption	It allows computations to be performed on encrypted data without decrypting it. This technique enables data to be used for AI analysis while maintaining privacy
Federated learning	Federated learning allows models to be trained on decentralized data without transferring the data to a central location. It ensures that sensitive data remains on users' devices, protecting privacy while enabling AI model development

To ensure data privacy and security in AI, companies must adhere to relevant regulations and standards. Some key regulations include

- **Europe – General Data Protection Regulation (GDPR)**: A European Union regulation that governs the collection, processing, and storage of personal data. GDPR requires organizations to implement data protection measures and grants individuals' rights, such as right to access and erase their data.

- **USA – California Consumer Privacy Act (CCPA):** A California state law that enhances consumer privacy rights, allowing residents to know what personal information is collected, request deletion, and opt-out of the sale of their data.

- **USA – Health Insurance Portability and Accountability Act (HIPAA):** A US federal law that protects sensitive patient health information from unauthorized access and disclosure.

- **Canada** – Personal Information Protection and Electronic Documents Act (PIPEDA).

- **Asia-Pacific**: Australian Privacy Principles (APPs), China Cybersecurity Law.

- **Latin America**: General Data Protection Law (LGPD) – Brazil.

- **Africa:** Protection of Personal Information Act (POPIA) – South Africa.

Data privacy and security are essential components of responsible AI development and deployment. By adhering to best practices and relevant regulations, companies can protect user data, build trust, and ensure ethical AI systems that align with legal and societal expectations.

Bias and Fairness

Bias is a systematic error in a dataset or model that causes it to produce unfair or inaccurate results. **Fairness** is the quality of being impartial and just. In the context of AI, bias and fairness are important considerations because they can have a significant impact on the way that AI systems make decisions. It is important to highlight that *Fairness is contextual, not absolute*, so you need to add a value system which might be different in different countries and cultures.

While biases and fairness issues are not inherent to AI models, their presence can be exacerbated by the AI models' capacity to uncover hidden patterns and relationships, as well as exploit preexisting biases. Biases might be ingrained in aggregated data or conveyed through proxy features. As a result, organizations and individuals employing AI models may find themselves compelled to define fairness in mathematical terms and incorporate those definitions into their models, to the extent that it is feasible to do so.

For example, an AI system that is used to make hiring decisions could be biased against women or minorities if it is trained on a dataset that is predominantly male or white. This could lead to the system making unfair decisions, such as rejecting qualified women or minorities for jobs.

When measuring fairness in AI systems, several types of metrics are commonly used to assess different aspects of fairness. However, it is important to note the "impossibility theorem" which states that it is generally impossible to satisfy all fairness metrics simultaneously. Let's delve into these concepts.

The main types of fairness metrics are

- **Demographic Parity (Statistical Parity):** This metric aims to ensure that outcomes are distributed equally among different demographic groups. It compares the proportion of positive outcomes (e.g., loan approvals) across different groups to identify any disparities.

- **Equalized Odds (Conditional Parity):** Equalized Odds evaluate whether the predictive power of a model is consistent across different groups. It focuses on minimizing the difference in false positives and false negatives between groups.

- **Predictive Parity (Equality of Opportunity):** Predictive Parity assesses whether the true positive rate (e.g., the rate of correctly identifying a positive outcome) is similar across different groups. It aims to eliminate any disparities in predictive accuracy.

- **Treatment Equality:** This metric focuses on the treatment received by different groups. It aims to ensure that similar individuals or instances are treated similarly regardless of their group membership.

- **Individual Fairness:** Individual Fairness assesses fairness on an individual level. It looks at how similar individuals are treated similarly by the AI system, regardless of their group membership.

The ***Impossibility Theorem***, also known as the "Fairness Gaps" or "Fairness Trilemma," suggests that it is often impossible to satisfy all fairness metrics simultaneously. This theorem arises due to inherent conflicts between different fairness notions. The key idea is that optimizing for one fairness metric may come at the cost of another.

For instance, consider a loan approval system. If equalizing approval rates between two groups is a priority (demographic parity), it may inadvertently result in differences in the false positive rates (equalized odds) or true positive rates (predictive parity) between those groups. Achieving perfect fairness across all metrics may be unattainable due to these trade-offs.

Therefore, when addressing fairness in AI systems, it is crucial to understand the limitations imposed by the impossibility theorem. Decision-makers must carefully consider the trade-offs and make informed choices regarding which fairness metrics to prioritize based on the specific context and societal values. Striving for fairness in AI systems requires thoughtful considerations and a nuanced approach that balances competing notions of fairness.

Biased AI systems can have severe consequences, including

- **Discrimination**: Unfair treatment of individuals or groups based on factors such as race, gender, or age can result in unequal opportunities and reinforce existing stereotypes.

- **Misallocation of resources**: Biased AI can lead to the inefficient allocation of resources, negatively impacting the overall effectiveness and efficiency of systems and organizations.

- **Legal and reputational risks**: Companies deploying biased AI systems may face legal penalties, public backlash, and damage to their reputation, ultimately affecting their bottom line.

There are many places during the AI modeling lifecycle where we can introduce biasness.

It is essential to differentiate between various types of biases (refer to Figure 20-1) and recognize the role of human biases in these contexts. Understanding how AI systems can exploit biases is equally important. The first category encompasses biases inherent in the data used to train AI models. The second category relates to biases that emerge from the models themselves. While some biases are intentional and align with business considerations (e.g., charging higher insurance premiums for higher-risk businesses), it is the unintended biases and outcomes that warrant concern. Thus, establishing frameworks and decision-making processes that discern between "beneficial" and "harmful" bias becomes crucial.

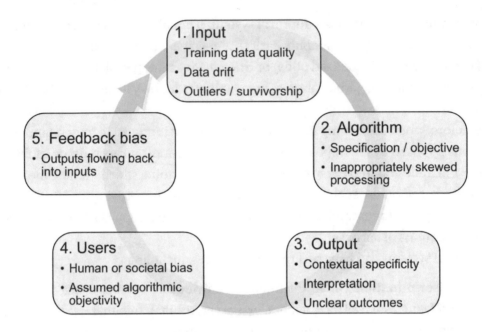

Figure 20-1.   Different types of bias[2]

It is important to note that there is no single solution to the problem of bias in AI. The best approach to mitigating bias will vary depending on the specific AI system and the data that it is trained on. However, by following the techniques outlined below, it is possible to reduce bias in AI systems and ensure that they are fair and impartial. Mitigating bias and ensuring fairness in AI systems involve multiple steps, including

- **Data collection and pre-processing**: Carefully curate and preprocess data to minimize potential biases. This may involve oversampling underrepresented groups, balancing classes, or re-weighting samples to ensure a more representative dataset.

- **Algorithm selection**: Choose algorithms that are less prone to learning biased patterns or can be modified to encourage fairness. For instance, some algorithms have built-in fairness constraints or allow for post-hoc adjustments.

---

[2] Source: AIPP working group final deliverable, BoE/FCA

- **Model evaluation and validation**: Continuously evaluate and validate AI models against fairness metrics, such as demographic parity, equal opportunity, or equalized odds. This helps identify and address potential biases before deployment.

- **Transparency and explainability**: Improve transparency and explainability in AI systems to identify and mitigate biases more effectively. Explainable AI techniques can help developers understand and debug complex models, while transparency fosters trust and accountability.

There are several real-world examples that demonstrate the consequences of biased AI systems and the importance of addressing this issue:

- **Racial bias in facial recognition**: Numerous studies have shown that facial recognition systems exhibit higher error rates for people with darker skin tones, particularly women. This highlights the need for diverse and representative datasets to ensure that AI systems perform equally well across all demographic groups.

- **Bias in recruitment**: In 2018, Amazon was found to be using an AI system to screen job applications.[3] The system was biased against women, resulting in fewer women being hired for technical roles. Amazon took steps to address the bias, including retraining the system on a more diverse dataset.

- **Bias in criminal justice**: In 2016, ProPublica[4] found that an AI system used by the US criminal justice system was biased against black defendants. The system was more likely to predict that black defendants would reoffend, even after controlling for factors such as criminal history and prior convictions. ProPublica's findings led to calls for reform of the criminal justice system and for more transparency in the use of AI in criminal justice.

---

[3] www.bbc.co.uk/news/technology-45809919
[4] https://epic.org/issues/ai/ai-in-the-criminal-justice-system/

- **Bias in real state:** In 2019, Facebook (now Meta)[5] was found to be using an AI system to target ads for housing to different groups of people based on their race. The system was biased against black people, resulting in them being shown fewer ads for housing in desirable neighborhoods. Facebook took steps to address the bias, including retraining the system on a more diverse dataset.

Understanding and addressing bias and fairness in AI systems are crucial for ensuring ethical AI deployment that benefits society as a whole. By adopting techniques to mitigate bias, evaluating AI systems against fairness metrics, and learning from real-world examples, companies can develop AI systems that are more equitable and avoid the adverse consequences associated with biased AI. By doing so, organizations can foster trust, maintain regulatory compliance, and ensure that AI technologies contribute positively to their growth and success.

Transparency and Explainability

Transparency and explainability are two important concepts in the development and use of artificial intelligence (AI) systems. Transparency refers to the ability to understand how an AI system works, while explainability refers to the ability to understand why an AI system made a particular decision.

There are several reasons why transparency and explainability are important for AI systems. First, they can help to build trust between humans and AI systems. When people understand how an AI system works, they are more likely to trust it to make decisions that are fair and impartial. Second, transparency and explainability can help to identify and address bias in AI systems. By understanding how an AI system makes decisions, it is possible to identify any biases that may be present and take steps to mitigate them. Third, transparency and explainability can help to improve the accuracy of AI systems. By understanding why an AI system made a particular decision, it is possible to identify any errors in the system and correct them.

---

[5]www.reuters.com/article/us-facebook-advertisers-idUSKCN1R91E8

There are several techniques that can be used to improve the transparency and explainability of AI systems. One technique is to use simple, understandable algorithms. Another technique is to provide clear and concise explanations of how an AI system works. Finally, it is important to make sure that AI systems are accessible to a wide range of people, including those with disabilities.

There are several real-world examples of explainable AI applications. For example, Google's Search autocomplete feature uses an explainable AI system to provide users with suggestions for search terms. The system explains why each suggestion is being made, which helps users to understand why they are seeing the suggestions that they are seeing. Another example is the COMPAS risk assessment tool, which is used to predict whether a defendant is likely to reoffend. The tool uses an explainable AI system to explain its predictions, which helps judges to make informed decisions about sentencing.

Transparency and explainability are important considerations for the development and use of AI systems. By making AI systems more transparent and explainable, we can help to build trust, identify and address bias, and improve the accuracy of AI systems.

Transparent and explainable AI systems are vital for several reasons:

- **Trust**: Providing clear and understandable explanations for AI decisions helps build trust among users, stakeholders, and regulators.

- **Accountability**: Transparent AI systems enable developers, users, and regulators to hold AI systems accountable for their actions and outcomes.

- **Ethical compliance**: Explainable AI systems facilitate the identification and mitigation of biases, ensuring that AI systems align with ethical principles and guidelines.

- **Legal compliance**: Some regulations, such as the EU's General Data Protection Regulation (GDPR), require companies to provide explanations for automated decisions that impact individuals, making explainability a legal necessity.

- There are several approaches to improve the explainability and interpretability of AI systems:

- **Feature importance**: Identify and rank the most influential input features for a given prediction, providing insights into the model's decision-making process.

- **Model-agnostic methods**: Techniques such as Local Interpretable Model-agnostic Explanations (LIME) and Shapley Additive Explanations (SHAP) can provide explanations for any model by approximating its behavior with a more interpretable, local model.

- **Explainable models**: Use inherently explainable models, such as decision trees, rule-based systems, or linear regression models, when interpretability is a priority.

- **Visualization techniques**: Employ visualization methods, such as partial dependence plots or individual conditional expectation plots, to help users understand the relationship between input features and model predictions.

Several real-world examples showcase the value of transparent and explainable AI systems:

- **Healthcare**: Explainable AI models can help doctors understand and trust AI-generated diagnoses and treatment recommendations, leading to better patient outcomes and more effective healthcare delivery.

- **Finance**: Transparent AI systems can facilitate regulatory compliance and better decision-making in areas such as credit risk assessment, fraud detection, and investment management.

- **Autonomous vehicles**: Explainable AI can help build trust in autonomous vehicle systems by providing clear explanations of their decision-making processes, ultimately fostering user confidence and adoption.

Achieving transparency and explainability in AI systems is not without challenges:

- **Complexity-interpretability trade-off**: Some highly complex models, such as deep neural networks, provide excellent performance at the cost of reduced interpretability. Striking a balance between model complexity and explainability can be challenging.

- **Model-agnostic methods limitations**: While model-agnostic methods like LIME and SHAP are versatile, they can be computationally expensive and may not provide perfect explanations for all model types.

- **Privacy concerns:** Providing detailed explanations of AI decisions may reveal sensitive information about the underlying data, potentially violating data privacy regulations or exposing proprietary information.

To overcome these challenges, organizations should consider the following strategies:

- **Balancing performance and explainability**: Depending on the specific use case and the importance of interpretability, organizations should carefully choose the AI models they deploy. In some cases, using a slightly less accurate but more interpretable model may be preferable.

- **Integrating explainability into the development process**: Developers should prioritize explainability as a core requirement from the beginning of the AI development process, ensuring that the final model is both effective and interpretable.

- **Leveraging interdisciplinary collaboration**: Bringing together experts from different domains, such as data scientists, domain experts, ethicists, and legal professionals, can help address the complexities and trade-offs involved in achieving transparency and explainability in AI systems.

Organizations can follow several best practices to implement transparent and explainable AI systems:

- **Establish clear objectives**: Define specific goals for transparency and explainability, considering the needs of various stakeholders, such as users, regulators, and decision-makers.

- **Document the AI system**: Maintain comprehensive documentation of the AI system's development process, including the choice of algorithms, data sources, feature engineering, and validation techniques. This documentation will help facilitate transparency and enable future audits.

- **Monitor and evaluate explainability**: Continuously assess the explainability of AI systems during their lifecycle, using appropriate metrics and methodologies to ensure that explanations remain accurate and relevant.

- **Communicate explanations effectively**: Tailor explanations to the intended audience, using clear language and visualization techniques to make AI decisions more understandable.

- **Provide training and support**: Educate users, stakeholders, and decision-makers on the importance of transparency and explainability, as well as the methods used to achieve them. This will help ensure that they can confidently interpret AI-generated explanations and make informed decisions.

- **Engage with the AI community**: Stay up-to-date with the latest research and developments in explainable AI and actively contribute to the broader AI community's efforts to improve transparency and explainability in AI systems.

Transparency and explainability are crucial aspects of responsible AI development and deployment. By understanding the importance of these principles, adopting suitable methods for improving AI explainability, and learning from real-world examples, organizations can build trust, ensure accountability, and comply with ethical and legal requirements.

One final point I would like to cover at the end of this section is the concept of **"Fairwashing,"** a term used to describe the practice where companies overstate the fairness of their AI systems, often as a part of their marketing or promotional efforts. However, the mere provision of explainability in an AI system does not necessarily ensure its fairness. Therefore, if you see any company saying their systems are not biased because they are fully explainable, you should be very careful!

For instance, let's consider a credit scoring AI model, which has been designed to be completely transparent and explainable. This model clearly outlines that it uses features like income, employment status, and credit history to determine credit scores. The transparency makes the AI system explainable, but it doesn't guarantee fairness. If the model systematically gives lower credit scores to certain demographic groups due to inherent biases in the historical data it was trained on, the model would be deemed unfair, despite its explainability.

In this case, fairness would require the model not only to be transparent but also to deliver outcomes that don't disproportionately disadvantage any particular group. Hence, while explainability is a vital feature for AI models, it is not a complete solution to prevent "fairwashing." Organizations need to implement rigorous testing and auditing procedures, and possibly engage third-party audits to ensure AI systems are not just explainable but also equitable in their operation and outcomes.

Observability

Observability, in the context of artificial intelligence (AI), refers to the ability to monitor, understand, and manage the performance, behavior, and decision-making processes of AI systems throughout their lifecycle. Observability is a critical aspect of responsible AI development and deployment, as it enables organizations to ensure the AI systems' compliance with ethical and regulatory standards, maintain their reliability and accuracy, and identify potential issues or biases that may arise.

Observability plays a vital role in responsible AI development and deployment for several reasons:

- **Accountability**: Observability allows organizations to track AI system decisions, behaviors, and performance, ensuring that they are held accountable for their actions and outcomes.

- **Trust**: By providing transparency into AI systems' inner workings, observability helps build trust among stakeholders, including customers, regulators, and the broader public.

- **Compliance**: Observability enables organizations to demonstrate compliance with ethical guidelines and regulatory requirements by monitoring AI systems and providing necessary documentation and evidence.

- **Continuous improvement**: Through observability, organizations can identify areas of improvement in AI systems, enabling iterative refinements and optimization over time.

- **Risk management**: Observability helps organizations detect and mitigate potential risks, such as unintended biases, privacy breaches, and security vulnerabilities, before they cause significant harm.

Several techniques can be employed to monitor AI systems and maintain observability throughout their lifecycle:

- **Data logging and collection**: Collect and store data related to the AI system's input, output, and internal states at various stages of processing. This information can be used to analyze the system's performance and behavior.

- **Metrics and indicators**: Define and track key performance indicators (KPIs) and metrics that reflect the AI system's performance, fairness, transparency, and other essential attributes. These metrics can help organizations identify issues and areas for improvement.

- **Visualization**: Employ visualization techniques to represent AI system behavior, decision-making processes, and performance metrics in a comprehensible manner. Visualization can help stakeholders better understand and interpret AI system dynamics.

- **Real-time monitoring**: Monitor AI systems in real-time to detect issues, anomalies, or deviations from expected behavior. Real-time monitoring allows organizations to address problems promptly and minimize potential negative consequences.

- **Audit trails**: Maintain comprehensive audit trails of AI system activities, including data sources, feature engineering, model training, and decision-making processes. Audit trails enable organizations to demonstrate compliance with ethical and regulatory requirements and facilitate future investigations if needed.

- **Automated testing**: Implement automated testing frameworks to continuously evaluate AI system performance, accuracy, and fairness. Automated testing can help organizations identify issues and refine AI models iteratively.

The following real-world examples demonstrate the importance of observability in AI systems:

- **Financial services**: In the financial sector, AI-based credit scoring models must be carefully monitored to ensure fairness, accuracy, and compliance with regulations. Observability techniques can be employed to track the performance of these models, identify potential biases, and generate reports for regulatory audits.

- **Healthcare**: AI systems used for diagnosing medical conditions must be closely observed to ensure their accuracy, safety, and compliance with data privacy regulations. By monitoring input data, model outputs, and performance metrics, healthcare organizations can maintain observability and promptly address any issues that may arise.

- **Autonomous vehicles**: Ensuring the safety and reliability of self-driving cars requires continuous monitoring and observability of the AI systems responsible for decision-making and control. Real-time monitoring, visualization, and performance metrics can help identify potential issues and optimize the system's performance.

- **Fraud detection**: AI systems employed for detecting fraudulent activities in banking, insurance, or e-commerce must be carefully observed to maintain accuracy and adapt to evolving patterns of fraud. Observability techniques can help organizations track the performance of these systems and refine them to improve detection capabilities.

- **Human resources**: AI-powered recruitment and talent management systems must be monitored for fairness and compliance with anti-discrimination regulations. Observability tools can help organizations track the performance of these systems, identify potential biases, and ensure fair decision-making processes.

Table 20-3 provides an overview of real-world examples of observability in AI systems, highlighting the importance of monitoring AI systems across different industries and applications.

Table 20-3. *Real-world examples of observability in AI systems*

Industry	AI application	Observability techniques
Financial services	Credit scoring	Performance tracking, bias identification, regulatory audit reports
Healthcare	Medical diagnostics	Monitoring input data, model outputs, performance metrics, data privacy compliance
Automotive	Autonomous vehicles	Real-time monitoring, visualization, performance metrics, safety assessment
Fraud detection	Fraud detection	Tracking system performance, refining models to improve detection capabilities, adapting to evolving fraud patterns
Human resources	Recruitment	Performance tracking, bias identification, fair decision-making processes, compliance with anti-discrimination laws

Observability is a crucial aspect of responsible AI development and deployment, as it enables organizations to monitor and manage the performance, behavior, and decision-making processes of AI systems throughout their lifecycle. By employing techniques such as data logging, metrics and indicators, visualization, real-time monitoring, audit trails, and automated testing, organizations can maintain observability and ensure their AI systems comply with ethical and regulatory standards, remain reliable and accurate, and address potential issues or biases.

Implementing observability in AI systems not only helps organizations build trust among stakeholders but also facilitates continuous improvement and risk management, ultimately contributing to the success and growth of enterprises leveraging AI technology.

Regulatory Efforts Around the World

As artificial intelligence (AI) continues to develop and evolve, governments around the world are taking steps to regulate its use. This is due to several factors, including the potential for AI to be used for malicious purposes, such as creating deepfakes or developing autonomous weapons systems.

There are a few different approaches to AI regulation that are being taken by governments around the world. Some governments, such as the European Union, are taking a top-down approach, developing comprehensive regulations that govern all aspects of AI development and use. Other governments, such as the United States, are taking a more piecemeal approach, developing regulations for specific applications of AI, such as self-driving cars.

As AI continues to permeate every aspect of modern life, governments worldwide are recognizing the need for regulation to address the ethical, privacy, and security concerns arising from AI's rapid advancements. The following list the latest – at the time of writing this book – development, which no doubt will continue over the next few years:

- **The European Union (EU)** has taken a leading role in regulating AI, with the European Commission proposing the Artificial Intelligence Act (AI Act) in April 2021.[6] The AI Act is a comprehensive legal framework designed to ensure that AI systems used in the EU respect fundamental rights, follow EU laws, and adhere to a high level of ethical standards.

- **The United States** has adopted a more sector-specific approach to AI regulation, focusing on guidelines and best practices rather than comprehensive legislation. The National Institute of Standards and Technology (NIST) has been tasked with developing a framework for trustworthy AI systems,[7] which includes elements such as explainability, fairness, and privacy.

- **Singapore** has adopted a voluntary approach to AI regulation, with the Infocomm Media Development Authority (IMDA) releasing the Model AI Governance Framework.[8] The framework provides guidance on how organizations can implement responsible AI practices, such as ensuring human involvement in AI-augmented decision-making, implementing a robust risk management process, promoting transparency and explainability, and ensuring AI system reliability.

---

[6] https://digital-strategy.ec.europa.eu/en/policies/european-approach-artificial-intelligence

[7] www.nist.gov/trustworthy-and-responsible-ai

[8] www.pdpc.gov.sg/help-and-resources/2020/01/model-ai-governance-framework

- **China** has also released guidelines for AI development, such as the Beijing AI Principles and the Governance Principles for the New Generation AI.[9] These guidelines focus on ethical AI development and call for international cooperation to address global AI governance challenges.

As AI regulation continues to evolve worldwide, businesses must stay informed about the changing legal and ethical landscape. By understanding and adhering to the regulatory efforts around the world, businesses can ensure responsible AI development and deployment, ultimately fostering trust and driving long-term success in the age of AI.

Here are some additional thoughts on AI regulation:

- **AI regulation is still in its early stages**, but it is likely to become more comprehensive and stringent in the years to come. Businesses should start planning for this now by developing an AI ethics framework and implementing responsible AI practices.

- **AI regulation is likely to vary from country to country**. Businesses that operate in multiple countries will need to be aware of the different regulatory requirements and adapt their practices accordingly.

- **AI regulation is not just about compliance**. It is also about building trust with customers and stakeholders. Businesses that can demonstrate that they are committed to responsible AI are more likely to succeed in the long run.

Navigating Ethical and Regulatory Implications

As artificial intelligence (AI) continues to develop and evolve, it is important for businesses to navigate the ethical and regulatory implications of AI. This is because AI has the potential to be used for both good and bad, and businesses need to be aware of the potential risks and benefits of using AI.

---

[9] www.loc.gov/item/global-legal-monitor/2019-09-09/china-ai-governance-principles-released/

One of the key ethical considerations for AI is bias. AI systems are trained on data, and if the data is biased, the AI system will be biased as well. This can lead to discrimination against certain groups of people. Businesses need to be aware of the potential for bias in their AI systems and take steps to mitigate it.

Another key ethical consideration for AI is privacy. AI systems can collect and store a lot of data about people, and this data needs to be protected. Businesses need to have clear policies in place for how they collect, use, and store data about people.

Finally, businesses need to be aware of the regulatory landscape for AI. Governments around the world are developing regulations for AI, and these regulations are likely to evolve over time. Businesses need to stay up-to-date on the latest regulatory developments so that they can comply with the law and protect their interests.

In today's rapidly evolving AI landscape, navigating the ethical and regulatory implications is essential for businesses to ensure responsible AI development and deployment. As AI technologies continue to transform industries and impact society, it is crucial for organizations to understand the potential challenges and risks associated with AI systems. This subsection will offer practical guidance on navigating the ethical and regulatory landscape of AI, discuss the role of interdisciplinary collaboration in addressing these challenges, and highlight the importance of continuous learning and staying up-to-date with regulatory changes.

To ensure compliance with ethical and regulatory requirements and foster trust in AI systems, organizations should adopt the following strategies:

- **Develop an AI ethics framework**: Establish a set of ethical principles and guidelines for AI development, deployment, and usage within your organization. This framework should address issues such as data privacy, security, transparency, fairness, and observability.

- **Appoint an AI ethics officer**: Designate a dedicated individual or team responsible for ensuring that AI systems adhere to your organization's ethical principles and comply with relevant regulations.

- **Conduct regular AI audits and ethical impact assessments**: Regularly review and assess the performance of your AI systems, including their fairness, transparency, and explainability. Implement any necessary changes to ensure compliance with ethical guidelines and regulatory requirements. This involves assessing the potential ethical impacts of AI systems before they are deployed.

- **Collaborate with external stakeholders**: Engage with industry peers, regulators, academia, and civil society to exchange insights and best practices on AI ethics and regulation. This can help foster a more informed and responsible AI ecosystem.

- **Monitor regulatory developments**: Stay up-to-date with the latest developments in AI regulation, both domestically and internationally. This will enable your organization to anticipate and adapt to changes in the regulatory environment. This could involve subscribing to industry publications, following government websites, and hiring a lawyer who specializes in AI law

- **Building in safeguards to mitigate bias and privacy risks**. This could include things like using fair data collection practices, building in explainability features, and having clear data privacy policies.

Addressing the complex ethical and regulatory challenges posed by AI requires an *interdisciplinary approach that brings together experts from various fields*, such as computer science, law, ethics, social sciences, and business. By fostering collaboration among these diverse disciplines, organizations can gain a comprehensive understanding of the potential risks and benefits of AI systems, as well as develop more robust and responsible AI solutions.

The benefits of interdisciplinary collaboration in addressing AI challenges include

- **Comprehensive understanding of AI risks and benefits**: By involving experts from different disciplines, organizations can better grasp the potential consequences of AI systems, both positive and negative.

- **Development of robust and responsible AI solutions**: Collaboration among diverse disciplines can lead to the creation of AI systems that are not only technologically advanced but also ethically sound and legally compliant.

- **Enhanced trust in AI systems**: Involving a diverse range of stakeholders in the development and deployment of AI systems can help foster trust in the technology among users and the wider public.

As AI technologies continue to advance and the regulatory landscape evolves, it is crucial for organizations *to stay informed about the latest developments and best practices in AI ethics and regulation*. Continuous learning and staying up-to-date with regulatory changes can help businesses anticipate and adapt to new requirements, ultimately ensuring the responsible development and deployment of AI systems.

To stay informed about the latest developments in AI regulation and ethics, organizations can

- **Participate in industry conferences and workshops**: Attend events focused on AI ethics and regulation to learn about the latest trends, research, and best practices.

- **Engage in online learning**: Utilize online courses, webinars to deepen your understanding of AI ethics, regulation, and best practices.

- **Subscribe to relevant newsletters and publications**: Stay informed about the latest developments in AI regulation and ethics by subscribing to newsletters, journals, and other publications focused on these topics.

- **Network with AI experts and professionals**: Connect with AI researchers, practitioners, and policymakers to exchange insights on AI ethics and regulation.

- **Foster a culture of continuous learning within your organization**: Encourage employees to participate in training programs and engage in ongoing professional development related to AI ethics and regulation.

Navigating the ethical and regulatory implications of AI is a critical aspect of responsible AI development and deployment. By following the practical guidance provided in this subsection, engaging in interdisciplinary collaboration, and staying informed about the latest developments in AI regulation and ethics, organizations can ensure that their AI systems are not only technologically advanced but also ethically sound and legally compliant. By doing so, businesses can build trust with users and the wider public, ultimately fostering the successful integration of AI technologies into their operations and contributing to a more responsible AI ecosystem.

Key Takeaways

In this chapter, we have discussed the ethical and regulatory implications of artificial intelligence (AI) and how organizations can navigate these challenges effectively. As the use of AI becomes more widespread, it is vital for businesses to adhere to responsible AI practices to ensure long-term success and maintain trust with users and the wider public.

1. **Key takeaway 1: Prioritize data privacy and security.**
   Organizations should implement appropriate security measures to protect personal data, such as encryption, access controls, and data backups.

   a. Do: Implement robust measures to protect user data privacy and security in AI systems. This includes adopting encryption, access controls, and data anonymization techniques.

       i. Example: Implementing end-to-end encryption to safeguard sensitive user information in a healthcare AI application.

   b. Don't: Neglect data privacy and security, as it can lead to breaches, loss of user trust, and potential legal ramifications.

       i. Example: Failing to secure user data in an e-commerce AI system, resulting in a data breach and compromised customer information.

2. **Key takeaway 2: Mitigate bias and ensure fairness:** AI systems can be biased if they are trained on data that is biased. This can lead to unfair outcomes, such as discrimination against certain groups of people. Organizations should take steps to mitigate bias in their AI systems, such as using a diverse dataset to train the models and monitoring the models for bias.

   a. Do: Be proactive in identifying and addressing biases in AI models. Employ techniques such as data preprocessing, algorithmic fairness, and diverse model evaluation.

       i. Example: Regularly auditing an AI-powered recruitment tool to ensure fair treatment of candidates from different demographic backgrounds.

    b. Don't: Overlook the potential consequences of biased AI systems, which can perpetuate discrimination and reinforce societal inequalities.

        i. Example: Deploying an AI-based credit scoring system that consistently denies loans to individuals from historically marginalized communities due to biased training data.

3. **Key takeaway 3: Foster transparency and explainability.** Users should be able to understand how AI systems work and make decisions. Organizations should make their AI systems transparent and explainable by providing documentation, user interfaces, and other tools that help users understand how the systems work:

    a. Do: Strive for transparency and explainability in AI systems. Employ techniques like model documentation, feature importance analysis, and algorithmic audits.

        i. Example: Providing a clear explanation of the factors considered by an AI-powered chatbot in making customer service recommendations.

    b. Don't: Rely solely on "black box" AI models without understanding how they reach decisions, as it can hinder trust and raise ethical concerns.

        i. Example: Using an opaque AI model for judicial decision-making without providing justification or explanation for the verdict.

These key takeaways underscore the significance of ethical and regulatory considerations in AI development and deployment. By prioritizing data privacy and security, mitigating bias, and fostering transparency and explainability, businesses can build responsible AI systems that inspire trust, minimize harm, and unlock the full potential of AI for their organizations.

CHAPTER 21

Scaling AI

This is the last chapter of Part IV, "The HOW," where we put everything together to provide guidance as to how to truly scale AI in any enterprise. We have explored "Thy WHY" most, if not all, companies should be embarking on an urgent AI Transformation. We have also gone deep into the intuition and First Principles of "The WHAT" of AI, so the reader should be able to evaluate different algorithms for different situations. We are now in the final chapter on "The HOW," how to bring to live all these capabilities, and in this last chapter, we will explore how to consistently deploy AI at scale across all types of organizations in different industries and sizes.

Artificial intelligence (AI) is rapidly transforming the business landscape, enabling companies to automate tasks, make data-driven decisions, and create new products and services. However, despite the potential benefits, we have seen why many companies struggle to implement AI at scale. Implementing AI requires a significant investment of resources, including technology, talent, and time. It also requires a thorough understanding of the business needs, the technology, and the processes involved. Last but not least, the importance of governance cannot be overstated, and its significance grows proportionally with the size of an organization.

Core Components of Scaling AI

To overcome these challenges, companies must address the five pillars of AI scaling, which are the core components from a First Principles perspective:

- Company AI cross adoption
- Governance and responsible AI
- Skills and diversity
- AI technology and infrastructure
- AI R&D

© Francisco Javier Campos Zabala 2023
F. J. Campos Zabala, *Grow Your Business with AI*, https://doi.org/10.1007/978-1-4842-9669-1_21

Despite the Potential, Most Companies Struggle to Deploy AI at Scale

AI is already delivering high ROI to a few large tech companies. The overall AI usage is also increasing year by year. But not all companies manage to extract the same value.

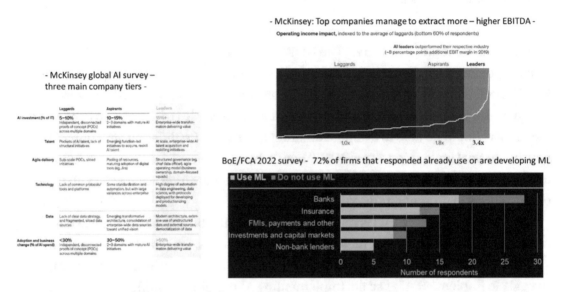

Figure 21-1. *AI adoption. Sources: Mckinsey reports[1] and Bank Of England/FCA 2022 Survey[2] on AI*

In the preceding graph (Figure 21-1) from McKinsey and Bank of England AI/ML survey, it is very clear that while some companies are indeed benefiting greatly, most struggle.

[1] www.mckinsey.com/~/media/McKinsey/Business%20Functions/McKinsey%20Analytics/ Our%20Insights/Global%20survey%20The%20state%20of%20AI%20in%202021/Global-survey-The-state-of-AI-in-2021.pdf

[2] www.bankofengland.co.uk/-/media/boe/files/report/2019/machine-learning-in-uk-financial-services.pdf

Why Is AI Implementation so Difficult?

Many companies struggle to implement AI because they lack a clear understanding of the business requirements and the technology involved. They also struggle to align their AI strategy with their overall business strategy, which results in disjointed efforts and suboptimal outcomes. Additionally, many companies are unable to attract and retain the necessary talent to implement and manage AI initiatives. The shortage of data scientists and AI experts has resulted in high salaries and intense competition for these resources. Moreover, companies often struggle to establish effective governance and responsible AI practices, which are critical to ensuring that AI initiatives are aligned with their values and ethical principles.

When you analyze deeply the challenges, as discussed widely in Chapter 4, most come from a core issue which is commonly overlooked; the "Elephant in the room" is the fact there are two groups of people, "business-minded" and "technical-Scientist" which effectively talk different languages and more importantly have different goals and motivation. Therefore, the role of a translator between the groups is extremely important, and when they are aligned the outcomes can indeed be incredible! The reality is that organizations, especially large ones, have legacy management structures which default in siloed behavior. This well-known issue is a massive barrier for any change to the organization, but especially AI as requires truly collaboration from many parts of the organization.

What AI Excellence Looks Like: What Large Tech Companies Do Differently for AI

Large tech companies like Google, Meta, Amazon, Microsoft, and Apple have set the standard for AI excellence. These companies have made significant investments in AI, many from their inception, and they have established a culture of innovation companywide that enables them to effectively implement and scale AI initiatives. They have also put in place robust governance and responsible AI practices, which ensure that AI is aligned with their values and ethical principles. Additionally, these companies have invested heavily in R&D, which allows them to develop new AI technologies and techniques and effectively be market leaders. In summary, these are the key areas that leading AI companies have:

- **AI-first mindset**: AI is not an afterthought, but something at the core of each company. For instance, all projects must consider AI from the get-go (although not all will use it) Amazon, Microsoft, etc. Right mixed teams, all separated R&D part, and deployed DS team within business units.

- **Scale AI infrastructure and engineering**: All have end-to-end proprietary tech stacks to facilitate AI. Some release the software stacks to the open community (Meta, Google, Microsoft).

- **Data centric**: All companies have data first strategies.

- **Focus on use cases**: Establishing baselines and having clear and constant business value-driven strategies.

- **Rapid interaction**: AI is quite different to standard software – you need to iterate/operate in a continuous way.

AI Maturity Level

Not all companies can imitate overnight the success of large AI tech ones. Where is your

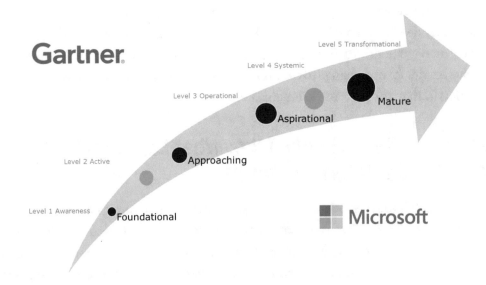

Figure 21-2. *AI maturity models. Sources: Gartner[3] and Microsoft[4]*
company in this process?

[3] www.gartner.com/en/documents/3982174

[4] https://query.prod.cms.rt.microsoft.com/cms/api/am/binary/RE4DIvg

This chapter will show you how to climb the maturity ladder (Figure 21-2), which is by creating a very specific targeted plan to your company that addresses all five pillars, each in a different way depending on your starting point in the maturity AI model and your desired target.

AI Maturity: How to Get to the Top Faster

I analyzed dozens of strategic AI roadmaps from top economies (the USA[5], China[6], the UK[7], Canada[8] up to 32 countries have an AI strategy so far) and large private tech AI organizations so you do not have to do it.

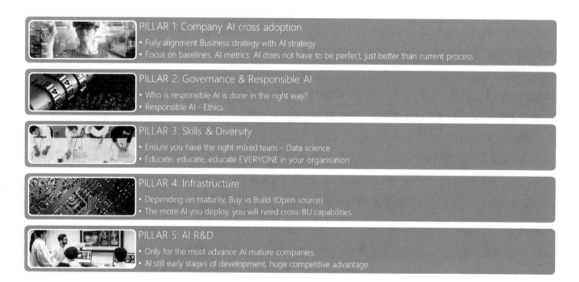

Figure 21-3. *Pillars to scale AI*

[5] www.ai.gov/

[6] https://digichina.stanford.edu/work/full-translation-chinas-new-generation-artificial-intelligence-development-plan-2017/

[7] www.gov.uk/government/publications/national-ai-strategy

[8] https://cifar.ca/ai/

To implement AI at scale, you will need to address the pillars presented in Figure 21-3. And a key step to achieve AI excellence is for companies to align their AI strategy with their overall business strategy and establish a culture of innovation. They must also establish effective governance and responsible AI practices, invest in R&D, and build the necessary skills and infrastructure to support AI initiatives. Companies must also focus on data and AI metrics, which are critical to measuring the impact of AI initiatives and determining whether they are delivering value.

Why Hardly Any Companies Included AI in Digital Transformation

Despite many companies undergoing digital transformation in recent years, very few have included AI as part of their transformation. This is due, in part, to a lack of understanding of the technology and the potential benefits. It is also due to a lack of investment in AI talent and infrastructure. Additionally, many companies struggle to align their AI strategy with their overall business strategy, which results in disjointed efforts and suboptimal outcomes. Finally, many companies lack the governance and responsible AI practices necessary to ensure that AI is aligned with their values and ethical. In summary, most of these transformations focus on doing a "lift and shift" moving apps from mainframes to the Cloud, but effectively the same business rules.

Tip   If your organization is either starting or in the middle of a digital transformation, challenge the "lift and shift" approach. Moving the same business rules from one platform to another will not fundamentally grow your business. However, whenever appropriated, transforming legacy rigid rules into AI-driven flexible applications can really catapult your business growth!

Pillar 1: Company AI Cross Adoption

In this section, we will focus on the first pillar, company-wide AI adoption, which is a critical step to ensure the whole organization benefits from AI whenever appropriated. The right use cases for AI must be uncovered. Not all projects will benefit, and some might not appear on the standard channels. You will need to make a few difficult decisions, depending on maturity and strategy.

There are two key areas to maximize companywide AI adoption:

1. **Fully aligning the business strategy with the AI strategy**: As discussed at length in Chapters 11 and 12, to ensure that AI technology is effectively used across the enterprise, it is critical to align AI capabilities, both present and future, with the overall business strategy. This requires a clear understanding of the company's business goals and objectives, as well as the ways in which AI can contribute to these goals. It is important to engage key stakeholders from across the organization in this process, including business leaders, data scientists, and IT teams, to ensure that all perspectives are considered. This can be achieved through several steps, including

   a. **Defining clear goals and objectives**: The first step is to define clear goals and objectives, using business outcome language, not technical. This includes identifying the specific business problems that AI can solve, as well as the potential revenue streams that can be generated from the deployment of AI.

   b. **Developing an AI roadmap**: Once clear goals and objectives have been defined, companies should develop an AI roadmap that outlines the steps that need to be taken to deploy AI solutions. This roadmap should include timelines, budgets, and resources, as well as a clear plan for integrating AI into each department's operations.

   c. **Engaging stakeholders**: To ensure company-wide AI adoption, it is important to engage all stakeholders, including senior leaders, employees, and customers. This includes involving them in the development of the AI roadmap and ensuring that they are aware of the benefits of AI and how it will impact their work.

   d. **Establish a governance framework** to ensure that AI is being used in a responsible and ethical manner.

2. **Focusing on business outcome baselines**: To ensure that AI technology is being used effectively and delivering value, it's important to focus on baselines and AI metrics. AI metrics are key performance indicators (KPIs) and objectives and key results

(OKRs) that help organizations to measure the impact of AI on the business. The goal is not necessarily to achieve perfect AI at all costs – being this a common mistake – but rather to demonstrate that AI can provide a better result than current business processes:

a. Defining key metrics: The first step in focusing on baselines, AI metrics is to define key metrics that will be used to measure the success of AI solutions. This includes identifying the specific business problems that AI can solve, as well as the potential revenue streams that can be generated from the deployment of AI.

b. Measuring and reporting results: Companies must measure and report on the results of the AI solutions deployed by each department. This includes tracking the benefits of AI, such as increased revenue, improved operational efficiency, and reduced costs. This data can be used to demonstrate the value of AI to the organization, and to encourage other departments to consider and deploy AI solutions. It is also very important to keep using these metrics over time, as per the following point.

c. Continuously improving: Companies must continuously improve their AI solutions by using data and metrics to identify areas for improvement. This includes using AI metrics to measure the effectiveness of AI solutions and using the results to make continuous improvements.

Tip   The larger the organization, the more important the governance became. Most organizations have legacy management structures which create unintended siloed behaviors – a bit of "Moloch" effect as we saw in the Introduction. You need to be fully aware of this underlying issue, so your project has the right support from senior management, but more importantly, there are the right metrics and cross-teams incentives to be successful. Just having top management is not enough.

Here are five sample KPIs and OKRs that can be used to measure the impact of AI on the business (please refer to Chapter 12 for a more extended coverage):

- **Improved customer satisfaction**: KPIs could include the number of customer complaints, the time it takes to resolve customer issues, and customer feedback scores. OKRs could be set to reduce customer complaints by X% over Y months.

- **Increased sales**: KPIs could include the number of new customers, the average order value, and the conversion rate. OKRs could be set to increase sales by X% over Y months.

- **Improved efficiency**: KPIs could include the time it takes to process an order, the number of errors in an order, and the number of manual interventions required. OKRs could be set to reduce manual interventions by X% over Y months.

- **Reduced costs**: KPIs could include the cost of goods sold, the cost of processing an order, and the cost of customer service. OKRs could be set to reduce the cost of processing an order by X% over Y months.

- **Improved employee engagement**: KPIs could include employee turnover, the number of hours worked, and employee feedback scores. OKRs could be set to increase employee engagement by X% over Y months.

While these are good examples of KPIs and OKRs for AI, it is important to avoid using KPIs and OKRs that are not directly related to the business goals. For example, using the accuracy of an AI model as a KPI is not as relevant as using the impact of the model on business outcomes, such as improved customer satisfaction or reduced costs.

Company AI cross-adoption is an important aspect of successfully scaling AI in the enterprise. By fully aligning the business strategy with the AI strategy and focusing on baselines and AI metrics, companies can ensure that AI is being used effectively to deliver real business value. This will ultimately lead to a company-wide commitment to AI, and a more successful scaling of AI in the enterprise.

Pillar 2: Governance and Responsible AI

Artificial Intelligence (AI) is rapidly transforming the business landscape, but with this transformation comes a need for proper governance and ethical considerations. The implementation of AI must be done in a responsible and ethical manner to ensure that it benefits both the company and society as a whole. As AI continues to play a larger role in the enterprise, companies must address the critical importance of governance and responsible AI adoption.

Who Is Responsible for Ensuring AI Is Done in the Right Way?

AI is a cross-functional and complex technology that requires the collaboration of various departments such as technology, legal, ethics, and human resources. It is crucial to establish clear ownership and accountability for AI governance within the organization. A dedicated AI governance team or a designated senior executive should be responsible for overseeing the implementation of AI and ensuring it aligns with the company's values and ethical principles.

While there is not a "silver-bullet" answer which fit to all companies, using first principals we need to ensure that (1) there is accountability/ownership and (2) all the right areas are implemented in the best pragmatic way to each unique organization context: culture, current organization, market position, and size. I strongly recommend the BoE/FCA industry guide advisory document about how to successfully implement and scale artificial intelligence within Financial Services. I had the privilege to be part of the expert industry group who contributed to the guidelines,[9] so I know it has considered all different perspectives from different stakeholders within the industry, which can be extended to most industries. Figures 21-4 and 21-5 explain the high level concept needed to implement AI in a responsible way.

Regardless of how you organize your AI teams, AI governance is best done centrally. Need to have a focus on explainable and responsible models.

---

[9] www.bankofengland.co.uk/research/fintech/ai-public-private-forum

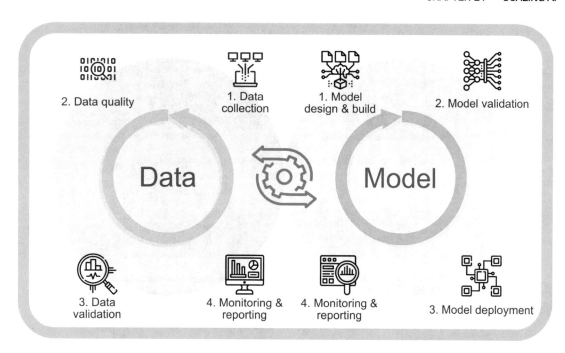

Figure 21-4. *AI governance model. Source: AIPP Bank Of England/FCA 2022*
AI report

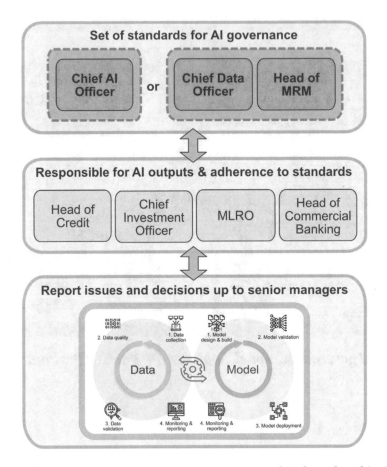

Figure 21-5. *AI governance model. Source: AIPP Bank Of England/FCA 2022 AI report*

Where to Put AI Organizations

No single silver bullet depends on many factors. Figure 21-6 shows the pros and cons of a centralized vs a distributed way. In many cases, the same company will change structures as they climb positions in the AI maturity models. When companies are small, it makes sense to have a central team but with clear alignment with the other teams. As the company – and AI project success – grows, at some point it might make sense to move the resources to the business units. This is what Meta did in a re-organization in 2022,[10] and despite still having pure R&D centralized, they moved the Applied Data Science teams to the business units to be more flexible, agile, and accelerate AI deployment across all business units.

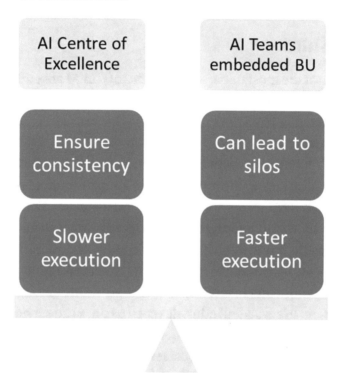

Figure 21-6. *Where to locate AI team – centralised vs distributed*

Responsible AI: Ethics

The implementation of AI must be done in a manner that respects ethical principles and values. Companies must consider the potential consequences of their AI systems and ensure that they do not violate privacy rights, perpetuate biases, or harm individuals. AI systems must also be transparent and explainable, so users can understand how

---

[10] https://ai.facebook.com/blog/building-with-ai-across-all-of-meta/

they make decisions. Companies can incorporate ethical considerations into the development process by conducting impact assessments, involving experts in ethics and human rights, and incorporating feedback from stakeholders. We expand this topic in Chapter 20.

Company Culture

This is probably one of the most underestimated factors. In AI governance, there is not a single answer that will fit all companies, and as well as maturity level, company size, and industry (whether regulated or not), many other factors will come into play when deciding the AI organization model.

The decision to centralize or decentralize AI resources should be based on the specific needs and culture of the organization. Company culture can have a significant impact on how AI teams are organized and managed. For example, in a hierarchical organization with a strong top-down management style, centralization may be more effective, as it provides clear lines of control and authority. In contrast, in a more decentralized, collaborative organization, decentralization may be more appropriate, as it fosters greater ownership and accountability among business units. Another consideration, in regulated industries such as financial services where most organizations implement the three lines of defense organization structure, a more centralized approach but with common business goals with the business lines provides the best organization structure.

Team Size

The size of an AI team can vary greatly depending on the specific needs and goals of a company. At its core, an AI team typically consists of data scientists, machine learning engineers, data engineers, and sometimes, AI research scientists. However, as an organization scales, other roles such as project managers, product managers, data analysts, data labeling specialists, or AI ethicists can become important.

When it comes to deciding the team size, communication plays a crucial role. According to the principle known as **Brooks' Law**[11], "Adding manpower to a late software project makes it later." The reasoning is that as the number of people in a team increases, the amount of communication needed to coordinate their efforts increases exponentially.

Amazon's "Two Pizza Rule"[12], which posits that teams should be small enough to be fed with two pizzas, further underlines the importance of keeping teams small for efficient communication and productivity. This usually translates to somewhere *between 5 and 7 individuals*, depending on appetites.

As your company grows and your projects multiply, you'll likely need to expand your team. If communication within the team starts becoming a major hurdle or if individuals start to wear too many hats, these are indications that the team may need to be split or increased in size.

While splitting a team, it's essential to ensure each team has a clear, defined purpose. Amazon's practice of establishing "single-threaded" teams, or teams that focus on one particular area, can be a good approach here. Each team needs to have enough skills to achieve its objectives and to operate with a high degree of autonomy.

Adding middle management usually becomes necessary when the number of teams starts to grow, and senior management can no longer efficiently handle direct communication with all individual teams or team members. Middle managers can help by taking over some of the communication, coordination, and decision-making tasks. They can also serve as vital communication bridges between the technical team members and the higher management, who might not be as deeply involved in the technical aspects of projects.

In the end, the right size for your AI team will depend on your company's specific circumstances. A small, well-functioning team can accomplish a lot when they have clear communication and a shared understanding of their goals. As the team grows, maintaining these principles becomes more challenging but also more important. Always remember that it's not just about having more people on the team, but how these individuals collaborate and drive the project towards its objectives.

---

[11] https://resources.sei.cmu.edu/asset_files/WhitePaper/2009_019_001_29000.pdf
[12] www.theguardian.com/technology/2018/apr/24/the-two-pizza-rule-and-the-secret-of-amazons-success

Common Pitfalls to Avoid

When implementing AI, it is important to avoid common pitfalls that can undermine governance and ethics. One common pitfall is the lack of transparency in AI systems, which can lead to a lack of accountability and trust. Another pitfall is the perpetuation of biases in AI systems, which can result in discriminatory outcomes. It is also crucial to avoid the over-reliance on AI systems, which can lead to the loss of human expertise and judgment. Companies must strike a balance between the benefits of AI and the need to respect ethical principles and values.

In conclusion, governance and responsible AI adoption are critical components of successfully scaling AI in the enterprise. Companies must establish clear ownership and accountability for AI governance and prioritize ethical considerations in the development and implementation of AI systems. By avoiding common pitfalls and incorporating best practices, companies can ensure that their AI systems are transparent, accountable, and respectful of ethical principles and values.

Pillar 3: Skills and Diversity

Scaling AI in the enterprise requires addressing several critical pillars, including skills and diversity. Ensuring the right mix of skills and promoting diversity in your organization can help drive AI adoption and support the successful implementation of AI projects.

1. **Ensure you have the right mixed team**: Having a team with a mix of expertise in data science, machine learning engineering, and AI product management is essential for successful AI implementation. Data scientists are responsible for analyzing data, selecting the right algorithms, and testing models to ensure accuracy. Machine learning engineers are responsible for implementing and deploying AI models. AI product managers are responsible for overseeing the entire AI project lifecycle, ensuring that it aligns with the company's goals and objectives.

   When building your AI team, it is essential to consider diversity in terms of gender, race, ethnicity, and other personal characteristics. A diverse team can bring new perspectives, fresh ideas, and different ways of thinking to the table, leading to more innovative and impactful AI solutions. Additionally, a diverse team can also better understand and serve the needs of diverse customer segments.

2. **Educate *everyone* in your organization**: While it is important to have the right mix of AI skills on your team, it is also crucial that everyone in your organization has a basic understanding of AI. This can help to ensure that AI is integrated into the company's overall strategy and that everyone can contribute to its success.

To achieve this, companies can offer AI training programs for all employees, regardless of their role or level within the organization. These programs can help to increase AI literacy and understanding, which can lead to more effective collaboration and problem-solving. Additionally, providing AI training can help to promote a culture of innovation, where employees are encouraged to embrace and leverage AI to drive business growth.

The following are best practices when it comes to have the right skillsets and diversity:

- **Foster a culture of continuous learning**: Encourage your team to stay up to date with the latest AI advancements and technologies by providing ongoing training and development opportunities.

- **Hire for potential and train for skills**: When hiring for AI roles, focus on the candidate's potential, not just their current skill set. With the right training and development, new hires can quickly become valuable contributors to your AI team.

- **Encourage cross-functional collaboration**: Encourage collaboration between your AI team and other departments, such as marketing, sales, and customer support. This can help to ensure that AI is integrated into the company's overall strategy and that everyone can contribute to its success.

Common Pitfalls to Avoid

Ensuring the right mix of skills and promoting diversity in your organization are critical components of successfully scaling AI in the enterprise. Below are some potential pitfalls to avoid:

- **Hiring solely based on technical skills**: While technical skills are important, they should not be the only factor considered when building your AI team. Soft skills, such as communication, teamwork, and problem-solving, are equally important and should also be considered when making hiring decisions.

- **Ignoring diversity**: Failing to promote diversity in your AI team can lead to a lack of diversity in thought and ideas, which can limit innovation and impact.

- **Neglecting employee education**: Failing to provide AI training to all employees can lead to a lack of understanding and a lack of adoption. This can also lead to a culture of fear and resistance toward AI, making it more difficult to integrate AI into your business strategy.

You will need to have the right team composition to execute the different AI data-driven projects and the right level of AI understanding across the organization. Having all the knowledge in one team can be inefficient. The following Figure 21-7 shows an ideal data science/AI team. Please note how it is very important to have all these four roles. Many organizations fail to include one or two, which can lead to project failure. While all teams will include data scientists, many organizations do not include anyone from the IT team. This will make the roll-out to production very complicated. Another mistake, it is not to include a "Business/Product Translator," which can create long delays, as scientists will by default try to do every model as performance as possible, but in many cases, as long as the new AI model is better than the baseline, it is always better to release quickly a minimum quality and then improve over time with actual data, rather than spending months and months on the "perfect" model with limited historical data.

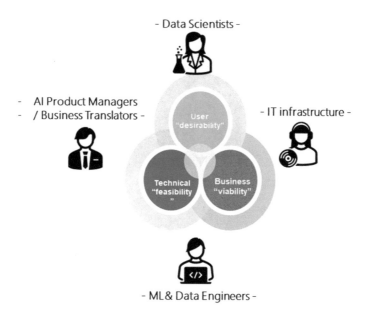

Figure 21-7. Key roles in a AI team – all must be part on an aligned team

Pillar 4: AI Infrastructure

When it comes to scaling AI in the enterprise, one of the most important aspects is having the right infrastructure in place. Without an effective AI infrastructure, it will be challenging to deploy and operate AI systems at scale, especially as your organization's AI footprint grows.

Figure 21-8 shows the three main components that any AI solution will need: AI needs data, most of your data will be in your legacy systems – hence the API's, and the best place to build in a future proven approach your solution is to use cloud infrastructure:

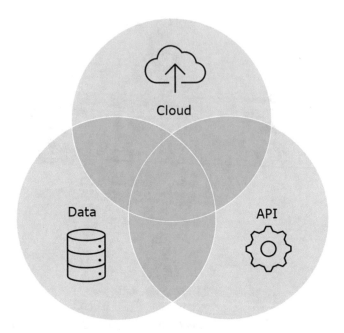

Figure 21-8. _AI core infrastructure components_

As we explain in Chapter 16, there are two main approaches to building an AI infrastructure: buying vs building. Depending on your organization's maturity level and the specific needs of your AI projects, you may opt for one approach over the other. For organizations that are just starting out with AI, buying pre-built infrastructure may be a more efficient and cost-effective solution. On the other hand, for organizations that have a mature AI program and a deep understanding of their specific requirements, building a custom infrastructure from the ground up may be a more suitable option. Hybrid approaches can also work for some organizations; they can provide some basic functionality using the market tools and customize specific functionality to their needs.

Open-source tools are becoming increasingly popular for organizations looking to build their AI infrastructure. These tools offer the flexibility and cost-effectiveness that organizations need to get started quickly, while also providing the ability to customize the infrastructure to meet their specific requirements. Some popular open-source tools for machine learning operations (MLOps) include Kubeflow, TensorFlow, and PyTorch.

As your organization's AI footprint grows, it is important to have a cross-business unit (BU) capability to manage the deployment and operation of AI systems. This involves having a centralized team that is responsible for overseeing the entire AI infrastructure, while also ensuring that the infrastructure is aligned with the overall business strategy. The centralized team should also work closely with other BUs to ensure that AI systems are deployed and operated in a consistent and scalable manner.

One of the biggest challenges when it comes to scaling AI in the enterprise is the need for data. AI systems require large amounts of data to train models and make accurate predictions. Most of this data is likely to be stored in legacy systems, which can make it difficult to access and use in AI systems. To overcome this challenge, organizations need to have a cloud-based infrastructure that provides access to the data, as well as APIs that can be used to interface with legacy systems.

When it comes to best practices for building/buying an AI infrastructure, it is important to focus on the following:

- **Start small and build incrementally**: When starting out with AI, it is important to build an infrastructure that can scale as your organization grows. This means starting with a small set of tools and systems and adding more as needed.

- **Focus on ease of use and scalability**: Your AI infrastructure should be easy to use and scalable, so that it can support the deployment and operation of AI systems at scale.

- **Invest in MLOps**: MLOps is a critical component of AI infrastructure, so it's important to invest in the tools and processes that are needed to manage the deployment and operation of AI systems. Also, your MLOps must be integrated with the rest of your system management operation, for instance, when an L1 alert is generated, this needs to be routed real-time to the right team looking at the right monitoring console.

- **Ensure data security and privacy**: Your AI infrastructure should have robust security and privacy controls in place to protect sensitive data and ensure that data is used in a responsible manner. This is especially important in multi-cloud environments.

- **Avoid silos**: Your AI infrastructure should be designed to promote collaboration and cross-BU capabilities, so that data and AI systems can be shared and reused effectively.

There are many cloud providers, AWS. Azure, Google, IBM, Oracle, and many other cloud providers have similar capabilities. Pick the right one for your organization, and large organizations might have multiple cloud providers. Figure 21-9 shows a sample cloud architecture with some key components. The cloud industry is moving at a very high pace, and new services and components are continuously released by major vendors which will accelerate application development. As an example where AWS launched, it had just a few services, and now have over 200 and growing.

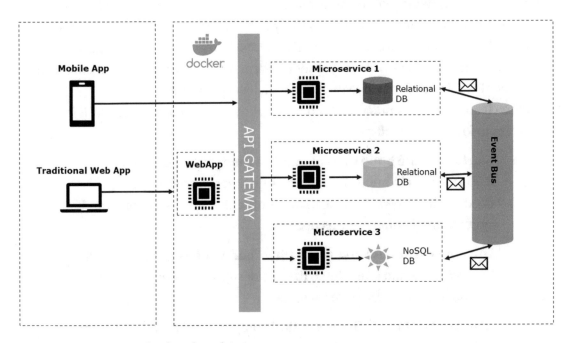

Figure 21-9. *Sample cloud architecture*

Building an effective AI infrastructure is a key factor in scaling AI in the enterprise. Whether you opt for a buy or build approach, it is important to focus on ease of use, scalability, data security, and privacy. With the right infrastructure in place, your organization will be well-positioned to achieve the benefits of AI at scale.

Pillar 5: AI R&D

AI R&D is an important component of scaling AI in the enterprise. However, it is not recommended for companies that are just starting to adopt AI. At the same time, for the most mature AI companies, a dedicated AI R&D team can provide a huge competitive advantage. This is because AI is still in the early stages of development, and companies that invest in AI R&D are likely to be ahead of their competition.

To take advantage of AI R&D, it is recommended to have a central team focused on researching AI. This team can focus on areas specific to the company's industry and investigate AI standards. By having a dedicated AI R&D team, the company can ensure that it is keeping up with the latest developments in the field, and that it is prepared to implement new technologies as they become available.

One best practice in AI R&D is to focus on solving specific problems facing the industry. For example, if the company is in the healthcare industry, the AI R&D team can focus on developing AI solutions that help with patient diagnosis or improve the efficiency of medical procedures. This way, the company can ensure that its AI R&D efforts are directly contributing to the company's bottom line.

Another best practice is to collaborate with universities, research institutions, and other companies to share knowledge and ideas. By working with others, the company can learn from their experiences, and gain access to new technologies and techniques that it may not have been able to develop on its own. Many countries have government-backed organizations which an objective to implement their particular national AI roadmap. In the UK, the Alan Turing (AT) institute[13] is tasked with fulfilling part of this R&D mandate of the UK's national AI roadmap[14]. It is also interesting to point out that the AT institute collaborates with top UK universities and industry to carry out applied research. Should your company be based in the UK or have a presence there, it is a very interesting route to explore. In any case, many other large countries will have similar schemes.

There are also common pitfalls to avoid when setting up an AI R&D team. One of the biggest is not having enough resources. AI R&D is a complex and resource-intensive process, and companies need to invest in it if they want to see results. Another pitfall is not having the right team. Companies need to ensure that their AI R&D team has the right mix of expertise, including data scientists, machine learning engineers, and AI product managers.

AI R&D is a critical component of scaling AI in the enterprise, and companies that invest in it are likely to be ahead of their competition. Companies should focus on solving specific problems, collaborating with others, and avoid common pitfalls such as not having enough resources or the right team. By doing so, they can ensure that their AI R&D efforts are contributing to the company's bottom line.

---

[13] www.turing.ac.uk/

[14] www.gov.uk/government/publications/national-ai-strategy

Putting All Together: Designing Your Company-Specific AI Roadmap

Now that we have discussed the five pillars that companies must address to successfully scale AI in their enterprise, it is time to put them all together and design a specific AI roadmap for your company. It is important to note that each company's roadmap will be unique and tailored to their specific needs based on their current AI maturity level, their target AI maturity level, and the investment required to cover the gap.

Assessing Your Company's AI Maturity Level

The first step in designing your AI roadmap is to assess your company's current AI maturity level. This assessment will help you determine where your company stands in terms of AI adoption and identify the gaps that need to be addressed to achieve your desired AI maturity level.

There are several AI maturity models available, including the AI Maturity Model by Cognizant, the AI Maturity Framework by IBM, the Microsoft AI maturity model, and the AI Readiness Assessment by Gartner. These models typically consist of several levels, ranging from basic AI adoption to advanced AI capabilities. By assessing your company's current AI capabilities, you can determine where you stand on the AI maturity model scale and identify the gaps that need to be addressed.

While it is not important which maturity model you select, it is important to do the exercise in a transparent way with the right governance and team skillset appropriate for your company size and culture. This will be heavily impacted by the culture of the company.

Tip   You should also be mindful of self-assessments by internal teams only without the right skillset, but also need to be careful not to engage only a third party (such as consultancy) so it does not seem a "negative audit." A mixed team approach, with the right objectives alignment across teams, will deliver the best outcomes.

Designing Your AI Roadmap

Once you have assessed your company's AI maturity level, you can begin designing your AI roadmap. This roadmap should include specific actions that need to be taken in each of the five pillars to achieve your desired AI maturity level.

The first pillar, company AI cross adoption, involves ensuring that AI is adopted and integrated into all aspects of the company's operations. This may include developing an AI strategy and governance framework, identifying use cases for AI, and promoting a culture of innovation and experimentation.

The second pillar, governance and responsible AI, involves ensuring that AI is developed and deployed in a responsible and ethical manner. This may include establishing ethical guidelines for AI development and deployment, ensuring transparency and accountability in AI decision-making, and addressing potential biases in AI algorithms.

The third pillar, skills and diversity, involves ensuring that the company has the necessary AI skills and diversity to support AI adoption and innovation. This may include investing in AI education and training programs, promoting diversity and inclusion in AI development teams, and attracting and retaining top AI talent.

The fourth pillar, Infrastructure, involves investing in the necessary AI infrastructure to support AI development and deployment. This may include investing in cloud computing, data storage and processing, and AI hardware and software.

The fifth and final pillar, AI R&D, involves investing in AI research and development to create innovative AI solutions. This may include developing new AI algorithms and models, exploring new AI applications, and investing in AI talent and partnerships.

Each company's roadmap will be unique, depending on their starting point in the maturity model, how ambitious their target AI maturity is, and the required investment to cover the gap. The roadmap should include specific actions and timelines for each pillar, as well as metrics for measuring progress and success.

Sample AI Roadmap: Using the Gartner AI Framework

The first step in designing your AI roadmap is to assess your company's current AI maturity level. This assessment will help you determine where your company stands in terms of AI adoption and identify the gaps that need to be addressed to achieve your desired AI maturity level.

An AI maturity model that is widely used is the Gartner AI Maturity Model, which consists of five levels, ranging from basic AI adoption to advanced AI capabilities. The following is a summary of the different levels in the Gartner AI Maturity Model:

- **Level 1 – No AI Adoption**: The organization has no experience or capability with AI.

- **Level 2 – Experimental**: The organization has started to experiment with AI and is beginning to develop basic skills and knowledge.

- **Level 3 – Operational**: The organization has deployed AI in some parts of the business and has developed some best practices for managing AI.

- **Level 4 – Embedded**: The organization has embedded AI into its operations and has developed a high level of AI expertise.

- **Level 5 – Innovative**: The organization is using AI to drive innovation and is constantly pushing the boundaries of what is possible with AI.

In this example, we will focus on a company that wants to go from level 2 (Experimental) to level 4 (Embedded) in the Gartner AI Maturity Model. The exact timings will depend on the way to fund the different initiatives and the actual level of resources and infrastructure when starting the program. The following roadmap detailed the different actions to execute for each of the key five pillars:

1. **Pillar 1: Company AI cross adoption**

    a. Develop an AI strategy that aligns with business objectives and identifies potential use cases for AI.

    b. Build cross-functional teams to develop and deploy AI solutions across the organization.

    c. Create a roadmap for AI adoption across the organization, prioritizing high-impact use cases.

2. **Pillar 2: Governance and responsible AI**

    a. Design the right AI organization for your company. In this case, when a company is in maturity level 2, it is very likely all the AI teams are centralized, as the company matures and goes to level 4, it might be better to move some resources to the business units, although keeping the AI function with dotted line to the central team to align on AI guidelines, common tooling, and model management.

b. Establish companywide ethical guidelines for AI development and deployment.

c. Ensure transparency and accountability in AI decision-making.

d. Develop a framework for assessing and managing AI risks, including potential biases in AI algorithms.

e. Algorithm development has a very challenging RoI that most companies cannot justify.

3. **Pillar 3: Skills and diversity**

a. Invest in AI education and training programs to upskill employees on AI technology and its applications.

b. Attract and retain top AI talent through competitive salaries and benefits.

c. Promote diversity and inclusion in AI development teams to drive innovation and avoid bias in AI algorithms.

4. **Pillar 4: Infrastructure**

a. Invest in cloud computing to support AI development and deployment. Ensure you have the right balance between on-premises and cloud environments.

b. Invest in AI hardware and software to support advanced AI capabilities. As the computing would be very intense, ensure you do very clear business cases why cloud would be more economical than in-house servers.

c. As the company moves away from level 2, develop a plan for scaling infrastructure to support growing AI capabilities.

5. **Pillar 5: AI R&D**

a. As the company starts in level 2, it is more efficient to leverage external resources and to establish the right level of partnerships with academia and key government organizations to drive innovation in AI.

b. As the company progresses toward 4 or even 5, start developing new AI algorithms and models in areas that are a unique differentiation to the business. Unless your company is a technology giant, doing research on research on pure generic.

Scaling AI in the enterprise is a complex process that requires a strategic and holistic approach. By addressing the five pillars of company AI cross adoption, governance and responsible AI, AI R&D, skills and diversity, and infrastructure, companies can successfully scale AI in their enterprise. It is important for each company to assess their current AI maturity level and design a personalized AI roadmap that is tailored to their specific needs and goals. With a well-designed AI roadmap, companies can realize the full potential of AI and drive growth and innovation.

Key Takeaways

Scaling AI in the enterprise is a complex and multifaceted challenge that requires a holistic approach. In this chapter, we covered five key pillars that companies must address to successfully scale AI: company AI cross-adoption, governance and responsible AI, AI R&D, skills and diversity, and infrastructure.

- **Takeaway point 1: Constant focus on business value**. It is important to keep the focus on business value throughout the entire AI journey, from planning and implementation to scaling and adoption. This means being clear about the objectives and outcomes that you want to achieve, and continuously evaluating the success of AI initiatives in terms of those goals.

- **Takeaway point 2: Have the right team with focus**. Building the right team with a mix of data scientists, machine learning engineers, AI product managers, and other roles is crucial for executing AI projects and ensuring success. Additionally, it's important to educate everyone in the organization about AI to build a culture of understanding and adoption.

- **Takeaway point 3: Where are we in the AI journey?** Understanding where your company is in the AI maturity journey is essential for making informed decisions about the resources, skills, and infrastructure you will need to scale AI effectively. For more mature companies, AI R&D can be a competitive advantage, but for early-stage companies, it may not yet be a priority. Many companies will benefit to establish a maturity AI gap roadmap, where they are at a particular point of time, their AI maturity ambition and a detailed roadmap which specify all the specific actions in each of the five pillars companies must pursue over time. This document should also be reviewed and adjusted regularly, at least twice a year.

In conclusion, to successfully scale AI in the enterprise, it is important to have a constant focus on business value, build the right team with a focus on skills and diversity, and understand where your company is in the AI maturity journey. You will need to address all five pillars we have seen, and organizations can move forward with confidence in their AI initiatives and reap the rewards of successful scaling.

As this chapter marks the end of Part IV, we will move into the final part of the book, Part V, "The Future of AI." Here we will explore some interesting developments, and as per the rest of the book, the objective will be to provide the reader with a set of future-proven First Principles to evaluate all the exciting new developments that no doubt will come over the next few years.

PART V

The Future

CHAPTER 22

How Younger Generations See the Future of AI

This chapter aims to provide insight into the perspectives of younger generations on the future of AI and its impact on society, industries, and daily life. By understanding how children and young adults envision AI shaping the future, we can better prepare for the evolving technological landscape and address concerns and expectations of the upcoming generations.

Welcome to a pivotal exploration of the minds of today's younger generation as they envision the future of AI. As we dive into this chapter, we venture into the thought processes of four young individuals, aged 12, twins of 16, and a 19-year-old, providing a fascinating snapshot of expectations, dreams, and potential fears related to the rapidly evolving AI landscape.

Our discussion is built on an interesting premise: As AI evolves at an unprecedented rate, how do young minds today envisage its role in shaping their personal lives, careers, and societal norms? How do they view AI's influence in their chosen fields of interest, ranging from architecture and interior design to armed forces and aeronautical engineering?

One crucial aspect we delve into is their perception of AI's potential ethical implications. From concerns related to privacy, security, and trust, to the broad questions about AI's societal impact, the young minds bring forth insightful views that represent a wide spectrum of future users, consumers, and leaders of AI technology.

Through their eyes, we'll understand the anticipation of AI advancements – both the aspirations and the apprehensions. This discussion isn't just about predicting the future; it's about understanding the future creators, users, and controllers of AI.

© Francisco Javier Campos Zabala 2023
F. J. Campos Zabala, *Grow Your Business with AI*, https://doi.org/10.1007/978-1-4842-9669-1_22

Join us as we embark on this journey through their perspectives. These youthful viewpoints, in the context of AI, are a profound reflection of tomorrow's world. A world where AI and human intelligence would coalesce to forge a new era of progress and innovation.

Remember, these younger generations are not just passive observers; they are active contributors to this exciting narrative. Their expectations and aspirations will shape the course of AI development and adoption. So, sit back, buckle up, and prepare for a thrilling ride into the future, seen through the eyes of its architects.

The Future of AI Seen Through the Eyes of a 12-Year-Old Female Y8 Student

So, I've been asked to tell you all about what a twelve-year-old thinks about AI. Yes, you heard it right, a twelve-year-old. And no, I'm not just going to talk about robot teachers (Figure 22-1) and self-tying shoes (although those would be helpful don't you think?)

Figure 22-1. *Robo-teacher (generated by OpenAI's DALL-E)*

AI is transforming society right before our eyes. I mean, have you ever thought about how incredible it is that we can just talk to our phones, and they can answer us? But I'm not just thinking about talking phones or walking robots. No, no. I'm thinking about how AI could help design our future homes, cities, and skyscrapers.

As a budding architect or interior designer, I can't help but get a bit starry-eyed imagining the possibilities. With AI, I could create digital designs of buildings, and maybe even whole cities (Figure 22-2), before a single brick is laid. I mean, how cool is that?

Figure 22-2. *3D futurist city (generated by OpenAI's DALL-E)*

But hold on a sec! It's not all roses and rainbows, right? I mean, what happens to the builders, the carpenters, the masons? And then there's the issue of military AI. I've seen enough movies to know that when you combine robots and weapons, things can get a bit messy.

So, my vision for AI is a bit of a mixed bag. I'm excited, of course, but also a bit cautious. We need to make sure we're creating a world that's fair and safe for everyone. After all, we don't want a world that's just awesome for the architects; we want a world that's awesome for everyone!

Alright, I'm off to doodle a blueprint for my AI-assisted dream treehouse. Catch you on the other side!

The Future of AI Seen Through the Eyes of a 16-Year-Old Male A-Level Student

In a world that feels more like an ongoing season of Black Mirror, with self-driving cars and home-assistant Alexa that seems to know more about my school schedule than I do, it's hard not to get a bit thrilled and scared about how AI will further infiltrate our lives. So let's get down to it; let me give you my piece of 16-year-old wisdom about what I think AI's future looks like.

Figure 22-3. *A full AI-driven futurist city[1]*

AI's impact on society? Well, imagine a society where no one has to do the dishes, fight over the remote, or figure out who is doing the laundry. I'm talking about AI-run households and people! Now that's a future I can get behind. Of course, I am biased since I am regularly on laundry duty at home. But seriously, the possibilities of AI in our everyday lives are mind-boggling and not just because they save us from chores. Improved healthcare, personalized education, streamlined transportation, the list goes on (Figure 22-3).

---

[1] Image by liuzishan on Freepik.com

Now, about my career plans. Yes, I'm seriously considering a life in the armed forces. No, not because of the snappy uniforms but because I see AI's potential to revolutionize defense strategies and enhance our country's security. Think about AI-powered drones for surveillance, cyber defense systems, and even robotic soldiers (Figure 22-4). It's kind of like an action movie, isn't it?

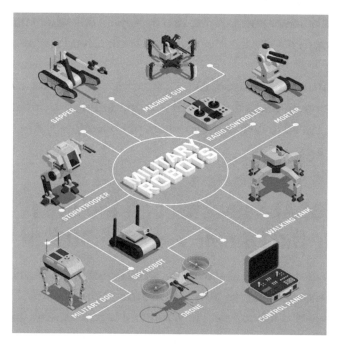

Figure 22-4. *AI military robots[2]*

But before you think I'm completely starry-eyed, let me assure you that I do have concerns. I sometimes lie awake at night wondering if AI would make humans obsolete. What happens to employment when jobs are automated? How do we ensure that AI doesn't widen the social divide? And more importantly, who's going to regulate the AI – a teenager who can't even be trusted to do his laundry regularly?

---

[2] Image: Freepik.com

Yes, we have to be cautious, like any good action movie, there's a potential villain lurking – the impact of AI on employment, politics, and societal structures. We've all heard of AI potentially taking jobs, but how about AI in politics? Could AI lead to better decision-making, or would it create a new form of divide – those who have access to AI and those who don't?

Moreover, how would AI reshape our society? Would we live in a utopian world where everything is efficient and smooth, or a dystopian one where our every move is watched and analyzed? It's like the plot of a good book, where you're both excited and anxious to turn the next page.

So, here's my take on the future of AI – a mix of high hopes, a dash of humor, and a dollop of healthy caution. And if this has got you pondering, I've done my job. And now, if you'll excuse me, I need to debate the future of politics with my AI-powered home assistant. Wish me luck!

The Future of AI Seen Through the Eyes of a 16-Year-Old Female A-Level Student

Growing up in an increasingly digital world, I, as a 16-year-old A-Level student in the UK, am marveling at the transformative potential of artificial intelligence (AI). I envision a future where AI could revolutionize society, influencing our careers, personal lives, and even our interaction with the natural world. At the same time, I acknowledge that this promise of progress is not without its pitfalls. Critical among my concerns is the potential impact of AI on privacy, security, and ethical standards.

In my view, AI holds a transformative potential for virtually every facet of our lives. AI-powered automation could relieve us of mundane tasks, freeing us up for more creative and meaningful endeavors. As an animal welfare enthusiast, I'm excited about the prospects of integrating AI into wildlife conservation efforts. With AI and data analytics, we could track endangered species more effectively, anticipate threats more accurately, and devise more strategic countermeasures (Figure 22-5).

Figure 22-5. *Wildlife conservation with AI[3]*

However, the AI-powered future we are advancing toward is not without its challenges. Among my greatest concerns is privacy, an aspect that could fundamentally be altered with increased reliance on AI. The data-intensive nature of AI systems poses a significant risk to personal privacy. With companies and governments able to collect, analyze, and store vast amounts of personal data, there's a real danger of misuse, be it intentional or accidental.

For example, personalized advertisements, while convenient, often come from companies collecting and analyzing your online behavior. On a more ominous note, the data we generate can be harnessed to influence our behavior or even predict our actions, a concept known as "predictive policing" in law enforcement circles. While there's a potential benefit in terms of security, it's a step toward a surveillance state if unchecked.

So, how do we strike a balance? How do we ensure that the benefits of AI are realized without trampling on individual privacy rights? The answer lies in a robust and forward-thinking regulatory framework that respects privacy while enabling innovation. Policies need to ensure that data is collected and used ethically, with explicit user consent, and only for stated purposes.

---

[3] Image: Freepik.com

As we navigate this AI-enhanced future, it's important to balance the immense potential of AI with the need to protect privacy and uphold ethical standards. By integrating policy, technology, and ethics, we can create an AI-enabled world that respects individual rights while advancing society as a whole. As a young adult stepping into this brave new world, I'm optimistic about our ability to shape this technology for the greater good.

The Future of AI Seen Through the Eyes of a 19-Year-Old Male Student

Okay, so here's the lowdown. I'm 19. No longer a kid but not quite the sage adult. Yet, for whatever reason, folks want to know what I think about AI. Well, buckle up, because I'm about to throw some hard truths at you (interspersed with the odd funny, of course).

Firstly, let's talk about AI in my future industry: aeronautical engineering. This isn't just "buzzword bingo"; AI has some serious potential here. I'm talking autonomous aircraft, predictive maintenance, optimizing flight paths, the whole nine yards (Figure 22-6). AI could, quite literally, help us reach for the stars.

However, I'm not oblivious to the issues. Like the need for trust, for instance. As someone who would love nothing more than to work with AI in aircraft, the prospect of an error in the code causing a tragic accident is quite sobering. We need to ensure safety and robustness in our AI systems.

Figure 22-6. *Autonomous aircraft[4]*

Then there's the societal cost. Just because we can implement AI everywhere, does it mean we should? And how do we make sure that the AI revolution isn't just benefiting the fat cats at the top, but everyone?

Picture this – AI revolutionizing sports, Rugby, in particular. Imagine sensors in rugby balls, player tracking, and strategies enhanced with AI – a total game-changer, right?

Finally, there's the whole matter of societal norms. Will AI redefine our norms? Could it even create new ones? It's a conundrum alright. I don't have the answers, but these are the questions that keep me up at night.

To fully realize the potential of AI, we need to focus on developing AI-based modeling techniques that can build automated, intelligent, and smart systems. These models should be analytical, functional, interactive, textual, and visual, to enable computers and machines to perform cognitive functions such as problem-solving,

---

[4] Image: Freepik.com

decision making, perception, and comprehension of human communication. We also need to ensure that AI is developed and implemented in an ethical and responsible manner, with a focus on transparency, accountability, and fairness.

So, as a 19-year-old future aeronautical engineer, that's my two cents on the future of AI. It's a complex picture, with plenty of exciting opportunities, but also significant challenges. As the saying goes, "with great power comes great responsibility." It's clear that AI is a great power; now we just need to make sure we handle it responsibly.

Chapter Summary/Key Takeaways

As we journeyed through Chapter 22, it was a refreshing exercise to immerse ourselves in the perspectives of four distinct youth voices. Through their anticipations and concerns, we gained invaluable insights into how AI might shape our world in the years to come.

This chapter delved into the visions of four children, each contemplating their futures amidst the rapid advancement of AI. The 12-year-old architect-to-be saw a world where AI unleashes unparalleled creativity in her chosen field. Meanwhile, the twin 16-year-olds, one planning to join the armed forces, another an animal welfare enthusiast, looked at AI as both a formidable force in defense and a tool to protect and preserve animal life. Lastly, our 19-year-old aeronautical engineering aspirant projected AI's influence on his industry and sport, simultaneously wrestling with ethical, societal, and safety concerns.

We have seen the following key points raised throughout the chapter:

- Younger generations are more familiar with AI than older generations.

- Younger generations see AI as a tool that can be used to solve problems and improve their lives.

- Younger generations are aware of the potential risks of AI, but they believe that the benefits outweigh the risks.

- There are challenges that need to be addressed in order to ensure that AI is used for good.

This will lead us to the three final key takeaways:

1. **Key takeaway 1: AI as a creative and practical tool**. AI is not just seen as a cold, computational technology but as a creative partner and practical tool for a broad range of applications – from architectural design to animal welfare, to enhanced defense capabilities.

2. **Key takeaway 2: Understanding ethical concerns**. As AI becomes more integrated into our lives, it's crucial to navigate potential pitfalls. These include privacy, job security, trust, code errors, and societal costs. The younger generation is cognizant and concerned about these issues.

3. **Key takeaway 3: AI as a potential equalizer or divider**. While AI presents opportunities to enhance life and work, there's a stark awareness of the potential for inequality. Ensuring AI benefits are distributed equitably across society, rather than accruing predominantly to the wealthy, will be a significant challenge for the future.

Through these youthful lenses, the future of AI is a blend of hope, pragmatism, and cautious optimism. Their unique insights should remind us all to shape AI in a way that enhances society while mitigating its potential risks.

CHAPTER 23

Future Trends in AI and Its Considerations for Business

The rapidly evolving landscape of AI technologies has brought forth a wave of unprecedented advancements in various domains. As we progress further into the 21st century, businesses must not only adapt to the current AI landscape but also anticipate and prepare for its future direction. This ability to foresee potential changes and harness emerging technologies will be the key to maintaining a competitive edge in an increasingly data-driven world.

"Those that fail to learn from history are doomed to repeat it."[1]

Most businesses which are not directly in the AI industry might be thinking: "why should I worry about how AI technology might evolve; it is not my core business." However, looking at history as the famous quote from Churchill, we can say this is quite a risky approach. In the constantly evolving landscape of technology, failing to anticipate, adapt to, and adopt transformational emerging innovations can mean the difference between thriving and disappearing. Let's look at *the demise of the ice industry*, which serves as an instructive case study.

---

[1] https://api.parliament.uk/historic-hansard/people/mr-winston-churchill/1948

© Francisco Javier Campos Zabala 2023
F. J. Campos Zabala, *Grow Your Business with AI*, https://doi.org/10.1007/978-1-4842-9669-1_23

The ice industry, at the end of the 19th century and into the early 20th, was a booming business. Companies, such as the **Knickerbocker**[2] Ice Company in the United States, capitalized on the demand for ice by owning frozen lakes and cutting massive ice blocks during the winter months, as shown in Figure 23-1. These blocks were then transported to cities where they were used for refrigeration in an era before modern refrigerators. These companies were large and prosperous, with the Knickerbocker Ice Company reportedly employing over 1,000 horses and over 100 wagons for transportation alone, becoming a pillar of the economy in the region.

Figure 23-1. *Workers guide a horse pulling an ice-cutting rig on the Hudson River, circa 1912*[3]

However, their dominance was short-lived. The advent of electrical refrigeration technology in the early 20th century marked the beginning of the end for the traditional ice industry. Companies that produced these new refrigeration units, such as Frigidaire[4]

---

[2] https://nystateparks.blog/tag/knickerbocker-ice-company/

[3] (Photo Credit – New York State Archives # A3045- 78_830)

[4] www.frigidaire.com/en/

and General Electric, offered a more convenient, reliable, and efficient method of food preservation and cooling. Suddenly, the logistics-heavy business of harvesting and transporting natural ice was no longer necessary.

Interestingly, the ice industry failed not because it couldn't have adapted to this new technology, but primarily because it didn't. The vast majority of these ice companies saw themselves in the business of harvesting and distributing natural ice, not in the broader business of refrigeration. As a result, they did not invest in the burgeoning field of ***artificial refrigeration***, allowing other companies to seize the opportunity.

This tale of the ice industry offers a stark warning for modern businesses: the cost of failing to keep an eye on future development of foundational technologies can be fatal. As AI evolves at a breakneck speed, businesses must stay alert to technological changes and prepare to pivot their strategies. If they do not, they risk going the way of the ice companies – becoming obsolete and outpaced by those who do embrace the new. In the age of AI, understanding the ***broader context of your business – not just the specifics of your current operation*** – will be critical to long-term survival and success.

Today, companies which core business models rely on information management are exposed to a fundamental revolution; AI capabilities can completely transform their industry. Many companies in the data business should remember that the clients/consumers are trying to achieve a task with their data, but the actual data is not the end, only a means to the end "job-to-be-done." And using AI, specially generative AI models, it is possible to achieve many tasks without using some of the existing datasets.

As AI technologies become more sophisticated and integrated into various processes, companies that successfully leverage these advancements will reap the benefits of increased efficiency, improved decision-making, and enhanced innovation.

One critical aspect of preparing for the future of AI is staying informed about emerging trends and potential breakthroughs. By keeping a finger on the pulse of AI advancements, business leaders can make informed decisions about adopting new technologies, investing in research and development, and upskilling their workforce.

Table 23-1. *Key AI advancements and their potential impact on various industries*

AI advancement	Potential impact	Industries affected
Quantum computing	Accelerated data processing, improved optimization	Finance, healthcare, science
Bioengineering	More efficient computing, accelerate AGI models	All industries
AGI research	More accurate "world models" will unlock new use cases	All industries
Human-AI collaboration	Improved decision-making, increased productivity	All industries
Brain-computer interfaces	Revolutionizing human-computer interaction, medical treatment	Healthcare, IT, entertainment
AI in key areas	Sustainability, cybersecurity. Healthcare, creativity	Energy, agriculture, NGOs, IT, finance, government

In this chapter, we will explore some of the most promising future trends in AI as per Table 23-1, as each of these trends has the potential to significantly impact various industries, redefine the way we work, and shape the future of our society.

Quantum Computing and AI

Quantum computing has the potential to revolutionize the field of artificial intelligence, offering unprecedented computational power and speed. By leveraging the core principles of quantum mechanics, quantum computers can solve certain complex problems far more efficiently than classical computers. Contrary to popular belief, quantum computing are not just super-fast classical computers, there work differently, and they are able to solve some problems in less time than classical computers, but they do it by operating differently rather than performing the same task as the classical computer quicker. Indeed, by harnessing the power of quantum mechanics, quantum computers can solve some problems that are currently intractable for classical computers. This could lead to major breakthroughs in areas such as drug discovery, materials science, and financial modeling.

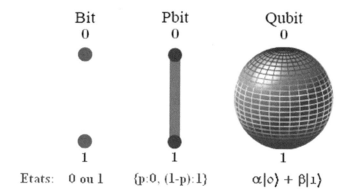

Figure 23-2. *Differences between bit, pbit, and qubit*

See the following core principles of quantum computers. For the more curious reader, I gave a full introduction to the topic in a developers' conference.[5] There is also a great book[6] for those would like to get far deeper into the details:

- **Qubits vs bits**: As per Figure 23-2, classical computers encode information as binary digits, or bits, which can take on one of two values, 0 or 1. Quantum computers, on the other hand, use quantum bits, or qubits. A qubit can exist in a state corresponding to 0 or 1, or in any superposition of these states.

- **Entanglement**: This is a quantum phenomenon where the state of one particle becomes linked to the state of another, no matter how far apart they are. In terms of quantum computing, when qubits become entangled, the state of one qubit will correlate with the state of another, enabling complex calculations to be performed more efficiently than classical computers.

- **Quantum gates**: Just as classical computers use logic gates to perform operations on bits, quantum computers use quantum gates to perform operations on qubits. However, unlike classical gates, quantum gates are reversible and involve complex numbers. They operate by changing the probabilities and phases of the quantum states.

---

[5] www.youtube.com/watch?v=oSi7T8AF3-s
[6] www.amazon.co.uk/Quantum-Computing-since-Democritus-Aaronson/dp/0521199565

- **Quantum superposition**: As mentioned earlier, a qubit can exist not just in a state corresponding to the logical state 0 or 1 as in a classical bit, but also in states that are superpositions of these. This means that a qubit can exist in multiple states at once, allowing it to perform multiple computations simultaneously.

- **Quantum error correction**: Quantum error correction is a technique used to protect qubits from errors. Errors can occur due to noise in the environment or due to interactions between qubits. Quantum error correction can be used to keep qubits in a consistent state and to prevent errors from accumulating.

- **Quantum algorithms**: Quantum algorithms are the programs that are run on quantum computers. They are designed to take advantage of the power of quantum computing to perform calculations that are impossible for classical computers. This is one of the areas with the most potential.

One of the most promising applications of quantum computing in AI is quantum machine learning (QML). QML algorithms can potentially process large datasets and optimize models much faster than their classical counterparts. This enhanced capability can lead to significant breakthroughs in various industries, including drug discovery, materials science, and financial modeling.

Table 23-2. *Potential applications of quantum computing in AI*

Industry	Application	Impact
Drug discovery	Molecular simulations, drug design	Accelerated development of new treatments and therapies
Materials science	Material property prediction, optimization	Discovery of advanced materials for various applications
Finance	Portfolio optimization, risk management	Improved decision-making and financial forecasting

In drug discovery, for example, quantum computing can help simulate the behavior of molecules and chemical reactions, enabling researchers to identify new compounds and predict their effectiveness more accurately (see Table 23-2). This can expedite the development of novel drugs and therapies, potentially saving lives and reducing healthcare costs.

Despite its enormous potential, there are several challenges and opportunities in harnessing quantum computing for AI. Some of these challenges include the current limitations in quantum hardware, the need for specialized quantum algorithms, and the integration of quantum computing with existing systems.

Quantum computing holds significant promise for the future of AI, with potential applications in various industries, such as drug discovery, materials science, and finance. Although there are challenges to overcome, businesses that stay informed about quantum computing advancements and invest in research can reap the benefits of this cutting-edge technology.

Bioengineering: Merging Biology with AI for Future Devices

When it comes to exploring the limits of computing, it is very useful to go to First Principles and remember from Chapter 6 the comparison of biological vs silicon brains. In the quest for a better computing future, we need to look no further than our own brains. A marvel of biological engineering, the human brain is a supercomputer in its own right, outperforming even the most powerful silicon-based machines in terms of efficiency. While it is estimated that the world's fastest supercomputer consumes around 20 megawatts to perform at its peak, the human brain does similar computational work using approximately 20 watts. This is about as much energy as a dim light bulb consumes, compared to 20 Mwatts, which could provide energy to a small city of around 10,000 homes for a year. Figure 23-3 shows a comparison from first principles (power-efficiency) between biological and silicon computing.

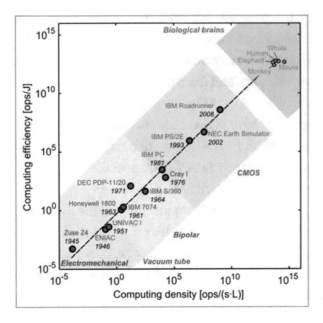

Figure 23-3. *Silicon vs biology in terms of power-efficient computing*

Such efficiency results from the brain's fundamentally different computing architecture. Instead of separate memory and processing units, the brain's billions of neurons and trillions of synapses concurrently store and process information. In essence, the brain is an analog computer, where computations occur in parallel, unlike in digital machines where computations are largely sequential. This has inspired a new wave of research in AI, focusing on building neuro-mimetic or neuromorphic devices that emulate the brain's.

Enter bioengineering, and more specifically, the revolutionary gene-editing tool, CRISPR. CRISPR enables precise modifications in the genetic code, making it possible to engineer biological organisms and systems at an unprecedented scale and detail. Leveraging CRISPR in conjunction with AI, we could potentially design hybrid bio-silicon devices that combine the high-speed processing power of silicon chips with the energy efficiency of biological systems.

There are many ways this could be achieved. For example, researchers might use CRISPR[7] to genetically engineer neurons to respond to light, effectively creating an interface between the digital and biological world. By linking these modified neurons with silicon chips, we could create a device that uses light signals to perform computations, similar to how neurons in our brains use electrical signals.

It's not just about creating efficient computers, though. Such hybrid devices could also revolutionize areas like drug discovery, environmental sensing, and even artificial tissue and organ growth. For instance, imagine an AI system that can guide the growth of complex biological structures, like human organs, for transplantation.

While this future is exciting, it is not without its challenges. Ethical considerations are paramount when dealing with genetic manipulation and blending biological and artificial systems. Regulatory frameworks must be put in place to guide these advancements responsibly, considering both the potential benefits and risks.

However, the potential is clear. By harnessing the power of bioengineering and AI, we could not only create devices that surpass the efficiency of today's computers but also open the door to a myriad of applications that could revolutionize industries and society as a whole. The future of AI and bioengineering combined is promising, if navigated judiciously, can bring unprecedented benefits to the world

AGI Research Areas

As we saw in earlier chapters, Artificial General Intelligence (AGI) represents highly autonomous systems that can outperform humans in the most economically valuable work. It is an area of research that aims to create machines that exhibit general intelligence similar to human intelligence. Here are the core components of AGI research from a first principles point of view:

- **Learning**: AGIs need to be able to learn from their environment. This means they need to be able to acquire new knowledge and skills, and they need to be able to adapt to new situations.

---

[7] www.broadinstitute.org/what-broad/areas-focus/project-spotlight/questions-and-answers-about-crispr

- **Reasoning**: AGIs need to be able to reason about their environment; they need to be able to make inferences, draw conclusions, and solve problems.

- **Decision-making**: AGIs need to be able to make decisions. This means they need to be able to weigh the pros and cons of different options, and they need to be able to choose the best option for a given situation.

Current AI systems do not exhibit behaviors in these three areas and might excel at one of them but not the others. It is expected we will need to solve all three. Here are the core areas of research involved:

- **World models**: World models are representations of the world that AGIs can use to reason about their environment. World models can be created by training an AGI on a large dataset of sensory data.[8]

- **Neural networks and deep learning**: AGI research builds heavily on advancements in deep learning and neural networks, which are computational models inspired by the human brain. Deep learning algorithms learn to recognize patterns and make decisions by being trained on large datasets.

- **Deep reinforcement learning**: Deep reinforcement learning is a type of machine learning that allows AGIs to learn how to behave in complex environments by trial and error. Deep reinforcement learning has been used to train AGIs to play games like Go and Dota 2.

- **Neuromorphic computing**: Neuromorphic computing is a type of computing that is inspired by the way the human brain works. Neuromorphic computing could be used to create AGIs that are more efficient and more energy-efficient than traditional computers.

---

[8] https://ai.facebook.com/blog/yann-lecun-advances-in-ai-research/

- **Causal inference**: Understanding cause-effect relationships is a crucial aspect of human intelligence that's largely missing in current AI models. Researchers like Yoshua Bengio[9] are focusing on this area, seeking to build machines that understand the underlying causal structure of the world.

- **Symbolic reasoning**: While current AI excels at pattern recognition, it struggles with high-level, abstract reasoning. The integration of symbolic reasoning with neural networks (neurosymbolic AI) addresses this.

- **AI safety and ethics**: As we move closer to AGI, issues of safety and ethics become increasingly important. This involves designing systems that behave as intended and are aligned with human values, and also considering the broader societal impacts of AGI.

- **Meta-learning and self-supervised learning**: Meta-learning, or learning to learn, involves building systems that can improve their own learning algorithms based on experience. Self-supervised learning, on the other hand, involves models learning from raw, unlabeled data.

- **Natural language processing (NLP)**: The ability to understand, generate, and respond to human language is a key aspect of AGI. OpenAI's GPT-3 is a major breakthrough in this area.

It's important to note that these areas are not distinct but rather closely intertwined. Achieving AGI will likely require significant progress and integration across all these areas. It is also important to note that we do not have a clear path to AGI, and plenty of different (and often strong!) views in the fields. For instance, some researchers think you only need deep learning to achieve AGI, just need to improve the architectures and keep adding more layers and data to do it effectively. And the success of ChatGPT and other LLM might provide an evidence point in this direction. However, there are also another

---

[9] https://medium.com/syncedreview/yoshua-bengio-team-proposes-causal-learning-to-solve-the-ml-model-generalization-problem-762c31b51e04

group of researchers who strongly disagree with this view, saying that you really need to have an internal "world view" that cannot be simply learned by using massive deep learning network. Time will tell who is right.

Brain-Computer Interfaces (BCIs)

Brain-computer interfaces (BCIs) are systems that enable direct communication between the human brain and external devices, such as computers or prosthetic limbs (Figure 23-4). BCIs have the potential to revolutionize various aspects of our lives, from assisting people with disabilities to enhancing cognitive capabilities and enabling new forms of human-machine interaction.

AI plays a crucial role in the development of BCIs, as machine learning algorithms can be used to interpret the complex neural signals generated by the brain and translate them into meaningful commands for external devices. Moreover, AI can be used to improve the accuracy, reliability, and responsiveness of BCIs, making them more practical and accessible for everyday use.

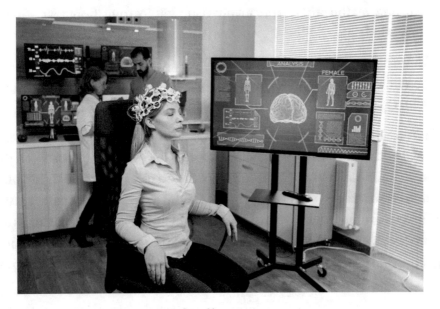

Figure 23-4. Brain-computer interface[10]

---

[10] Image by DCStudio on Freepik

Potential applications of BCIs include

- **Medical and rehabilitation**: BCIs can be used to help people with disabilities regain control over their bodies, such as controlling prosthetic limbs or wheelchair navigation. Additionally, BCIs can be used to facilitate communication for people with severe speech or motor impairments.

- **Human augmentation**: BCIs have the potential to enhance human cognitive capabilities, such as memory, attention, or problem-solving. For example, AI-powered BCIs could be used to augment human decision-making in high-stress environments, such as military operations or emergency situations.

- **Entertainment and gaming**: BCIs can be used to create more immersive and interactive gaming experiences, enabling players to control virtual environments using only their thoughts.

- **Workplace productivity**: BCIs could be integrated into workplace environments to improve productivity, such as enabling workers to control computers or machinery using their thoughts or enhancing focus and concentration during complex tasks.

- **BCIs could be used to create new types of AI** that are able to interact with the world in new ways. For example, BCIs could be used to create AI that is able to control robots or other machines, or that is able to communicate with other people using their thoughts.

- **BCIs could be used to improve the performance of existing AI systems**. For example, BCIs could be used to give AI systems access to more information, such as the user's thoughts and feelings. This could help AI systems to make better decisions and to learn more effectively.

- **BCIs could raise ethical concerns**. For example, some people worry that BCIs could be used to control people's thoughts or to manipulate their behavior. It is important to carefully consider the ethical implications of BCIs before they are widely used.

The field is moving quickly and at the time of writing the FDA just approved human trials to Neuralink.[11] Once again, multiple trends developing in parallel could converge to unexpected new technologies. This is another area to keep an active eye on it.

Future of AI in Key Areas

In this subsection, we delve into the future of AI in specific areas that are crucial to both business and societal landscapes. Here are some of the key areas where AI is expected to have a significant impact in the future:

Sustainability and Social Good

AI can be used to address global challenges such as climate change, poverty, and inequality. The application of AI for sustainability and social good is forecasted to grow substantially, with AI having the potential to significantly contribute to the United Nations' Sustainable Development Goals (SDGs).[12] For example, AI can be used to

- **Optimize energy use**: AI can be used to develop more efficient ways to generate and use energy, such as by optimizing power grids and designing energy-efficient buildings.

- **Develop new sources of renewable energy**: AI can be used to identify new sources of renewable energy, such as solar and wind power, and to develop more efficient ways to harness these resources.

- **Improve healthcare delivery in developing countries**: AI can be used to develop new diagnostic tools, identify potential drug targets, and personalize treatment plans.

---

[11] www.forbes.com/sites/roberthart/2023/06/05/elon-musks-neuralink-wants-to-put-chips-in-our-brains---how-it-works-and-who-else-is-doing-it/?sh=fa6def8babb9

[12] www.un.org/sustainabledevelopment/

Healthcare

AI is already being used in healthcare to improve diagnosis, treatment, and patient care. In the future, AI is expected to play a greater role in healthcare, for example, by

- **Developing new drugs and treatments**: AI can be used to screen large datasets of molecules to identify potential new drugs and treatments. There are several companies[13] pioneering AI research to understand diseases at a molecular level, potentially revolutionizing drug discovery.

- **Personalizing treatment plans**: AI can be used to analyze individual patient data to identify the most effective treatments and optimize care.

- **Providing remote patient monitoring**: AI-powered devices and applications can be used to monitor patients remotely, enabling healthcare providers to identify potential health issues and intervene early.

Cybersecurity and Warfare

As digital threats become more complex, AI is predicted to play a central role in cybersecurity. Through machine learning algorithms, systems can learn to detect anomalies, identify potential threats, and respond promptly, thus significantly enhancing cybersecurity infrastructure. AI is increasingly being used in cybersecurity and warfare. In cybersecurity, AI can be used to

- **Identify and respond to threats**: AI can be used to analyze large datasets of data to identify potential threats and to develop automated responses to these threats.

- **Manage vulnerabilities**: AI can be used to identify and manage vulnerabilities in computer systems and networks.

---

[13] www.ncbi.nlm.nih.gov/pmc/articles/PMC7577280/

- **Train employees on cybersecurity best practices**: AI can be used to create interactive training modules that help employees learn about cybersecurity best practices.

In warfare, AI is being used for tasks such as target identification, autonomous weapons, and cyberwarfare. The use of AI in warfare raises ethical concerns, such as the potential for autonomous weapons to kill without human intervention.

AI-Driven Creativity

AI is also being used to create new forms of art, music, and literature. In the future, AI is expected to play an even greater role in AI-driven creativity, for example, by

- **Generating new ideas**: AI can be used to generate new ideas for art, music, and literature by analyzing large datasets of existing creative works.

- **Collaborating with humans**: AI can be used to collaborate with humans to create new creative works.

- **Evaluating creative works**: AI can be used to evaluate creative works, such as by identifying patterns and trends in creative output.

The future of AI is full of promise, but it also raises important ethical and social concerns. It is important to consider these concerns as AI continues to evolve.

Table 23-3. *Real-world examples*

Key area	Potential impact	Challenges	Real-world examples
Sustainability and social good	Optimize resource management, combat climate change	Data privacy, achieving cooperation between entities	Google's AI for social good program
Healthcare	Enhance patient care, Advance precision medicine	Regulatory compliance, data security	DeepMind's AlphaFold
Cybersecurity and warfare	Enhance cybersecurity infrastructure, redefine warfare	Ethical considerations, risk of autonomous weapons	Defense Advanced Research Projects Agency's (DARPA) AI programs
AI-driven creativity	Redefine creativity, collaborate to produce innovative works	Quality control, intellectual property rights	OpenAI's MuseNet[14]

Harnessing the potential of AI in these key areas (Table 23-3) will require concerted efforts from businesses, governments, and societies. As AI continues to evolve, businesses will need to adapt their strategies to embrace the transformative potential of AI while managing associated risks.

Enhancing Business Efficacy: Human-AI Synergy and Augmentation

Artificial intelligence (AI) has begun to shape workplaces and societies in unprecedented ways. This chapter focuses on the enhancement of human capabilities and decision-making through AI integration, the fostering of effective human-AI collaboration, and risk mitigation strategies.

---

[14] https://openai.com/research/musenet

The Human-AI Evolution in the Workplace and Society

AI's incorporation in numerous industries and societal sectors has the potential to improve human performance and empower decision-making. This transformative relationship between humans and AI can be classified into three primary stages:

- **Human-led AI**: In this initial phase, AI serves as an instrumental resource for humans, assisting in decision-making by processing data and offering insights. Control over AI systems remains predominantly with humans.

- **Human-AI collaboration**: As AI evolves, it assumes an active role alongside humans, contributing its strengths and balancing human limitations. The collaboration yields shared responsibilities and enhances task performance.

- **AI-driven human augmentation**: In this advanced phase, AI expands human decision-making and abilities. Acting as cognitive assistants, the AI elevate human capacity to tackle complex problems and boost creativity.

Leveraging AI for Human Augmentation and Decision-Making

AI can significantly amplify human capacities and improve decision-making:

- **Data analysis and pattern recognition**: AI can process large datasets, identifying patterns that might otherwise elude human observation. This functionality facilitates data-driven, informed decision-making.

- **Automation of mundane tasks**: AI can handle repetitive tasks, liberating humans to concentrate on strategic operations.

- **Enhanced decision-making under uncertainty**: By providing probabilistic outcome estimations, AI assists in decision-making during complex situations with ambiguous conditions.

- **Boosted creativity and innovation**: AI contributes to idea generation, solution exploration, and identification of untapped options, thus fostering creativity and innovation.

- **Personalized learning and skill development**: AI can customize educational content and training programs to cater to individual learning styles and requirements, enabling efficient learning and skill advancement.

Strategies for Successful Human-AI Synergy and Risk Mitigation

Several strategies can ensure a productive human-AI partnership and address potential risks:

- **AI developer-end-user collaboration**: Building a collaborative environment between AI developers and end users can lead to human-centric AI design, fostering more effective human-AI synergy.

- **Investment in AI education and training**: To enable successful human-AI collaboration, individuals must be equipped with both technical and ethical knowledge concerning AI, and be informed of its potential societal impacts.

- **Transparent and explainable AI**: AI systems must be developed to provide transparent and explainable decision-making processes. This transparency builds trust, aiding more effective collaboration.

- **Ethical guidelines and regulatory framework**s: These clear frameworks can help mitigate potential risks such as job displacement, privacy concerns, and algorithmic bias. Regular review and updating of these guidelines are crucial as AI technology evolves.

- **Interdisciplinary collaboration**: Encouraging interaction between disciplines, including computer science, psychology, and social sciences, can lead to a more comprehensive understanding of the complex interplay between humans and AI, helping to identify potential risks and develop effective human-AI collaboration strategies.

- **Human-centric AI design**: AI systems should prioritize the well-being and needs of humans, respecting values such as privacy, fairness, and autonomy.

The symbiotic relationship between humans and AI holds immense potential for enhancing human capabilities, transforming industries, and addressing complex societal issues. However, the successful realization of this potential hinges on effective collaboration and risk mitigation strategies, including AI education and training, interdisciplinary collaboration, and ethical and regulatory frameworks.

Staying Ahead of the Curve: Innovating and Adapting to the AI Landscape

In the thrilling drama of technological advancement, AI plays the leading role. To ride the crest of this wave, businesses must not only adopt AI but also adapt and innovate within its ever-changing landscape. Imagine a game of chess, where not just the pieces, but the rules and the board itself are constantly evolving. You need to strategize, recalibrate, and anticipate future moves to win.

Let's consider a three-pronged approach to stay ahead in this game: harnessing the power of first principles thinking, championing continuous innovation, and learning from the trailblazers in the field:

1. **The power of First Principles in shaping AI strategy**: We discussed in Chapter 11 how to create an AI roadmap that fulfills the business strategy. As a reminder, First Principles thinking empowers businesses to crack the code of AI's complexity. Like Sherlock Holmes solving a mystery, it involves drilling down to the fundamental truths, peeling away layers of assumptions, and then building innovative solutions based on these irrefutable facts. Here is how you can harness this power:

   a. **Define clear AI goals**: What do you want AI to achieve? Improved efficiency? Stellar customer experiences? Innovation? Define these objectives with laser precision.

   b. **Understand AI's building blocks**: Dive into the core technologies driving AI - ML, NLP, computer vision, and others.

   c. **Forge a unique AI path**: With clear business objectives, carve out an AI strategy tailored to your business's unique needs.

   d. **Stay flexible and ready to evolve**: Review and revise your strategy regularly to adapt to the dynamic AI landscape.

2. **Keeping the innovation engine running:** To stay ahead, it's crucial to transform your business into a hothouse of innovation. Think of it as a two-pronged strategy:

   a. **Nurture an in-house AI R&D culture**: Allocate resources, encourage cross-departmental collaboration, foster a learning spirit, and let your people experiment with new ideas and technologies.

   b. **Forge partnerships with external AI wizards**: Collaborate with AI-centric organizations, research institutions, startups, and experts. This can turbocharge your innovation engine, opening doors to fresh opportunities and knowledge.

3. **Lessons from the AI frontlines.** Learning from pioneers who have blazed the AI trail can be immensely rewarding.

   a. **Take Tesla**, for instance. By applying First Principles thinking, Tesla has broken new ground in AI-driven autonomous driving technology, questioning traditional notions.

   b. **Other AI-driven giants like Google, Amazon, and Netflix** have embraced a culture of relentless innovation, translating into breakthroughs in AI technologies. This has led to the birth of innovative, AI-powered products and services like Google Assistant, Amazon's Alexa and Go, and Netflix's highly personalized content recommendations.

The rapidly evolving world of AI is like a high-stakes, ever-changing game of chess. To thrive, businesses must learn to continuously strategize with First Principles thinking, fuel continuous innovation, and learn valuable lessons from the front-runners.

Cultivating a Future Proven AI-Ready Workforce

In the era of AI, it is crucial for businesses to prepare their workforce for the challenges and opportunities that AI-driven technologies bring. By upskilling and reskilling employees, organizations can remain competitive, enhance productivity, and foster a culture of innovation. This section will discuss the importance of upskilling and reskilling the workforce and explore strategies for fostering a culture of learning and innovation using a First Principles approach.

As AI technologies continue to evolve and integrate with various business functions, the skill sets required for employees to excel in their roles will also change. The benefits of having an AI-ready workforce include

- **Increased productivity**: AI-trained employees can leverage AI tools and technologies to automate repetitive tasks, enhance decision-making, and increase overall efficiency.

- **Enhanced competitiveness**: Companies with a workforce skilled in AI will be better positioned to stay ahead of competitors, as they can effectively capitalize on AI-driven opportunities and innovations.

- **Improved employee engagement**: When employees are equipped with the necessary skills to thrive in an AI-driven environment, they are more likely to feel engaged, motivated, and empowered, ultimately leading to higher job satisfaction and retention rates.

- **Better adaptability to change**: A workforce proficient in AI skills will be better prepared to adapt to changing business environments and capitalize on new opportunities.

There are several best practices to cultivate a future proven AI-ready workforce. A First Principles approach can be instrumental in creating a learning culture that empowers employees to embrace AI-driven technologies. Here are some strategies to consider:

- **Align workforce development with business objectives**: By using a First Principles approach, identify the core objectives of your organization and analyze the skills your workforce will need to achieve these goals. Create a skills development plan that aligns with your overall business strategy, focusing on critical AI competencies such as data analysis, machine learning, natural language processing, and computer vision.

- **Invest in personalized learning experiences**: Design and implement AI-driven personalized learning experiences for employees, taking into account their individual strengths, weaknesses, and learning styles. A First Principles approach can help identify the most effective learning methods for each employee, ensuring that upskilling and reskilling efforts yield optimal results.

- **Leverage partnerships and collaborations**: Collaborate with academic institutions, industry experts, and AI-driven businesses to access cutting-edge knowledge and resources in AI. These collaborations can help your workforce stay updated on the latest AI trends and techniques.

- **Promote a growth mindset**: Encourage employees to adopt a growth mindset, embracing challenges, and viewing failure as an opportunity to learn and grow. A First Principles approach can help employees question existing assumptions, explore new ideas, and develop innovative solutions.

- **Encourage cross-functional collaboration**: Foster a culture of collaboration and knowledge sharing across different departments, enabling employees to learn from each other and develop a holistic understanding of AI-driven technologies. This approach can help break down silos and promote the adoption of AI across the entire organization.

- **Recognize and reward learning and innovation**: Establish a system for recognizing and rewarding employees who demonstrate a commitment to learning and innovation in the AI realm. This can help motivate employees to continuously upskill and reskill, ensuring your workforce remains AI-ready.

Several organizations have embraced the importance of cultivating an AI-ready workforce and have implemented strategies to upskill and reskill their employees. Here are some real-world examples:

- **IBM**: They invested heavily in AI training for its employees, offering personalized learning experiences through its AI Skills Academy. The company also collaborates with academic institutions to ensure that its workforce stays updated on the latest AI trends and techniques.

- **Google**: They encourage a culture of learning and innovation by offering various AI and machine learning courses to its employees, fostering cross-functional collaboration, and recognizing and rewarding employees who demonstrate a commitment to learning and innovation.

- **Microsoft**: They have established an AI School that offers a range of AI courses, workshops, and resources for its employees. The company also collaborates with external partners to access cutting-edge AI knowledge and resources, helping its workforce stay ahead in the AI race.

Key Takeaways

In this chapter, we have explored the many ways in which AI technology is set to shape the future of various domains, from quantum computing and bioengineering to human-AI collaboration. The potential transformative impact of these AI trends cannot be understated, as they will likely redefine how businesses operate and how society functions at large. These are the three key takeaways:

1. **Takeaway 1: AI's potential to revolutionize industries and transform society is immense, and we have only scratched the surface of what is possible**. Business executives must understand and anticipate these changes to stay ahead of the competition and capitalize on the potential benefits that AI can bring.

   a. **Do**: Start small. Don't try to do too much too soon. Start with small projects and gradually scale up as you gain experience.

   b. **Don't**: Dismiss emerging trends as mere hype or assume that they will not have a significant impact on your organization.

2. **Takeaway 2: Staying informed about AI's latest advancements and trends is crucial for business executives**, as it will help them make informed decisions and adapt to the ever-changing landscape.

   a. **Do**: Ensure you keep track of the adjacent fields, such as quantum computing, bioengineering, and other new ones that might appear.

   b. **Don't**: Repeat history and follow first generation of ice industry companies – AI is the new electricity and will heavily impact your industry, in ways that might not be obvious now.

3. **Takeaway 3: Cultivating a future proven AI-ready workforce**: By aligning workforce development with business objectives and promoting a culture of continuous learning, organizations can ensure their employees are prepared for the challenges and opportunities presented by AI technologies.

   a. **Do**: Implement personalized learning experiences and promote a growth mindset.

   b. **Don't**: Neglect workforce development and risk losing the competitive advantage.

The future of AI presents both remarkable opportunities and significant challenges. By staying informed, engaging with the AI community, and adhering to best practices, business executives can help shape the future of AI in a manner that promotes growth, innovation, and ethical responsibility. The potential for AI to transform businesses and society is immense, and it is up to us to ensure that this technology is harnessed for the betterment of all.

CHAPTER 24

Conclusions

In today's rapidly evolving technological landscape, artificial intelligence (AI) has emerged as a game-changing force, poised to reshape the way businesses operate and grow. This book has explored the why, the what, and the how of growing your company with AI (Figure 24-1). We have discussed the potential of AI to drive growth and innovation, the essential AI concepts and technologies, and the steps involved in implementing AI in your organization. As we reach the conclusion of this book, it is crucial to reflect on the key takeaways and consider the future outlook for AI in business.

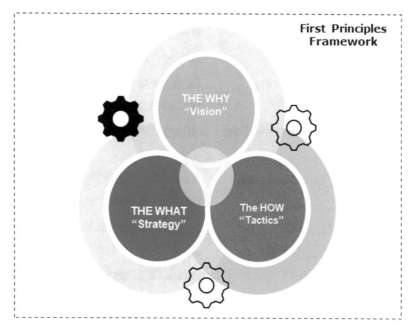

Figure 24-1. *The AI adoption journey*

© Francisco Javier Campos Zabala 2023
F. J. Campos Zabala, *Grow Your Business with AI*, https://doi.org/10.1007/978-1-4842-9669-1_24

Throughout the book, we have discussed the immense potential of AI to drive growth, streamline processes, and foster innovation. By leveraging AI, businesses can gain a competitive edge in the market, improve efficiency, and address pressing global challenges such as climate change and economic inequality. Furthermore, the book has provided a solid foundation in core AI concepts, such as machine learning, deep learning, and natural language processing, as well as a detailed exploration of AI technologies and their applications across various industries (Table 24-1).

Table 24-1. *AI technologies and applications*

AI technology	Industry	Application
Machine learning	Retail	Personalized customer experience, inventory management, pricing, and discount strategy
Deep learning	Healthcare	Disease diagnosis, personalized treatment, drug discovery
Natural language processing (NLP)	Customer service	Chatbots for customer queries, sentiment analysis
Reinforcement learning	Gaming	Strategy development, player behavior analysis
Computer vision	Manufacturing	Quality control, automated inspection, predictive maintenance
Speech recognition	Telecommunications	Voice-activated virtual assistants, transcription services
Robotics process automation (RPA)	Finance and banking	Automating repetitive tasks, fraud detection, customer service
Generative adversarial networks (GANs)	Media and entertainment	Content creation, virtual reality experiences
Transfer learning	Education	Personalized learning, intelligent tutoring
Predictive analytics	Supply chain management	Demand forecasting, logistics optimization

As we move forward, it is essential for business executives to stay informed about advancements in AI research and applications, prepare for emerging trends, and drive ethical practices and responsible innovation in the AI landscape. By reflecting on the key takeaways from this book and embracing the opportunities and challenges of AI, you will be well-equipped to harness the power of AI in growing your company and shaping the future of business. The AI data framework depicted in Figure 24-2, which we've discussed in previous chapters, can serve as an effective tool for unlocking value through AI.

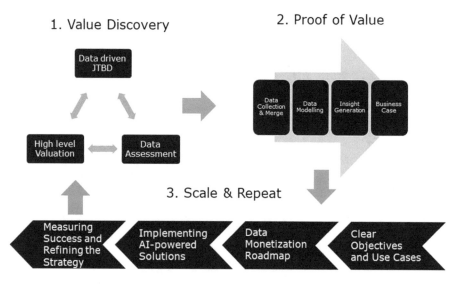

Figure 24-2. *An AI data framework*

As we look toward the future of AI in business, it is important to consider the rapidly evolving landscape of AI technologies. The ongoing advancements in AI research and applications are expected to unlock new opportunities and transform industries further. Business leaders must anticipate these developments and adapt their strategies accordingly to stay competitive in the market. Emerging trends, such as quantum computing, bioengineering and brain-computer interfaces, have the potential to revolutionize AI's capabilities and open up new avenues for innovation.

In this context, the role of business leaders in shaping the future of AI cannot be overstated. By driving ethical AI practices and responsible innovation, executives can ensure that the transformative power of AI is harnessed for the greater good while minimizing the risks associated with its deployment. Collaboration with stakeholders, including governments, academia, and civil society organizations, will be crucial in maximizing the impact of AI while addressing potential concerns surrounding privacy, security, and job displacement. Figure 24-3 shows the key elements which needs to be addressed for a successful AI implementation.

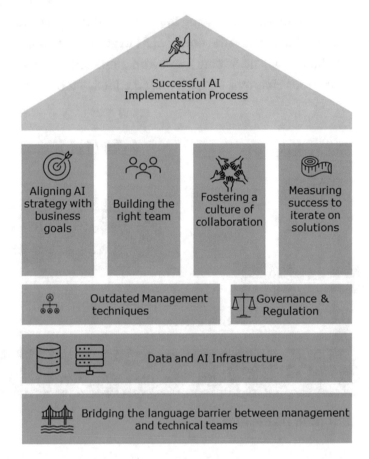

Figure 24-3. *The AI implementation process*

Furthermore, **the importance of continuous learning and adaptation in the age of AI cannot be emphasized enough**. Business leaders and their teams must stay informed about the latest AI advancements and trends, embracing change and fostering a culture of lifelong learning. This will not only help organizations stay ahead of the curve but also empower them to leverage AI's full potential in driving growth and innovation.

Key Takeaways

In this conclusion chapter, we consolidate the key takeaways from the book, focusing on understanding the importance of AI in business, essential AI concepts and technologies, and practical guidance for implementing AI in your organization.

i. **The Why: Understanding the Importance of AI in Business**. AI has the potential to drive growth and innovation in business. AI can be used to automate tasks, improve decision-making, and create new products and services:

    a. **AI's potential to drive growth and innovation**: AI has the power to revolutionize industries, streamline processes, and unlock new opportunities, enabling businesses to grow and innovate. By leveraging AI, companies can develop new products and services, optimize decision-making, and enhance customer experiences.

    b. **Competitive advantages and efficiency gains**: AI helps businesses gain a competitive edge by automating routine tasks, reducing human error, and improving efficiency. By implementing AI, companies can cut costs, increase productivity, and make data-driven decisions to stay ahead in the market.

    c. **Addressing global challenges and promoting sustainability**: AI has the potential to tackle pressing global issues, such as climate change, resource management, and economic inequality. By utilizing AI, businesses can contribute to a more sustainable and equitable future.

ii. **The What: Essential AI Concepts and Technologies**. There are a number of essential AI concepts and technologies that businesses need to understand in order to implement AI successfully. These include

    a. **Core AI concepts**: The book has introduced foundational AI concepts such as machine learning, deep learning, and natural language processing. These concepts form the building blocks of AI applications, allowing machines to learn, adapt, and perform tasks that typically require human intelligence.

    b. **AI technologies and their applications in various industries**: AI has far-reaching applications across diverse industries, from healthcare and finance to retail and manufacturing. By understanding the different AI technologies and their potential use cases, businesses can identify opportunities for growth and innovation.

c. **Ethical considerations and guidelines for AI implementation**: As AI becomes increasingly pervasive, it is crucial for businesses to adhere to ethical guidelines and best practices to ensure responsible AI deployment. This includes addressing concerns related to privacy, security, fairness, and transparency.

iii. **The How: Implementing AI in Your Organization**. Implementing AI in your organization is a complex process that requires careful planning and execution. There are a number of steps involved, including

a. **Understand the current management techniques limitations to take advantage of AI**: Many management guidelines in use today were established in the 1950s and 1970s, and they do not fully account for the rapid advancements in technology and data processing capabilities. Additionally, most organizations' operating models create unintended siloes, where budgets, resources, and goals are isolated and not joined up. Data and AI needs a truly enterprise-wide approach.

b. **Developing an AI strategy aligned with business goals**: To successfully implement AI, businesses must develop a clear AI strategy that aligns with their overarching objectives. This involves identifying key use cases, setting measurable targets, and outlining a roadmap for AI integration.

c. **Building the right team and fostering a culture of collaboration**: Implementing AI requires a multidisciplinary team with diverse skills and expertise. Fostering a culture of collaboration among data scientists, engineers, and domain experts is essential for ensuring successful AI deployment.

d. **Bridging the language barrier between management and technical teams**: To effectively implement AI, business leaders must have a basic understanding of AI concepts and technologies. Educating management on AI fundamentals can help bridge the language barrier and enable more informed decision-making.

e. **Measuring AI success and iterating on solutions**: Tracking the performance of AI initiatives and measuring their impact on business outcomes is crucial for ensuring long-term success. By regularly evaluating and iterating on AI solutions, businesses can optimize their AI strategy and maximize ROI.

Future Outlook

As we look toward the future of AI in business, it is essential to remain aware of the evolving landscape of AI technologies and their potential impact on various industries.

    i. **The Evolving Landscape of AI Technologies**

        a. Anticipating advancements in AI research and applications: The field of AI is constantly advancing, with new research and applications emerging regularly. Business leaders must stay informed about these developments and adapt their strategies accordingly to maintain a competitive edge in the market.

        b. Preparing for emerging trends: As AI technology continues to advance, new trends such as quantum computing and brain-computer interfaces will become increasingly relevant. Business leaders should be prepared to explore and adopt these emerging technologies to drive further innovation and growth.

    ii. **The Role of Business Leaders in Shaping the Future of AI**

        a. Driving ethical AI practices and responsible innovation: As AI becomes more pervasive, it is crucial for business leaders to champion ethical practices and responsible innovation. This includes addressing concerns related to privacy, security, fairness, and transparency, and ensuring that AI is used for the greater good.

        b. Collaborating with stakeholders to maximize impact and minimize risks: Business leaders must collaborate with various stakeholders, including governments, academia, and civil society organizations, to maximize the impact of AI and minimize potential risks. This collaboration will be key to creating a sustainable and equitable AI ecosystem.

    iii. **The Importance of Continuous Learning and Adaptation**

        a. Staying informed about the latest AI advancements and trends: Business leaders and their teams must keep up-to-date with the latest AI advancements and trends to stay ahead of the curve and effectively harness the power of AI in their organizations.

b. Embracing change and fostering a culture of lifelong learning: As AI
    technologies continue to evolve, businesses must embrace change and
    foster a culture of lifelong learning. This will empower organizations to
    adapt and thrive in the ever-changing AI landscape.

By reflecting on these key takeaways and anticipating future developments in the
world of AI, business leaders can effectively navigate the challenges and opportunities
that lie ahead. Embracing the potential of AI and remaining committed to ethical
practices and continuous learning will enable organizations to successfully grow and
innovate in this exciting new era of technological innovation.

Closing Thoughts

As we reach the conclusion of this book, it is essential to reflect on the insights gained
and consider the ways in which you can apply this knowledge to grow your company
with AI. From understanding the importance of AI in business, grasping essential AI
concepts and technologies, to implementing AI in your organization, we have covered
a comprehensive overview of AI from a First Principles point of view. In this closing
section, we will encourage you to take action and reinforce the importance of staying
informed and engaged in shaping the future of AI in business.

Taking Action

Having acquired an understanding of the potential of AI and its applications across
industries, it is crucial to take the next steps in leveraging this technology for your
organization. To begin, consider the following actions:

- **Above all, understand the challenges associated with the outdated
  management techniques and different languages within teams**.
  The first step to solve a problem is to understand it, and it is truly
  remarkable how most people in organizations are unaware of this
  divide – therefore failing to resolve it.

- **Assess your organization's AI readiness**: Review your company's current state, including its data infrastructure, technological capabilities, and workforce skills, to identify areas where AI can be beneficial. This assessment will help you develop a roadmap for AI implementation that aligns with your business goals.

- **Create an AI strategy**: Develop a comprehensive AI strategy that outlines your organization's objectives, the AI technologies and tools you will adopt, and the required resources and investments. Be sure to involve key stakeholders and decision-makers in this process to ensure buy-in and support for AI initiatives.

- **Foster a culture of collaboration**: Encourage cross-functional collaboration between technical and non-technical teams to bridge the language barrier and facilitate knowledge sharing. This collaboration will help create an environment where AI can thrive and contribute to your company's growth.

- **Invest in talent development**: Provide training and development opportunities for your employees to acquire AI and data science skills. This investment will help create a skilled workforce capable of driving AI initiatives and adapting to the ever-evolving technological landscape.

- **Measure success and iterate**: Regularly evaluate the performance of your AI initiatives using relevant metrics to measure their success. Use these insights to fine-tune your AI strategy and make data-driven decisions that contribute to continuous improvement.

Staying Informed and Engaged

The world of AI is constantly evolving, with new technologies and applications emerging at a rapid pace. To stay ahead of the curve and ensure the continued success of your AI initiatives, it is crucial to remain informed and engaged in the AI community. Here are some ways to achieve this:

- **Continuous learning**: Embrace a culture of lifelong learning by regularly updating your knowledge of AI advancements and trends. This can be achieved through reading books and articles, taking online courses, attending conferences and networking events, and participating in professional organizations and communities.

- **Collaboration with stakeholders**: Engage with various stakeholders, including customers, employees, partners, and suppliers, to understand their perspectives on AI and its potential impact on your business. This collaboration will help you make informed decisions and develop strategies that maximize the benefits of AI while minimizing risks.

- **Ethical and responsible AI**: As AI technologies become increasingly integrated into various aspects of our lives, it is essential to ensure that they are developed and implemented ethically and responsibly. Stay informed about ethical guidelines and best practices for AI implementation and actively promote these principles within your organization.

- **Advocacy for AI**: Become an advocate for AI in your industry and share your insights and experiences with others. By doing so, you can contribute to the broader understanding of AI and its potential, inspiring others to explore and adopt this transformative technology.

By taking action and remaining engaged in the AI community, you will be better positioned to harness the power of AI and drive your company's growth. As you embark on your AI journey, remember that the road to success may be filled with challenges and setbacks, but with persistence, adaptability, and continuous learning, you can overcome these obstacles and realize the full potential of AI in your organization.

Embracing Change and Innovation

The insights gained from this book are just the beginning. There is much more to learn about AI and how to implement it successfully in your business. I encourage you to continue learning and exploring the possibilities of AI. Encourage your teams to think creatively and experiment with new ideas, approaches, and technologies.

- **Encourage experimentation**: Provide your employees with the resources and support needed to explore and experiment with AI technologies. This may include allocating time for research and development, offering financial support for pilot projects, and celebrating successes and learnings from failures.

- **Adapt to new technologies**: As new AI technologies emerge, be open to adopting and integrating them into your business processes. This adaptability will help your organization stay at the forefront of technological advancements and maintain a competitive edge.

- **Support diversity and inclusion**: A diverse and inclusive workforce can bring fresh perspectives, ideas, and insights to your organization. Encourage diversity in your teams and ensure that all employees have equal opportunities to contribute their unique talents and perspectives to your AI initiatives.

Growing your company with AI requires a deep understanding of the technology's potential and a commitment to integrating it into your organization's strategy, culture, and processes. By taking action and staying informed, you can harness the power of AI to drive growth, innovation, and success. As you embark on your AI journey, remember that the road ahead may be filled with challenges, but with persistence, adaptability, and continuous learning, you can overcome these obstacles and realize the full potential of AI in your organization.

As we close this book, we hope that you have gained valuable insights and knowledge that will empower you to make informed decisions about AI and its role in your company's future. We encourage you to continue learning, stay engaged with the AI community, and embrace the exciting opportunities that this technology presents. Together, let us shape a future where AI drives growth, innovation, and positive impact for businesses and society as a whole.

I hope you have enjoyed reading this book. Thank you for your time.

APPENDIX A

References and Resources

As a business executive, it is essential to expand your knowledge and stay up to date with the latest developments in AI and business strategy. In this section, we provide a comprehensive list of additional resources, including books and articles, online courses and training programs, conferences and networking events, and professional organizations and communities that can help you stay informed and engaged in shaping the future of AI in business.

The best source for the latest scientific papers is **arXiv**[1] – free, common for most authors to publish there before they are fully peer-reviewed. Most papers are very technical but a great way to keep up to the latest. Another good place **Papers with Code**[2], latest papers plus links to GitHub repositories.

Finally, a great hands-on source is **Google Colaboratory (Colab)**. I have used this through the book to automatically export the output of the LLM (Bard) to running the code. It is a cloud free Jupyter Notebook environment which requires no setup.

Books and Articles

Recommended reading on AI, machine learning, and business strategy:

- ***"The Hundred-Page Machine Learning Book"*** by Andriy Burkov: This book provides an excellent introduction to machine learning, offering a concise yet comprehensive overview of essential concepts and techniques.

---

[1] https://arxiv.org/

[2] https://paperswithcode.com/

- ***"Deep Learning"*** by Ian Goodfellow, Yoshua Bengio, and Aaron Courville: Covers foundations of neural networks and latest advancements in the field.

- ***"Superintelligence: Paths, Dangers, Strategies"*** by Nick Bostrom: This book discusses the potential development of superintelligent AI, its implications for humanity, and strategies to ensure that AI remains beneficial.

- ***"Human Compatible: Artificial Intelligence and the Problem of Control"*** by Stuart Russell: This book offers an insightful look at the challenges of creating AI systems that are aligned with human values and interests.

- ***"AI Superpowers: China, Silicon Valley, and the New World Order"*** by Kai-Fu Lee: This book explores the global race for AI dominance.

- **"Artificial Intelligence for Business: A Practical Introduction"** by Thomas H. Davenport and D.J. Patil.

- **"Machine Learning for Business: What You Need to Know"** by Andreas C. Müller and Sarah Guido.

- **"The AI Revolution: Reshaping Business, Society, and Our Lives"** by Thomas L. Friedman.

- ***"The Master Algorithm: How the Quest for the Ultimate Learning Machine Will Remake Our World"*** by Pedro Domingos.

- ***"Pattern Recognition and Machine Learning"*** by Christopher M. Bishop.

Online Courses and Training Programs

Educational platforms and resources for learning AI and data science skills:

- **Coursera**: This platform offers a wide range of courses in AI, machine learning, including the popular "Deep Learning Specialization" by Andrew Ng. There is also the more basic, "AI for everyone"[3].

---

[3] AI For Everyone | Coursera

- **Udacity**: Udacity offers numerous AI-focused Nanodegree programs, such as the "AI Product Manager," "Machine Learning Engineer," and "Deep Learning" programs.

- **edX**: With courses from top universities, edX provides a variety of AI, machine learning, and data science courses, including the "CS50's Introduction to Artificial Intelligence with Python" from Harvard University.

- **DataCamp**: This platform offers interactive courses in data science, machine learning, and AI, with a focus on hands-on learning and practical skills.

- **Fast.ai**: Fast.ai offers free, practical deep learning courses for coders, with a focus on making AI accessible and easy to understand.

- **Google AI**: Learn AI and machine learning – with Google.[4]

Conferences and Networking Events

Opportunities to engage with AI experts and professionals in the field:

- **NeurIPS (Conference on Neural Information Processing Systems)**: One of the largest annual AI conferences, NeurIPS focuses on the latest research in neural information processing and machine learning.

- **ICML (International Conference on Machine Learning)**: This annual conference covers a wide range of machine learning topics and brings together leading researchers and practitioners.

- **AAAI (Association for Computational Linguistics) Conference**: This conference, organized by the AAAI, focuses on advancements in natural language processing and related fields.

- **AI Summit**: A global series of conferences that bring together business leaders, AI experts, and industry professionals to discuss the latest trends and applications of AI in business.

---

[4] Learn AI & machine learning - Grow with Google

- **AI for Good Global Summit**: This annual event focuses on the use of AI to address global challenges and promote sustainable development.

Professional Organizations and Communities

AI-focused groups and forums for sharing knowledge and staying informed:

- **Association for Computational Linguistics (ACL)**: This organization promotes research in natural language processing and computational linguistics, offering conferences, workshops, and publications,

- **Association for the Advancement of Artificial Intelligence (AAAI)**: The AAAI is dedicated to advancing the understanding of AI and its potential impact on society. They offer conferences, publications, and a variety of resources for AI professionals and researchers.

- **Institute of Electrical and Electronics Engineers (IEEE)**: With a dedicated AI community, the IEEE offers conferences, workshops, and publications on AI and related fields, providing opportunities for collaboration

- **International Machine Learning Society (IMLS)**: They host the ICML conference and provide resources for researchers, professionals in the field.

- **Machine Learning subreddit (r/MachineLearning)**: This online community on Reddit is a valuable resource for machine learning and AI.

- **AI Stack Exchange**: A question and answer community for professionals, academics, and enthusiasts in AI, this platform allows users to seek expert advice and share their knowledge on various AI topics.

- **AI-focused groups and forums** for sharing knowledge and staying informed:

  - Medium https://medium.com/tag/artificial-intelligence

- Towards Data Science `https://towardsdatascience.com/`

- Machine Learning Mastery Machine Learning Mastery

- The AI Alignment Forum `https://www.alignmentforum.org/`

- The Future of Life Institute `https://futureoflife.org/`

- The OpenAI Blog `https://openai.com/blog/`

- Google AI Blog `https://ai.googleblog.com/`

Miscellaneous

The following are a set of resources that I found interesting – this list will be maintained updated in my GitHub site (`http://github.com/javcamposz`):

- Beginner's guide to AI[5]

- Making friends with ML. Cazzie Kozyrkov[6]

- What Is ChatGPT Doing, and Why Does It Work [7]

- Prompt Engineering Guide[8]

- Links to multiple AI resources from the famous VC A16z company[9]

- Updated list to all the ML/AI courses[10]

---

[5] A free online introduction to artificial intelligence for non-experts (elementsofai.com)

[6] `https://towardsdatascience.com/making-friends-with-machine-learning-5e28d5205a29`

[7] What Is ChatGPT Doing … and Why Does It Work?—Stephen Wolfram Writings

[8] Prompt Engineering Guide | Prompt Engineering Guide (promptingguide.ai)

[9] `https://a16z.com/2023/05/25/ai-canon/`

[10] GitHub - dair-ai/ML-YouTube-Courses: 📺 Discover the latest machine learning / AI courses on YouTube.

Index

A

Actor-Critic methods, 236
Agile methodologies, 362–364
AI-driven development (AID), 154
AlphaGo, 237
Amazon's AI recruiting tool, 449–451
Amazon Web Services (AWS), 378
Application programming interfaces
    (APIs), 381–385
  authentication/authorization, 422
  components/applications, 421
  documentation, 423
  error handling, 423
  gateway, 404
  logging/monitoring
    implementation, 423
  microservices architecture, 399–400
  RESTful, 421, 422
  security, 423
  testing, 423
  versioning, 422
Artificial general intelligence (AGI), 124,
    125, 531–534
Artificial intelligence (AI), 85, 307
  accessibility tools, 155
  action process, 556
  adoption, 549
  algorithms, 119
  algorithm selection, 118
  applications, 550
  automation, 132
  autonomous aircraft, 519–521

back-propagating errors, 127
backpropagation/gradient descent, 205
barriers (*see* Barriers)
big data technologies, 146
budding architect or interior designer,
    513, 514
business considerations, 523
business leaders, 555
business strategy, 134, 281, 561,
    (*see also* Business strategies)
business/strategy alignment, 13
business/tech executives, 113
change management, 13
chatbots and virtual assistants, 132
ChatGPT, 142
cloud-based platforms, 147, 211–214
cloud-native applications, 391
comprehensive models
    taxonomy, 207–212
computational power/hardware, 129
computer vision/image
    recognition, 144
concepts/technologies, 549, 552–554
conferences and networking
    events, 563
continuous learning and
    adaptation, 555
core components, 114, 137, 197, 199
corporate environments, 22
cost/complexity, 15
costs/efficiency, 9, 10
cultures/scientific revolution, 15

F. J. Campos Zabala, *Grow Your Business with AI*, https://doi.org/10.1007/978-1-4842-9669-1

Printed in the United States
by Baker & Taylor Publisher Services